EXPLORER'S GUIDE

BUFFALO & NIAGARA FALLS

EXPLORER'S GUIDE

BUFFALO & NIAGARA FALLS

FIRST EDITION

CHRISTINE A. SMYCZYNSKI

THE COUNTRYMAN PRESS
A division of W. W. Norton & Company
Independent Publishers Since 1923

For information about permission to reproduce selections from this book, write to
Permissions, The Countryman Press, 500 Fifth Avenue, New York, NY 10110

For information about special discounts for bulk purchases, please contact
W. W. Norton Special Sales at specialsales@wwnorton.com or 800-233-4830

The Countryman Press
www.countrymanpress.com

A division of W. W. Norton & Company, Inc.
500 Fifth Avenue, New York, NY 10110
www.wwnorton.com

978-1-58157-446-3 (pbk.)

10 9 8 7 6 5 4 3 2 1

To my family—thank you for supporting my writing
and helping me complete this book.

EXPLORE WITH US!

Welcome to the first edition of *Explorer's Guide Buffalo & Niagara Falls*. There is so much to see and do in the Buffalo Niagara region that the publisher decided to release a book focusing just on this region, rather than the entire western part of the state, as in the previous book (*Explorer's Guide Western New York*, The Countryman Press 2008). Note that all entries are based on merit, not on paid advertising, so the author has included information on places that are the best of the best.

WHAT'S WHERE At the beginning of the book is a listing of special highlights and important information regarding items unique to the Buffalo Niagara area, including the best places to enjoy the outdoors, the must-see attractions to visit, and where to find the tastiest local cuisine.

LODGING Accommodations included in this book are based on merit; we do not charge innkeepers to be listed. Many of the accommodations were personally checked out by the author.

PRICES Please don't hold innkeepers or other establishments responsible for rates and prices listed as of press time in 2018. Unfortunately, change is inevitable; always call ahead to verify rates and make lodging reservations well in advance. Also keep in mind that higher rates may be charged during peak seasons.

RESTAURANTS There is a distinction between *Dining Out* and *Eating Out*. Those restaurants listed under *Dining Out* are generally more formal and can be pricey, while those listed under *Eating Out* are usually more casual and less expensive.

Keep in mind that as of press time, all information was current and accurate. However, as with anything in life, change is inevitable. Some new businesses will open, others may close, or change hours or ownership. Please be sure to call ahead if you are traveling any distance to a particular establishment to avoid disappointment. If you discover a business or attraction not reviewed in this book that you feel should be included, please inform the publisher or author so that it can be considered for inclusion in future editions. The Countryman Press, a division of W. W. Norton & Company, is located at 500 Fifth Avenue, New York, New York 10110, and can be found online at www.countrymanpress.com. The author may be contacted at explorewny@att.net.

KEY TO SYMBOLS

⚜ **Special Value.** The blue-ribbon icon appears next to lodging, restaurants, and attractions that combine quality and moderate prices.

✎ **Child-Friendly.** The crayon icon appears next to lodging, restaurants, and activities that appeal to families with young children.

♿ **Handicapped Access.** The wheelchair symbol appears next to establishments that are wheelchair accessible.

🐾 **Pet Friendly.** The dog paw symbol appears next to lodgings that accept pets. Not all establishments advertise the fact that they do accept pets, so be sure to inquire when making reservations if you are bringing a pet. Some establishments may charge a rather nominal fee, while others may charge quite a bit to accommodate a pet.

☂ **Rainy-Day Activities.** The umbrella symbol indicates activities and places that are appropriate on bad-weather days.

💍 **Weddings.** The wedding ring symbol appears next to wedding chapels and lodgings that specialize in weddings. The listings included in this book are all in the Niagara Falls area.

🍸 **Nightlife.** The martini glass icon appears in front of restaurants and other establishments with good bars.

✪ **National Historic Landmark.** This icon appears in front of designated National Historic Landmarks in the United States and designated National Historic Sites in Canada.

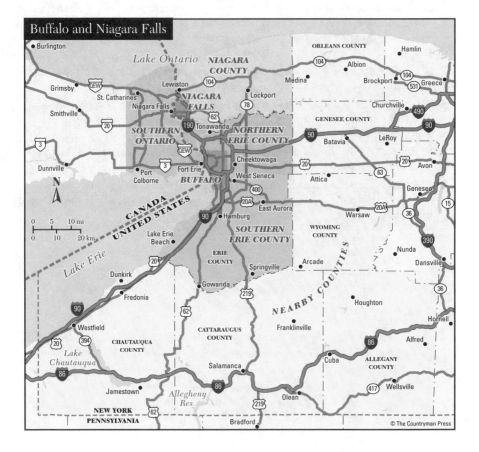

Buffalo and Niagara Falls

CONTENTS

ACKNOWLEDGMENTS | 12

INTRODUCTION | 13

WHAT'S WHERE IN BUFFALO NIAGARA | 15

CITY OF BUFFALO | 31

NORTHERN ERIE COUNTY | 85

GRAND ISLAND, CITY AND TOWN OF TONAWANDA, AND KENMORE | 88

AMHERST | 96

CLARENCE AND AKRON | 110

LANCASTER, DEPEW, AND CHEEKTOWAGA | 117

SOUTHERN ERIE COUNTY | 123

TOWN OF AURORA: EAST AURORA, MARILLA, AND ELMA | 126

ORCHARD PARK AND WEST SENECA | 135

LAKE ERIE TOWNS: HAMBURG, BLASDELL, EDEN, ANGOLA, AND DERBY (ALSO NORTH COLLINS) | 141

SKI COUNTRY: BOSTON, HOLLAND, COLDEN, GLENWOOD, SPRINGVILLE, AND WEST FALLS | 149

CITY OF NIAGARA FALLS, NEW YORK | 155

NIAGARA COUNTY | 169

NORTH OF THE FALLS: LEWISTON, YOUNGSTOWN, SANBORN, RANSOMVILLE, AND PORTER | 172

NORTH TONAWANDA AND WHEATFIELD | 187

LAKE ONTARIO SHORE: WILSON, OLCOTT, BURT, NEWFANE, AND BARKER | 195

CANAL TOWNS: LOCKPORT, MIDDLEPORT, AND GASPORT | 204

SOUTHERN ONTARIO | 215

FORT ERIE | 218

NIAGARA FALLS, ONTARIO | 226

NIAGARA-ON-THE-LAKE AND QUEENSTON | 241

WELLAND CANAL CORRIDOR: ST. CATHARINES/PORT DALHOUSIE, THOROLD, WELLAND, AND PORT COLBORNE | 258

OVERVIEW OF NEARBY COUNTIES | 271

GENESEE | 272

ORLEANS | 274

WYOMING | 275

CHAUTAUQUA | 276

CATTARAUGUS | 278

ALLEGANY | 279

INDEX | 281

MAPS

OVERALL MAP: BUFFALO AND NIAGARA FALLS | 8
BUFFALO | 32
NORTHERN ERIE COUNTY | 86
SOUTHERN ERIE COUNTY | 124
NIAGARA FALLS, NEW YORK | 156
NIAGARA COUNTY | 170
SOUTHERN ONTARIO | 216
GENESEE COUNTY | 273
ORLEANS COUNTY | 274
WYOMING COUNTY | 275
CHAUTAUQUA COUNTY | 277
CATTARAUGUS COUNTY | 278
ALLEGANY COUNTY | 280

ACKNOWLEDGMENTS

I couldn't have written a book of this magnitude without help. Friends, family, and strangers alike supplied me with moral support as well as information. I could fill a book just with the names of people who were so generous and accommodating in sharing information.

First and foremost, I'd like to thank God, for giving me the writing ability, as well as the strength and patience, to see this project through. On more than one occasion, I think divine intervention must have been at work as I did my research. Often I would strike up a conversation with a shopkeeper or restaurant owner, and they would be exactly the right person I needed to talk to in order to find the information I was seeking.

Next, I'd like to thank my husband, Jim, and my children, Andy, Peter, Jennifer, and Joey, who had to put up with me while I wrote this book. My special thanks to Jim, who offered encouragement and suggestions as well as a second set of eyes to proofread the book. I would have never completed it without his love and support.

A very special thanks goes to my daughter, Jennifer, who was always willing to accompany me on day trips, try new restaurants, and of course, visit stores! She made working on this book a fun experience, and I couldn't have done it without her as my sidekick as well as an extra set of eyes to observe things I missed. Plus, we had a lot of mother-daughter bonding time! My lifelong friends, Mary and Linda, also joined me on some of my adventurers.

Of course, I must thank my late parents, Joseph and Adele Kloch, who sparked my interest in local travel when I was a young child and encouraged me in my writing career.

The folks at local chambers of commerce and visitors bureaus, as well as business owners, were invaluable. I would like to thank every single one of them by name, but space will not permit. If you helped me in any way at all, I extend my sincere thanks.

Finally, thanks to the folks at the Countryman Press, a division of W. W. Norton & Company, for allowing me to write this guide.

INTRODUCTION

You hold in your hands the first comprehensive book on the market to describe all there is to see and do in the Buffalo Niagara region, from the grandeur of Niagara Falls to new attractions and restaurants in the City of Buffalo to small out-of-the-way villages in the outlying areas. Whatever your interest is, you can find it in Buffalo Niagara. This book includes information on the City of Buffalo, Erie County, Niagara County, and Niagara Falls, New York, as well as Niagara Falls, Ontario, and its vicinity, including Fort Erie, Niagara-on-the-Lake, and the Welland Canal Corridor.

If history is your thing, in Buffalo Niagara you will find hundreds of museums, both big and small, along with numerous designated National Historic Landmarks, including the site of a presidential inauguration. The area also has one of the oldest structures in the Great Lakes region, the French Castle at Old Fort Niagara.

Closely entwined with the region's history is its unique architecture, including Buffalo structures designed by three of the nineteenth century's most prominent architects: Frank Lloyd Wright, Louis Sullivan, and Henry Hobson Richardson. Buffalo also has park systems designed by noted landscape architect Frederick Law Olmsted. Many of the small towns throughout the area have historic downtown business districts that have been virtually untouched since the early 1900s.

If you enjoy arts and culture, Buffalo Niagara offers a wide array of theaters, art galleries, and other cultural institutions. This region has the largest concentration of theaters in the state, outside of New York City.

Buffalo Niagara has a lot to offer in the way of outdoor recreational activities. With its abundance of lakes, rivers, and streams, it is a boaters'—as well as anglers'—paradise. If you like getting close to nature, the area has numerous parks and nature centers, as well as campgrounds. You don't have to head south to enjoy good golfing; there are many top-rated courses right in the area. With the region's legendary winters, skiing is one of the most popular cold-weather activities. And just for the record, it's not always snowy and cold in Buffalo—there are four distinct seasons!

Across the border, you can enjoy Niagara-on-the-Lake, Canada's prettiest town, take a drive along the Welland Canal Corridor or the scenic Niagara Parkway, or enjoy all the attractions and nightlife in Niagara Falls, Ontario.

If you are inclined to more leisurely recreational activities, this book also describes numerous wineries and breweries in the Buffalo Niagara region of New York State, as well as those in southern Ontario. Other interesting places listed include country stores, bed & breakfast inns, and of course, hundreds of restaurants, along with annual events and festivals.

This book was written with a wide audience in mind, including tourists and travelers to the area, who want to know what else there is to do once they've seen Niagara Falls and eaten chicken wings. Natives will also enjoy the book, as it describes many little-known, out-of-the-way places they may wish to explore. Parents looking for places to take the kids on school breaks and summer vacations will appreciate the "kid-friendly" icons used throughout the book. If you are seeking a getaway without the kids, you'll find many romantic bed & breakfast inns and sophisticated restaurants included here. History buffs will enjoy the little-known historical facts presented in the introduction to each chapter, as well as the descriptions of the many museums located throughout the region. If you are a tour operator or plan trips for school, youth, or senior citizens' groups, you will find this book to be an invaluable resource.

The basic format of each chapter begins with an overview of that area—including a brief history and helpful information on where to go for guidance, travel directions, locations of hospitals, etc.—as well as a brief history of the towns.

Each chapter is then broken down into sections that cover a specific town or group of towns. These sections describe things to see—such as museums and historic sites—and things to do—including boat excursions, golf courses, and family activities. In the *Green Space* sections, you will find parks, beaches, and nature centers. Each section also has descriptions of available lodging, restaurants, entertainment venues, and shops. I have personally visited or contacted each business listed and have included only those establishments that offer quality goods and services. Concluding each section are highlights of that county's annual events and festivals.

While I have tried to include as much information as possible about the Buffalo Niagara region, any travel guide has space limitations, so it would be impossible to include every town, attraction, restaurant, lodging, and store. I therefore picked places that have wide appeal and are generally welcoming to visitors.

Enjoy exploring Buffalo Niagara!

—Christine A. Smyczynski, Getzville, NY

WHAT'S WHERE IN BUFFALO NIAGARA

General Information

TOURISM Contact information for local convention and visitor's bureaus and other tourism information centers is listed at the beginning of each chapter.

AIRPORTS AND AIR SERVICE The **Buffalo Niagara International Airport** (716-630-6000; www.buffaloairport.com) is served by most major airlines, including American, Delta, Jet Blue, Southwest, and United. The **Niagara Falls International Airport** (716-855-7300; www.niagarafallsairport.com) has flights by Spirit Airlines and Allegiant Air to Myrtle Beach and several Florida cities.

AMTRAK The train service has regularly scheduled stops at stations on Dick Road in **Depew** (716-683-8440), on Exchange Street in downtown **Buffalo** (716-856-2075), and in **Niagara Falls**. For detailed information, check out www.amtrak.com, or call 800-872-7245.

AREA CODES The area code in Buffalo and surrounding areas is 716. When calling southern Ontario, Canada, the area code is either 905 or 289.

BUS SERVICE New York Trailways Bus Service operates throughout New York State (800-295-5555; trailwaysny.com). **Greyhound** (800-231-2222; www.greyhound.com) also operates throughout the state. The **Niagara Frontier Transportation Authority** (NFTA) (716-855-7211; www.nfta.com), 181 Ellicott Street, Buffalo, operates buses in Buffalo,

Niagara Falls, Lockport, and their outlying suburbs.

CANADIAN CUSTOMS For information on entering Canada, see the introduction to the *Southern Ontario* chapter.

CASINO GAMBLING While high-stakes casino gambling is not permitted in New York State per se, it is legal on Native American tribal reservations. The **Seneca Niagara Casino** in Niagara Falls is built on land owned by the Seneca

FALLSVIEW CASINO RESORT, NIAGARA FALLS, ONTARIO

Nation of Indians. They also operate the **Seneca Allegany Casino** in Salamanca and the **Seneca Buffalo Creek Casino** in the City of Buffalo. Across the border in Niagara Falls, Ontario, **Casino Niagara** and the **Niagara Fallsview Casino Resort** draw patrons from both sides of the border. In Canada you must be 19 years old to enter a casino; in New York State, you must be 21.

EMERGENCIES Dial 911 in both the United States and Canada for emergencies.

HANDICAPPED ACCESSIBLE While most new buildings are accessible, some of the older historic sites described in this book may not be accessible or have only partial access.

LOCAL LINGO When folks who live in the Buffalo Niagara region want a carbonated beverage to drink, they ask for a "pop," meaning soda pop. If they order a "blue" at a bar, they mean a Labatt's Blue beer, a Canadian import very popular in these parts. While the rest of the country refers to the region's most famous

culinary food as "Buffalo wings" or "chicken wings," they are merely called "wings" by locals. "Weck," as in "beef on weck," refers to the kimmelweck roll, a local specialty, similar to a Kaiser roll but topped with coarse salt and caraway seeds. The big blue water tower is a local landmark located where the New York State Thruway (I-90) and the Youngmann Expressway (I-290) converge, often the site of much traffic congestion. Lastly, if someone tells you they are going to the "Canadian Ballet," they are not as cultured as you think; that is a commonly used euphemism for the strip clubs located on the seamier side of Niagara Falls, Ontario.

LODGING There are many choices listed under lodging, from cottages to bed & breakfast inns to four-star resort hotels. Some of the bed & breakfast establishments have age restrictions for children, and most lodgings, except for those noted with the 🐾 icon at the margin, do not accept pets.

LODGING—RATES Please do not hold the innkeepers or author to the lodging rates listed in this book, as price increases are often inevitable, and prices may vary seasonally, so call ahead to confirm rates. Reservations are generally recommended, especially during peak seasons. Below is a chart used in this book to show average lodging rates.

$	Less than $100 per night
$$	$100–200 per night
$$$	$200–300 per night
$$$$	More than $300 per night

NATIVE AMERICAN CULTURE A book about western New York would not be complete without mentioning Native American heritage and culture. All of New York State was once occupied by the Iroquois Nation. One of the five original Iroquois Nations, the Seneca Nation—known as the Keepers of the Western Door—lived in the western portion of the state.

GUEST ROOM AT THE INN BUFFALO OFF ELMWOOD

LAKE-EFFECT SNOW

If you are visiting western New York during the winter, most likely you'll hear the words "lake-effect snow" uttered during a weather forecast. This weather phenomenon, common in the Great Lakes Region from November through January, occurs when Lake Erie is not frozen. Cold arctic air moves over the relatively warm lake water and picks up moisture as it crosses Lake Erie. This moisture is deposited as heavy snow on the downwind shores of the lake. This type of snowfall often comes down in narrow bands, resulting in heavy snowfall in one area and clear skies a few miles away. Most communities in western New York have the snow-fighting equipment to keep up with this heavy snowfall, but lake-effect snow is often responsible for hazardous driving conditions and school closings.

After the Holland Land Purchase and the arrival of European settlers, life changed dramatically for the Seneca. Treaties had to be negotiated to protect Seneca lands. The Big Tree Treaty in 1797 established several reservations for the Native Americans. Today four Seneca reservations and one Tuscarora reservation are located in the western part of the state. Three of the larger Seneca reservation are the Tonawanda Reservation near Akron, the Cattaraugus Reservation near Gowanda, and the Allegany Reservation in Salamanca. The fourth is the Oil Springs Reservation near Cuba in Allegany County, a one-mile square area surrounding a natural oil spring with a large amount of medicinal herbs growing nearby. The Tuscarora Reservation is located near Lewiston in Niagara County.

SUNDAYS AND MONDAYS Many shops and restaurants, along with some museums, may be closed on Sunday and/ or Monday. If you'll be traveling any distance to a particular listing, always call ahead to check the hours because many establishments change their hours seasonally.

SMOKING Smoking is not permitted in most restaurants and bars in both the United States and Canada, except for the casinos on Native American tribal reservations.

TRAFFIC AND HIGHWAY TRAVEL TIPS Locals often joke that there are really only two seasons in western New York: winter and road construction. Allow extra time when traveling during the warmer months, due to construction delays. In winter, the major roads are generally in good shape due to the region's top-notch snow-fighting equipment, but side streets—even in the cities—may prove challenging after a big storm.

WEATHER Western New York has four distinct seasons despite its reputation as the snow capital of the nation, earned as a result of a major blizzard that hit the Buffalo area in 1977. While the metro Buffalo area does get its fair share of snow in the winter—an average of 93 inches annually, measured at the Buffalo Airport—the regions south of the city, where the ski resorts are located, usually get around 180 inches, making this some of the best ski country in the northeast. Summers in western New York are beautiful, with temperatures in the 70s and 80s, lots of sunshine, and very low humidity. Spring and fall are cool but pleasant.

WEDDINGS Several wedding chapels are located in both Niagara Falls, New York, and Niagara Falls, Ontario. They are identified with the ♂ symbol. Please note that wedding arrangements must generally be made well in advance—these are not Las Vegas–style elopement chapels—although some will perform ceremonies, including same-sex, on short notice. Refer to the chapters that cover these cities for more information about obtaining a marriage license.

Arts

ART ASSOCIATIONS AND COUNCILS **Arts Service Initiative of WNY** (716-363-8389; www.asiwny.com) is the local arts council serving the five counties of Erie, Niagara, Chautauqua, Cattaraugus, and Allegany. **Niagara Arts and Cultural Center** (716-282-7530; www.thenacc.org) in Niagara Falls, is home to over 70 visual and performing artists' studios.

ARTISTS AND GALLERIES One of the larger art centers in Buffalo is **Hallwalls Contemporary Arts Center** (716-835-7362; www.hallwalls.org). This arts center focuses on visual, performing, media, and literary arts. Dozens of smaller galleries can be found in Buffalo, many located in and around the Allentown and Elmwood Village areas. Lockport's **Kenan Center** (716-433-2617; www.kenancenter.org) is an arts, education,

and recreation center. **The Art 247** (716-404-9884; theart247.com), located in a historic building on the banks of the Erie Canal in Lockport, features several art galleries showcasing the work of Niagara County artists, along with 20 working artists' studios.

ART MUSEUMS The larger museums in the region include the **Albright-Knox Art Gallery** (716-882-8700; www.albrightknox.org) on Elmwood Avenue in Buffalo. The gallery, which opened in 1905, is one of the nation's oldest public art organizations. Across the street, the **Burchfield-Penney Art Center** (716-878-6011; www.burchfield-penney.org) showcases the talents of western New York artists. The **Castellani Art Museum** (716-286-8200; www.castellaniartmuseum.org), on the campus of Niagara University in Lewiston, has over 5,000 pieces of mostly modern art.

THEATER From summer stock to large professional companies, there are numerous theaters throughout the region. The Buffalo Niagara region alone has the highest concentration of theaters in the state, outside of New York City.

ALBRIGHT KNOX ART GALLERY

THE ERIE COUNTY FAIR IS THE LARGEST COUNTY FAIR IN THE UNITED STATES

You'll find theaters listed under the Entertainment heading, right after the restaurant listings.

Food and Drink

AGRICULTURAL FAIRS The Erie County Fair, held in the town of Hamburg each August, is the largest county fair in the United States. Niagara County also hosts an agricultural fair each summer, as do most other nearby counties.

APPLES New York State is the second largest apple-producing state—first in the number of varieties—and the Lake Ontario shore, particularly Niagara County, is one of the state's principal apple-growing regions. Locally grown apples and apple cider are available at farm markets and at u-pick farms throughout the region. For more information, visit the **New York State Apple Association** website: www .nyapplecountry.com.

BEER, WINE, AND SPIRITS More than 70 wineries in western New York and southern Ontario are highlighted in this book. Many are located near Lake Erie and Lake Ontario's shorelines. Most offer tastings and sales of their products, and many also offer tours. Several wine trails—associations of wineries, retailers,

YOU CAN TOUR THE WINE CELLARS AT MANY LOCAL WINERIES

inns and restaurants located in a particular area—run throughout western New York. These trails include **Niagara County Wine Trail**, **Chautauqua–Lake Erie Wine Trail**, and the wineries of **Niagara-on-the-Lake**. There are also a number of breweries and distilleries listed in this book.

FARM MARKETS New York State rates in the top five producers of many crops, including apples, cabbage, and pumpkins. Designated farmland occupies 25 percent of the state. For a complete listing of farmers' markets, visit farmsandfood.agriculture.ny.gov/farmsandfood/consumer/viewHome.do.

FISH FRY If you're not a native western New Yorker, you'll probably wonder why so many restaurants are noted for their Friday night fish fries. This tradition harkens back to the days when the area's largely Catholic population was required to abstain from eating meat on Fridays. Since the Second Vatican Council in 1962, abstinence needed only to be observed on Fridays during Lent and on Ash Wednesday and Good Friday, and yet the tradition continues. Local bars and restaurants serve up over 100,000 pounds of fish each week.

MAPLE SUGARING New York State is the third-largest maple producer in the world. About 17 percent of all syrup made in America—about 700,000 gallons—is produced in New York. In 1995 a group of Wyoming County maple producers decided to open their facilities to showcase the making of maple products. The event, referred to as **Maple Weekend** (www.mapleweekend.com), demonstrates the maple-sugaring process, from tapping the trees and collecting the sap to boiling it into syrup. Most producers offer a variety of other activities that weekend, from pancake breakfasts to children's activities. This event takes place on working farms, so dress according to the weather, and wear boots or old shoes, because conditions are often muddy and visitors may have to walk a distance from their cars to the sugar shacks.

RESTAURANTS—REGIONAL CHAINS Several regional chain restaurants were founded in the area and have expanded to include multiple locations. Stop by one of these if you want to experience a true taste of western New York. Some of the popular chains in the Buffalo area include **John and Mary's**, which has specialized in submarine sandwiches, wings, and pizza for nearly 50 years; **Ted's Hot Dogs** (www.tedsonline.com), famous for over 75 years for their foot-long Sahlen's hot dogs as well as hamburgers; and **Anderson's** (www.andersonscustard.com), known for roast beef on kimmelweck and soft custard.

Of course, let's not forget the Canadian-based chains, like **Tim Horton's** (www.timhortons.com), popular for their coffee and donuts, as well as sandwiches. It was founded in Canada in the 1960s by Tim Horton, who played hockey for the Buffalo Sabres in the early 1970s. You will find one about every 4 or 5 miles in more populated areas. Then there is **Swiss Chalet** (www.swisschalet.com), a Canadian chain which used to have several locations in the Buffalo area. However,

TIM HORTON'S IS POPULAR FOR COFFEE

CHICKEN WINGS

Better known as "Buffalo wings," or merely "wings" to locals, these are a must-taste item when visiting the region. No other culinary creation has put Buffalo on the map like the chicken wing. The once lowly wing, which was relegated to the stockpot in the past, has become wildly popular not only in Buffalo but throughout the United States, Canada, and many other countries.

This phenomenon started on a Friday night back in 1964 at Frank and Theresa Bellissimo's Anchor Bar in Buffalo. Their son, Dom, arrived with a bunch of hungry friends and he asked his mom to fix them something to eat. Theresa spotted a plate of chicken wings in the kitchen that were about to go into the soup pot. Thinking they looked too nice to be put into soup, she deep fried them, poured on some hot sauce, and, well, the rest is history. Chicken wings can be found on most menus throughout western New York. Some of the best known wing places include the Anchor Bar, where Buffalo wings made their debut; La Nova Pizzeria, which is equally well-known for its pizza as it is for wings; and Duffs, a popular wing spot in the suburbs.

the chain pulled out of the United States and is now only in Canada. There are two locations in Niagara Falls, Ontario, and folks from the Buffalo area are known to make regular pilgrimages there to get their fix. Yes, the chicken is that good!

Museums and Historic Sites

AFRICAN AMERICAN HISTORICAL AND CULTURAL SITES The Buffalo Niagara area has many significant African American cultural sites. The region played an important role in assisting escaped slaves on the Underground Railroad. The Niagara Movement, the forerunner of the NAACP, was founded in this region and they held their first conference in Niagara Falls, Ontario, in 1905.

AVIATION MUSEUMS For a time the center of aviation in the United States was Buffalo, New York, where the world's largest aircraft plant was built in 1917. The **Niagara Aerospace Museum** in Niagara Falls, features vintage aircraft and memorabilia as well as an overview of aviation history.

HISTORIC HOMES, MUSEUMS, AND HISTORIC SITES Almost every city, town, and village in the area has a historical society and historic homes, along with unique museums. Some of the "must-sees" for history buffs include: the **Buffalo History Museum, Darwin Martin House, Theodore Roosevelt Inaugural Site**, and **Buffalo and Erie County Naval and Military Park** in Buffalo; **Graycliff** in

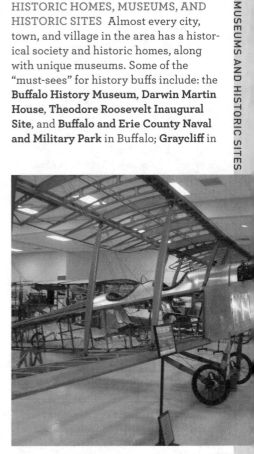

VINTAGE AIRCRAFT AT THE NIAGARA AEROSPACE MUSEUM

LOCAL CUISINE

Besides the previously mentioned chicken wings, other western New York culinary favorites include beef on weck—thinly sliced beef served on a salty kimmelweck roll. When craving a hot dog, Buffalonians prefer Sahlen's or Wardynski's, preferably topped with Weber's horseradish mustard. Buffalo natives who now live in other parts of the country have been known to take home a care package of local favorites after coming home to visit friends and relatives.

Another popular chicken in western New York is Chiavetta's chicken, which can be found at events and fund raisers throughout the summer. Their famous BBQ marinade and salad dressings can be purchased at local supermarkets.

Speaking of local cuisine, the place where many people purchase ingredients is Wegmans, a local family-owned supermarket chain founded in nearby Rochester in 1916. With close to 50 stores throughout the region, it is more than just a supermarket; to some it's a tourist destination!

Derby; and the **Niagara Historical Society** in Niagara-on-the-Lake.

NATIONAL HISTORIC LANDMARKS These sites commemorate significant historical events, places where prominent Americans lived or worked, important ideals of our past, or outstanding architectural design. National Historic Landmarks featured in this guide are marked with the symbol ✪. Also mentioned in the book are buildings listed on the **National Register of Historic Places**. While not as significant as the National Historic Landmarks, these are buildings and places that are considered cultural resources worthy of preservation.

Nature

BEACHES With two Great Lakes, abundant rivers, and numerous other large and small lakes, there are many beaches in the region. Some of the more popular ones include: **Beaver Island State Park** on the Niagara River; **Woodlawn Beach**; **Wendt Beach, Bennett Beach, Evangola,** and **Sunset Bay** on Lake Erie; **Wilson Tuscarora** and **Olcott Beach** on Lake Ontario in Niagara County; and **Bay Beach, Crystal Beach, Crescent Beach,**

Thunder Bay, and **Wavery Beach** in southern Ontario.

EMPIRE PASS This annual all-season park pass, which can be purchased from the New York State Parks, allows the purchaser access to most state parks and recreational facilities. For New York State residents over age 62, the Golden Park Program allows free access to state parks on non-holiday weekdays. For information about all park admission programs, call 518-474-0456 or visit parks.ny.gov/admission/empire-passport.

GARDENS Horticulturists will enjoy the beautiful botanical gardens located in Buffalo Niagara, including the **Buffalo and Erie County Botanical Gardens** in Buffalo and the **Niagara Parks Botanical Gardens** in Niagara Falls, Ontario.

NATURE PRESERVES Many areas in western New York have been set aside as nature preserves. Some of them include **Tifft Nature Preserve** in Buffalo; **Buckhorn Island State Park** on Grand Island; **Reinstein Woods Nature Preserve** in Depew, a 300-acre preserve with an undisturbed ancient forest; and **Penn Dixie Paleontological Site** in Hamburg, which has an abundance of fossils.

NIAGARA ESCARPMENT Throughout this book there are references to the Niagara Escarpment, a ledge of solid rock running through New York State that created Niagara Falls. The city of Lockport is also located along the escarpment, which necessitated the construction of the "flight of five" locks on the Erie Canal to raise boats traveling west to the top of the escarpment and lower those traveling east. Route 104 is known as "the Ridge," meaning the ridge of the Niagara Escarpment. The ridge was once the shoreline of ancient Lake Iroquois, created by Canadian glaciers. Over time this lake receded to become present-day Lake Ontario.

PARKS There are thousands of parks in the Buffalo Niagara region, from small neighborhood parks to huge state parks. Since it's impossible to list every single park, I have listed—in the Green Space sections—those that offer the most diverse recreational attractions, have the best scenery, are historic in nature, or just are great places to spend some free time. For detailed information on the New York State parks mentioned in this book, check out www.nysparks.com.

FRANK LLOYD WRIGHT

Considered by many to be America's greatest architect, Wright designed more than 420 buildings during his illustrious career. Some of his nationally known designs include the Guggenheim Museum in New York City and Fallingwater in Pennsylvania. Wright is especially known for his Prairie Style buildings, which have low horizontal lines and pick up the features found in the surrounding landscape. He was the first US architect to design homes with open spaces, often eliminating the walls between rooms. Several Wright-designed structures can be found in Buffalo and western New York, including the **Darwin D. Martin House** and **Graycliff**, which both offer tours.

NATURE

SCENIC HIGHWAYS The **Great Lakes Seaway Trail** is a 518-mile scenic route

ENJOY NATURE A SHORT DISTANCE FROM DOWNTOWN BUFFALO AT TIFFT NATURE PRESERVE

PAN-AMERICAN EXPOSITION

The eyes of the world were focused on Buffalo in 1901, when the Pan-American Exposition took place. Three hundred fifty acres of farmland were converted into a wonderland of exhibits, midways rides, and unusual attractions. The centerpiece of the exposition was the nearly 400-foot-tall Electric Tower, which soared over the grounds. At night the exposition was transformed into a "City of Light" as the buildings were illuminated. This was considered quite a feat at the turn of the twentieth century, when electric lighting was considered a novelty. Buffalo's close proximity to the power-generating facilities in Niagara Falls made this possible.

The exposition ended tragically when US President William McKinley, who was visiting the exposition, was shot at the Temple of Music on September 5, 1901, by self-proclaimed anarchist Leon Czolgosz. McKinley died of his gunshot wounds little more than a week later on September 14, and Vice President Theodore Roosevelt was sworn into office at the home of his friend Ansley Wilcox. To learn more about the Pan-American Exposition, visit the **Buffalo History Museum** (the only surviving building from the Exposition) or the **Theodore Roosevelt Inaugural National Historic Site** (Wilcox Mansion), which has an in-depth display on the assassination.

THEODORE ROOSEVELT INAUGURAL NATIONAL HISTORIC SITE

NATURE

that goes through New York and Pennsylvania, running parallel to Lake Erie, the Niagara River, Lake Ontario, and the Saint Lawrence River. The trail runs through ten counties and is the state's only National Scenic Byway. Marked with green Great Lakes Seaway Trail signs, the trail takes you through quaint villages and other scenic sites that would be missed if you traveled on a superhighway. There are also 42 War of 1812 sites along the trail, marked with brown War of 1812 signs. For more information www.seawaytrail.com.

Besides the previously mentioned Great Lakes Seaway Trail, several other roadways in the region offer scenic vistas, along with historic sites and unusual landmarks. If you're looking for a ride in the country, try **Route 104** from Niagara

Falls to Rochester, where you'll pass farms, farm markets, and antiques stores, as well as numerous homes of cobblestone construction. Looking for spectacular scenery? Take a drive along the 38-mile-long **Niagara Parkway** in Canada from Fort Erie to Niagara-on-the-Lake, once described by Winston Churchill as the "world's prettiest Sunday afternoon drive."

WATERFALLS While **Niagara Falls** is by far the most well-known waterfall in the region, numerous other waterfalls throughout western New York offer scenic vistas. These falls were formed when water began to flow over the Onandaga Escarpment, a 67-mile-long rock layer running from Buffalo to Rochester. It is about 20 miles south of the Niagara Escarpment, over which Niagara Falls flows. If you like waterfalls, be sure to check out: **Glen Falls** in Williamsville, a 27-foot-high falls located in a beautiful park; **Akron Falls**, a 50-foot lower falls and a 20-foot upper falls over the escarpment in Akron Park; and **Indian Falls**, a 30-foot-high falls, in Tonawanda Creek near the Tonawanda Indian reservation ("Tonawanda" is the Iroquois word for "swift water").

Outdoors and Family Fun

AMUSEMENT PARKS The region's largest amusement park, **Darien Lake Theme Park Resort** (585-599-4641; www.darienlake.com) in nearby Genesee County, has hundreds of rides and attractions, including a huge waterpark complex. **Fantasy Island** (716-773-7591; www.fantasyislandny.com) on Grand Island, is just the right size for families with young children; **Marineland** (905-356 9565), in Niagara Falls, Ontario, offers amusement rides along with live dolphin, seal, and whale shows.

AQUARIUMS The **Aquarium of Niagara** (716-285-3575; www.aquariumofniagara.org), in Niagara Falls, New York, has over 1,500 types of aquatic animals including sharks, piranhas, moray eels,

AQUARIUM OF NIAGARA, NIAGARA FALLS, NY

NATURE / OUTDOORS AND FAMILY FUN

along with a state-of-the-art Humboldt Penguin exhibit. Across the border in Niagara Falls, Ontario, **Marineland** (905-356-2142; www.marinelandcanada.com) is one of the largest aquariums in the world, featuring a huge variety of aquatic life.

BICYCLING The **Greater Buffalo Niagara Regional Transportation Council** (GBNRTC) has a bicycle map of the Buffalo Niagara region on their website, www.gbnrtc.org. Walking, hiking, and biking trails are listed under the *Green Space* heading of each section.

BOATING With its abundance of lakes, rivers, and streams, Buffalo Niagara is a boater's paradise, for pleasure crafts, fishermen, kayakers, and canoers. Public marinas are listed under *Green Space* in each section.

BOAT TOURS AND EXCURSIONS There are numerous scenic boat excursions to choose from across Buffalo Niagara, including the **Buffalo Harbor Cruises** (Miss Buffalo) and the **Grand Lady** in the City of Buffalo, the **Maid of the Mist** in Niagara Falls, New York, **Hornblower Niagara Cruises** in Niagara Falls, Ontario, and the **Lockport Locks & Canal Cruises** and the **Lockport Cave and Underground Boat Ride** in Lockport.

CAMPING Private, public, and state-run campsites abound in western New York. See *Other Lodging* in each chapter. For more information on camping in New York State parks, call 800-456-CAMP.

FISHING With its abundance of lakes, rivers, and streams, Buffalo Niagara is an angler's paradise, with catches including small- and large-mouth bass, walleye,

THE *MAID OF THE MIST*, NIAGARA FALLS, NY

ERIE CANAL

The Erie Canal, the most well-known canal in America, is a 350-mile waterway that threads its way through New York State from Buffalo to Albany. When it opened in 1825, it was considered the greatest engineering marvel of the world. It was originally 40 feet wide, 4 feet deep, and 363 miles long. It had 83 locks and 18 aqueducts over rivers. Over the years the canal has been widened, rerouted, and shortened. Today the waterway has 35 locks and four aqueducts remaining.

It is now part of the 524-mile New York State Canal System, which also includes the Cayuga Seneca Canal, Oswego Canal, Champlain Canal, and Hudson River. While transportation was the main application of the canal when it first opened, today's focus is on recreational boating, fishing, and tourism. Towns located along the canal feature quaint shops, restaurants, canal side parks, and walking trails.

To learn more about the Erie Canal (800-422-6254), refer to the New York State Canal System website at www.canals.ny.gov.

trout, salmon, muskellunge, and pike. New York State fishing licenses can be obtained at most county clerk's offices as well as at local sporting goods establishments. A state fishing license can be applied for online at www.dec.ny.gov/permits/6091.html.

GOLF Golf courses are listed under *To Do* sections. Some of the finest courses in the Northeast can be found in Buffalo Niagara. For further information on golf in the area, check out Buffalo Golf Guide at buffalogolfer.com/wordpress.

HUNTING For questions on New York's hunting seasons and regulations, contact the DEC (800-933-2257; www.dec.ny.gov/permits/6094.html). Licenses can be purchased over the counter at certain sporting goods stores, some major discount stores, and at town clerk's offices.

RAINY-DAY ACTIVITIES The ⊤ icon indicates places that are good to visit when the weather is inclement.

SKIING AND SNOWSHOEING The following alpine ski resorts, located south of the city, have downhill trails: **Holiday Valley**, **Kissing Bridge**, and **Peek 'n Peak**. **Bryncliff Resort** in Varysburg offers cross-country skiing and snow-shoeing, as do Holiday Valley and Peek n' Peak. Most of the larger state and county parks have cross-country and snowshoe trails.

SNOWMOBILING One of the more popular winter activities in New York State is snowmobiling, with over 10,000 miles of state-funded snowmobile trails winding through the state, many in state parks. Riders under 18 are required to take a snowmobile safety course. For information on the course or for a trail map, go to parks.ny.gov/recreation/snowmobiles.

SPORTS You can find all sorts of sports in western New York: amateur, college, and professional. Some of the better-known pro teams that play here include the **Buffalo Bills**, **Buffalo Bisons**, and **Buffalo Sabres**, The larger college teams hail from Niagara University, Canisius College, Saint Bonaventure, and the University at Buffalo. Check each chapter's *Entertainment* listings to find sports teams.

WHITE WATER RAFTING There are locations south and east of Buffalo that lend themselves well to white water rafting. One of the more popular white water tour operators is **Adventure Calls** (585-343-4710; www.adventure-calls.com). They offer beginner and intermediate levels of white water rafting with licensed, experienced guides. White water rides are offered in two locations: the Genesee River at Letchworth State Park, perfect for novice paddlers and families, and Cattaraugus Creek in Gowanda, for more adventurous souls.

Sights to See

ARCHITECTURE The works of many well-known architects can be found in western New York, including designs in the city of Buffalo by three leading nineteenth-century architects: Frank Lloyd Wright, H. H. Richardson, and Louis Sullivan.

FALL FOLIAGE Autumn in western New York is an especially beautiful time, particularly in the southern part of the region, with its mountain peaks and valleys. Some of the more popular spots to view fall foliage are just a short drive from Buffalo. These include Letchworth State Park on the border of Wyoming and Livingston Counties, the Zoar Valley outside Gowanda, and Ellicottville in central Cattaraugus County.

FORTS History buffs will want to check out the historic forts located in the region. **Old Fort Niagara** in Youngstown boasts the "French Castle," the oldest structure in the Great Lakes region. Across the Niagara River in Canada, **Fort George** played an important role in the War of 1812. **Old Fort Erie** also features War of 1812 memorabilia.

LIGHTHOUSES The **Buffalo Main Light** can be found at the Buffalo Harbor, while the **Fort Niagara Light** is on the grounds of Old Fort Niagara. Along Lake Ontario, you'll find the **Thirty Mile Point Lighthouse** at Golden Hill State Park. The **Port Abino Lighthouse** is located along Lake Erie in Fort Erie, Ontario.

RELIGIOUS SITES Those seeking the spiritual will want to visit these sites that offer solace and beauty, including **Our Lady of Victory Basilica** in Lackawanna, home of Father Baker, and **Our Lady of**

THE BUFFALO MAIN LIGHT IS AT THE ENTRANCE TO THE BUFFALO HARBOR

Fatima Shrine in Lewiston. There are also many historic churches in the city of Buffalo, including **Saint Joseph's Cathedral**, **Saint Louis Church**, and **Saint Paul's Episcopal**.

UNDERGROUND RAILROAD The Underground Railroad was not an actual rail line but a series of safe houses where people escaping slavery in the South could find refuge on their path to freedom in Canada. With western New York's close proximity to Canada, there were many "stations" in the region. Organized tours of Underground Railroad sites are organized by **Motherland Connextions** (716-282-1028; www .motherlandconnextions.com). Some noted sites include the Michigan Street Baptist Church in Buffalo and Murphy Orchards in Burt. Many slaves crossed the Niagara River on the ferry that operated from Broderick Park, at the foot of

Ferry Street, to Fort Erie, in Canada. There were many more sites in the area, but since aiding runaway slaves was illegal, they are usually not well documented but passed down through oral history.

Shopping

The section on shopping near the end of each chapter highlights a variety of local retail businesses, including antique shops, book stores, art galleries, farmers' markets, gift shops, and more.

Further Reading

You may want to refer to some of these weekly and monthly publications to find out up-to-the-minute information about local festivals, events, and more:

Buffalo News "Gusto" section: Published every Thursday, with listings of what is happening that week, www.buffalonews.com.

Buffalo Spree: A monthly magazine focusing on people and places in the Buffalo area at www.buffalospree.com.

Forever Young magazine: A free monthly publication geared towards people over age 50, www.foreveryoungwny.com.

Western New York Family magazine: A free monthly publication for families with children, www.wnyfamilymagazine.com.

Western New York Wares: A book publisher and distributor which carries books focusing on western New York, www.wnybooks.com.

You may also want to check out the following websites, which have listings of weekly events taking place in the Buffalo area, as well as email newsletters you can sign up to receive:

Buffalo Vibe/Buffalo Citybration: www.buffalovibe.com

Elmwood Village Association: www.elmwoodvillage.org

Step Out Buffalo: www.stepoutbuffalo.com

If you want to learn more about attractions throughout New York State, pick up a copy of my other recently published book, **Backroads and Byways of Upstate New York**, which features twenty drives and day trips throughout upstate New York (www.christinesmyczynski.com).

CITY OF BUFFALO

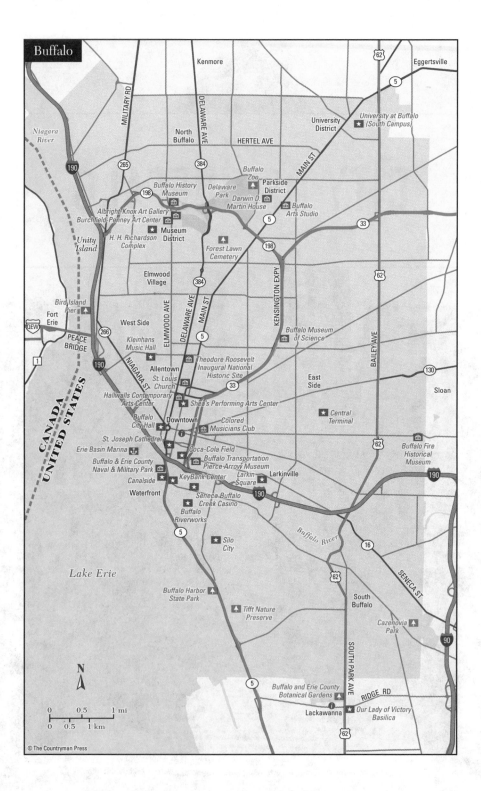

INTRODUCTION

Buffalo, one of New York State's best kept secrets, is a shining jewel on the shores of Lake Erie. The city, which over the past few years has been undergoing a renaissance of sorts, has transformed from an aging rust belt city to a cool place to live, work, and play. Neighborhoods that were once derelict are being transformed into attractive hot spots that people want to go to.

The city is home to dozens of museums, cultural institutions, and theaters, along with an abundance of parks and recreational activities. In addition, Buffalo has some of the finest architecture in the United States; it is the only city besides Chicago to have major works by the three greatest architects of the nineteenth and twentieth centuries: Frank Lloyd Wright, H. H. Richardson, and Louis Sullivan. There are nine National Historic Landmarks within the city limits.

Buffalo's extensive parks and parkway system, designed by the noted nineteenth-century landscape architect Frederick Law Olmsted, the "Father of Landscape Architecture," was Olmsted's first park system designed for any city. Listed on the National Register of Historic Places, the parks represent the largest body of Olmsted's work.

Hundreds of wonderful restaurants, from fine dining to casual eateries, offer locally inspired foods as well as cuisine from around the world. Fast-food junkies know Buffalo as the birthplace of that deep-fried delicacy, the Buffalo chicken wing, which is a must-try when visiting the city. Because of the chicken wings, Buffalo has been recently ranked the third best food city in the nation by *National Geographic* magazine.

BUFFALO'S ART DECO-STYLE CITY HALL TOWERS OVER NIAGARA SQUARE

CITY OF BUFFALO

Including South Buffalo and Lackawanna

✳ A Bit of City History

European settlement began in the region in the late 1700s. Prior to this, the area was home to several Native American tribes. All of western New York west of the Genesee River was part of what is known as the Holland Land Purchase. In 1804, Joseph Ellicott, who was hired by the Dutch Land Purchase Investors to survey the territory, established the grid-like street system of the new settlement at the crossroads of Lake Erie and the Niagara River which he named—in honor of his employers—"New Amsterdam," later renamed Buffalo.

There are several theories as to where the name "Buffalo" came from. One is that Buffalo is a mispronunciation of the French *beau fleuve*, or beautiful river, referring to the scenic river. Another theory is that an Indian named Buffaloe lived at the crossroads, and the area was known as "Buffaloe's Creek." While some may think the area was named after the American bison—or buffalo—there is no evidence that these creatures ever roamed the area.

By 1809 there were over a dozen homes, two taverns, and several businesses in the village; by 1813, over 100 buildings. During the War of 1812, the area became a military post due to its strategic location. The village was burned by the British during the war. Only four buildings remained, and many residents fled to the nearby villages of Williamsville and Clarence. After the war the village slowly rebuilt. Buffalo was incorporated in 1822, and by 1825 there were over 400 structures in town.

The completion of the Erie Canal in 1825, which connected Lake Erie and points west with the Eastern Seaboard, contributed greatly to the city's growth. As the western terminus of the Erie Canal, Buffalo became the nation's busiest inland port by the turn of the twentieth century. Finished goods or raw materials bound for factories would be transferred from the canal boats to freighters that sailed the Great Lakes and the Eastern Seaboard. Buffalo, officially incorporated as a city in 1832, was also the busiest grain transfer port in the world and the world's second largest milling center. The grain elevator, which revolutionized the grain industry, was invented in Buffalo in 1842 by Joseph Dart. "Elevator Alley," lining the Buffalo River, is the world's largest collection of grain elevators.

Harnessing hydroelectric power from nearby Niagara Falls, beginning in 1896, made Buffalo one of the world's most technically advanced cities. The 1901 Pan-American Exposition brought national attention to the city, encouraged industrial progress, and was the largest-scale display of electrical illumination seen up until that time. Unfortunately the Pan-American Exposition also brought about one of the most tragic events to befall the city, the assassination of President William McKinley. Vice President Theodore Roosevelt took the presidential oath of office in Buffalo, making it one of only a handful of presidential inauguration sites outside of Washington, DC.

Buffalo is also rich in African American history. Given its proximity to Canada, it was an important last stop on the Underground Railroad, a means by which escaping slaves could reach freedom. The Niagara Movement, the forerunner to the NAACP, was founded in the city in 1905.

By 1910 Buffalo was the eighth largest city in the United States in terms of population and commerce. Immigrants seeking new lives in the Midwest passed through Buffalo in the nineteenth and early twentieth centuries, giving the city the nickname "Inland Ellis Island." Many of these immigrants remained in Buffalo and established neighborhoods that continue to flavor the city's traditions. As with many other American cities after the 1950s, Buffalo saw a marked decline in population due to changes in transportation and industry.

Fortunately, today's Buffalo is on the upswing, a result of its cultural, historical, and architectural assets, as well as forward-thinking individuals who have invested in the city's future. New developments in the city include a redeveloped waterfront, a state-of-the-art medical campus, expansions at some of the many museums and cultural institutions, and the building of new upscale housing, as people are moving back into the city, since it is a "cool" place to live. Visitors are also flocking to the city, necessitating the building of new hotels and an explosion of new restaurants, brewpubs, and recreational activities.

✳ Getting to Know the City

The city of Buffalo can be broken down into several identifiable sections, each with its own focus and flavor.

DOWNTOWN/CENTER CITY

The downtown area is the business and financial heart of the city as well as the Theatre and Entertainment District. There are numerous theaters as well as restaurants and bars, especially in the areas around Main Street and Chippewa Street. The Buffalo Niagara Medical Campus, which includes the Buffalo General Hospital/Gates Vascular Institute, the Roswell Park Cancer Institute, and the John R. Oishei Children's Hospital, as well as the University at Buffalo Medical School, is also downtown.

WATERFRONT/INNER HARBOR (CANALSIDE, COBBLESTONE DISTRICT, AND RIVERWORKS)

Over the last several years, the Buffalo waterfront has had millions of dollars of new development, the focal point being **Canalside** (44 Prime Street, www.canalsidebuffalo.com), where the terminus of the Erie Canal was located back in the day. Today it is a multi-use entertainment district and the site of festivals, concerts, and year-round activities, from ice skating in winter and paddleboats in summer. Don't forget to take a picture with *Shark Girl*, a sculpture by Casey Riordan located at Canalside.

You can also view illuminated grain elevators, a public art project, across the Buffalo River from Canalside; the display changes with the season. New at Canalside for summer 2018 is the circa-1924 carousel and the Explore & More Children's Museum, formerly in East Aurora.

Adjacent to Canalside, the **Harborcenter** hockey and entertainment complex (www.harborcenter.com) includes two NHL size hockey rinks, a 200-room Marriott Hotel, and several restaurants. Although the rinks are used mainly for armature and college hockey, there is also limited open skating for the general public.

Less than a mile away, **Buffalo River-works** (716-342-2292, www.buffaloriver works.com, 359 Ganson Street) is a former warehouse and grain silo complex that has been transformed into a venue that includes a concert hall, restaurant, and roller derby arena, home to the Queen City Roller Girls. There are also two large outdoor ice rinks. The six ten-story tall silos that tower over Riverworks have been painted to look like a six-pack of Labatt Blue beer, a Canadian beer very popular with folks in Buffalo. A fully functioning brewery recently opened within the "six-pack."

MAKE SURE YOU TAKE A PHOTO WITH SHARK GIRL AT CANALSIDE

WATERFRONT/OUTER HARBOR (WILKESON POINT, GALLAGHER BEACH, TIMES BEACH, BUFFALO HARBOR STATE PARK)

The Outer Harbor (outerharborbuffalo .com) includes Wilkeson Point, a 21-acre park that has biking and walking trails as well as space for festivals and other events. Also in the Outer Harbor are Times Beach Nature Preserve (www.friendsoftimesbeachnp.org/index.html), the Buffalo lighthouse, Gallagher Beach, and Buffalo Harbor State Park.

LARKINVILLE

The area referred to as "Larkinville," also called Larkin Square (www.larkinsquare .com, 745 Seneca Street) was once the site of the Larkin Soap Company warehouse. This public space is a popular community gathering spot for food, music, and fun. Weekly events happening May to October include *Food Truck Tuesdays*, *Live at Larkin* (music) on Wednesdays, and Larkin Farmers' Market on Thursdays. Larkin Square also has two pickleball courts; pickleball combines badminton, tennis, volleyball, and ping pong.

ELMWOOD VILLAGE

Over 250 unique shops, art galleries, restaurants, and bars are located along Elmwood Avenue between Forest Avenue and Allen Street. For a map/brochure, contact Elmwood Village Association, 875 Elmwood Avenue, Buffalo, 716-881-0707 (www.elmwoodvillage.org).

BUFFALO RIVERWORKS

ALLENTOWN

Located on the southern end of the Elmwood Village, Allentown is an eclectic collection of art galleries, antique shops, bars, and restaurants. The neighborhood, which runs along Allen Street from Main to Wadsworth, and a few blocks to the north, south, and west of Allen, was named for Lewis Allen, the uncle of Grover Cleveland, who lived in this area in the early nineteenth century. It is listed on the National Register of Historic Places and is one of the largest urban preservation districts in the nation. It is the site of the Allentown Art Festival in June. (Allentown Association, 716-881-1024; www.allentown.org)

LARKINVILLE IS A POPULAR COMMUNITY GATHERING SPOT

NORTH BUFFALO/HERTEL AVENUE

Hertel Avenue, Buffalo's unofficial "Little Italy," is a walkable urban shopping area lined with an array of shops, restaurants, and other businesses. Since many of the residents in the area are of Italian descent, numerous Italian restaurants can be found here. (Hertel–North Buffalo Business Association, 716-877-6607)

MUSEUM DISTRICT

This area, located near Olmsted-designed Delaware Park, has three major Buffalo cultural institutions within its borders: the Albright-Knox Art Gallery, the Buffalo History

BUFFALO HISTORY MUSEUM

Museum, and the Burchfield-Penney Art Center. The neighborhood is surrounded by spacious parkways lined with elegant mansions, including Lincoln Parkway and Nottingham Terrace. The district is also referred to as the **Olmsted Crescent**. Adjacent to this area is the **Parkside District**, which contains the acclaimed Frank Lloyd Wright–designed Darwin D. Martin House, along with tree-lined streets and restored homes of various architectural styles.

THE EAST SIDE

The East Side of Buffalo is mostly residential and has not yet seen the renaissance that other parts of the city have in recent years. While there are a few places in this area you don't want to venture into at night, there are a number of places of interest that make a trip to the East Side worthwhile, including the Central Terminal and the Broadway Market. Superman fans will want to stroll one block up Kent Street by the Broadway Market to the corner of Clark Street and look at the street sign; you will be standing at the corner of Clark and Kent! In addition to a large African American population, the East Side is home to Buffalo's Polonia, with many historic churches and other Polish heritage sites (broadwayfillmorealive.org/2.0). Many of the annual Dyngus Day events take place in Polonia the day after Easter.

WEST SIDE/BLACK ROCK

This section of town, which is mostly residential, has a very diverse population, with many recent immigrants from Asia and Southeast Asia, a large Hispanic community, as well as Italian-American families who have lived here for several generations. Grant Street, Connecticut Street, and especially Niagara Street are some of the areas that have seen an increase in businesses, housing, and restaurants in recent years. The world-renowned Kleinhan's Music Hall is on the West Side.

UNIVERSITY DISTRICT

The area located near the Main Street (South Campus) of the University at Buffalo is mainly residential, along with a number of restaurants and businesses located along Main Street.

CORNER OF CLARK AND KENT STREETS ON THE EAST SIDE

SOUTH BUFFALO/LACKAWANNA

For the purposes of this book, South Buffalo and Lackawanna are included in the Buffalo section. Located just south of Buffalo is the City of Lackawanna, home of Father Nelson Baker, who oversaw the construction of the massive Our Lady of Victory Basilica in 1926. It is also the location of the century-old Victorian glass conservatory that houses the area's botanical gardens. The city of Lackawanna was once known as the "Steel City of the Great Lakes," taking its name from Lackawanna County, Pennsylvania, where the steel industry began. The steel industry was the major employer in the city from about 1900 until the early 1980s, when massive layoffs forced the plants to shut down. At one point in time, Bethlehem Steel employed about 24,000 workers and was the largest steel plant in the world.

South Buffalo is also home to a large Irish-American population; there is even an Official Irish Heritage District along Abbott Road, including the Buffalo Irish Center (245 Abbott Road, 716-825-9535; www.buffaloirishcenter.com).

AREA CODE The area code for the city is 716.

GUIDANCE ♿ **Buffalo Niagara Convention and Visitors Bureau** (716-852-0511 or 800-283-3256; www.visitbuffaloniagara.com), 403 Main Street, Buffalo.

Buffalo Place (www.buffaloplace.com). This organization has information about places and events in the downtown area.

Lackawanna Area Chamber of Commerce (716-823-8841; www.lackawannachamber .com), 638 Ridge Road, Lackawanna. Open 9 AM–4 PM Monday–Friday.

GETTING THERE *By air:* **Buffalo Niagara International Airport** (716-630-6000; www .buffaloairport.com), 4200 Genesee Street, Cheektowaga. The airport is served by most major airlines.

By bus: **Greyhound Lines** (716-855-7533 or 800-231-2222; www.greyhound.com) operates out of the Ellicott Street Bus Terminal, 181 Ellicott Street at North Division, Buffalo.

By car: There are several approaches to the city. From Rochester and east, take the New York State Thruway (I-90) to I-290 (Youngmann Expressway), where you can connect to either the 33 (Kensington Expressway) or the I-190. The 219 and the I-90 from Erie, Pennsylvania, approach the city from the south. From Canada, take the Queen Elizabeth Way (QEW) to the Peace Bridge. Special note: The Peace Bridge, built in 1927 to commemorate the long-standing friendship between the United States and Canada, is the sixth busiest international border crossing in North America.

By train: **Amtrak** (800-872-7245; www.amtrak.com) has two stations in the Buffalo area, one at 75 Exchange Street, Buffalo (716-856-2075), the other at 55 Dick Rd, Depew (716-683-8440).

GETTING AROUND Buffalo has been referred to as the "20-minute city" because that's how long it usually takes to get from the city to the outlying areas.

By car: The major streets in Buffalo branch out in a radial pattern from the downtown business district.

By bike: **Reddy Bike Share** (716-407-7474; reddybikeshare.socialbicycles.com) has bicycle rentals available within the city of Buffalo and at the north campus of the University at Buffalo.

By bus: **Niagara Frontier Transportation Authority** (716-855-7211; www.nfta .com), 181 Ellicott Street, Buffalo. Numerous routes run throughout the city and to the outlying suburbs, Niagara Falls, and

USE REDDY BIKESHARE TO TRAVEL AROUND THE CITY

Lockport. NFTA also operates the metro rail system, the Buffalo and Niagara Falls International Airports, and the Buffalo Harbor.

By subway: **Light Rail Rapid Transit System** This system travels from the foot of Main Street to the Main Street campus of the University at Buffalo.

By taxi: **Airport Taxi Service** (716-633-8294 or 800-551-9369; www.buffaloairport taxi.com) serves major downtown hotels and the airport. Taxis are available 24 hours.

MEDICAL EMERGENCY Call 911.

HOSPITALS Buffalo General Medical Center/Gates Vascular Institute (716-859-5600; www.kaleidahealth.org), 100 High Street, Buffalo.

Erie County Medical Center (716-898-3000; www.ecmc.edu), 462 Grider Street, Buffalo.

Mercy Hospital of Buffalo (716-826-7000; www.chsbuffalo.org), 565 Abbott Road, Buffalo.

John R. Oishei Children's Hospital (716-859-KIDS; www.kaleidahealth.org), 818 Ellicott Street, Buffalo.

Sisters of Charity Hospital (716-862-2000; www.chsbuffalo.org), 2157 Main Street, Buffalo.

✳ To See

ART MUSEUMS AND GALLERIES ♿ ⬆ **Albright-Knox Art Gallery** (716-882-8700; www.albrightknox.org), 1285 Elmwood Avenue, Buffalo. Tuesday–Sunday 10 AM–5 PM. The gallery is one of the nation's oldest public art organizations. The original 1905 building was designed by Edward B. Green, a distinguished Buffalo architect, and construction was funded by Buffalo philanthropist John J. Albright. The newer wing, designed by Gordon Bunshaft, dedicated in 1962, was constructed thanks to a generous donation by the Seymour H. Knox Jr. family. The exhibits focus mainly on contemporary art, especially post-war American and European art. The gallery's Muse Restaurant is open for lunch, and the gallery also has an extensive gift shop.

The museum is currently undergoing a multimillion dollar expansion, with an additional 23,000 feet of new gallery space in two new buildings. When completed in 2021, it will be known as the Albright Knox Gunderlach Art Museum; Buffalo-born billionaire Jeffrey Gunderlach contributed over $42 million toward the expansion.

Anderson Gallery of the University at Buffalo (716-834-2579; ubartgalleries.buffalo .edu), 1 Martha Jackson Place, Buffalo. Wednesday–Saturday 11 AM–5 PM, Sunday 1–5 PM. Free admission. Home to the university's permanent art collection, the gallery's exhibits include contemporary paintings, sculptures, and graphics.

Art Dialogue Gallery (716-885-2251; www.artdialoguegallery.com), 5 Linwood Avenue, Buffalo. Tuesday–Friday 11 AM–5 PM, Saturday 11 AM–3 PM. Founded in 1985, the exhibits at this gallery feature the works of artists, composers, musicians, poets, and writers living in western New York.

Big Orbit Art Gallery (716-712-4355; www.cepagallery.org), 30D Essex Street, Buffalo. This gallery, part of the CEPA art gallery, focuses on contemporary art created by western New York artists, featuring visual art, music, performance theater, video, and public art projects.

Buffalo Arts Studio (716-833-4450; www.buffaloartsstudio.org), Tri-Main Center, 2495 Main Street, Suite 500, Buffalo. Tuesday–Friday 11 AM–5 PM, Saturday 10 AM–2 PM. The Buffalo Arts Studio features two galleries exhibiting regional, national,

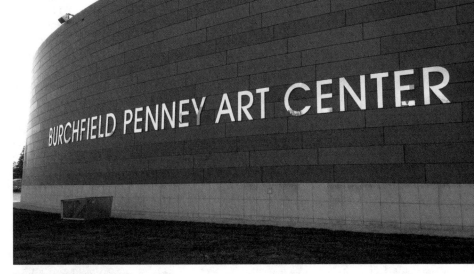

BURCHFIELD PENNEY ART CENTER

and international artists. Forty-five resident artists specialize in painting, printmaking, photography, sculpture, pottery, metalworking, woodworking, and installations.

   ♿ **Burchfield-Penney Art Center** (716-878-6011; www.burchfield-penney.org), 1300 Elmwood Avenue, Buffalo. Tuesday–Saturday 10 AM–5 PM, Thursday until 9 PM, Sunday 1–5 PM, closed holidays. This art museum showcases paintings, photographs, sculptures, and folk art objects by western New York artists, including an extensive collection of works by renowned watercolorist Charles Burchfield, who created the museum in 1966. Art collector Charles Rand Penney gifted the center with more than 1,300 works by western New York artists, including works by Burchfield and by the Roycroft Arts and Crafts Community of East Aurora.

   ♿ **CEPA Gallery** (716-856-2717; www.cepagallery.org), 617 Main Street, Buffalo. The CEPA Gallery was founded in 1974 as a resource for photographic creation, education, and presentation.

   Hallwalls Contemporary Arts Center (716-835-7362; www.hallwalls.org), 341 Delaware Avenue, Buffalo. Tuesday–Friday 11 AM–6 PM, Saturday 11 AM–2 PM. Free admission. This arts center, located in the former Asbury Delaware United Methodist Church, focuses on visual, performing, media, and literary arts. Their mission is to bring new and challenging contemporary art to the public.

   WNY Book Art Center (716-348-1430; www.wnybookarts.org), 468 Washington Street, Buffalo. The center provides understanding of printing and book related arts through education, workshops and exhibits.

PUBLIC LIBRARY ♿ T / **Buffalo and Erie County Public Library** (716-858-8900; www.buffalolib.org), 1 Lafayette Square, Buffalo. This modern library, headquarters to the Buffalo and Erie County Public Library System, houses over three million books on 58 miles of shelves. The 40,000-square-foot building covers more than two city blocks. The Mark Twain Room features a rare book collection, including Twain's *The Adventures of Huckleberry Finn* manuscript and other memorabilia. There is even a small café on the first floor. See *Eating Out*.

MUSEUMS AND HISTORIC HOMES (✪ designates National Historic Landmark)

✪ ✎ ♿ **Buffalo History Museum** (716-873-9644; www.buffalohistory.org), 1 Museum Court, Buffalo. Tuesday, Thursday–Saturday 10 AM–5 PM, Wednesday 10 AM–8 PM, Sunday 12–5 PM. The museum, one of the country's oldest regional historical institutions, is housed in the only remaining structure from Buffalo's 1901 Pan-American Exposition. The white Vermont marble, Greek Revival–style building, a National Historic Landmark, was designed by well-known Buffalo architect George Cary. Displays include the world's largest Pan-American exhibit, as well as changing exhibits focusing on Buffalo and western New York.

✪ **Darwin D. Martin House** (716-856-3858; www.darwinmartinhouse.org), 125 Jewett Parkway, Buffalo. Docent-led tours by reservation only, times vary. The structures located in this complex were designed by well-known architect Frank Lloyd Wright in 1904 for one of his loyal clients, Darwin D. Martin, a wealthy industrialist. The prairie-style Martin House is regarded as one of the greatest residences in the world. The smaller Barton House was built for Martin's sister and her husband. After the Martin family moved out in 1938, the home was vacant for years, then changed hands several times until the 1980s, when the home was given National Historic Landmark status. The Buffalo area has the largest collection of Wright-designed structures east of the Mississippi. Two nearby private residences, the **William R. Heath House** (76 Soldiers Place) and the **Davidson House** (57 Tillinghast Place), were also designed by Wright.

Nash House Museum (716-856-4490; www.nashhousemuseum.org), 36 Nash Street, Buffalo. Thursday and Saturday 11:30 AM–4 PM. This museum features documents, photos, books, and correspondence that relate to the Civil Rights movement. This was the home of the Reverend J. Edward Nash (1868–1957) and his family from 1925 until 1987. Rev. Nash, pastor of the Michigan Avenue Baptist Church from 1892 to 1953, was influential in the Civil Rights Movement.

THE DARWIN D. MARTIN HOUSE WAS DESIGNED BY NOTED ARCHITECT FRANK LLOYD WRIGHT

THE *EDWARD M. COTTER* IS THE OLDEST OPERATING FIREBOAT IN THE WORLD

HISTORIC SITES **Coit House**, 414 Virginia Street, Buffalo. The Coit House, built by George Coit in 1814, is the oldest house in Buffalo. Coit, a prosperous businessman, built the two-story clapboard house on the corner of Pearl and Swan Streets after the fire that devastated the city during the War of 1812. The house was moved to its present location in the 1870s. It is now a private residence.

Colored Musicians Club (716-855-9383), 145 Broadway, Buffalo. Established in 1917 and designated a historic preservation site in 1999, is the longest continuously operating African American musicians club in the entire United States.

✪ **Edward M. Cotter Fireboat**, foot of Ohio Street on the Buffalo River. The *Edward M. Cotter*, built in 1900, is the oldest operating fireboat in the world, which has earned it a National Historic Landmark designation. The boat, which is used to fight fires on floating ships and in waterfront buildings, serves the Buffalo Harbor, Niagara River, and Lake Erie.

Michigan Street Baptist Church, 511 Michigan Street, Buffalo. This brick church, built in 1845, was placed on the National Register of Historic Places in 1974. The church played an important role in the history of the African American community and was a station on the Underground Railroad during the early 1800s. Many noted black abolitionists, like Frederick Douglass and William Wells Brown, made frequent stops here.

✪ **Theodore Roosevelt Inaugural National Historic Site** (716-884-0095; www.nps.gov/thri), 641 Delaware Avenue, Buffalo. Monday–Friday 9 AM–5 PM, Saturday–Sunday 12–5 PM. This National Historic Site, operated by the National Parks Service, also known as the Wilcox Mansion, was the home of Ansley Wilcox, a close friend of Theodore Roosevelt. Following the assassination of President William McKinley at the 1901 Pan-American Exposition in Buffalo, Vice President Roosevelt was sworn in as president in the library of this Victorian-era home; one of only six presidents who took the oath of office outside of Washington, DC.

UNIQUE ARCHITECTURE Buffalo has one of the finest collections of late nine-teenth- and early-twentieth-century buildings and homes in the country. There are nine National Historic Landmarks within the city of Buffalo. It's one of only two cities in the nation that has structures designed by all three of America's greatest architects: Frank Lloyd Wright, Louis Sullivan, and H. H. Richardson. Some architectural gems you don't want to miss include:

Central Terminal (www.buffalocentralterminal.org), 495 Paderewski Drive, Buffalo. This former train station, designed by Stewart Wagner and Alfred Fellheimer in 1929, is a prime example of art deco architecture popular during the 1920s and 1930s. The building, on both the National and State Registers of Historic Places, opened four months before the stock market crash in 1929 and closed in 1979. The 523,000-square-foot building has a massive 225-foot by 66-foot concourse that's just shy of 60 feet high. It is the tallest train station in the country, with a 17-story office tower that's 271 feet high. Currently it is only open for special events and tours.

"Electric Building": Niagara Mohawk Power Building, 535 Washington Street, Buffalo. The design for this 1912 structure was inspired by the Electric Tower at the 1901 Pan-American Exposition.

&. **Ellicott Square Building,** 295 Main Street, Buffalo. The Ellicott Square Building, designed by Burnham and Company, which takes up a whole city block, was the largest office complex in the world when it was completed in 1896. Commemorating Joseph Ellicott, the founder of Buffalo, the building is constructed around a large interior court with inlaid marble floors, one of the most ornate public spaces in the city. The first movie theater in the world, built by Mitchell Mark, was once located in the basement of this building.

THE CENTRAL TERMINAL, BUILT IN 1929, IS A PRIME EXAMPLE OF ART DECO ARCHITECTURE

♧ **Erie Community College City Campus (Old Post Office Building)**, 121 Ellicott Street, Buffalo. The Flemish Gothic Revival structure, designed by James Knox Taylor, has a 245-foot central tower, complete with gargoyles and shallow gothic arched windows. The interior, with its six-story sky lighted courtyard, is magnificent.

✕ **H. H. Richardson Complex (Buffalo Psychiatric Center)**, 400 Forest Avenue, Buffalo. This structure, which has two 184-foot red Medina sandstone towers, was designed by noted architect Henry Hudson Richardson, who considered this building to be his greatest work. It was built between 1879 and 1896 to house New York State's fifth asylum for the insane. Frederick Law Olmsted designed the formal landscaping surrounding the buildings. It has been renovated and contains the Hotel Henry Urban Resort Conference Center. See *Lodging*.

✕ **Kleinhans Music Hall** (716-883-3560; for Buffalo Philharmonic tickets and info: 716-885-5000 or 800-699-3168; www.bpo.org), 71 Symphony Circle, Buffalo. The permanent home of the Buffalo Philharmonic Orchestra, Kleinhans Music Hall is world-renowned for its acoustic excellence. This designated National Historic Landmark is a great setting for the many performances scheduled here throughout the year, including concerts by the BPO and an assortment of other local and national musical, dance, and variety acts. Designed by the architecture firms of F. J. and W. A. Kidd (interior) and Eliel and Eero Saarinen (exterior), it is considered one of the finest works by the Saarinens.

Old County Hall, 92 Franklin Street, Buffalo. Built between 1871 and 1876, this Gothic Revival structure's most notable feature is the clock tower, with sculptures representing justice, agriculture, commerce, and the mechanical arts.

✕ **Prudential Building (Guaranty Building)**, 28 Church Street, Buffalo. This building, designed in 1895 by Louis Henry Sullivan and Dakmar Adler, was cutting edge when it opened. The first steel-supported, curtain-walled building in the world, its features included steel frames, elevators, fireproofing, and electric lights. The outside of the building is decorated with intricate art nouveau red terra-cotta ornaments. There is a museum in the lobby that focuses on the building's history.

St. Joseph Roman Catholic Cathedral (716-854-5844), 50 Franklin Street, Buffalo. The Gothic Revival–style cathedral designed by prominent New York City architect Patrick Keeley was constructed of gray limestone between 1851 and 1862. One of the cathedral's interesting features is the three-story-tall Hook & Hasting pipe organ that was originally built for the 1876 Centennial exposition in Philadelphia, which the diocese purchased at the close of the exposition.

St. Louis Church, Main and Edward Streets, Buffalo. This renovated 1,900-seat church was built in 1889. The fourteenth-century-style Gothic church, one of the largest churches in the city, was modeled after a cathedral in Cologne, Germany. The parish actually was formed in 1829, when land was donated to the city for a church to be built on this spot. It is the oldest Catholic congregation in Buffalo. Several church buildings were erected before this landmark church was built.

✕ **St. Paul's Episcopal Cathedral** (716-855-0900; www.spcbuffalo.org), 128 Pearl Street, Buffalo. This Gothic Revival–style church, Buffalo's first National Architectural Landmark, was designed by Richard Upjohn in 1851. Upjohn, who also designed Trinity Episcopal Church in New York City, regarded St. Paul's as his finest church. The cathedral is open Monday–Saturday 8:30 AM–3:30 PM and Sunday 7:30 AM–2 PM for self-guided tours. (Note that church services are at 12:05 PM weekdays and Sundays at 8 AM and 10:15 AM.) You can also make arrangements for archivist-led group tours.

Frank Lloyd Wright Fontana Boathouse (716-362-3140; www.wrightboathouse.com, www.wrightsboathouse.org), 1 Rotary Row, at the foot of Porter Avenue, Buffalo. This rowing boathouse was originally designed by Wright in 1905 for the University of Wisconsin Boat Club, but was never built in that location. It was built in Buffalo in 2007

FRANK LLOYD WRIGHT DESIGNED FONTANA BOATHOUSE

as a working boathouse for the West Side Rowing Club. It is open for tours and can be rented for events.

Silo City (www.silo.city), Silo City Row, off Ohio Street. The historic grain elevators here are open for special events and also for tours, through Explore Buffalo Tours.

ARCHITECTURAL TOURS See *To Do—Guided Tours.*

SPECIAL INTEREST MUSEUMS AND SITES **Black Rock Historical Society** (www .blackrockhistoricalsociety.com), 1902 Niagara Street, Buffalo. Established in 2011 to preserve the heritage and history of the Black Rock area of Buffalo.

GRAIN ELEVATORS LINE THE BUFFALO RIVER

✪ **Buffalo & Erie County Naval and Military Park** (716-847-1773; www .buffalonavalpark.org), 1 Naval Park Cove, Buffalo. April–October daily 10 AM–5 PM, November Saturday and Sunday 10 AM–4 PM. This six-acre waterfront site is the largest inland park of its kind in the nation. The museum features exhibits representing all branches of the armed services. Start by viewing video presentations about the park and about the on-site submarine, the USS *Croaker.* Visitors have the opportunity to climb aboard the cruiser USS *Little Rock* and the destroyer USS *Sullivans*, named after five brothers killed while serving during World War II.

The USS *Sullivans* has been dedicated a National Historic Landmark. Note: vessels are not stroller or handicapped accessible.

✍ **Buffalo Fire Historical Museum** (716-892-8400; www.bfhsmuseum.com), 1850 William Street, Buffalo. Saturday 10 AM–4 PM or by appointment. Free admission. Learn about the history of firefighting in Buffalo from the 1800s until the present time. This museum has many photos and artifacts depicting the early days of the Buffalo Fire Department, including an 1893 parade carriage and an 1831 hand pumper.

Buffalo Harbor Museum (716-849-0914; www.buffaloharbor.org), 66 Erie Street, Buffalo. Thursday and Saturday 10 AM–3 PM; also open Tuesday June–September. Donation. This museum, located in an 1896 building that once housed the Howard H. Baker Company ship chandlery, focuses on the maritime history of Buffalo and the Great Lakes region.

✍ ♿ ⚓ **Buffalo Museum of Science** (716-896-5200; www.sciencebuff.org), 1020 Humboldt Parkway, Buffalo. Daily 10 AM–4 PM. This Buffalo institution features over 600,000 exhibits on permanent display, from anthropology to zoology, along with short-term traveling exhibits. There are over a dozen exhibit halls, many with hands-on learning displays.

Buffalo Religious Arts Center (716-481-2350; www.buffaloreligiousarts.org), 157 East Avenue, Buffalo. Tours by appointment. Established in 2008 in the former St. Francis Xavier Church, their mission is to collect and preserve artifacts from local churches that have closed.

⚓ **Buffalo Transportation Pierce-Arrow Museum** (716-853-0084; www.pierce-arrow .com), 263 Michigan Avenue, Buffalo. Hours vary. A visit to this 20,000-square-foot museum takes visitors back to a time when Buffalo was a booming industrial center, with special focus on the Buffalo-made Pierce-Arrow automobile, with several Pierce-Arrows on display, along with other classic cars like the Buffalo-made Thomas

BUFFALO & ERIE COUNTY NAVAL AND MILITARY PARK

BUFFALO TRANSPORTATION PIERCE-ARROW MUSEUM

Flyer. Many of the vehicles on display are from the collection of museum founder James T. Sandoro; others are on loan from various collectors across the country. Also on display are other items related to the transportation history of Buffalo, including a large collection of vintage bicycles.

Iron Island Museum (716-892-3084; www.ironislandmuseum.com), 998 Lovejoy Street, Buffalo. Thursday 6–8:30 PM, Friday–Saturday 10 AM–12:30 PM. This small neighborhood museum is located in the East Buffalo neighborhood of Lovejoy, or "Iron Island"—so dubbed because the area used to be surrounded by railroad tracks; it is no surprise that railroad memorabilia is prominent. The museum also features a "Red, White, and Blue" corner that salutes veterans and artifacts from days gone by, including many old photos of the New York Central Terminal, a dominant landmark in the neighborhood.

☊ **Karpeles Manuscript Library Museum** (716-885-4139; www.karpeles.com). Two locations: 453 Porter Avenue and 220 North Street, Buffalo. Tuesday–Sunday 11 AM–4 PM. Free admission. Karpeles Manuscript Museums are the world's largest private holdings of important original manuscripts and documents. There are eight such libraries across the country, including the two in Buffalo. Every three months the exhibits are rotated between all eight museums before being returned to the archive.

& ☊ **Our Lady of Victory National Shrine and Basilica** (716-828-9648; www .ourladyofvictory.org), 780 Ridge Road, Lackawanna. Open daily 7 AM–7 PM. This magnificent Italian Renaissance–style basilica, completed in 1926, was the great dream of the late Father Nelson H. Baker—being considered for canonization to Catholic sainthood—who named it Our Lady of Victory to honor the Blessed Virgin Mary. The basilica is constructed almost entirely of marble. Its most prominent feature is its 165-foot copper-topped dome. When it was built, the dome was second in size only to the US Capitol. A museum in the basilica's lower level chronicles Father Baker's life and contains some of his personal belongings.

Steel Plant Museum (716-821-9361; www.steelplantmuseumwny.org), 100 Lee

OUR LADY OF VICTORY NATIONAL SHRINE AND BASILICA

FATHER NELSON BAKER: A SAINT AMONG US

Born in western New York in 1841, Nelson Baker started out as a businessman. However, he heard the calling to the priesthood at age 27 and was ordained at 34. His first assignment was St. Patrick's parish, which was also responsible for two orphanages. Father Baker, known as the "Padre of the Poor," was especially concerned about young people, particularly orphans and abandoned children, and founded several institutions in the early 1900s, including a home for infants and unwed mothers, a hospital, and an orphanage. He established a home for boys, where they could learn a trade. These boys were affectionately referred to as Father Baker's Boys—a few of them are still alive today.

Father Baker died in 1936 at age 95. The funeral director preserved Father Baker's body fluids in glass vials, and these were buried with him. This was done because many people considered the priest to be a saint while he was alive, so there was the hope that he would one day be canonized.

In March 1999 his body was exhumed and reburied within the basilica. The vials of the body fluids were found to be in the same condition as when he was buried 60 years earlier. Doctors confirmed that this was impossible; Rome considered it a miracle. Father Baker is currently being considered for canonization in the Catholic Church.

Street, Buffalo. Tuesday, Thursday, and Saturday 10 AM–5 PM. This museum focuses on the steel-making history in western New York.

LIGHTHOUSES **Buffalo Main Light** (716-856-6696; www.buffalolight.org), Buffalo Lighthouse Association, US Coast Guard Base, 1 Fuhrmann Boulevard, Buffalo. This 76-foot octagonal lighthouse, built in 1823 to replace an 1818 lighthouse, is also known as "Chinaman's Light" after a turn-of the-twentieth-century pagoda-like tower that was located nearby and was used to monitor the harbor for illegal immigrants.

BUFFALO LIGHTHOUSE

Although the light has not been in service since 1914, it has been maintained by the Buffalo Lighthouse Association since 1985. The tower, located on Coast Guard property, is open during festivals and special events. The lighthouse can also be viewed from the Erie Basin Marina.

✳ To Do

BOAT EXCURSIONS/PADDLING/KAYAKING **Buffalo Cycleboats** (716-392-1753; www .buffalocycleboats.com), 329 Erie Street (Erie Basin Marina), Buffalo. Enjoy a unique boating/biking experience on a 14-passenger, 31-foot-long catamaran that is propelled by pedal power. Purchase individual tickets or rent the whole vessel for parties, corporate functions, and more. It's bring your own food and drink and age 21 and over, except for special family-friendly cruises.

Buffalo Harbor Cruises (716-856-6696; www.buffaloharborcruises.com), 79 Marine Drive, Buffalo. May–October, hours vary throughout the season. This is a unique way to view Buffalo's skyline, historic landmarks, and the Canadian shoreline, including Old Fort Erie. The *Miss Buffalo II* cruises under the Peace Bridge and "locks through" the historic Black Rock Locks and Canal. During your two-hour narrated tour you'll see Buffalo's lighthouse, the navy vessels USS *Sullivans* and USS *Little Rock*, and many other local landmarks.

Buffalo Harbor Kayak (716-288-5309; www.bfloharborkayak.com). Enjoy kayaking or stand up paddle boarding on the Buffalo waterfront.

Buffalo Tiki Tours (716-800-7568; www.buffalotikitours.com). Cruise along the Buffalo River and Canalside on a one-hour tour with up to six people on your own personal floating Tiki Bar, with food and drink packages available from Buffalo Riverworks.

Elevator Alley Kayak (716-997-7925; www.elevatoralleykayak.com). Kayak rentals, lessons, and guided tours are offered.

Grand Lady Cruises (716-873-4630; www.grandlady.com), 359 Ganson Street, Buffalo (Riverworks). Since 1998 Captain Rick Deegan has been offering a variety of public and charter cruises on the 80-foot *Grand Lady.*

RIDE A WATERBIKE ON THE BUFFALO RIVER

Spirit of Buffalo (716-796-7210; www .spiritofbuffalo.com), 1 Naval Park Cove, Buffalo. Both public and chartered sailing cruises are offered on a classic 73-foot topsail schooner.

Moondance Catamaran (716-854-7245; www.moondancecat.com). Group charters and individuals sails available.

Queen City Bike Ferry (Canalside) (www.queencitybikeferry.com). Operating Memorial Day through Labor Day, this bike and pedestrian ferry links the inner and outer harbors. Cost is $1 each way, including bicycle.

Waterbikes of Buffalo at Canalside (716-681-4643; www.waterbikesofbuffalo .com). Rent waterbikes and paddle boats by the hour; in winter, rent an icebike to ride at the ice rink at Canalside.

QUEEN CITY BIKE FERRY

BREWERIES, DISTILLERIES, AND WINERIES There are two dozen (and growing) local beer and spirit producers in and around the Buffalo area. Additional information about area breweries can be found at the following sources:

Buffalo Brewery District (www.buffalobrewerydistrict.com).

Buffalo Niagara Brewers Association (www.Buffaloniagarabrewersassociation .org); Buffalo Beer Week (www.buffalobeerweek.com).

Buffalo Brewing Company (716-868-2218; www.buffalo-brewing-company.com), 314 Myrtle Avenue, Buffalo. Thursday, Thursday, Friday 4–8 PM, Saturday 12–8 PM, Sunday 12–5 PM. A family-run microbrewery, with the slogan "Good Neighbors, Great Beer."

Big Ditch Brewery (716-854-5050; www.bigditchbrewing.com), 55 East Huron Street, Buffalo. Tuesday–Wednesday 11 AM–10 PM, Thursday–Friday 11 AM–12 AM, Saturday 12 PM–12 AM, Sunday 12–8 PM. Named after the Erie Canal, which was referred to as the "Big Ditch" by skeptics when it opened in 1825, this 15,000-square-foot facility has an on-site brewery and a two-level tap room serving burgers, pizza, soups, and more.

Black Button Distillery (www.blackbuttondistilling.com), 149 Swan Street, Buffalo. Open Thursday–Saturday 11 AM–12 AM, Sunday 11 AM–4 PM. This tasting room for Rochester-based Black Button Distillery features gin, vodka, three bourbons, a bourbon cream, and apple pie moonshine. You can sample their products, along with craft beer, wines, and ciders. A limited food menu is available.

Black Squirrel Distillery (716-249-1122; www.blacksquirreldistillery.com), 1595 Elmwood, Buffalo. Retail sales Saturday 12–5 PM. The first distillery to make rum in Buffalo and the first in the country to use maple syrup, instead of sugarcane, to make rum.

Buffalo Distilling (www.bflodistilling.com), 860 Seneca Street (Larkinville), Buffalo. This distillery moved to Buffalo from Bennington, NY; they make bourbon, apple brandy, and vodka.

Chateau Buffalo (716-704-4671; www.chateaubuffalo.com), 175 Niagara Frontier Food Terminal, 500 Clinton Street, Buffalo. Thursday–Saturday 12–7 PM. Enjoy tasting craft ciders, along with red and white wines, at Buffalo's urban winery.

Community Beer Works (716-759-4677; www.communitybeerworks.com), 15 Lafayette Avenue, Buffalo. Thursday 3–7 PM, Friday–Saturday 3–8 PM. This nanobrewery produces high-quality beer that can be found on tap at many local restaurants. They also sell it at the brewery, along with merchandise like hats and glasses.

Flying Bison Brewery (716-873-1557; www.flyingbisonbrewing.com), 840 Seneca Street, Buffalo. Retail sales and tastings Thursday–Saturday 12–8 PM, tours offered Thursday–Friday at 6 PM, Saturday at 1 and 4 PM. This brewery was the first stand-alone brewery to operate in the city since 1972.

Old First Ward Brewing and Gene McCarthy's (716-855-8948; www.genemccarthys .com), 73 Hamburg Street, Buffalo. Kitchen open Monday–Saturday 11 AM–10 PM, Sunday 12–9 PM. Enjoy beer from Old First Ward Brewing, established in 2014, and pub food like wings and burgers from the adjacent Gene McCarthy's.

Lakeward Spirits Craft Distillery at the Barrel Factory (716-541-1454; www .barrelfactory.com/lakeward-spirits.html), 65 Vandalia Street, Buffalo. Thursday–Saturday 12–10 PM, Sunday 12–5 PM. Tours are offered Thursday–Saturday at 1, 3, and 5 PM and Sunday at 1 and 3 PM.

Lockhouse Distillery (716-768-4898; www.lockhousedistillery.com), 41 Columbia Street, Buffalo. Tuesday–Friday 12 PM–12 AM, Saturday 4–12 PM. The first distillery to open in Buffalo after Prohibition, they craft fine spirits, like vodka, gin, and coffee liqueur using local ingredients.

Niagara Distillery (716-246-4100; www.niagaradistillery.com), 459 Ellicott Street, Buffalo. Tuesday–Thursday 5–10 PM, Friday–Saturday 4–12 PM. Established in 2015, they are a farm-to-bottle distillery. They have a 1,500-square-foot retail and tasting room.

Resurgence Brewing Company (716-381-9868; www.resurgencebrewing.com), 1250 Niagara Street, Buffalo. Tuesday–Thursday 4–10 PM, Friday 4–11:30 PM, Saturday 12–11:30 PM, Sunday 12–5 PM. A craft brewery, tap room, and outdoor beer garden. They have a rotating selection of beers, as well as snack foods for purchase. Tours by appointment.

Riverworks Brewery (716-342-2292; www.buffaloriverworks.com), 359 Ganson Street, Buffalo. First brewery in the world to be built inside a grain elevator.

Thin Man Microbrewery/Restaurant (716-423-4100; www.thinmanbrewery.com), 492 Elmwood Avenue, Buffalo. Tuesday–Thursday 3–10 PM, Friday 3–11 PM, Saturday 11 AM–11 PM, Sunday brunch 11 AM–3:30 PM, and dinner 4–9 PM. This brewery/restaurant has a thin man crash dummy theme. The three-story building features a rooftop patio.

Tommyrotter Distillery (716-312-1252; www.tommyrotter.com), 500 Seneca Street, Suite 110, Buffalo. Open Spring–Fall. Located in the Hydraulics District, they craft small batches of gin and vodka using natural grains.

CASINOS **Seneca Buffalo Creek Casino** (877-8-SENECA; www.senecabuffalocreek casino.com), 1 Fulton Street, Buffalo. Operated by the Seneca Nation of Indians, this casino, which is open 24 hours, features over 800 slot machines and over 20 gaming tables.

CROSS-COUNTRY SKIING See **Tifft Nature Preserve** in *Green Space.*

FAMILY FUN ✿ **Buffalo City Hall Observation Deck** (716-851-5891), 65 Niagara Square, Buffalo. Monday–Friday 9 AM–4 PM, closed holidays. Free admission. The observation deck offers one of the best views in the city. Buffalo City Hall, listed on

THIN MAN BREWERY HAS A CRASH DUMMY THEME

the National Register of Historic Places, is an outstanding example of the art deco architecture popular in the 1920s and 1930s. The frieze above the building's entrance has figures illustrating different facets of the history of Buffalo. Take the elevator to the 25th floor, then go up three flights to the observation deck, where you can view the city, Lake Erie, and the Niagara River from 330 feet up.

✏️ ♿ **Buffalo Zoo** (716-837-3900; www.buffalozoo.org), 300 Parkside Avenue, Buffalo. June 1–September 30, daily 10 AM–5 PM; October 1–May 31, daily 10 AM–4 PM. The 23-acre Buffalo Zoo—established in 1875, the third oldest zoo in the United States—has been undergoing major renovations over the last several years. Animals are viewed in exhibit areas similar to their natural habitats as opposed to cages. Some of the more than 1,000 animals include lowland gorillas, polar bears, giraffes, and elephants, as well as exotic bird species in an aviary.

FISHING The Buffalo Niagara region has some of the best fishing in the state. Catches include smallmouth bass, muskie king salmon, steelhead, walleye, and lake trout.

Bird Island Pier, end of West Ferry Street over bridge to Bird Island (see *Green Space—Walking and Hiking* trails). Other popular fishing spots include Lake Kirsty at Tifft Nature Preserve and the Safe Harbor Marina.

A BUFFALO AT THE BUFFALO ZOO

GOLF **Cazenovia Golf Course** (716-825-9811), 1 Willink Avenue, Buffalo. A public

9-hole, par-3 course, with a driving range located in Olmsted-designed Cazenovia Park.

Delaware Park (716-851-5806 or 835-2533), Delaware Park, Buffalo. A public 18-hole, par-71 course located in Buffalo's best-known park.

South Park (716-851-5806), 3284 South Park Avenue. Open May 1–October 31. A well-maintained 9-hole, par-36 course, which is great for beginners because the fairways are wide open.

GUIDED TOURS There are a variety of tours offered in the Buffalo area. No matter what your interests, you'll find the perfect tour.

Buffalo Bites Food Tours (1-800-656-0713; www.buffalobitesfoodtours.com). Enjoy samples from local eateries, while you learn the history of the neighborhood on a three-hour walking tour of the Elmwood Village or East Aurora. Advanced reservations required.

Buffalo Double Decker Bus Tours (716-246-9080; www.buffalodoubledeckerbus .com). Take a tour of Buffalo in a 1980 Leyland Olympian bus imported from England. Tour guide Joel Dombrowski, a writer and former stand-up comic, offers several tour options including a Best of Buffalo Tour, Canalside Tour, Murder Mystery Tour, Tavern Tour, and even a Drunk Buffalo Tour.

Buffalo History Tours (buffalohistorytours.com). Historic, yet humorous, tours of Buffalo led by a former stand-up comic. Included are haunted pub crawls and murder mystery tours.

Buffalo Pedal Tours (716-984-3834; www.buffalopedaltours.com). Get to know Buffalo on a pedal-powered party bus that takes you from pub to pub.

Buffalo River Keeper Tours (716-852-7483; www.bnriverkeeper.org). Paddling and bicycle tours offered in the summer months; snowshoe tours in winter; see website for more information.

Buffalo River History Tours (716-796-4556; www.buffaloriverhistorytours.com). Take a cruise through history on the Buffalo River.

Buffalo Touring Company (www.buffalotouringcompany.com). Tour Buffalo's museum district on a Segway. Tours last about three hours.

Consumer Beverages Craft Cruiser (716-249-1499; www.craftcruiser.com). Downtown, East Aurora, and Hamburg. Explore the area on a pedal-powered megacycle for 8–15 people.

Explore Buffalo (716-245-3032; www.explorebuffalo.org). This organization offers a variety of architectural and history tours.

Fly Buffalo Aerial Photo Tours (716-574-5581; www.flybuffalony.com). Take an aerial helicopter tour of Buffalo and/or Niagara Falls.

Forgotten Buffalo Tours (www.forgottenbuffalo.com). Explore unique landmarks, taverns, and old world neighborhoods on this tour that takes you off the beaten trail.

Historic Buffalo River Tours of the Industrial Heritage Committee, Inc. (716-856-6696—*Buffalo Harbor Cruise* phone—for reservations; visit www.buffaloindustrial heritage.com; www.historicbuffalorivertours.net). About six times a year the Industrial Heritage Committee offers two-hour narrated boat tours of the grain elevator district aboard the *Miss Buffalo*. The tour covers the invention of the grain elevator, its architectural significance, and the current uses of the grain elevators.

Preservation Buffalo Niagara/Buffalo Tours (716-852-3300; www.preservation buffaloniagara.org), 617 Main Street, Buffalo. Scheduled and group tours. The Preservation Coalition offers a broad range of tours, including tours of Main Street buildings, Buffalo churches, and special tours of historic sites.

GRAIN ELEVATORS LINE THE BUFFALO RIVER

Motherland Connextions (716-282-1028; www.motherlandconnextions.com). Fees and hours vary. The western New York area played a major role in the Underground Railroad—it was not an actual railway but a network of roads and safe houses used by slaves seeking freedom in the 1850s. Motherland Connextions provides an educational and enlightening experience. "Conductors" dressed in period clothing take groups to stops along the Underground Railroad in both western New York and southern Ontario.

Open Air Autobus Tours (716-854-3749; www.openairbuffalo.org). A variety of architectural and history tours are offered.

Polonia Trail (www.poloniatrail.com). Visit, either physically or virtually, the places that were prominent in the growth of western New York's *Polonia* or Polish community. Go to clubs, churches, cemeteries, and other locations on this self-guided tour that covers over 50 locations throughout Buffalo's East Side and Erie County.

ICE SKATING ⛸ **Ice at Canalside** (www.canalsidebuffalo.com), 44 Prime Street, Buffalo. Monday–Wednesday 3–7 PM, Thursday 11 AM–7 PM, Friday–Saturday 10 AM–10 PM, Sunday 10 AM–8 PM until mid-March. At 35,000 square feet, it is the largest outdoor ice surface in the state. Don't like ice skating? Rent an icebike (716-681-4643; www.icebikesofbuffalo.com) or try your hand at curling.

⛸ **Rotary Rink at Fountain Plaza** (www.buffaloplace.com). Main Street between Chippewa and Huron Streets. Open December–March, weather permitting.

See also **Harborcenter** and **Riverworks** for ice skating.

MARINAS **Erie Basin Marina** (716-851-6503), 329 Erie Street, Buffalo. Located along Buffalo's waterfront, the marina is popular during the warmer months. It has 278 slips used by a variety of boats, along with a public boat launch. Even if you don't have a boat, the marina is a fun spot to people watch or catch a pleasant breeze on a warm summer day. An observation tower located at one end of the marina offers a view of the city, as well as the Niagara River and Lake Erie. There is even a small beach at the end of the Marina for sunning and playing in the sand; swimming not permitted.

First Buffalo River Marina (716-849-0740; www.firstbuffalomarina.com), 32 Fuhrmann Boulevard, Buffalo. Located on the Buffalo River near the Buffalo Lighthouse.

Safe Harbor Marina at Buffalo Harbor State Park. (716-828-0027; www.safeharbormarina.com), 1111 Fuhrmann Boulevard, Buffalo. This full-service marina has over 1,000 slips. They also have boat rentals, sales, and service. Charlie's Boatyard Restaurant is located here.

ICE SKATING AT CANALSIDE

✳ Green Space

BEACHES AND POOLS Several City of Buffalo parks (716-884-9660) have pools, wading pools, and splash pads which are open to residents and nonresidents alike. Visit the City of Buffalo website for a complete listing: www.ci.buffalo.ny.us /Home/City_Departments/Public_Works_Parks_Streets/ParksDepartment.

CEMETERIES **Forest Lawn Cemetery & Garden Mausoleums** (716-885-1600; www .forest-lawn.com), 1411 Delaware Avenue, Buffalo. Grounds open daily 8 AM–5 PM; until 6 PM Memorial Day–Labor Day. Forest Lawn is a place for peaceful repose for the departed and a place of beauty and tranquility for the living. The cemetery, which opened in 1849, has a number of prominent people buried here, including Millard Fillmore (1800–1874), the 13th President of the United States. Trolley and walking tours of the cemetery are offered during the warmer months; concerts and lectures take place during the winter.

GARDENS 🐾 🍴 ♿ 👕 **Buffalo and Erie County Botanical Gardens** (716-827-1584; www .buffalogardens.com), 2655 South Park Avenue, Buffalo. Daily 10 AM–5 PM. The showplace of the gardens, an over-100-year-old Victorian-style glass conservatory—350 feet long and 60 feet high—is listed on the New York State and National Register of Historic Places. Two smaller palm domes are connected to the central dome by glass growing ranges. The 11.3 acre site features plants from around the world, including cacti, fruit trees, palms, and many beautiful flowers.

NATURE PRESERVES 🍴 ♿ **Tifft Nature Preserve** (716-825-1289; www.tifft.org), 1200 Fuhrmann Boulevard, Buffalo. Visitor center open Wednesday–Saturday 10 AM–4 PM, Sunday 12–4 PM; grounds open daily, dawn to dusk. Donation. This 264-acre refuge, less than 3 miles from downtown, is dedicated to environmental education and conservation. It's a great place to watch migrating birds and other wildlife, such as beaver and deer. Get close to nature on 5 miles of hiking trails, and do some fishing along the preserve's Lake Kirsty. In winter, cross-country skiing and snowshoeing are popular.

Times Beach Nature Preserve and Wilkeson Point along Buffalo Outer Harbor, off Fuhrmann Boulevard, Buffalo. Open Open daily, dawn to dusk. Free admission. This 50-acre site, adjacent to the Coast Guard Station and the Buffalo Lighthouse, was once a disposal area for Buffalo Harbor sediment dredging. It's a good spot to view waterfowl in spring and fall.

PARKS, OLMSTED **Cazenovia Park**, Cazenovia and Abbott Roads, Buffalo. Open daily, dawn to dusk. This 191-acre Olmsted Park, originally constructed in 1897, features a nine-hole golf course, indoor swimming pool, community center, sports fields, ice rinks, and outdoor spray pool. Cazenovia Creek is a popular launch site for canoe trips.

⚓ **Delaware Park** (716-884-9660), Lincoln Parkway, Buffalo. Open daily, dawn to dusk. This 350-acre park, the centerpiece of the Buffalo Parks system, was designed in the late 1800s by Frederick Law Olmsted. It was designed with three distinct features: a 42-acre lake, a large meadow, and several wooded areas. Over the years there have been changes to Olmsted's design. The meadow is now an 18-hole golf course, and the Buffalo Zoo, the Buffalo History Museum, and the Albright-Knox Art Gallery are located on what was originally park land. The park's Rose Garden features award-wining roses, including a collection of antique roses dating back to the 1800s. In winter, visitors can enjoy cross-country skiing and ice skating.

BUFFALO & ERIE COUNTY BOTANICAL GARDENS

OLMSTED PARKS

Buffalo's park and parkway system, designed in 1868 by America's first landscape architect, Frederick Law Olmsted, is made up of six parks linked with eight circles and eight landscaped parkways. Olmsted, often referred to as the "Father of Landscape Architecture," also designed New York's Central Park. Along with Calvert Vaux, Olmstead designed the parks not only to offer beautiful scenery but to offer people a place to walk and be active—which is especially important in an industrial city like Buffalo. The system of parks and parkways in Buffalo, whose parks are listed on the National Register of Historic Places, is of historical significance because it represents the largest body of Olmsted's work; the parks were the first of their kind in the nation. The city's parkland is 75 percent Olmsted-designed, and Buffalo is one of only five cities in the country that has an Olmsted park system that is still intact. The **Buffalo Olmsted Parks Conservancy** (716-838-1249; www.bfloparks.org, 84 Parkside Avenue, Buffalo), founded in 1978, is a not-for-profit organization that works with the city and community to ensure that the Olmsted-designed parks are preserved and maintained.

The parkways designed by Olmsted include **Lincoln, Bidwell, Chapin, Richmond, Porter, Red Jacket,** and **McKinley.** Humboldt Parkway was lost as a result of the construction of the Kensington Expressway. The seven circles are **Soldiers, Gates, Colonial, Ferry,** and **Symphony Circle,** all located near Delaware Park, and **McClellan** and **McKinley Circles** in South Buffalo.

Front Park, Porter Avenue at the Peace Bridge. Open daily, dawn to dusk. Originally known as "The Front," Front Park was considered the most formal of Olmsted's first three Buffalo parks (Front, Martin Luther King, and Delaware). When it was constructed in 1868, it had 32 acres and its main feature was its commanding view of the Niagara River, Lake Erie, and Canada. However, much of its parkland was lost due to the construction of the Peace Bridge and the New York State Thruway.

Martin Luther King Jr. Park (716-851-5806), Best Street and Fillmore Avenue, Buffalo. Open daily, dawn to dusk. Also known as Humboldt Park, this 50-acre Olmsted-designed park is adjacent to the Buffalo Museum of Science. The park was originally known as "The Parade," and was designed by Olmsted to be the site of military drills and large gatherings. It was later called Humboldt Park, then renamed Martin Luther King Jr. Park in 1977. Facilities include tennis courts, hockey rink, picnic shelters, and a 500-foot-diameter wading pool.

Riverside Park (716-877-5972), 2607 Niagara Street, near Tonawanda Street and Crowley Avenue, Buffalo. Open daily, dawn to dusk. This 37-acre park was the final park designed in Buffalo by Olmsted. Originally the park overlooked the Erie Canal and the Niagara River, but it was cut off from the river by the Niagara section of the Thruway in the 1950s. Facilities include a swimming pool and a wading pool.

South Park (716-838-1249), South Park Avenue, South Buffalo. Open daily, dawn to dusk. The design for South Park was first proposed by Olmsted in 1892, its central feature being a circuit drive to enjoy views of the entire park—now popular with walkers, joggers, and in-line skaters, instead of carriage riders. Today the park features 155 acres of green space, including a shrub garden, a lake, and a golf course. The park's focal point is the circa-1900 Victorian glass conservatory, home to the Buffalo and Erie Country Botanical Gardens.

PARKS, OTHER **Buffalo Harbor State Park** (716-882-1207; parks.ny.gov/parks/191/details.aspx), 1111 Fuhrmann Boulevard, Buffalo. This 190-acre park and 1,000-slip marina features great views of Lake Erie, Gallagher Beach, a sunbathing beach (no swimming permitted), and a nautical theme playground.

Buffalo Riverfest Park (716-823-4707; www.thevalleycenter.com), 249 Ohio Street, Buffalo. A three-acre public access area along the Buffalo River across from Riverworks. Enjoy concerts on Wednesdays, June–September. The park's Tewksbury Lodge restaurant and banquet facility has salads, sandwiches, burgers.

LaSalle Park (716-884-9660), Porter Avenue at Amvets Drive, Buffalo. Open daily, dawn to dusk. This 77-acre city park is located on Lake Erie at the mouth of the Niagara River. Facilities include a swimming pool, sports fields, snack bar, and picnic area. The Riverwalk Bike Path goes through it. LaSalle Park is a good place for bird watching.

HAVE A BITE TO EAT AT TEWKSBURY LODGE IN BUFFALO RIVERFEST PARK

Cathedral Park, Main Street next to St. Paul's Cathedral, downtown Buffalo. A small, shady urban park, this is a popular spot for downtown office workers to eat lunch.

Numerous small neighborhood parks are located throughout the city. Contact the Buffalo Parks Department for more information (716-884-9660; www.ci.buffalo.ny.us).

WALKING AND HIKING TRAILS Bird Island Pier (at the end of West Ferry Street, go over lift bridge to Bird Island). This path is on a 1-mile long cement barrier that separates the Black Rock Canal and the Niagara River. Walkers, joggers, and in-line skaters enjoy this trail, as do fishermen who try their luck from the rocks along the pier. This is also a good spot to watch rowers from the West Side Rowing Club on the Black Rock Canal.

Riverwalk Bike Path (716-858-8352). Riverwalk is a 14-mile county-owned paved pathway for walking, biking, jogging, and rollerblading. It starts on Commercial Street by the Naval Park in downtown Buffalo near the Erie Basin Marina, then travels along the Niagara River, through several parks, ending on Main Street in the City of Tonawanda along the Erie Canal.

See also Tifft Nature Preserve, Delaware Park, and South Park in *Green Space*.

✳ Lodging

INNS AND RESORTS Inn Buffalo (716-867-7777 or 716-432-1030; www.innbuffalo.com), 619 Lafayette, Buffalo. Just a half-block from Elmwood Avenue in the Elmwood Village, this nine-suite upscale boutique inn, located in an 1898 home, is within walking distance of unique shops and restaurants. $$$.

&. The Mansion on Delaware Avenue (716-886-3300; www.mansionondelaware.com), 414 Delaware Avenue, Buffalo. The 28 guest rooms in this 1869 Second Empire–style mansion have been carefully restored to reflect the inn's Victorian splendor. The building, known as "The House of Light" when it was first constructed, has over 175 windows, 14 of them large bay windows. The amenities that set this hotel apart from others include 24-hour-a-day butlers, round-the-clock in-room dining, and an upscale complimentary continental breakfast. Reservations are strongly recommended as this place is often fully booked. $$$$.

Oscar's Bed & Breakfast (716-381-8605; www.oscarsbnb.com), 288 Linwood Avenue, Buffalo. Three suites are available in this Second Empire–style home, which is in the Linwood Historic

THE MANSION ON DELAWARE OFFERS UPSCALE ACCOMMODATIONS

Preservation District and close to the Elmwood Village. $$.

Parkside House Bed & Breakfast (716-480-9507; www.theparksidehouse.com), 462 Woodward Avenue, Buffalo. Three guestrooms, named after streets in the Parkside District, are available in this inn, which is within walking distance of the National Historic Landmark Darwin Martin House. $$.

MOTELS AND HOTELS & **Adams Mark** (716-845-5100; www.adamsmark.com), 120 Church Street, Buffalo. This waterfront hotel offers 486 guest rooms, including six multilevel suites. The hotel has an indoor pool, a health club, 24-hour room service, and airport shuttle service. $$.

Courtyard Marriott (716-840-966), 125 Main Street, Buffalo. This 96-room hotel is located on the lower four levels of the building. It is a great location, being walking distance to the waterfront, Canalside, and many downtown attractions, including KeyBank Center and Coca Cola Field. $$$.

Curtiss Hotel (716-208-1215; www.curtisshotel.com), 210 Franklin at Huron, This 68-room full-service boutique hotel is built inside the landmark Harlow Curtiss building. It features many amenities, including a revolving bar, the 200-seat Chez Ami restaurant, a rooftop lounge overlooking the city and a spa with a hot spring soaking pool. $$$.

& **Doubletree Club** (716-845-0112), 125 High Street, Buffalo (on the Buffalo Niagara Medical Campus). This hotel has secure walkways to both Buffalo General Hospital and Roswell Park Cancer Institute. Amenities include signature warm chocolate chip cookies upon check-in, a fitness center, free Wi-Fi, and a complimentary downtown shuttle. $$.

Embassy Suites at the Avanti (716-842-1000; www.embassysuitesbuffalo.com), 200 Delaware Avenue, Buffalo. Located on the first eight floors of the Avanti Building, it is close to downtown restaurants and attractions. A free breakfast is included. $$$.

Foundry Suites Hotel (716-240-9693; www.foundrysuites.com), 1738 Elmwood

THE ROOMS AT THE CURTISS HOTEL ARE STATE-OF-THE-ART

Avenue, Buffalo. A boutique hotel with ten luxurious suites located in a former early 1900s manufacturing plant. It also has banquet and meeting spaces. $$$.

 ♿ **Hampton Inn & Suites** (716-855-2223, 800-HAMPTON), 220 Delaware Avenue, Buffalo. This 137-room inn combines modern amenities with a historic feel; it was constructed inside an existing vintage downtown building. In addition to regular rooms, the hotel has 31 suites, some as large as 1,500 square feet. It also has an indoor pool, Jacuzzi, workout area, and a complimentary weekday breakfast buffet. $$.

Hilton Garden Inn (716-848-1000), 10 Lafayette Square, Buffalo. This hotel, which overlooks Lafayette Square, has views of the city and Lake Erie. Amenities include in-room microwaves and mini-fridges, Wi-Fi, an indoor pool, and a fitness center. A restaurant and bar are on-premises. $$.

Hotel at the Lafayette (716-853-1505) 391 Washington Street, Buffalo. This beautifully restored French Renaissance style hotel was built in 1904 and designed by Louise Blanchard Bethune, America's first female architect. Located in the heart of downtown Buffalo it offers luxurious accommodations as well as on-site dining. Free breakfast and wi-fi are part of the amenities. $$.

Hotel Henry Urban Resort Conference Center (716-882-1970; www.hotelhenry.com), 444 Forest Avenue, Buffalo. Located in the National Historic Landmark Richardson complex, this 88-room boutique hotel has rooms with 18-foot ceilings and 14-foot windows with a view of the hotel grounds. Modern amenities include outlets with USB and tablets to control functions in the room. The hotel is just steps away from the Burchfield-Penney Art Center and the Albright-Knox Art Gallery. See also *Dining Out*. $$.

 ♿ **Hyatt Regency** (716-856-1234), 2 Fountain Plaza, Buffalo. This 395-room luxury hotel is located in the heart of the entertainment and business district and is connected to the Buffalo Convention Center by an enclosed walkway. It is unique in its architecture; the Hyatt Corporation utilized the 15-story circa-1923 Genesee Building, designed by E. B. Green and William Wicks, and added to it when building the hotel. The marble doorway of the old building serves as the entrance to the hotel's glass atrium. $$.

Buffalo Marriott Harborcenter (716-852-0049), 95 Main Street, Buffalo. This hotel, which opened in 2016, has 205 rooms which overlook the city or Lake Erie. It is within walking distance of Canalside, the waterfront, and downtown businesses. An indoor walkway connects the hotel to the Harborcenter ice rinks and the KeyBank arena. $$$.

Westin Buffalo (716-854-9000; www.westinbuffalo.com), 250 Delaware Avenue, Buffalo. Located on the lower five floors of the Delaware North corporate headquarters, this high-end hotel, which is known for its plush "heavenly beds," features 119 upscale rooms and a two-story fitness facility. It's the first hotel in New York State to install Amazon Echo devices in each room so that guests can request services. It works in tandem with "Chip," the hotel's robot butler, who delivers room service to guests. $$$.

✳ Where to Eat

DINING OUT

DOWNTOWN

⅄ **31 Club** (716-332-3131; www.the31club.com), 31 North Johnson Park, Buffalo. Upscale restaurant and bar with 1940s feel. Opens daily at 5 PM for dinner, Sunday brunch 11 AM–3 PM. Menu includes steak, seafood, and pasta. Live music featured Friday and Saturday evenings.

Buffalo Chop House (716-842-6900; www.buffalochophouse.com), 282 Franklin Street, Buffalo. Sunday–Thursday 4 PM–12 AM, Friday and Saturday 4 PM–2 AM. This steak house, located in an 1870 carriage house, is known for its large cuts of meat, like a 48-ounce porterhouse. The menu, modeled after the best steak houses in Manhattan, also offers chicken, pasta, and seafood if you are not in the mood for meat.

⅄ **Buffalo Proper** (716-783-8699; www.buffaloproper.com), 333 Franklin Street, Buffalo Tuesday–Thursday 5 PM–12 AM, Friday–Saturday 5 PM–2 AM, Sunday 11:30 AM–11 PM. This restaurant is known for farm-to-table dishes and craft cocktails.

Cabaret (716-842-4181; www.cabaretrestaurant.com), 490 Pearl Street, Buffalo. Monday–Thursday 11 AM–9 PM, Friday 11 AM–10 PM, Saturday 4–10 PM. A large well-lit restaurant popular with the theater and downtown lunch crowd. Lunch items include wraps, burgers and sandwiches. Dinner includes steak, fish, and Italian entrees.

Coco Bar and Bistro (716-885-1885; www.cocobuffalo.com), 888 Main Street, Buffalo. Named after the French fashion designer Coco Chanel, this cozy bistro features European-inspired menu items.

Encore (716-931-5001; www.encorebuffalo.com), 492 Pearl Street, Buffalo. Tuesday–Thursday 5–10 PM, Friday–Saturday 5–11 PM, Also open Sundays 4–8 PM, when there are major productions at Shea's. This is the perfect spot to get a bite to eat before attending a performance at Shea's. The seasonal menu features steak, seafood, and sushi.

Greystone (716-858-4363), 445 Delaware Avenue, Buffalo. Wednesday–Saturday 5–10 pm, also open Saturday–Sunday 11 AM–3 PM for brunch. Enjoy fine dining, with entrees like rack of lamb, chateaubriand, and crispy cauliflower steak.

♿ **Hutch's** (716-885-0074; www.hutchsrestaurant.com), 1375 Delaware Avenue, Buffalo. Monday–Thursday 5–10 pm, Friday and Saturday 5–11:30 PM, Sunday 4–9 PM. This romantic eatery features cuisine with a hint of the southwest and Pacific Rim. With its brick walls adorned with posters and paintings, it has the feel of a European bistro. It is known for its seafood dishes, as well as for pastas and meat selections.

The Mahony (716-783-8009; www.themahony.com), 199 Scott Street, Buffalo. Lunch Monday–Friday 11 AM–4 PM, dinner Monday–Saturday 4 PM–close. Chef Brian Mahony has created a menu of fusion ethnic cuisines, with Italian, Asian, and Mexican dishes on the menu, as well as burgers, salads, and sandwiches.

Marble & Rye (716-853-1390, www.marbleandrye.net), 112 Genesee Street, Buffalo. Tuesday–Thursday 5–10 PM, Friday–Saturday 5–11 PM. Featuring craft cocktails, along with a large selection of rye whiskey. The dining menu features from-scratch dishes with locally supplied seasonal ingredients.

Papaya (716-856-2444; www.papayarestaurant.biz), 118 West Chippewa Street, Buffalo (adjacent to the Hampton Inn). This sophisticated, yet casual, restaurant features Southeast Asian cuisine, along with a full service bar.

Patina 250 (716-290-0600), 250 Delaware (in the Westin Hotel), Buffalo. Daily 7 AM–11:30 PM. Enjoy fine dining at this very popular hotel restaurant, with menu selections like sea bass, rib eye steak, and crispy chicken. An outdoor dining patio is available.

OUTDOOR DINING PATIO AT PATINA 250

Seabar (716-332-2928), 475 Ellicott Street, Buffalo. Chef Mike Andrzejewski is known for innovative sushi creations like the beef on weck sushi roll.

Sear Steakhouse (716-319-1090; www .searbuffalo.com), 200 Delaware Avenue, Buffalo. (Embassy Suites in the Avanti Building.) This 10,000-square-foot restaurant and bar has a 2,500-bottle wine wall. Lunch selections include small plates, salads, and sandwiches, while dinner focuses mainly on steak, chops, and seafood.

Tempo (716-885-1594; www.tempo buffalo.com), 581 Delaware Avenue, Buffalo. Monday–Thursday 5–10 PM, Friday–Saturday 5–11 PM. This upscale restaurant is located in a vintage home. Menu selections include seafood and steak with an Italian accent.

WATERFRONT/LARKINVILLE

Hydraulic Hearth (716-248-2216; www .hydraulichearth.com), 716 Swan Street, Buffalo. Tuesday–Thursday 4:30–10 PM, Friday–Saturday 4:30–11 PM. Enjoy brews from Community Beer Works, craft cocktails, and brick-oven pizza.

♿ **Panorama on 7** at the Marriott Harborcenter (716-852-0049), 95 Main Street, Buffalo. Open daily 6 AM–10 PM. Located just off the seventh floor lobby of

the hotel, this restaurant has a great view of the waterfront.

Templeton Landing (716-852-7337), 2 Templeton Terrace, Buffalo. Open May–October. Enjoy patio dining and drinks with waterfront views at this popular seasonal restaurant.

William K's (716-852-0500; www .williamksrestaurant.com), 329 Erie Street, Buffalo (Erie Basin Marina). Open seasonally for Sunday brunch and dinner. Enjoy fine dining on the waterfront, overlooking the Buffalo Lighthouse. Menu features locally sourced cuisine and wood-fired pizza.

ELMWOOD VILLAGE/ ALLENTOWN

♿ **Saigon Café** (716-883-1252; www .thesaigoncafe.com), 520 Elmwood Avenue, Buffalo. Monday–Saturday 11 AM–10 PM, Sunday 12–9 PM. This small, intimate restaurant, its tables adorned with white-linen tablecloths, cloth napkins, and fine china, offers diners fine Vietnamese and Thai cuisine.

Sato (716-931-9146; www.satobuffalo .com), 739 Elmwood Avenue, Buffalo. Monday–Thursday 4–10 PM, Friday–Saturday 11:30 AM–10:30 PM. Featuring

ENJOY THAI AND VIETNAMESE CUISINE AT SAIGON CAFE

upscale yet casual dining. Enjoy authentic Japanese cuisine, including ramen, sushi, and sashimi.

Trattoria Aroma (716-881-7592), 307 Bryant Street, Buffalo. Monday–Thursday 11:30 AM–10 PM, Friday 11:30 AM–11 PM, Saturday 5–11 PM, Sunday 11 AM–2:30 PM and 5–10 PM. This restaurant features fine Italian foods and wines. Enjoy traditional dishes, as well as unique offerings.

NORTH BUFFALO/HERTEL AVENUE

100 Acres: The Kitchens at Hotel Henry (716-955-1511; www.100acresbflo.com), 444 Forest Avenue, Buffalo. Open for breakfast daily 7–10:30 AM and for dinner Tuesday–Thursday 5–9:30 PM and Friday–Saturday 5–10 PM. This restaurant features a menu with emphasis on regional products. See also *Lodging*.

The Terrace at Delaware Park (716-886-0089; www.terracebuffalo.com), 199 Lincoln Parkway, Buffalo. Daily 11:30 AM–9:30 PM. Located on the upper floor of the circa-1901 Macy Casino in Delaware Park, this restaurant has great views of the surrounding museum district. The menu features contemporary global cuisine, with selections like Argentinian skirt steak and Lebanese chicken kabobs. The restaurant also has a patio which is popular during the warmer months.

Oliver's (716-877-9662; www.oliverscuisine.com), 2095 Delaware Avenue, Buffalo. Tuesday–Thursday 5–10 pm, Friday and Saturday 5–11 PM, Sunday 4:30–9:30 PM. This Buffalo restaurant has been a fine-dining destination for over 70 years. It's definitely a special-occasion restaurant, with its contemporary decor, distinctive entrees, and extensive wine list. Specialties include New York strip steak, seafood, and fresh fish.

Ristorante Lombardo (716-873-4291; www.ristorantelombardo.com), 1198 Hertel Avenue, Buffalo. Monday–Thursday 5–10 PM, Friday 11:30 AM–2:30 PM and 5–11 PM, Saturday 5–11 PM. Enjoy dining on regional Italian fare in a Tuscan-style dining room or outdoors in an intimate, private courtyard.

WEST SIDE

The Dapper Goose (716-551-0716; www.thedappergoose.com), 491 Amherst Street, Buffalo. Tuesday–Thursday 5–10 PM, Friday–Saturday 5–11 PM, Sunday 11 AM–4 PM. Enjoy creative craft cocktails, plus small and large plate dishes like Korean fried chicken and confit duck.

Left Bank (716-882-3509; www.leftbankrestaurant.com), 511 Rhode Island Street, Buffalo. Monday–Thursday 5–11 PM, Friday–Saturday 5 PM–12 AM, Sunday brunch 11 AM–2:30 PM, dinner 4–10 PM. This casually elegant American bistro is one of Buffalo's more popular dining spots. The menu features pastas, vegetarian steaks, and Mediterranean dishes. Signature dishes include pork tenderloins with a Grand Marnier sauce.

Viking Lobster Company (716-873-1079; www.vikinglobster.biz), 366 Tonawanda Street, Buffalo (Black Rock). Wednesday–Saturday 5–10 PM. This restaurant, located in an old house, is the only restaurant in Buffalo that specializes in affordable lobster, as well as fish and shrimp. They also serve steak, ribs, and chicken. It's BYOB and cash only.

ENJOY LOBSTER AND MORE AT VIKING LOBSTER COMPANY

UNIVERSITY DISTRICT

Shango (716-837-2326), 3260 Main Street, Buffalo. Monday–Thursday 5–10 pm, Friday–Saturday 5–11 PM, Sunday brunch 11 AM–3 PM. A New Orleans–inspired bistro with authentic Cajun Creole cuisine, including gumbo and desserts like Southern pecan pie served with homemade coconut ice cream.

EATING OUT

DOWNTOWN

Ŷ **Anchor Bar** (716-886-8920; www.anchorbar.com), 1047 Main Street, Buffalo. Open Monday–Thursday 11 AM–10 PM, Friday 11 AM–11 PM, Saturday 12–11 PM, Sunday 12–10 PM. No trip to Buffalo is complete without a stop at the famous Anchor Bar, where Buffalo wings were first served back in 1964. While wings are the most popular menu item, a variety of other dishes are also offered. While you're waiting for your wings, take a look at the photos of notable people and celebrities who have visited this Buffalo institution over the years.

&. **Bijou Grille** (716-847-1512; www.bijougrille.com), 643 Main Street, Buffalo. Open Monday–Saturday 11:30 AM–9 PM (hours may vary; call first). This theater-district eatery is decorated to resemble Hollywood in the 1950s. The menu has a decidedly California influence, along with many Mexican dishes.

Casa Azul (716-807-1141; www.casaazulbuffalo.com), 128 Genesee Street, Buffalo. Monday–Saturday 11:30 AM–9 PM. The menu features tacos and Mexican street food.

Charlie's Boatyard (716-828-1600; www.charliesboatyard.com), 1111 Fuhrman Boulevard, Buffalo. Open April through mid-October. Enjoy wings, seafood, and burgers, with a view of Lake Erie.

🍽 ♪ **Chefs** (716-856-9187; www.ilovechefs.com), 291 Seneca Street, Buffalo. Open Monday–Saturday 11 AM–9 PM. Buffalo's best-known Italian restaurant for over 80 years. Dine on red-and-white

checkered tablecloths under grape chandeliers. Their red sauce, which can be purchased by the quart to take home, is one of the best in the city. Specialties include spaghetti parmigiana, lasagna, and ravioli. Desserts are baked fresh daily at a local bakery.

Chris's NY Sandwich Company (716-854-6642; www.chrisnysandwichco.com), 395 Delaware Avenue, Buffalo. Monday–Friday 11 AM–2:30 PM. This restaurant is known for its large sandwiches, the size of New York City, hence the name. The menu includes over 30 different sandwiches, along with over a dozen salads and a Friday fish fry.

Ŷ **The Chocolate Bar** (716-332-0484; www.thechocolatebar.com), 114 West Chippewa Street, Buffalo. Monday–Thursday 11 AM–12 AM, Friday–Saturday 11 AM–2 AM, Sunday 3 PM–12 AM. While they have a great selection of sandwiches, salads and soups, the reason you come here is for chocolate. The desserts are outstanding; try a Belgian chocolate pyramid or perhaps a frozen hot chocolate. In the evening, indulge in a chocolate martini.

Deep South Taco (716-235-8464; www.deepsouthtaco.com), 271 Ellicott Street, Buffalo. Enjoy authentic Mexican cuisine including tacos with house-made corn and flour tortillas and an array of tapas. Their other locations are on Hertel Avenue and Transit Road.

Ŷ **Dinosaur Bar-B-Que** (716-880-1677; www.dinosaurbarbque.com/bbq-buffalo), 301 Franklin Street, Buffalo.

MUST DO

FOOD TRUCKS

Buffalo has over two dozen (and growing) food trucks, some an offshoot of established brick-and-mortar restaurants, others just operating as food trucks. The best place to check out area food trucks is at Food Truck Tuesday, which takes place at Larkin Square April–October (www.larkinsquare.com, 745 Seneca Street, Buffalo).

Monday–Thursday 11 AM–10 PM, Friday–Saturday 11 AM–12 AM, Sunday 12–10 PM. This award-winning regional barbecue chain (the original opened in Syracuse in the 1980s) features traditional Southern barbecue, including ribs and brisket. Live music is featured on Friday and Saturday evenings.

Expo Food Market (716-855-3976; www.expobuffalo.com), 617 Main Street, Buffalo. Monday–Friday 10 AM–9 PM, Saturday 11 AM–8 PM. A locally inspired food hall, similar to a food court, with several up-and-coming restaurants serving diverse cuisine.

&. **Fables Café** (716-858-7127), 1 Lafayette Square in the Buffalo and Erie Country Central Library, Buffalo. This popular coffee café and lunch spot, located in the library, offers sandwiches, along with an assortment of salads and soups, daily specials, and baked goods.

Frankie Primo's +39 (716-855-3739; www.frankieprimos39.com), 51 Chippewa, Buffalo. Sunday 11 AM–9 PM, Monday–Thursday 11 AM–11 PM, Friday–Saturday 11 AM–12 AM. Enjoy authentic Italian fare and more.

&. **JJ's Casa di Pizza** (716-883-8200; www.casadipizza.com), 11 East Mohawk, Buffalo. Monday–Saturday 11:30 AM–12 AM, Sunday 12 PM–12 AM. Since 1953, folks living in Buffalo have come to love pizza from this establishment. Choose from a full menu of Italian and American dishes. Take-out and delivery is also available.

Jerk's Ice Cream (716-436-2395; www.jerkssoda.com), 523 Main Street, Buffalo. Monday–Thursday 11:30 AM–9 PM, Friday 11:30 AM–11 PM, Saturday 1–11 PM, Sunday 1–8 PM. Enjoy a variety of ice cream treats like black and brown cows, New York egg creams, and black and white ice cream sodas, along with milkshakes, sundaes, and even hot chocolate.

Just Fries (716-436-2395; www.justfriesusa.com), 523 Main Street, Buffalo. Monday–Thursday 11:30 AM–8 PM, Friday 11 AM–9 PM, Saturday 1 -10 PM, Sunday 1–7 PM. The menu features French fries ranging from plain to a variety of toppings.

Lagerhaus 95 (716-200-1798; www.lagerhaus95.com), 95 Perry Street, Buffalo. This gastropub restaurant is located next to the KeyBank Center and a short walk to Canalside. Burgers, sandwiches, and other pub foods dominate the menu.

Lenox Grill (716-884-1700; www.lenoxgrill.com), 140 North Street, Buffalo. Located downstairs in the Hotel Lenox. Open daily 11 AM–11 PM, Friday–Saturday until 3 AM. An upscale yet cozy, urban restaurant specializing in a variety of foods from wings to steak.

Osteria 166 (716-858-3118; www.osteriabuffalo.com), 166 Franklin Street, Buffalo. Open Monday–Thursday 11 AM–10 PM, Friday 11 AM–11 PM, and Saturday 5–11 PM. Nani's (mother of owner) famous Sunday sauce tops the pasta dishes at this casual Italian eatery.

Pan American Grill and Brewery (716-856-0062; buffalobrewerydistrict.com/panam/node/28), 391 Washington Street, Buffalo. Daily 11 AM–11 PM. Enjoy pub grab and craft beers in the historic Hotel Lafayette.

Y **Pearl Street Grill & Brewery** (716-856-2337; www.pearlstreetgrill.com), 76 Pearl Street, Buffalo. Monday–Saturday 11 AM–closing, Sunday noon–closing. This restored 1870 building in the old Erie Canal district features brick walls, tin ceilings, and an antique pulley fan system. A microbrewery is located on the first floor of the restaurant.

Raclettes (716-436-3244; www.raclettesbuffalo.com), 537 Main Street, Buffalo. Monday 8 AM–9 PM, Tuesday–Thursday 8 AM–10 PM, Friday 8 AM–11 PM, Saturday 12–11 PM, Sunday 11 AM–3 PM. Their specialty is melted cheese served with, and then spread on, meat and vegetables.

Y **Sato Brewpub** (716-248-1436; www.satobrewpub.com), 110 Pearl Street, Buffalo. Tuesday–Thursday 11 AM–12 AM, Friday–Saturday 11:30 AM–1 AM. Located in the historic Dun building, this casual Japanese gastropub, referred to as *izakaya* in Japanese, specializes in ramen, skewered yakitori items, and small plate selections. They brew their own Japanese-inspired beers on site. It is the first Japanese brewpub outside of Japan.

Soho Burger Bar (716-856-7646; www .sohoburgerbar.com), 64 West Chippewa, Buffalo, Monday–Thursday 11 AM–11 PM, Friday–Saturday 11 AM–12 AM, Sunday 12–9 PM. Featuring custom-blended and hand-formed burgers, hand-cut fries, and house-made chips.

Swannie House (716-847-2898), 170 Ohio Street, Buffalo. This Irish tavern, originally established in 1886, was popular with sailors at the turn of the century. The menu features pub food along with a Friday fish fry.

Tappo (716-259-8130;www .tappoitalian.com), 338 Ellicott Street, Buffalo. Open for lunch and dinner. This restaurant offers traditional red sauce favorites, a reasonably priced wine list, and a rooftop patio.

Toutant (716-342-2901; www .toutantbuffalo.com), 437 Ellicott Street, Buffalo. Sunday–Monday 5 PM–12 AM, Thursday–Saturday 5 PM–2 AM, also Sunday brunch 11:30 AM–2:30 PM. This Southern-inspired restaurant features dishes like fried chicken, jambalaya, and barbecue favorites.

Ulrich's Tavern (716-855-8409; www .ulrichstavern.com), 674 Ellicott Street, Buffalo. Monday–Saturday 11 AM–midnight. Established in 1868, Ulrich's is Buffalo's oldest tavern. This bar/restaurant features a German-American menu, with beers from Buffalo and Germany. Menu selections include beef on weck, burgers, and potato pancakes, as well as German fare like bratwurst and wiener schnitzel.

WATERFRONT/LARKINVILLE

♈ **716 Food and Sport** (716-855-4716; www .716foodandsport.com), 7 Scott Street, Buffalo. Sunday–Thursday 11 AM–1 AM, Friday–Saturday 11 AM–2 AM. This sports bar, a popular place to go before or after Buffalo Sabres games, has a 38-foot video screen over the main bar, along with over 70 big screen TVs throughout. The menu features Buffalo favorites like wings and beef on weck, along with pizza, sandwiches, and salads.

Filling Station (716-362-2665), 745 Seneca Street, Buffalo. Monday–Friday 11 AM–3 PM. Enjoy homemade soup, salads, sandwiches, quiche, and more in the heart of Larkinville.

🖉 🕭 🍴 **The Hatch** (716-851-6501), 329 Erie Street (at the Erie Basin Marina), Buffalo. Seasonal, May–mid-October, seven days a week, 7:30 AM–9 PM. While the food here is good—burgers, sandwiches, hot dogs, and a standard-fare breakfast menu—you should really come here for the view. The restaurant offers a picturesque vista of the Buffalo River and Lake Erie. They also serve ice cream and have a clam bar that sells beer and wine. Special note: Don't leave your food unattended; there are many hungry seagulls nearby.

Healthy Scratch (716-855-4404; www .thehealthyscratch.com), 75 Main Street (Harborcenter), Buffalo. This eatery offers organic and clean eating options, like smoothies and cold-pressed juice, toast topped with healthy ingredients, and grab-and-go salads, wraps, and snacks.

Liberty Hound (716-845-9173; www .libertyhoundbuffalo.com), 1 Naval Park Cove, Buffalo. Open daily in summer, 11:30 AM–10 PM, limited hours the rest of the year. This waterfront restaurant, located at the Buffalo Naval Park, features seafood and craft beers, along with other menu choices.

Pizza Plant (716-626-5566; www .pizzaplant.com), 125 Main Street (Courtyard Marriott), Buffalo. Monday–Thursday 11 AM–11 PM, Friday–Saturday 12 PM–12 AM, Sunday 11 AM–10 PM. This pizza restaurant is known for its "pods," as well as a variety of pizzas, including some gluten-free options. They also have over 30 beers on tap.

Swan Street Diner (716-768-1823; www.swanstreetdiner.com) 700 Swan Street, Buffalo. Tuesday–Sunday 7 AM–3 PM. Enjoy breakfast and lunch in a fully restored 1937 diner in the heart of the

Larkinville District. The menu includes an all-day breakfast, sandwiches, burgers and more.

ELMWOOD VILLAGE/ ALLENTOWN

Allen Burger Venture (716-768-0386; www.allenburgerventure.com), 175 Allen Street, Buffalo. Daily 11:30 AM–12 AM; until 1 AM on Friday and Saturday. This restaurant has tap beer, along with the first tap wine system in the city. The menu features 15–20 different varieties of burgers.

    Allen Street Poutine (716-883-7437; www.allenstreetpoutine.com), 242 Allen Street, Buffalo. Monday–Thursday 11:30 AM–1 AM, Friday–Saturday 11:30 AM–4 AM Sunday 11:30 AM–11 PM. This is the first poutinerie in Buffalo. They serve about 20 varieties of the Canadian dish, which consists of French fries topped with cheese curds and gravy.

    Allen Street Hardware Company (716-882-8843; www.allenstreethardware.com), 245 Allen Street, Buffalo. Kitchen open Sunday–Thursday 5–11 PM, Friday–Saturday 5 PM–midnight, bar open until 4 AM. This small café and bar gets its name from the hardware store that formerly occupied this space. This

HEALTHY EATING CHOICES ARE ON THE MENU AT ASHKERS JUICE BAR

neighborhood pub features wine, beer, and an assortment of soups, salads, and sandwiches, including wraps and panini.

    ♿ **Ashkers Juice Bar** (716-886-2233), 1002 Elmwood Avenue, Buffalo. Monday–Saturday 7 AM–10 PM, Sunday 9 AM–5 PM. Enjoy healthy eating choices, including vegan and vegetarian options, along with fresh juices and smoothies, in a comfortable and welcoming atmosphere.

    Betty's (716-362-0633; www.bettys buffalo.com), 370 Virginia Street, Buffalo. Tuesday–Saturday 8 AM–3 PM and 5–8 PM, Sunday 9 AM–2 PM. An eclectic restaurant located in a restored nineteenth-century home that features made-from-scratch items, including many vegetarian selections.

    Billy Club (716-331-3047; www.billy clubbuffalo.com), 228 Allen Street, Buffalo. Monday, Wednesday, and Thursday 5 PM–1 AM, dinner service until 10; Friday–Saturday 5 PM–2 AM, dinner service until 11 PM; Sunday brunch 11 AM–3 PM. A small upscale restaurant serving locally inspired American cuisine and craft cocktails.

    Cantina Loco (716-551-0160), 191 Allen Street, Buffalo. Lunch Tuesday–Friday 11:30 AM–4 PM, dinner Monday–Thursday 4–10 PM, Friday–Saturday 4 PM–12 AM, brunch Saturday–Sunday 11:30 AM–3 PM. Enjoy a variety of Mexican dishes along with an extensive selection of tequilas and cocktails.

    Giacobbi's Cucina Citta (716-834-4000; www.giacobbis.com), 59 Allen Street, Buffalo. Monday–Wednesday 11:30 AM–10 PM. Thursday–Friday 11:30 AM–11 PM, Saturday 4–10 PM, Sunday 4–9 PM. An upscale family restaurant that has a variety of authentic Italian dishes.

    ♿ **Cecelia's** (716-883-8066; www.ceceliasristorante.com), 716 Elmwood Avenue, Buffalo. Monday 4:30–10 PM, Tuesday–Thursday 11 AM–10 PM, Friday–Saturday 10 AM–11 PM, Sunday 10 AM–9 PM. Offering the largest open-air patio along Elmwood Avenue, this restaurant features numerous Italian entrees like manicotti and pizza, along with specialty dishes like chicken or veal Cecelia. Other popular menu selections are the panini sandwiches. Also on the menu are over fifty varieties of martinis, from classic to unusual.

♈ & **Cole's** (716-886-1449; www .colesonelmwood.com), 1104 Elmwood Avenue, Buffalo. Monday–Thursday 11 AM–11 PM, Friday–Saturday, 11 AM–12 AM, Sunday 11 AM–10 PM. This popular restaurant/bar has been a neighborhood fixture since 1934. Enjoy your meal in the dining room, in the wicker-furnished atrium, or on the outdoor patio. Enjoy burgers, sandwiches, salads, and even a Sunday brunch.

Colter Bay Grill (716-882-1330; www .colterbaygrill.com), 561 Delaware Avenue, Buffalo. Named after Colter Bay on Jackson Lake in Wyoming, this popular brewpub has over thirty craft beers on tap and an American West–influenced menu, with offerings like bison meatloaf and elk burgers.

Gatur's Fast and Tasty (716-881-1832), 69 Allen Street, Buffalo. Monday–Saturday 6 AM–10 PM, Friday–Saturday 6 AM–midnight. This ethnic restaurant features vegetarian and Ethiopian cuisine.

Fat Bob's Smokehouse (716-887-2971; www.fatbobs.com), 41 Virginia Place, Buffalo. Monday–Wednesday 11:30 AM–10 PM, Thursday 11:30 AM–11 PM, Friday–Saturday 11:30 AM–12 AM, Sunday 1–10 PM. Dine in or take out. Enjoy BBQ and smokehouse-style foods. Fat Bob's specializes in "slow and low" cooking. Meats are dry rubbed and cooked for several hours on low heat in their 24-foot, 7,000-pound smoker.

Gabriel's Gate (716-886-0602), 145 Allen Street, Buffalo. Sunday–Wednesday 11:30 AM–12 AM, Thursday 11:30 AM–1 AM, Friday–Saturday 11:30 AM–2 AM. This high-quality, casual dining establishment is located in a historic 1864 row house. Menu selections include burgers, salads, and steaks. Their French onion soup is outstanding, as is their Friday fish fry. They have some of the best wings in the city.

Grindhaus Café (716-725-6300), 160 Allen Street, Buffalo. A vegetarian restaurant that also features pour-over coffee and loose tea.

& ❧ **India Gate** (716-886-4000; www .indiagatebuffalony.com), 1116 Elmwood Avenue, Buffalo. Open daily for lunch 11:30 AM–2:30 PM, dinner 4:30–10 PM. This bright and cheery restaurant features naturally healthy and high-quality Indian cuisine. It offers a mix of vegetarian and non-vegetarian dishes, including delicacies from their clay oven like chicken tikka and fish tandoori. The lunch buffet is very popular.

& ❧ **Jim's Steak Out** (www.jims steakout.com). Eleven locations in the Buffalo area, including 938 Elmwood (885-2900), 3094 Main (838-6666), 92 Chippewa (854-6666), and 196 Allen (886-2222). Open daily 10:30 AM–5 AM. This locally owned and operated restaurant chain, the place to go once the bars close, is famous for their steak hoagies and other subs.

Kuni's (716-881-3800; www.kunis buffalo.com), 226 Lexington Avenue, Buffalo. Tuesday–Thursday 5–9:45 PM, Friday–Saturday 5–10:45 PM. A very popular sushi place that features sushi and sashimi and house specialties, along with a selection of soups and salads. Voted best sushi in Buffalo by *Buffalo Spree* magazine.

Melting Point (716-768-0426; www .buffalomeltingpoint.com), 244 Allen Street, Buffalo. Tuesday–Thursday 11 AM–10 PM, Friday–Saturday 11 AM–2 AM, Sunday 3–9 PM. Their specialty is gourmet grilled cheese sandwiches, plus other sandwich options.

Merge (716-842-0600; www.merge buffalo.com), 439 Delaware Avenue, Buffalo. A café that offers vegan and gluten-free dishes, along with fresh juices. They also have live music on select evenings.

Mezza (716-885-4400; www.mezza buffalo.com), 929 Elmwood Avenue, Buffalo. Monday–Thursday 11 AM–11 PM, Friday–Saturday 11 AM–12 PM, Sunday 11 AM–9 PM. Mediterranean and Lebanese food is featured on the menu.

Midtown Kitchen (MTK) (716-322-1960; www.mtkbuffalo.com), 451 Elmwood Avenue, Buffalo. Monday–Thursday 5–10 PM, Friday 12–11 PM, Saturday 11 AM–3 PM and 5–11 PM, Sunday 11 AM–3 PM, and 5–9 PM. This sleek restaurant with glass walls overlooks Elmwood Avenue. They offer a variety of snack plates to share, as well as entrees like burgers and bourbon glazed hangar steak.

Mother's (716-882-2989), 33 Virginia Place, Buffalo. 2 PM–4 AM. This has been a popular pub and restaurant in Allentown for many years. Located in a former carriage house, Mother's offers fine dining in a relaxed atmosphere.

Mythos (716-886-9175; www.mythos buffalo.com), 510 Elmwood Avenue, Buffalo. Monday–Saturday 7 AM–11 PM, Sunday 7 AM–9 PM. The menu features Greek food at affordable prices, including some of the best chicken souvlaki in the city.

Pano's (716-886-9081; www.panos onelmwood.com), 1081 Elmwood Avenue, Buffalo. Open daily 7 AM–11 PM. A popular Greek restaurant that has been a fixture on Elmwood for over 35 years. Enjoy dining outdoors on the deck in summer.

Sweet Temptations du Jour (716-536-0567; www.sweettemptationsbuffalo .com), 220 Allen Street, Buffalo. Tuesday–Thursday 10 AM–6 PM, Friday 10 AM–7 PM, Saturday 10 AM–4 PM. This bakery has strudel, cheesecake, brownies, mini pies, and sugar waffles. They even offer a Croatian apple strudel workshop.

Taste of Siam (716-886-0746; www .taste-of-siam.com), 810 Elmwood Avenue, Buffalo. Monday–Saturday 12–10 PM, Sunday 4–9 PM. Enjoy authentic Thai cuisine at this family-owned and -operated restaurant.

The Place (716-882-7522; www .theplacebuffalo.com), 229 Lexington Avenue, Buffalo. This neighborhood pub is located in one of the oldest taverns in the city. The menu features everything from wings to pan-roasted salmon.

Thirsty Buffalo (716-878-0344; www .thirstybuffalo.com), 555 Elmwood Avenue, Buffalo. This bar and restaurant has 22 TVs throughout the bar. The menu features pub favorites, like handmade burgers and wings, as well as sandwiches and wraps.

Tokyo Shanghai Bistro (716-886-3839; www.tokyoshanghainy.com), 494 Elmwood Avenue, Buffalo. Monday–Thursday 11 AM–10:30 PM, Friday–Saturday 11 am–11:30 PM, Sunday 12–10 PM. Enjoy sushi, as well as a variety of Chinese and Asian dishes.

Towne Restaurant (716-884-5128), 186 Allen Street, Buffalo. Monday–Saturday 7 AM–5 AM, Sunday–Wednesday 7 AM–10 PM, Thursday 7 AM–1 AM, Friday–Saturday 7 AM–3 AM. This Greek restaurant, a fixture in Allentown for over 30 years, is known for its souvlaki and rice pudding. Breakfast is available all day.

Vera Pizzeria (716-551-6262; www .verapizzeria.com), 220 Lexington Avenue, Buffalo. This neighborhood bar is known for classic cocktails and thin crust pizza.

Vinos (716-332-2166), 1652 Elmwood Avenue, Buffalo. Wednesday–Saturday 5 PM–close. A family-run Italian eatery where everything is made fresh daily, from appetizers to desserts.

HERTEL AVENUE/NORTH BUFFALO

Bertha's Diner (716-836-3100), 1430 Hertel Avenue, Buffalo. Monday–Saturday for breakfast and lunch 7 AM–2 PM, Sunday 8 AM–2 PM. This cozy diner will take you back to the 1950s. Enjoy a specialty sandwich, such as the Elvis, Marilyn Monroe, or James Dean, along with burgers, homemade soups, and salads. Breakfast is served anytime.

Blackbird Sweets (716-253-1115; www .blackbirdsweets.com), 1547 Hertel Avenue, Buffalo. Tuesday–Friday 9 AM–7 PM, Saturday 9 AM–4 PM. Indulge in cupcakes, pies, muffins, and other sweets.

BERTHA'S DINER TAKES YOU BACK TO THE 1950S

Bob & John's La Hacienda (716-836-5411; www.bobandjohns.com), 1545 Hertel Avenue, Buffalo. Sunday–Thursday 11 AM–11 PM, Friday 11 AM–11 PM, Saturday 11 AM–12 AM. Bob and John's has been a fixture on Hertel Avenue for over 30 years. They specialize in Italian cuisine, along with pizza, wings, sandwiches, and salads. Eat in the dining room or outdoors on the sidewalk patio in the warmer months.

Burning Buffalo Bar & Grille (716-259-9060; www.theburningbuffalo.com), 1504 Hertel Avenue, Buffalo. This bar and grill has 16 taps, craft beer, cocktails and pub fare like wings, burgers, and a fish fry.

Café on the Avenue (716-877-2233), 1240 Hertel, Avenue, Buffalo. Open daily 7 AM–3 PM. American diner menu, breakfast and lunch, along with Buffalo's first donut robot, making fresh donuts every day with almost a dozen varieties.

Cravings (716-883-1675; www.cravingbuffalo.com), 1472 Hertel Avenue, Buffalo. The menu features local delicacies made with fresh ingredients, including handmade pasta and gourmet pizza.

Daily Planet Coffee (716-551-0661; www.dailyplanetcoffee.com), 1862 Hertel Avenue, Buffalo. Monday–Thursday 7 AM–9 PM, Friday–Saturday 7 AM–10 PM, Sunday 8 AM–7 PM. Enjoy organic fair-trade coffee, specialty coffees, breakfast fare, sweets, sandwiches and more. Live music is featured several evenings a week and at lunch time.

Deep South Taco (716-235-8464; deepsouthtaco.com/about), 1707 Hertel Avenue, Buffalo. Enjoy authentic Mexican cuisine, including tacos with house-made corn and flour tortillas and an array of tapas. Their other locations are on Ellicott Street and Transit Road.

♿ **Franks Sunny Italy** (716-876-5449), 2491 Delaware Avenue (one block north of Hertel), Buffalo. Monday 11 AM–10 PM, Tuesday–Saturday 11 AM–11 PM, Sunday 12–11 PM. A casual family restaurant specializing in authentic Italian home-cooking. Menu selections include veal, chicken and pasta dishes, along with a large selection of pizzas. This restaurant has been operated since 1990 by the Sclafani family, who hail from Montemaggiore Belsitoa, a small town in Sicily.

♿ **Gramma Mora's** (716-837-6703; www.grammamorasbuffalo.com), 1465 Hertel Avenue, Buffalo. Monday–Tuesday 4–10 PM, Wednesday–Thursday

DAILY PLANET COFFEE

11 AM–10 PM, Friday 11 AM–11 PM, Saturday 12–11 PM, Sunday 11 AM–9 PM. Well-known for the most authentic Mexican cuisine in the city, this friendly restaurant offers homemade food made from recipes handed down for generations.

Joe's Deli (716-875-5637; www .joesdelionline.com), 1322 Hertel Avenue, Buffalo. Monday–Friday 10:30 AM–8:30 PM, Sunday 10:30 AM–4:30 PM. This corner deli serves an assortment of homemade deli sandwiches, wraps, and soups.

Kostas Restaurant (716-838-5225; www.kostasfamilyrestaurant.com), 1561 Hertel Avenue, Buffalo. Monday–Thursday 7 AM–11 PM, Friday–Saturday 7 AM–12 AM, Sunday 8 AM–11 PM. This popular Greek restaurant has been a landmark on Hertel Avenue since 1977. Try the Greek combo platter, which is big enough for two people.

La Tavola Trattoria (716-837-3267; latavolabuffalo.com). 1458 Hertel Avenue, Buffalo. Monday–Thursday 4–10 PM, Friday–Saturday 4–11 PM, Sunday 4–9 PM. La Tavola means "table" in Italian. Enjoy pizza from a wood-fired oven, along with small and large plate selections that change seasonally.

Lloyd's Taco Factory (www .whereslloyd.com), 1503 Hertel Avenue, Buffalo. Monday–Thursday 11 AM–11 PM, Friday–Saturday 11 AM–2 AM This restaurant, the brick-and-mortar version of Lloyd's popular food trucks, features freshly prepared Mexican street food along with craft beers and specialty cocktails. Next door, **Lloyd's Churn** has soft serve ice cream made from scratch, with milk from grass-fed cows, sugar, and very little stabilizer. Choose from vanilla, chocolate, and strawberry, as well as a vegan coconut soft serve.

Macs on Hertel (716-833-6227; www .macsbuffalo.com), 1435 Hertel Avenue, Buffalo. Monday–Thursday 4 PM–12 AM, Friday–Saturday 11 AM–2 AM, Sunday 11 AM–3 PM. This large family-friendly restaurant offers dishes like rotisserie chicken and a Friday fish fry, along with wings, flatbreads, and even a house-made veggie burger.

Mes Que (716-836-8800, www.mesque .com), 1420 Hertel Avenue, Buffalo.

GRAMMA MORA'S HAS AUTHENTIC MEXICAN CUISINE

Monday–Saturday 5–11 PM, Sunday 5–10 PM. This is Buffalo's original soccer bar, with a game on TV most of the time. The menu features casual fare like sandwiches, pizza and pasta, as well as craft cocktails.

Marco's Italian Deli (716-862-9117; www.marcosbuffalo.com), 1744 Hertel Avenue, Buffalo. Monday–Saturday 11 AM–8 PM. This restaurant is best known for its "sangwiches" with names like *Forget About It*, a turkey sub with red peppers, provolone cheese, and Marco's chili mustard, and the *Try It*, made with roast beef, onions, hot peppers, and melted swiss.

New Moon Café (716-481-8397), 1685 Hertel Avenue, Buffalo. Tuesday–Sunday 7 AM–3 PM. Enjoy creative breakfast burritos, Belgian waffles, and French toast croissants to start your day. For lunch, there are a variety of panini and sandwiches to choose from, including vegetarian options.

Parkside Meadow (716-834-8348; www.parksidemeadow.com), 2 Russell Street, Buffalo. Monday–Saturday 11 AM–11 PM, Sunday 11 AM–7 PM. Located across the street from the Buffalo Zoo, this restored neighborhood pub is decorated with all sorts of Buffalo memorabilia. Menu selections include beef on weck, wings, meatloaf, and pot roast.

The Public House (716-551-6208; www.publichousebuffalo.com), 1206 Hertel Avenue, Buffalo. Tuesday–Thursday 12–11 PM, Friday–Sunday 12 PM–2:30 AM. The bar features 20 taps and 60 bottled beers. Menu items include items like Flying Bison's Rusty Chain beer-battered fish fry, chicken wings, and a variety of sandwiches.

♿ **Romeo's & Juliet's Bakery Café** (873-5730; www.rjcaffe.com), 1292 Hertel Avenue, Buffalo. Tuesday–Thursday 10:30 AM–9 PM, Friday–Saturday 10:30 AM–10 PM. When you step into this small corner café, with soft Italian music playing in the background and the smells of authentic Italian cooking, you feel like you've been transported to Italy. Selections include gourmet pizza, specialty sandwiches served on focaccia bread, appetizers like bruschetta, and wonderful desserts like cannoli and biscotti.

The Wellington Pub (716-833-9899; www.wellingtonpub.com), 1541 Hertel Avenue, Buffalo. Monday–Saturday 11 AM–12 AM, Sunday 12 PM–12 AM. Traditional American cuisine is served in this casual restaurant. It's also a great place to enjoy an order of wings or a bowl of chili while watching the Bills or Sabres on TV.

UNIVERSITY DISTRICT

♿ 🐾 ⚓ **Lake Effect Diner** (716-833-1952; www.curtinrestaurants.com/lake-effect.html), 3165 Main Street, Buffalo. Daily 7 AM–10 PM. Take a trip back to the 1950s when you visit the Lake Effect Diner, an authentic 1952 diner originally erected in Wayne, Pennsylvania, and moved in the 1990s to its present location. Breakfast selections include eggs, bacon, and stuffed pancakes. For lunch or dinner choose from burgers, sandwiches, beef on weck, salads, souvlaki, or homestyle entrees like meatloaf, roast beef, or turkey.

Parkside Candy (716-833-7540; www.parksidecandy.com), 3208 Main Street, Buffalo. Monday–Thursday 11 AM–6 PM, Friday–Saturday 11 AM–9 PM. This sweets shop, established in 1927, is an architectural treasure listed on the National Register of Historic Places. Known for their ice cream sundaes and signature sponge candy, they have been voted the best ice cream shop in the city by *Buffalo Spree* magazine.

Sato Ramen (716-835-7286; www.sato-ramen.com), 3268 Main Street, Buffalo. Monday–Thursday 11:30 AM–10 PM Friday–Saturday 11:30 AM–10:30 PM. Enjoy authentic Japanese ramen—not the kind you make in the microwave—and Japanese soul food in this University District restaurant.

The Steer (716-838-0478;. www.curtinrestaurants.com), 3151 Main

Street, Buffalo. Daily 11 AM–4 AM. Long-time University District restaurant that offers vegan, raw, and gluten-free choices, along with burgers and steaks.

WEST SIDE

The Black Sheep (716-884-1100; www.blacksheepbuffalo.com), 367 Connecticut Street, Buffalo. Tuesday–Thursday 5–10 PM, Friday–Saturday 5–11 PM, Sunday 11 AM–2 PM. Enjoy farm-to-table dining on Buffalo's West Side. They have a small plate and appetizer menu, as well as larger entrees and daily specials, including pork dishes from pigs raised on a T-Meadow Farm in Lockport.

Bread Hive Bakery (716-980-LOAF; www.breadhive.com), 402 Connecticut Street, Buffalo. Tuesday 8 AM–6 PM, Wednesday–Sunday 8 AM–3 PM. A worker cooperative bakery and café which offers homemade breads and sandwiches with locally sourced products.

Five Points Bakery and Toast Café (716-884-8888; www.fivepointsbakery.com), 44 Braylon Street, Buffalo. Monday–Wednesday, Friday 7 AM–3 PM, Thursday 7 AM–6 PM, Saturday–Sunday 9 AM–3 PM. Feast on whole grain breads and pastries made from local ingredients.

Gypsy Parlor (716-551-0001; www.thegypsyparlor.com), 376 Grant Street. Buffalo. Monday–Thursday and Saturday 5 PM–12 AM, Friday 2:30 PM–12 AM, Sunday 4 PM–12 AM. Enjoy pub fare and local west side specialties as well as international cuisine. They also have entertainment, such as open mic night, trivia night, karaoke, and local bands.

Lait Cru Brasserie (716-462-4100; www.laitcrubrasserie.com), 346 Connecticut Street, Buffalo. Tuesday–Wednesday 9 AM–6 PM, Thursday–Saturday 9 AM–2:30 PM and 5–9 PM, Sunday 11 AM–3 PM. This cafe, located in the Horsefeathers building, features French-inspired cuisine that is locally sourced. Next door, **Nickel City Cheese &**

Mercantile (716-882-3068) carries a variety of cheese and specialty foods.

Lin Restaurant (716-260-2625; www.linrestaurant.com), 927 Tonawanda Street. Monday–Friday 11 AM–10 PM, Saturday–Sunday 9 AM–10 PM. Authentic Thai and Burmese cuisine is served in this nicely decorated restaurant located across the street from Riverside Park. An all-you-can-eat Burmese and Thai brunch is served on Sundays. The adjacent Lin Market has imported food items from Thailand and Burma.

Roost (716-259-9306), 1502 Niagara Street, Buffalo. Wednesday–Saturday 11 AM–10 PM, Sunday 11 AM–3 PM. Chef Martin Danilowicz's restaurant, which is located in the former Bison Storage building, features a seasonal, eclectic menu, which includes pizza made in a four-ton rotating deck pizza oven.

Ru Pierogi Restaurant (716-235-8243; www.ruspierogi.com), 295 Niagara Street, Buffalo. Monday–Thursday 11 AM–10 PM, Friday–Saturday 11 AM–11 PM. Traditional and experimental fillings can be found in the pierogi, which are made on-site in their production plant. Other menu items include kielbasa, fried bologna, and barbecued hamburgers, along with locally brewed beers, wines, and ciders. They also have a food truck.

🍴 **Santasieros** (716-886-9197)1329 Niagara Street, Buffalo. Daily 11 AM–10 PM. Opened in 1921 and owned by the same family for four generations, this casual Italian restaurant features Italian comfort food topped with the family recipe sauce. Cash only.

West Side Bazaar (716-464-6389; www.westsidebazaar.com), 25 Grant Street, Buffalo. Tuesday–Thursday 11 AM–7 PM, Friday 11 AM–8 PM, Saturday 10 AM–8 PM. This small business incubator for immigrants and refugees offers handcrafted items and a food court with ethnic dishes from Burma, Thailand, Jamaica, Ethopia, Laos, India, and Pakistan.

La Nova Pizzeria (716-881-3355; www
.lanova.com), 371 West Ferry Street,
Buffalo. Sunday–Thursday 10 AM–1 AM,
Friday–Saturday 10 AM–2 AM. Owned
and operated by the Todaro family since
1957, this Buffalo institution serves pizzas, along with wings, subs, and more.
A second location is at 5151 Main Street,
Williamsville (716-634-5151).

EAST SIDE

R & L Lounge (716-896-5982), 23 Mills
Street, Buffalo (just off Broadway). This
bar and restaurant, located around
the corner from the Broadway Market,
is known for homemade pierogi and
golabki, as well as a Friday fish fry.

SOUTH BUFFALO/LACKAWANNA

The Blackthorn (716-825-9327;
blackthornrestaurant.com), 2134 Seneca
Street, South Buffalo. Daily 11:30 AM–
10 PM. This casual pub, open since 1977,
is a local hangout. Specialties include
beef on weck and Irish beer cheddar
soup.

Curly's Grill (716-824-9716; www
.curlysgrille.com), 647 Ridge Road,
Lackawanna. A popular Lackawanna
restaurant that has a variety of innovative American dishes and Caribbean
inspired dishes, like Jamaican jerk
chicken.

✿ ♿ ✿ **Daisies Café** (716-826-3410),
2711 South Park Avenue, Lackawanna.
Tuesday–Saturday 7:30 AM–2 PM. Start
your day with omelets, pancakes, and
other breakfast favorites at this kid-
friendly restaurant. Lunch selections
include burgers, club sandwiches, hot
sandwiches, and even some ethnic
favorites.

Mess Hall (716-827-1134; www
.messhallbuffalo.com), 717 Ridge
Road, Lackawanna. Tuesday–Thursday
11:30 AM–9 PM, Friday–Saturday
11:30 AM–9:30 PM. The menu features
pizza, homemade spaghetti, goulash, and
tortellini, along with unusual dishes like
oxtail pierogi.

Mulberry Italian Ristorante (716-822-
4292; www.mulberryitalianristorante
.com), 64 Jackson Avenue, Lackawanna.
Monday–Thursday 11:30 AM–9 PM, Friday
11:30 AM–9:30 PM, Saturday 4–9:30 PM,
Sunday 3–8 PM. Hidden in an unassum-
ing residential neighborhood, this Italian
restaurant is noted for their authentic
cuisine, homemade pasta, huge base-
ball-sized meatballs, and friendly service.

✿ ✿ **Steve's Ox and Pig Roast** (716-
824-8601), 951 Ridge Road, Lackawanna.
Open Monday–Saturday 11 AM–9 PM.
This place may not be fancy, but it has
been voted to have one of the best beef
on weck in the Buffalo area. They are
equally well-known for their roast pork,
lamb, and turkey sandwiches.

✳ Entertainment

MUSIC **Buffalo Chamber Music Society**
(716-838-2383; www.bflochambermusic
.org), Kleinhans Music Hall, 71 Symphony Circle, Buffalo. For over 80 years
this group of musicians has been enter-
taining Buffalo audiences. Performances

MULBERRY ITALIAN RISTORANTE IS A HIDDEN GEM IN
LACKAWANNA

are held Thursday evenings in the **Mary Seaton Room** at Kleinhans Music Hall.

Buffalo Philharmonic Orchestra (716-885-5000 or 800-699-3168; www .bpo.org), Kleinhans Music Hall, 71 Symphony Circle, Buffalo. The acoustically perfect Kleinhans Music Hall is the permanent home of the internationally renowned Buffalo Philharmonic Orchestra, under the direction of conductor JoAnn Falletta. The orchestra performs classical as well as pops and children's concerts. Kleinhans is also a popular venue for concerts for local and national acts. See also *Unique Architecture.*

Waiting Room (716-853-5483; www .waitingroombuffalo.com), 334 Delaware Avenue, Buffalo. Music venue for rock and roll and alternative rock bands. Live band karaoke is featured on Thursday and Friday evenings upstairs in the studio.

NIGHTLIFE While clubs come and clubs go, the most popular nightspots in the city can be found on Chippewa Street and the theater district in downtown, and along Elmwood Avenue in the Elmwood Village and Allen Street in Allentown.

THEATERS For complete up-to-date information about Buffalo area theaters, visit www.theatreallianceofbuffalo.com. Below are some of the theaters in and around the Buffalo area.

African American Cultural Center/ Paul Robeson Theatre (716-884-2013; www.aaccbuffalo.org/paul-robeson-theatre), 350 Masten Avenue, Buffalo. The African American Cultural Center, founded in 1958, was the first Black educational cultural institution in the City of Buffalo. The facility contains the African World Studies Archive and the 110-seat Paul Robeson Theatre, the oldest African American theater in Western New York.

Theatre of Youth Company (TOY) (716-884-4400; www.theatreofyouth .org), Allendale Theater, 203 Allen Street, Buffalo. The mission of the Theater of Youth (TOY), founded in 1972, is to bring quality entertainment to young audiences. Performances take place in the restored 469-seat **Allendale Theater**, built in 1913.

Alleyway Theatre (716-852-2600; www.alleyway.com), 1 Curtain Up Alley, Buffalo. Founded in 1980 by Neal Radice, this theater is located in Buffalo's former bus terminal. Four or five productions are featured each theater season.

Ashbury Hall/Babeville (716-852-3835; www.babevillebuffalo.com) 341 Delaware Avenue, Buffalo. This 130-year-old renovated former church has a concert hall with seating capacity for 1,200 people. It is the headquarters of singer Ani DiFranco's Righteous Babe Records and also houses Hallwalls Contemporary Arts Center.

Road Less Traveled Productions at the Forbes Theatre (716-629-3069; roadlesstraveledproductions.org), 500 Pearl Street, Buffalo. This theater company features works by playwrights in western New York and southern Ontario.

Irish Classical Theater (716-853-4282; www.irishclassicaltheatre.com), 625 Main Street, Buffalo. This theater-in-the-round was founded in 1990 by Dublin natives Chris O'Neill and James Warde.

Kavinoky Theatre (716-881-7668; www.kavinokytheatre.com), 320 Porter Avenue, Buffalo. This 250-seat 1908 Victorian auditorium is located on the campus of D'Youville College. Since 1981 the resident professional theater company has been presenting productions from September through May.

New Phoenix Theatre (716-853-1334; www.newphoenixtheatre.org), 95 North Johnson Park, Buffalo. This theater, which resembles an off-Broadway theater, presents productions a bit edgier and more avant-garde than most Buffalo theater groups. It started out as a gay-themed theater but has since expanded to include other themes.

♧ **Rockwell Hall** (716-878-3005; buffalostatepac.org), Buffalo State College, 1300 Elmwood Avenue, Buffalo. The performing arts center at Rockwell

Hall hosts a variety of events each season, including dance, vocal, and musical performances.

Shakespeare in Delaware Park (716-856-4533; www.shakespearein delawarepark.org), Shakespeare Hill in Delaware Park, behind the Albright-Knox, near the Rose Garden and Casino. Late June–August. Performances Tuesday–Sunday at 7:30 PM. Free admission. For over 40 years, works by the Bard have been presented in this open-air theater located on a grassy knoll in Delaware Park—one of the largest free Shakespeare events in the United States.

 ♿ **Shea's Performing Arts Center** (716-847-1410; www.sheas.org), 646 Main Street, Buffalo. This cultural institution, listed on the National Register of Historic Places, is one of only four theaters still in existence that were designed by Louis Comfort Tiffany, and one of the most ornate theaters of the 13 operated by Michael Shea. It opened in 1926 as a movie house and later hosted live stage shows. Shea's presents a wide variety of entertainment: Broadway productions, concerts, opera, ballet, and even classic films. One of the notable fixtures in the theater is the restored custom-built 1926 Mighty Wurlitzer pipe organ, the second-largest organ of its type in the state. Two other smaller, more intimate venues are part of the theater complex: Shea's Smith Theater, 658 Main Street, and Shea's 710 Theater, 710 Main Street.

Ujima Theatre Company (716-281-0092; www.ujimacoinc.org), 515 Main Street, Buffalo. The only professional theater company in western New York that focuses on works by African Americans and other artists of color.

PROFESSIONAL SPORTS **Buffalo Bandits Lacrosse** (716-855-4100; www .bandits.com), KeyBank Center, 1 Seymour H. Knox III Plaza, Buffalo.

Buffalo Bills Football (716-648-1800, tickets: 877-BB-TICKS; www.buffalobills .com), New Era Field, 1 Bills Drive, Orchard Park.

Buffalo Bisons Baseball (716-846-2003, 888-223-6000; www.bisons.com), Coca-Cola Field, 275 Washington Street, Buffalo. The Bisons are the AAA farm team of the Toronto Blue Jays.

Buffalo Sabres Hockey (716-855-4110 or 888-GO-SABRES; www.sabres.com), KeyBank Center, 1 Seymour H. Knox III Plaza, Buffalo.

✳ Selective Shopping

ANTIQUES

ELMWOOD VILLAGE/ ALLENTOWN

Antiques Allentown (716-882-9535), 146 Elmwood Avenue, Buffalo. Thursday–Saturday 12–5 PM. This shop specializes in mid-century primitives and miniatures.

Antique Man (716-883-2121), 234 Allen Street, Buffalo. Monday–Saturday 12–6 PM. This shop features art and other collectibles.

Carl Stone (716-884-0211), 65 Elmwood Avenue, Buffalo. Friday and Saturday 11 AM–5 PM or by appointment. Specializes in stained glass and period lighting.

HERTEL AVENUE

The Antique Lamp (716-871-0508; www .antiquelampco.com), 1213 Hertel Avenue, Buffalo. Wednesday–Saturday 11 AM–4 PM. This shop has antique and vintage lighting, along with gifts and jewelry.

Buffalo Antiques (716-832-4231; www .buffaloantique.com), 1539 Hertel Avenue, Buffalo. Wednesday–Saturday 12–5 PM. Features furniture, rugs, carved items, and art objects.

Dana Tillou Fine Arts (716-854-5285; www.danatilloufinearts.com), 1478 Hertel, Buffalo. Wednesday–Friday 10:30 AM–5 PM, Saturday 10:30 AM–4 PM. This shop specializes in American and British art from 1800–1940 and period antiques.

The Second Reader (716-862-0001), 1419 Hertel Avenue, Buffalo.

THE ANTIQUE LAMP ON HERTEL AVENUE SPECIALIZES IN VINTAGE LIGHTING AND GIFTS

Tuesday–Thursday 11 AM–5 PM, Friday and Saturday 10 AM–7 PM. Used books, prints, and ephemera.

WEST SIDE

Gothic City (716-874-4479; www.gothic city.com), 1940 Niagara Street, Buffalo. Thursday–Sunday 11 AM–5 PM. Specializes in architectural items for the home, including iron fencing, gates, garden furnishings, and more.

ART GALLERIES **Benjamin's Art Gallery** (716-886-0898; www.thebenjaman gallery.com), 419 Elmwood Avenue, Buffalo. Thursday–Saturday 11 AM–5 PM. This gallery specializes in fine art, from antique to contemporary.

  ♿ **Buffalo Big Print** (716-884-1777; buffalobigprint.com), 78 Allen Street, Buffalo. Art Gallery and custom display work.

  Nina Freudenheim Gallery (716-882-5777; www.ninafreudenheimgallery .com), Hotel Lenox, 140 North Street, Buffalo. Tuesday–Friday 10 AM–5 PM, Sunday and Monday by appointment. This gallery showcases a variety of national and international contemporary artists.

  ♿ **El Buen Amigo** (885-6343; elbuenamigo.org), 114 Elmwood Avenue,

Buffalo. Monday–Saturday 11 AM–7 PM, Sunday 11 AM–5 PM. This art and crafts gallery operated by the Latin American Cultural Association features finely crafted jewelry, pottery, clothing, masks, musical instruments, and other hand-made items from South and Central America.

  El Museo Francisco Oller y Diego Rivera (716-884-9693; www .elmuseobuffalo.org), 91 Allen Street, Buffalo. Wednesday–Saturday 12–6 PM. Works of art by Latinos, African Americans, and other artists of color, many who are local.

  Michael Morgulis Studio–Local Color Gallery (716-885-5188; www.cafepress .com/newbuffalo), 1417 Hertel Avenue, Buffalo. Tuesday–Saturday 12–6 PM. This gallery features the work of Buffalo artist Michael Morgulis.

BOOKSTORES **Old Editions Book Shop & Café** (716-842-1734; www.oldeditions .com), 72 East Huron Street, Buffalo. Tuesday–Saturday 10 AM–5:30 PM. One of the largest antique bookstores in upstate New York, the 12,000 square-foot shop, housed in a vintage 1896 building, contains an array of old, rare, and collectible books, prints, maps, autographs, and engravings.

  Talking Leaves Books (716-884-9524; www.tleavesbooks.com), 951 Elmwood Avenue, Buffalo. Open Monday–Saturday 10 AM–9 PM, Sunday 10 AM–6 PM. Buffalo's largest independent bookstore features a large selection of poetry, along with the latest bestsellers, local interest books, Native American studies books, and more.

FARM MARKETS **Clinton-Bailey Market** (716-208-0003; clintonbaileymarket .com), 1443–1517 Clinton Street, Buffalo. Open May 1–November 1, Sunday–Friday 7 AM–6 PM, Saturday 6 AM–6 PM, remainder of the year Saturdays only 6 AM–6 PM. Since 1931 this establishment has been the largest privately owned farmers' market in New York State.

During the growing season, thousands of people flock here for the best selection of locally grown produce. During the off-season, produce from other parts of the country is available.

Downtown Buffalo Country Market (716-856-3150), Main Street (between Church and Court Streets), Buffalo. Open mid-May–late October Tuesday and Thursday 10 AM–2:30 PM. For over 30 years, local farmers, gardeners, and florists have been bringing their goods to downtown office workers and residents.

Elmwood Village Farmers' Market (contact Elmwood Village Association, 716-881-0707; www.elmwoodmarket .org), corner of Elmwood Avenue and Bidwell Parkway, Buffalo. Open end of May–November, Saturday 8 AM–1 PM. This market, located in the heart of the Elmwood Village, features organic fruits, vegetables, and flowers.

SPECIAL SHOPS

DOWNTOWN/CENTER CITY/ WATERFRONT

Buffalo Niagara Convention and Visitors Bureau (716-852-0511 or 800-283-3256; www.visitbuffaloniagara.com), 403 Main Street, Buffalo. They carry a large selection of Buffalo-themed items, from key chains to hats and shirts.

New Era Cap (716-604-9000; www .neweracap.com), 160 Delaware Avenue, Buffalo. Monday–Saturday 10 AM–6 PM. You can find a large selection of caps in their flagship store, located in the former Federal Reserve building. New Era is the exclusive cap supplier to Major League Baseball.

EAST SIDE

🍴 ✐ **Broadway Market** (716-893-2216; www.broadwaymarket.com), 999

ENJOY FINE ART ALONG ELMWOOD AVENUE

Broadway, Buffalo. Monday–Saturday 8 AM–5 PM. This market is a regional treasure, noted for its ethnic Old World shopping atmosphere. Many family-owned businesses, including butchers, sausage makers, bakeries, candy makers, and greengrocers, have been passed from generation to generation since the market opened in 1888. It's an especially popular place to shop before Easter or Christmas.

HERTEL AVENUE/NORTH BUFFALO

Conley Interiors (716-838-1000; www.conleyinteriors.com), 1425 Hertel Avenue, Buffalo. Monday–Friday 10 AM–5 PM, Saturday by appointment. This 25,000-square-foot showroom, established in 1925, offers fine furniture, unusual lighting, fine art, accessories, and antiques.

Globe Market on Hertel (716-783-9955; www.theglobemarket.com), 1416 Hertel Avenue, Buffalo. A gourmet grocery and cookware store that also offers fresh entrees, soups, and salads to eat in or take out from their café.

THERE IS AN ETHNIC OLD-WORLD SHOPPING ATMOSPHERE AT THE BROADWAY MARKET

Cone Five Pottery (716-332-0486; www.conefivepottery.com), 1508 Hertel Avenue, Buffalo. Tuesday–Sunday, opens at 11 AM. For over 20 years Cone Five has featured the work of over 100 American crafts artists including pottery, blown glass, jewelry, wood, candles, and more. In addition, pottery classes are offered, from beginner to advanced.

Modern Nostalgia (716-844-8435; www.shopmodnos.com), 1382 Hertel Avenue, Buffalo. Opens daily at 11 AM. Men's and women's fashions and accessories from local designers.

North Park Florist (716-838-1123; www.northparkflorist.com), 1514 Hertel Avenue, Buffalo. Monday–Friday 9 AM–5 PM, Saturday 10 AM–2 PM. A variety of floral items and gifts are sold here.

ELMWOOD VILLAGE/ ALLENTOWN

Anna Grace (716-332-7069; annagracebuffalo.tumblr.com), 799 Elmwood Avenue, Buffalo. Monday–Friday 11 AM–6 PM, Friday–Saturday 12–5 PM. Dresses, jeans, jackets, and more can be found in this boutique.

Blue Mountain Coffees (716-883-5983), 509 Elmwood Avenue, Buffalo. Monday–Friday 8 AM–6 PM, Saturday 8 AM–5 PM, Sunday 8 AM–2 PM. Since 1981 this has been a popular shop to buy freshly roasted coffees from all over the world, a variety of loose teas, brewing accessories, gift items, magazines, and greeting cards.

Blush Boutique (716-768-0110; www.shopblushny.com), 1005 Elmwood Avenue, Buffalo. Choose from an array of designer women's clothing, accessories, jewelry, and sunglasses.

Dolci Bakery (716-310-4918; www.dolcibakery.com), 802 Elmwood Avenue, Buffalo. Specializing in hand-crafted Italian desserts, including gelato. They also make vegan and gluten free desserts.

SHOP AT CONE FIVE ON HERTEL AVENUE

Everything Elmwood (716-883-0607), 740 Elmwood Avenue, Buffalo. Monday–Friday 10 AM–8 PM, Saturday 10 AM–6 PM, Sunday 12–5 PM. A mix of eclectic upscale items, including glassware, home decor, jewelry, stained glass, cards, clothing, and cards.

Fern & Arrow (716-882-5858), 773 Elmwood Avenue, Buffalo. A gift shop that carries an array of items from clothing and specialty soaps to books and kitchen items.

Her Story Boutique (716-886-6457; www.herstorybuffalo.com), 779 Elmwood Avenue, Buffalo. This boutique shop specializes in jewelry, bath and body items, clothing and accessories.

Globe Market on Elmwood (716-886-5242; www.theglobemarket.com), 762 Elmwood Avenue, Buffalo. Monday–Saturday 10 AM–8 PM, Sunday 10 AM–6 PM. A gourmet grocery and cookware store that also offers fresh entrees, soups, and salads to eat in or take out from their café.

Lexington Co-op Market (716-886-COOP; lexington.coop), 807 Elmwood Avenue, Buffalo. Open daily 7 AM–11 PM. A natural and organic cooperative grocery market.

Neo Gift Studio (716-884-1119), 905 Elmwood Avenue, Buffalo.

Monday–Friday 10 AM–5:30 PM, Saturday 10 AM–5 PM. This store offers an eclectic mix of gifts, jewelry, furniture, and home decor. Its renowned signature gift wrap includes handmade bows and silk flowers.

Spoiled Rotten (716-884-3883), 831 Elmwood Avenue, Buffalo. Monday–Friday 10 AM–8 PM, Saturday 10 AM–6 PM, Sunday 1–5 PM. A great place to get jewelry, stuffed animals, and home decor items for that spoiled rotten person in your life.

Thin Ice Gift Shop (716-881-4321; www.thiniceonline.com), 719 Elmwood Avenue, Buffalo. Sunday–Monday 11 AM–6 PM, Tuesday–Saturday 10:30 AM–7 PM. Choose from one of a kind items handmade by local artisans, including jewelry, metal, glass, pottery, wooden items, and more.

✐ **The Treehouse**, 754 Elmwood Avenue, Buffalo. Open Sunday 12–4 PM, Tuesday, Wednesday, Saturday 10 AM–6 PM, Thursday and Friday 10 AM–7 PM. Choose from all sorts of educational toys, stuffed animals, and other special playthings. The vintage shop features decorative copper and tin ceilings.

THIN ICE HAS ITEMS MADE BY LOCAL ARTISANS

Village Designs (716-881-7800; www
.villagedesignselmwood.com), 448
Elmwood Ave. Tuesday–Saturday 11
AM–6 PM, Sunday–Monday 12–4 PM.
They carry women's designer fashions
that you won't find anywhere else in
the city.

Wild Things (716-882-3324; www
.wildthingsartisans.com), 224 Lexington Avenue, Buffalo. Monday–Saturday
11 AM–6 PM. This unique shop features
locally made hand-crafted jewelry, pottery, clothing, scarves and more, including custom bridal headdresses.

SOUTH BUFFALO/LACKAWANNA

Dog Ears Bookstore and Café (716-823-2665; www.dogearsbookstore.org),
688 Abbott Road, South Buffalo. Bookstore open Monday–Saturday 10 AM–8
PM, Sunday 11 AM–3 PM; café open Monday–Friday 6:30 AM–8 PM, Saturday 8
AM–8 PM, Sunday 9 AM–3 PM. The bookstore has a variety of books, from new
releases to classics, for both children
and adults. Proceeds go to programs
promoting children's creativity and literacy. The café has a variety of soups and
sandwiches.

Ko-Ed Candies (716-824-3489; www
.koedcandies.com), 285 Abbott Road,
South Buffalo. Open seasonally. This
candy shop has been a fixture in South
Buffalo since 1947. Enjoy sponge candy,
fine chocolates, and other specialties.

Tara Gift Shoppe (716-825-6700;
www.taragiftshoppe.com), 250 Abbott
Road, South Buffalo. Monday–Saturday
10 AM–5:30 PM, Thursday until 8 PM.
Named after a type of brooch that fastens the cloaks of Irish dancers, this shop
is a fixture in South Buffalo's Irish community. They carry Irish-themed apparel,
jewelry, music, and other items.

Woyshner's Christmas Shoppe (716-821-0416), 880 Ridge Road, Lackawanna.
Open Seasonally July-December. Choose
from a large selection of imported glass
ornaments, Santas, snowmen, custom-made wreaths and centerpieces,

Irish gift items, Dept. 56 Villages, and
more.

✳ Special Events

Here is just a sampling of annual festivals
and events held in Buffalo:

January: **Chillibration** (www
.canalsidebuffalo.com). A family-friendly
event with ice skating, curling, kids
activities, ice carving and more.

February: **Mardi Gras Festival**,
Downtown Buffalo and Allentown. This
annual Mardi Gras Festival, held on "Fat
Tuesday" features over 40 parade floats
and more than 30 participating bars and
restaurants.

March: **St. Patrick's Day Parade** (716-875-0282; www.buffaloirish.com), Delaware Avenue. An annual event where
everyone in Buffalo is Irish.

Spring: **Dyngus Day Celebrations**
(716-668-6888; www.dyngusdaybuffalo
.com). Buffalo's large Polish community
holds this traditional post-Lenten celebration the day after Easter in numerous
locations throughout the city, especially
on the east side of Buffalo. It is the largest Dyngus Day celebration in the United
States.

June: **Allentown Art Festival** (716-881-4269; allentownartfestival.com).
More than 400 artists display their
works in Buffalo's historic Allentown district. **Juneteenth Festival**, MLK Jr. Park
(716-891-8801; www.juneteenthofbuffalo
.com). A celebration of African American
culture, featuring ethnic foods, wares,
entertainment, and family activities.

July: **Friendship Festival** (905-871-6454 or 888-333-1987; www
.friendshipfestival.com), Buffalo and
Fort Erie, Ontario. One of the largest
international events in the Niagara
region, this festival commemorates the
friendship between the United States
and Canada. Activities include concerts,
children's rides, and an international
air show over the Niagara River. **Italian
Heritage Festival** (716-512-1878; www

THE NATIONAL BUFFALO WING FESTIVAL

Held on Labor Day Weekend, the National Buffalo Wing Festival revolves around eating chicken wings—lots of them; over 20 tons are consumed in two days. More than two dozen restaurants from all over the United States serve up traditional, Cajun, BBQ, and other uniquely flavored wings. The festival, which began in 2002, was inspired by the 2001 movie *Osmosis Jones*, which featured a junk-food addict (played by actor Bill Murray) going to the National Chicken Wing Festival in Buffalo—though, in fact, no such event existed at that time. After the release of the movie, Donn Esmonde, a reporter for the Buffalo News, wrote a column asking why Buffalo didn't actually have a National Chicken Wing festival. Buffalo-based food promoter Drew Cerza saw the column and decided to make this concept a reality. Besides eating, activities include musical entertainment, the Miss Chicken Wing competition, and—the climax of the festival—the chicken wing eating contest, sanctioned by the International Federation of Competitive Eating.

THE NATIONAL BUFFALO WING FESTIVAL TAKES PLACE ON LABOR DAY WEEKEND

.buffaloitalianfestival.com), Outer Harbor. This five-day festival has been a Buffalo favorite since the 1930s. Enjoy musical entertainment, cultural displays, Italian foods, rides, games, and vendors. **Taste of Buffalo** (www.tasteofbuffalo .com), Delaware Avenue, downtown Buffalo. The largest two-day food festival in the country, offering a weekend of food and entertainment for the entire family. **Garden Walk** (716-247-5004; www.gardenwalkbuffalo.com), Elmwood Village and Buffalo's West Side. Almost

400 city gardens are open to the public for viewing, with many of the gardeners themselves available to offer horticultural advice.

August: **Elmwood Avenue Festival of the Arts** (716-830-2484; www .elmwoodartfest.org), Elmwood Avenue, between Lafayette and West Ferry. A family-friendly summer street festival focusing on the artists and craftspeople located on and around Elmwood Avenue. Live musical performances and foods from local restaurants are also

featured. **Buffalo Irish Festival** (www
.buffaloirish.com), Outer Harbor. Celebrating Irish heritage.

Labor Day Weekend: **National Buffalo Wing Festival** (716-565-4141; www
.buffalowing.com), Coca Cola Field,
275 Washington Street, Buffalo. What
more natural place to have the National
Chicken Wing Festival than the birthplace of the Buffalo wing?

Fall: **Buffalo International Film Festival** (www.buffalointernationalfilmfest
ival.com). Various locations throughout
western NY. All types of films will be
shown at this multiday event; see website
for specifics.

September: **Curtain Up!** (tda-wny
.com), Theater District. The opening
of Buffalo's theater season starts with
a black-tie dinner and ends with a
post-theater street party.

November: **Rail Barons Model Train
Exhibit,** Buffalo History Museum
(716-873-9644; www.buffalohistory
.org), 1 Museum Court. This exhibit
runs from the day after Thanksgiving until February, featuring period

locomotives on 200 feet of track and
over 80 handcrafted miniature ver-
sions of notable western New York
buildings. **World's Largest Disco**
(theworldslargestdisco.com), Buffalo
Convention Center. This retro party
features 72,000 watts of sound on the
largest disco floor in New York. **Turkey
Trot** (www.ymcabuffaloniagara.org/
annual-events/ymca-turkey-trot). The
oldest continually run race in America,
it first started in 1896. It takes place on
Thanksgiving Day.

December: **Victorian Christmas,** Theodore Roosevelt Inaugural
National Historic Site (716-884-0095;
www.nps.gov/thri), 641 Delaware
Avenue, Buffalo. This event features
Victorian seasonal decorations and
gifts, vintage fashion shows, entertainment, lunches, and dinners. **First
Night Buffalo** (716-635-4959; www
.firstnightbuffalo.org), Elmwood
Avenue (Museum District). A family-oriented New Year's celebration
that features music, rides, games, and
fireworks.

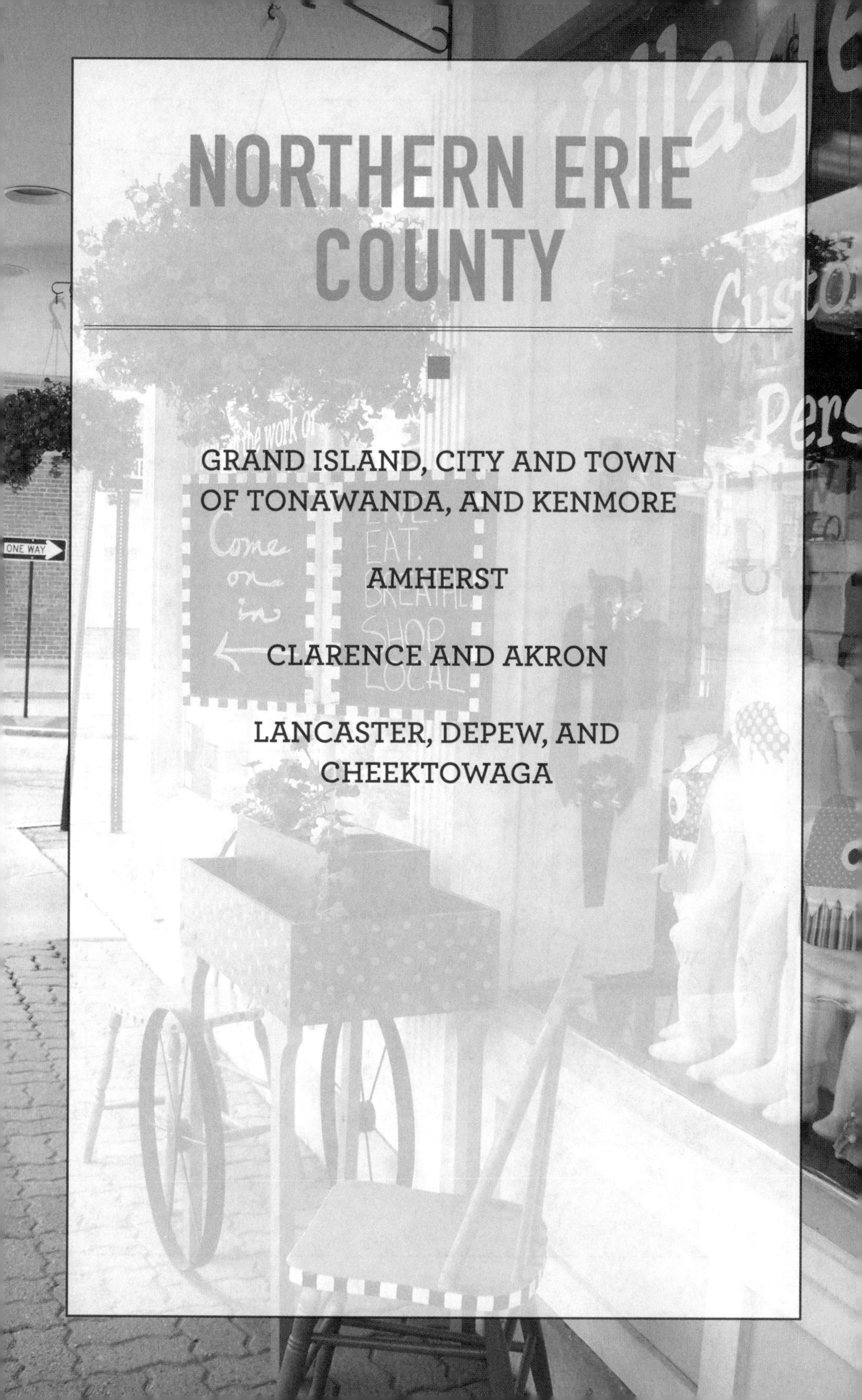

NORTHERN ERIE COUNTY

GRAND ISLAND, CITY AND TOWN OF TONAWANDA, AND KENMORE

AMHERST

CLARENCE AND AKRON

LANCASTER, DEPEW, AND CHEEKTOWAGA

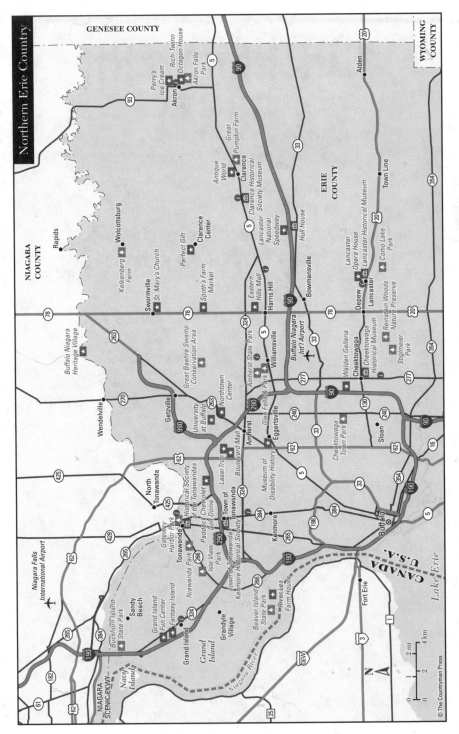

Northern Erie Country

GENESEE COUNTY

WYOMING COUNTY

NIAGARA COUNTY

ERIE COUNTY

© The Countryman Press

INTRODUCTION

Northern Erie County, known as the "Northtowns" by locals, is made up mainly of Buffalo bedroom communities and upscale suburbs, but it also has many interesting historical museums, and lots of recreational activities. There are also many eating establishments, from fine dining to hot dog joints. If you like to shop, you'll find a wide variety of stores, from the Walden Galleria, the area's largest shopping mall, to quaint shops in the town of Clarence, the antiques capital of western New York.

GRAND ISLAND, CITY AND TOWN OF TONAWANDA, AND KENMORE

Grand Island is one of 19 islands in the upper Niagara River. At 7.5 miles long and 6 miles wide, it is one of the largest freshwater islands in the world. The Seneca Indians called the island *Ga-We-Not*: the great island; French explorers referred to it as *La Grande Isle*. In 1815 the land was purchased from the Seneca Indians by the state of New York for a thousand dollars. Originally part of the city of Buffalo, it became part of Tonawanda in 1836. The town of Grand Island, which became a separate entity in 1852, was known for its farms and orchards during its early days. Today, with 25 miles of shoreline, Grand Island is an ideal location for fishing, boating, swimming, and other recreational activities.

Before pioneer settlers arrived in the area which is now the three Tonawandas (Town and City in Erie County and the City of North Tonawanda in Niagara County) in the early 1800s, it was a forested land traveled by Native Americans. But after the construction of the Erie Canal in 1825, the community which is now the City of Tonawanda and the City of North Tonawanda, known commonly now as "The Twin Cities," developed rapidly. The Tonawandas are located where the Erie Canal meets the Niagara River, and lumber shipped from the western US and Canada passed eastward through here on the Erie Canal. By 1890 the then–Village of North Tonawanda and the Village of Tonawanda were together considered the lumber capital of the world. While the cities of Tonawanda and North Tonawanda are two separate cities located in two different counties, they have always worked together as one community—in the past as a manufacturing center and today as a tourist destination. North Tonawanda became a city in 1897 and Tonawanda followed in 1903. The Town of Tonawanda to the south of the City of Tonawanda was incorporated in 1836. (See *Niagara County—North Tonawanda and Wheatfield* for more information and listings.)

Located next door to Tonawanda is Kenmore, one of the first planned bedroom communities in western New York. In the late nineteenth century, Louis Phillip Adolph Eberhardt came up with the idea of creating a community away from the hustle and bustle of Buffalo, yet close enough for people to commute to their jobs in the city. Kenmore, incorporated in 1899, was the first suburb in western New York and one of the earliest established in the United States.

AREA CODE The area code is 716.

GUIDANCE **Chamber of Commerce of the Tonawandas** (716-692-5120; www.the-tonawandas.com), 254 Sweeney Street, North Tonawanda. Monday–Friday 8:30 AM–4:30 PM.

Grand Island Chamber of Commerce (716-773-3651; www.gichamber.org), 1870 Whitehaven Road, Grand Island.

Kenmore–Town of Tonawanda Chamber of Commerce (716-874-1202; www.ken-ton.org), 3411 Delaware Avenue, Kenmore. Open Monday–Friday 9 AM–5 PM.

GETTING THERE *By bus:* The #40 NFTA bus between Niagara Falls and Buffalo has a stop in Grand Island; buses #61 (North Tonawanda) and #79 (Tonawanda) offer express service to and from Buffalo.

By car: Grand Island is accessible from I-90 from either Buffalo or Niagara Falls. The major expressways running through the Tonawandas include the I-290 (Youngmann Memorial Highway) and Route 425 (Twin Cities Memorial Highway).

MEDICAL EMERGENCY Call 911.

DeGraff Memorial Hospital (716-694-4500; www.kaleidahealth.org), 445 Tremont Street, North Tonawanda.

Kenmore Mercy Hospital (716-447-6100; www.chsbuffalo.org), 2950 Elmwood Avenue, Kenmore.

✳ To See

MUSEUMS **Historical Society of the Tonawandas** (716-694-7406; www.tonawandas history.org/index.html), 113 Main Street, Tonawanda. Open Wednesday–Saturday. Displays inside this circa-1886 former New York Central & Hudson Valley Railroad station depict the area's early lumber days and Erie Canal history. The research center has over 6,000 indexed photos and obituaries dating back to 1877.

Long Homestead (716-694-7406; www.tonawandashistory.org/index.html), 24 East Niagara Street, Tonawanda. Open Sunday 1–4 PM, May–October; also open the first three Sundays in December. The restored Pennsylvania German-style 1829 home of Benjamin and Mary Long, who came to this area from Lancaster County, Pennsylvania, in 1828, is constructed of hand-hewn timber. The decorating reflects the style of home built by a relatively well-to-do family of the era, furnished with period furnishings from the early 1800s. Mr. Long was a farmer, businessman, and politician and was one of the organizers of the Town of Tonawanda.

River Lea Farm House (716-773-3817, Grand Island Historical Society), 2136 Oakfield Road, Grand Island. Open for special events and a monthly open house; call for details. This historic Victorian farmhouse, constructed in 1849, was once the home of Lewis Allen, founder of the Erie County Fair and uncle of Grover Cleveland, the 22nd and 24th president of the United States. Mr. Allen provided a young Mr. Cleveland with his first job working on the farm. The museum, maintained by the Grand Island Historical Society and furnished in the Victorian style, houses a collection of books, documents, and pictures related to Grand Island in the 1800s.

Town of Tonawanda–Kenmore Historical Society (716-873-5774; www .tonawanda.ny.us/community/historical-society), 100 Knoche Road, Tonawanda. Open alternating Sundays 2–5 PM, May–October. The historical society is housed in a brick church built in 1849. Displays include a collection of stained-glass windows from the Eberhardt mansion, books, and other memorabilia from the town, including genealogy records. There is even a display dedicated to the resident ghost. Several town residents have reportedly seen the ghost of a young girl who is buried in the cemetery next to the museum. Some have even offered the girl a ride home, only to discover that she disappears on the way there.

✳ To Do

AMUSEMENT PARKS 🐾 ✎ ♿ **Fantasy Island** (716-773-7591; www.fantasyislandny .com), 2400 Grand Island Boulevard, Grand Island. Open mid-May–mid-September.

Hours vary. Fantasy Island is a family-oriented park with rides, shows, and attractions that will please everyone from tots to teens. The park is home to a classic wooden roller coaster, the Silver Comet, and the popular Fantasy Island Iron Horse #1 train ride. Live shows include the Wild West Shoot-Out and the crowd-pleasing Western Musical Review. Catch a wave at the wave pool, ride the giant water slide, or cool down on the log flume ride.

FAMILY FUN ✍ ♿ **Adventure Landing** (716-832-6248; www.adventurelanding.com), 2400 Sheridan Drive, Tonawanda. Enjoy miniature golf and a video arcade.

✍ **Island Fun Center** (716-775-0180; www.islandfuncenter.com), 2660 Grand Island Boulevard, Grand Island. Daily 11 AM–11 PM, May–September. The Island Fun Center offers a world of family fun. There are many activities to keep the whole family busy, including laser tag, an 18-hole miniature golf course, batting cages, an arcade, and a snack bar.

♿ ✍ ⚲ **Tonawanda Aquatic and Fitness Center** (716-876-7424), 1 Pool Plaza, Tonawanda. Open Monday–Friday 6 AM–9 PM, Saturday 8 AM–6 PM, Sunday 9 AM–5 PM. Admission fee charged. This 48,000-square-foot, state-of-the-art pool and fitness facility offers a wide variety of aquatic and fitness activities.

Waterbike & Boat Adventure (716-316-3905; www.waterbikeadventures.com) Gateway Harbor, Tonawanda. Rent a kayak, stand up Paddleboard, hydrobike, or even an electric boat.

GOLF **Beaver Island State Park Golf Course** (716-773-4668, pro shop 716-773-7143), 2136 West Oakfield Road, Grand Island. An 18-hole, par-72 golf course and driving range. See also *Parks*.

WILD WEST SHOOT OUT AT FANTASY ISLAND ON GRAND ISLAND

Brighton Park Golf Course (716-695-2580), 70 Brompton Road, Tonawanda. A public 18-hole, par-72 course with driving range.

 ♿ ⛳ **Paddock Chevrolet Golf Dome** (716-504-3663), 175 Brompton Road, Tonawanda. Hours vary. You can practice your swing no matter what the weather at the Paddock Chevrolet Golf Dome. Inside the 82-foot high dome are 48 tee stations on two levels plus a 3,500-square-foot putting and chipping green. Kids will enjoy the 18-hole miniature golf course. The golf dome also has a pro shop, a restaurant, and a private party room.

Sheridan Park Golf Course (716-875-1811), Center Park Drive, Tonawanda. A public 18-hole, par-71 course with restaurant and snack bar.

MARINAS **Anchor Marine** (716-773-7063), 1501 Ferry Road, Grand Island. A full-service marina.

Blue Water Marina (716-773-7884), 340 East River Road, Grand Island. A full-service marina with a boat launch, boating and fishing supplies, and boat storage.

River Oaks Marina (716-774-0050), 101 Whitehaven Road at East River, Grand Island.

Six Mile Creek Marine (716-773-3270), West River and Whitehaven Road, Grand Island.

✳ Green Space

BEACHES See *Beaver Island State Park.*

NATURE PRESERVES **Buckhorn Island State Park** (716-773-3271), 2136 West Oakfield Road, Grand Island (c/o Beaver Island State Park). This 895-acre preserve, on the northern tip of the island, consists of marsh, meadows, and woods, including wetlands which are home to great blue herons and other waterfowl. The public is invited to walk the nature trails, hike, fish, and cross-country ski in the winter.

PARKS ♿ **Beaver Island State Park** (716-773-3271), 2136 West Oakfield Road, Grand Island. This 950-acre park is located at the south end of Grand Island. Playgrounds, picnic facilities, an 80-slip marina, fishing access, an 18-hole golf course and a half-mile-long sandy beach make this a popular spot on summer weekends. Also located in the park is the historic River Lea Farm House. (See *Museums and Historic Homes.*)

Ellicott Creek Park (716-693-2971), Niagara Falls Boulevard at Ellicott Creek Road, Tonawanda. This park, which opened in 1926, is located along Ellicott Creek. Park activities include baseball, fishing, ice skating, picnicking, sledding, cross-country skiing, softball, and tennis.

Gateway Harbor Park (716-695-8520, North Tonawanda; 716-743-8189, Tonawanda), Main and Webster Streets, Tonawanda/North Tonawanda. Gateway Harbor Park is a two-block park bordering the Erie Canal along Niagara Street in the City of Tonawanda and Sweeney Street in North Tonawanda. One of seven major harbors along the New York State Canal System, the park is the site of the annual Canal Fest each July. Docking facilities are equipped with electricity and water, and showers and rest rooms are available for boaters at the Harbor Master's Station on the Tonawanda side.

Isle View Park (716-692-1890), 796 Niagara Street, Tonawanda. This park, located along the Niagara River overlooking Grand Island, offers a variety of activities, including biking, hiking, and rollerblading on the Riverwalk trail, which passes through the

TONAWANDAS GATEWAY HARBOR

park. Isle View is also a popular place for fishing; a boat launch is available. A pedestrian foot bridge connects Isle View Park with Niawanda Park.

Lincoln Park (716-831-1009), Decatur Avenue, Tonawanda. A 65-acre park that includes picnic shelters, sports fields, and a swimming pool.

Niawanda Park (716-852-1921), Route 266 and River Road, Tonawanda. A long, narrow park with picnic tables and a boat launch on the Niagara River. A paved biking and walking trail connects with the Riverwalk Trail, which goes all the way to Buffalo.

WALKING, HIKING, AND BIKING TRAILS **Blueways and Greenways Intermodal Depot**, Young Street, between Main and Delaware, Tonawanda. This transit hub for bicyclists and boaters alike is located close to bike trails and the Erie Canal. This rest stop, which resembles a turn-of-the-century train station, has restrooms, a changing area, a bike repair shop, bike racks, and vending machines.

Niagara River Walk and Bicycle Trail This 10-foot-wide, 2-mile blacktop trail winds in and out of Gratwick Park, Fisherman's Park in adjacent North Tonawanda, and Gateway Harbor Park, as well as the downtown business district. It connects with the **Buffalo and Erie County Riverwalk**.

Tonawanda Rails to Trails An almost 4-mile-long trail along a former railroad bed runs from Kenmore Avenue in Kenmore to State Street in the City of Tonawanda, with small parking lots on either end. The Kenmore Avenue end connects to the much shorter North Buffalo Rails to Trails, which goes to the LaSalle subway station on Main Street.

✳ Lodging

INNS AND RESORTS Radisson Hotel Niagara Falls-Grand Island (716-773-1111), 100 Whitehaven Road, Grand Island. This hotel, located on the shores of the upper Niagara River, is located about 15 minutes from either Buffalo or Niagara Falls. Many of the 263 rooms and suites have balconies with a view of the river. $$.

OTHER LODGING KOA Kamping Kabins and Kampsites (716-773-7583), 2570 Grand Island Boulevard, Grand Island. Facilities include 60 cabins, almost 200 trailer sites (70 with water and electric), and 43 tent sites with electric hookups. They have two pools, two fishing ponds, canoes, and miniature golf. $.

✳ Where to Eat

DINING OUT Amici (716-874-0143; www.amicibuffalony.com) 2516 Elmwood, Kenmore. Monday–Saturday 4–9:30 PM, Sunday 4–8:30 PM. Since 1995, Amici, which means "friend" in Italian, has been serving authentic Italian fare, including homemade sauce and freshly baked bread.

Dick and Jenny's Bake and Brew (716-775-5047; www.dickandjennysny.com), 1270 Baseline Road, Grand Island. Tuesday–Saturday 8 AM–2 PM and 5–10 PM. Enjoy New Orleans style cuisine including gumbo and shrimp poboys.

Saigon Bangkok (716-837-2115; www.saigon-bangkok.com), 512 Niagara Falls Boulevard, Tonawanda. Open Sunday–Thursday 11 AM–10 PM, Friday and Saturday 11 AM–11 PM. This upscale Thai and Vietnamese restaurant offer selections like Spicy Rainbow (a vegetarian dish), chicken satay, and pad Thai, the national dish of Thailand. The restaurant's ambience includes soft music and cloth napkins and tablecloths.

Sinatra's (716-877-9419; www.sinatraswny.com), 938 Kenmore Avenue, Kenmore. Daily 5–10 PM. Enjoy classic southern Italian dishes, veal and seafood at this popular Kenmore restaurant. Sinatra's is moving to 945 Kenmore Avenue in December 2018.

Riverstone Grill (716-775-9079; www.theriverstonegrill.com), 971 East River Road, Grand Island. Sunday 11 AM–9 PM, Tuesday–Thursday 4–10 PM, Friday–Saturday 11 AM–10 PM. This restaurant specializes in steak, ribs, barbecue, and seafood. They are known for their signature "Bone in the Stone," a 50-ounce rib eye steak.

EATING OUT Adrian's Custard & Beef (716-773-9242), 2335 Grand Island Boulevard, Grand Island. Open seasonally 11 AM–9 PM. Cash only. This locally owned restaurant is a great place to stop for a beef on weck, as well as soft serve custard and other ice cream treats.

🍴 **The Beach House** (716-773-7119; www.grandislandbeachhouse.com), 5584 East River Road, Grand Island. Monday–Friday 11 AM–10 PM, Saturday–Sunday 3–10 PM. A small restaurant serving reasonably priced food, located near the river with indoor and outdoor dining. Homemade soup is served daily, along with lunch and dinner specials. A fish fry is served Wednesday and Friday.

Donut Kraze (716-836-2160; www.donutkrazebuffalo.com), 365 Somerville Avenue, Tonawanda. Open 24 hours. Enjoy breakfast sandwiches, lunch sandwiches, and, of course, donuts; their specialty is maple bacon. They have a second location in Cheektowaga.

Ling Ling (716-877-6802; linglingbuffalo.com), 2758 Elmwood Avenue, Kenmore. Monday–Thursday 11 AM–10 PM, Friday–Saturday 11 AM–11 PM, Sunday 12–10 PM. This small takeout restaurant, with just a few eat-in seats, has some of the best Chinese food in the Buffalo area. Be sure to try their Crab Rangoons.

MISSISSIPPI MUDDS OVERLOOKS THE NIAGARA RIVER

✍ **Mississippi Mudds** (716-694-0787; mississippimuddswny.com), 313 Niagara Street, Tonawanda. Open March–October, 11 AM–7:30 PM daily. This two-tiered restaurant, overlooking the Niagara River, is usually packed on a hot summer day. Enjoy hot dogs, burgers, chicken, roast beef, and more. End your meal with a homemade waffle cone topped with soft-serve custard or locally made Perry's ice cream.

✍ **Old Man River** (716-693-5558; oldmanriverwny.com), 375 Niagara Street, Tonawanda. Open April–September, 11 AM–7:30 PM daily. Enjoy burgers, hot dogs, and ice cream, along with sweet potato fries, grilled carrots (better known as "bunny dogs"), and more. The rear seafood shack serves up clams, shrimp cocktails, crab legs, and chowder. This eatery is located across the street from the Niagara River, so the view is great.

Mooney's Sports Bar & Grill (716-877-1800; www.mooneyssportsbarandgrill .com), 1531 Military Road, Kenmore. (Six other locations throughout the area.) If you like mac and cheese, this is the place to come, with almost 20 varieties to choose from. They also serve up burgers, sandwiches, pizza, wings, and more.

Paula's Donuts (716-862-4246; www .paulasdonuts.com), 2319 Sheridan Drive, Tonawanda. (There are also locations in Clarence and West Seneca.) A very popular family-owned donut shop known for their large donuts, including their Texas donut, which serves 6 to 8 people.

Pizza Amore (716-775-5975; www .pizzaamorewoodfire.com), 2024 Grand Island Boulevard, Grand Island. Sunday 4–9 PM, Monday and Wednesday 11 AM–9 PM, Tuesday and Thursday 10 AM–9 PM, Friday–Saturday 11 AM–10 PM. This popular pizzeria is known for its wood-fired pizza and wood-fired baked wings, as well as dessert pizzas, calzones, and subs.

Reid's on Elmwood (716-877-7343), 2800 Elmwood Avenue, Kenmore. Seasonally Monday–Saturday 11 AM–7 PM. Since 1970 Reid's has been a popular spot for hamburger, hot dogs, ice cream, and milkshakes.

River Grill (716-873-2553; www .rivergrilltonawanda.com), 70 Aqua Lane, Tonawanda. Opens Monday–Friday at 11 AM, Saturday and Sunday at 12 PM. This casual eatery overlooks the Niagara River. Enjoy menu items like salad, seafood, and ribs.

Smoke on the Water (716-692-4227; www.sotw77.com), 77 Young Street, Tonawanda. Tuesday–Thursday 11:30 AM–9 PM, Friday–Saturday 11:30 AM–10 PM. If you enjoy barbecue, this is the place to eat. They smoke their own brisket, ribs, pulled pork, and

OLD MAN RIVERS HAS HOT DOGS

chicken. The dining room is tiny, but you can also eat outdoors on their patio.

Sophia's (716-447-9661), 749 Military Road, Kenmore. Daily 7 AM–3 PM. This restaurant, popular with locals, is known for its made-from-scratch, all-day breakfasts. Its breakfast has been voted Best Diner Breakfast by *Buffalo Spree* magazine.

Switson's Beef & Keg (716-692-9723; www.swistonsbeefandkeg.com), 101 Young Street, Tonawanda. This tavern is noted for its beef on weck. During warmer weather you can enjoy a cold beer on the patio overlooking a marina.

✳ Selective Shopping

ANTIQUES **Attic to Basement Repeats** (716-957-3885; www.atbrepeats.com), 83 Broad Street, Tonawanda. Tuesday–Friday 11 AM–6 PM, Saturday 2–6 PM. Browse through 7,500 square feet of antique and vintage items.

The Mulberry Tree (716-693-7235), 49 Main Street, Tonawanda. Call for hours. This shop has quality antique furniture, glassware, and handmade linens.

SPECIAL SHOPS **Cats Like Us** (716-694-6600; www.catslikeus.com), 67 Main Street, Tonawanda. Wednesday–Saturday 11 AM–6 PM, Thursday until 8 PM. This shop specializes in retro clothing and accessories.

Janie's Emporium (716-573-6456; www.facebook.com/janiesemporium), 2943 Delaware Avenue, Kenmore. Tuesday–Thursday 11 AM–6 PM, Friday 11 AM–5 PM, Saturday 10 AM–4 PM. A specialty boutique selling hand-crafted jewelry and accessories.

✎ **Kelly's Country Store** (716-773-0003; www.kellyscountrystore.com), 3121 Grand Island Boulevard, Grand Island. Kelly's Country Store has been a Grand Island landmark since 1962. Chose from old-fashioned candy, scented candles, brass and crystal giftware, and much more. The "Christmas Room" features visits with Santa on weekends after Thanksgiving, along with gifts, stocking stuffers, and toys. At Easter enjoy homemade candies, along with a visit from the Easter Bunny.

✎ **King Condrells** (716-877-4485; www.condrells.com), 2805 Delaware Avenue, Kenmore. This recently renovated candy and ice cream shop is known for its high-quality chocolates and sponge candy.

Paths, Peaks, and Paddles (716-213-0350; www.pathspeakspaddles.com), 1000 Ellicott Creek Road, Tonawanda. They refer to themselves as "the candy store for outdoor people." It is one of the state's largest outdoor specialty shops. They also offer guide services for canoeing, kayaking, and snowshoeing.

✳ Special Events

July: **Canal Fest of the Tonawandas** (716-692-3292; www.canalfest.org). This eight-day festival is the largest of its kind along the Erie Canal. Events include parades, youth activities, midway rides, musical entertainment, tours of historical sites, gaming, lots of food, an arts and crafts show, a car show, and much more.

AMHERST

A mherst, population 121,000, is a 54-square-mile suburban community that includes the village of Williamsville plus the hamlets of Eggertsville, Getzville, Snyder, Swormville, and East Amherst.

The first inhabitants of the region were Native Americans, who found the area good for hunting and fishing. Later, though western New York was considered by most Europeans to be a wilderness frontier, the title to 3,300,000 acres was acquired in 1798 by the Holland Land Company, a group of Dutch financiers. Joseph Ellicott, an experienced land surveyor, was hired to oversee the task of surveying the land acquired in what is known as the Holland Land purchase.

Ellicott and his crew were responsible for improving some of the Indian trails so that settlers could come into the area in their wagons. Some of these roads include what was referred to as the Buffalo Road, now Main Street, and Transit Road, which was named after the surveyors' instrument used to help make a straight line.

Early settlers included John Thompson and Benjamin Ellicott, brother of Joseph, who in 1799 purchased 300 acres of land around the Ellicott Creek waterfall, known today as Glen Falls. By 1803 some six homes had been constructed in the vicinity. Jonas Williams, traveling through the area, realized the potential of water power in the area and decided to acquire the land. In 1811 he built a gristmill on the west side of the waterfall and the location became known as Williams Mills, later changed to Williamsville. It was the first and biggest settlement in the town, which was officially incorporated as the town of Amherst in 1818. At that time the town also included Cheektowaga and part of West Seneca. Amherst may have been named for Sir Jeffrey Amherst, commander in chief of the British troops in America before the American Revolution, or it may have been named after Amherst, Massachusetts.

Life was hard for the early pioneers—the land needed to be cleared, and much of the area was swampy, so roads were hard to build. The opening of the Erie Canal helped the town prosper since it gave farmers a means to send their crops to larger markets. It was also easier for new settlers to reach the area, many of whom were German or "Pennsylvania Dutch."

By the late 1870s Amherst's main occupation was farming, which continued up until the 1920s, when farmland was sold to make room for housing subdivisions. While only four working farms remain in Amherst, many areas of the town still maintain a rural feel.

(For more information on Amherst history, consult *Glancing Back: A Pictorial History of Amherst, New York* by Joseph A. Grande, PhD.)

AREA CODE The area code is 716.

GUIDANCE **Amherst Chamber of Commerce** (716-632-6905; www.amherst.org), 400 Essjay Road, Suite 150, Williamsville. Open Monday–Friday 9 AM–5 PM.

Village of Williamsville (716-632-4120; www.village.williamsville.ny.us), 5565 Main Street, Williamsville. Open Monday–Friday 8 AM–4 PM.

Village of Williamsville Business and Professional Organization (www.willvill .com).

GETTING THERE *By bus:* There are several bus routes between Amherst and downtown Buffalo. Some of these routes take passengers to the Light Rail Rapid Transit station at the University at Buffalo Main Street Campus.

By car: From I-90 take I-290 (exit 50). The next several exits feed into various parts of Amherst.

MEDICAL EMERGENCY Dial 911

Millard Fillmore Suburban Hospital (688-3100; www.kaleidahealth.org), 1540 Maple Road, Williamsville.

✻ To See

ART MUSEUMS **University at Buffalo Art Gallery** (716-645-6912; www.ubartgalleries .buffalo.edu) 201-A Center for the Arts, University at Buffalo North Campus, Amherst. Tuesday–Friday 11 AM–5 PM, Saturday 1–5 PM. A gallery with changing exhibits dealing with current issues.

MUSEUMS AND HISTORIC HOMES ♿ ✑ **Buffalo Niagara Heritage Village** (716-689-1440; www.bnhv.org), 3755 Tonawanda Creek Road, Amherst. Open April–October, Wednesday and Friday 9:30 AM–4:30 PM, Thursday 9:30 AM–8 PM, Saturday 12–4 PM. This museum is a 35-acre historical park, with 12 restored buildings decorated with period furnishings. In addition to the historic structures, a modern exhibit building focuses on local history, antique radios, decorative arts, and more, including a children's Discovery Room featuring a replica Erie Canal packet boat. It has a research library with over 3,000 books and other records pertinent to western New York.

♿ **Museum of Disability History** (716-629-3626; www.museumofdisability.org), 3826 Main Street, Amherst. Open Monday–Friday 10 AM–4 PM, Saturday 10 AM–2 PM. This one-of-a-kind museum, operated by People Inc., focuses on the treatment of people with disabilities throughout the ages. The museum's mission is to help others understand and accept those with disabilities.

HISTORIC SITES **Williamsville Water Mill** 56 Spring Street, Williamsville. This mill, built in 1811, is the oldest building in Amherst. One of seven mills built by Jonas Williams, it is the only one still in existence. Sweet Jenny's Ice Cream and Candy is located in the mill.

✻ To Do

BREWERIES AND BREWPUBS **12 Gates Brewing Company** (716-906-6600; www .12gatesbrewing.com), 80 Earhart Drive, Williamsville. Monday–Thursday 4–10 PM, Friday–Saturday 12–11 PM, Sunday 12–6 PM. Sample beer in their taproom, which also serves light fare such as flatbread pizza, salads, and sandwiches.

✑ ♿ **Buffalo Brew Pub** (716-632-0552; www.buffalobrewpub.com), 6861 Main Street, Williamsville. Open Sunday–Thursday 11:30 AM–midnight, Friday and Saturday 11:30 AM–1 AM. This popular, casual family restaurant is Buffalo's original brew pub and the oldest brew pub in New York State. Enjoy a selection of in-house-brewed draft beer with your meal. Entrees include typical pub food like sandwiches, pizza, ribs, wings, and chicken dishes.

Moor Pat (716-810-9957; moorpat.com), 78 East Spring Street, Williamsville. Monday–Thursday 4–11 PM, Friday–Saturday 12 PM–1 AM, Sunday 12–10 PM. A craft beer and whiskey bar also serving a limited menu that includes, wings, sausages, and hand-cut fries.

FAMILY FUN ✍ **LaserTron** (716-833-8766; buffalo.lasertron.us), 5101 North Bailey Avenue, Amherst. Open 10 AM–midnight daily, Friday and Saturday until 2 AM. Admission fees vary. Reservations suggested. Each player entering the arena has a vest with sensors, vibrators, identification lights, and LED readout, and everyone is equipped with a phaser—ready to zap the enemy. In addition to the laser games, they have arcade games, mini-golf, cybersport (a combination of lacrosse and basketball played on moveable cars), a snack bar, and a party room.

GOLF **Audubon Golf Course** (716-631-7139), 500, Maple Road, Williamsville. An 18-hole, par-71 public course.
  Audubon Par-3 Golf Course (716-631-7124), 475 Maple Road, Williamsville. A public 9-hole, par-3 course.
  Glen Oak Golf Course (716-688-4400 or 716-688-5454; www.glenoak.com), 711 Smith Road, East Amherst. A public 18-hole, par-72 course with driving range.
  Oakwood Golf Course (716-689-1421), 3575 Tonawanda Creek Road, East Amherst. A 9-hole, par-34 golf course with snack bar.
  Grover Cleveland Park (716-836-7398), 3781 Main Street, Amherst. The clubhouse of this course was originally built by the Buffalo County Club in 1901. It was purchased by the city in 1925 and named after Grover Cleveland, former mayor of Buffalo, governor of New York, and president of the United States. The 18-hole course is owned and operated by Erie County.

MARINAS **Amherst Marine Center** (716-691-6707), 1900 Campbell Boulevard, Amherst. A full-service marina located on the Erie Canal.

RECREATIONAL FACILITIES ♿ ✍ ⛄ **Northtown Center** (716-631-7555), 1615 Amherst Manor Drive, Williamsville. Call for skating hours as they vary from month to month. This 182,000-square-foot, two-story facility is one of the largest recreational ice complexes in the country, offering four ice surfaces. Outdoors there are baseball and soccer fields as well as a junior football field.

SLEDDING **Billy Wilson Park**, Hopkins Road (between Dodge and West Klein), Williamsville. A very popular spot to take the kids after a snowfall, this hill is big enough to be fun for older kids, yet small enough to be safe for younger children.

✳ Green Space

NATURE PRESERVES ♿ ✍ **Great Baehre Swamp Conservation Area/Billy Wilson Park**, Hopkins Road (between Dodge and West Klein), Williamsville. Open daily, dawn to dusk. Free admission. Get up close to nature when you walk on the boardwalk through the Great Baehre Swamp. A variety of waterfowl, turtles, deer, and other wildlife can be observed, along with plants native to the area. There is an accessible playground located in Billy Wilson Park.

PARKS **Amherst State Park**, 400 Mill Street, Williamsville. This 77-acre undeveloped park was the former site of the St. Mary of the Angels convent. Enjoy walking and biking trails along Ellicott Creek.

Bassett Park, Klein and Youngs Road, Williamsville. A 40-acre park with a small lake, band shell, playground, and rest room facilities. Free concerts take place in the band shell during the summer.

Garrison Park, Garrison Road and South Ellicott Street, Williamsville. This small neighborhood park has playground equipment, a wading pool, and a gazebo.

Glen Park, Between Main Street and Glen Avenue, Williamsville. Glen Park is the most scenic site in the village. Ellicott Creek, cascading over the Onondaga Escarpment, forms Glen Falls. The ten acre park and natural wildlife area is a place to enjoy picnicking, fishing, or just strolling the trails. Back in the 1940s and '50s, Glen Park was the site of an amusement park and the Glen Casino, which attracted nationally known performers. That complex was destroyed in a spectacular fire in 1968. The property was converted into parkland in 1976.

Island Park (716-632-4120), 5565 Main Street, Williamsville. This triangle-shaped park is actually an island, formed in 1841 when Jonas Williams built a raceway to divert water to power his gristmill. The park features a large pavilion, a playground, and a wading pool. It's the site of Old Home Days and the Taste of Williamsville each summer.

POOLS ✐ ♿ **Clearfield Recreation Center** (716-689-1418), 15 Plaza Drive (off Hopkins Road), Williamsville. Open daily late June until just before Labor Day. Enjoy a wading pool with a large splash park plus a large swimming pool, with a handicapped access ramp. The recreation area also has tennis courts, a playground, baseball diamonds, a basketball court, and an indoor multi-use sports court.

GLEN FALLS IS A SCENIC SIGHT IN GLEN PARK IN THE VILLAGE OF WILLIAMSVILLE

⚲ **North Forest Park and Pool** (716-631-7275), 85 North Forest Road, Williamsville. Open daily late June until just before Labor Day. This park has a swimming pool, a wading pool, and a recreation area.

WATERFALLS **Glen Falls.** Glen Park, Williamsville. A 27-foot-high falls is located in a beautiful park used by people of all ages. The viewing spot next to the falls is considered to be quite a romantic location, a popular place for both marriage proposals and wedding pictures.

WALKING, HIKING, AND BIKING Trails Note for all bike trails: Pets must be on a leash not exceeding six feet in length, speed limit is 15 MPH, no motor vehicles, trails are closed 10 PM–6 AM.

Bailey Campus to Amherst Campus (a.k.a. Inter-Campus Bikeway). This marked urban trail, designed with students at the University at Buffalo in mind, starts on the southwest corner of Main Street and Bailey Avenue by the University at Buffalo South Campus. It follows Bailey Avenue down several side streets, to Sweet Home Road, where a 5-foot-wide restricted lane starts on the east side of the road and continues to the North Campus.

Amherst Canalway Trail (a.k.a. Tonawanda Creek Bike Path). This 6-mile path starts by Tonawanda Creek Road and New Road, near the Buffalo Niagara Heritage Village, and runs along the Erie Canal.

Ellicott Creek Bike Path. This 5-mile-long paved trail follows Ellicott Creek from a parking lot on North Forest Road in Williamsville to Niagara Falls Boulevard near Ellicott Creek Park. It is popular with walkers, bikers, and in-line skaters, especially on the weekend. There are many secluded areas along the trail, so for safety it is strongly recommended that you travel with a friend.

Lehigh Valley Railroad Path. Access it by the old Lehigh Valley Railroad depot on South Long Street in Williamsville. This paved walking and biking path in the village of Williamsville is about 1.5 miles long.

Village of Williamsville Walking Tour (www.willvill.com). A printable version of a walking tour through historic Williamsville can be found on this website.

Walton Woods Bike Path. This bike and walking path, located in a wooded area behind Amherst Police headquarters, loops around Lake Audubon, a small pond that's home to native waterfowl. It has 6 acres of old-growth forest, including several 150-year-old trees.

Willow Ridge Bike Path. This short bike trail runs between Ellicott Creek Road and Sweet Home Road in Amherst with a bridge crossing over the I-990 Expressway.

✳ Lodging

MOTELS AND HOTELS **Buffalo Niagara Marriott** (716-689-6900; www.buffaloniagaramarriott.com), 1340 Millersport Highway, Amherst. Convenient to both downtown Buffalo and Niagara Falls, the Marriott offers quality accommodations to business travelers as well as vacationers. It features 356 guest rooms, a fully-equipped fitness center, and an indoor/outdoor pool. $$.

Note: There are also a number of national chain motels located adjacent to the Marriott.

Hampton Inn Williamsville (716-632-0900; www.hamptoninnwilliamsville.com), 5455 Main Street, Williamsville. This hotel, located right in the village of Williamsville, blends Old-World charm with modern amenities. Each guest room has custom-designed Thomasville furniture that includes a large desk plus high-speed Internet access. Suites include whirlpools, decorative fireplaces, and full kitchens. Included is a complimentary buffet breakfast, a fitness room, and an indoor pool. $$.

Hyatt Place Buffalo Amherst (716-839-4040; www.hyattplacebuffalo amherst.com), 5020 Main Street, Amherst. This 137-room hotel is convenient to the village of Williamsville and the I-290 expressway. Breakfast is included in your stay. $$.

Reikart House (716-839-2000; www.reikarthouse.com), 5000 Main Street, Amherst. A 93-room upscale boutique hotel named after the Reikart family, known for their hospitality in the town of Amherst back in the early 1900s. $$$.

Salvatore's Grand Hotel (716-636-4900; www.salvatoresgrand.com), 6675 Transit Road, Williamsville. This spacious and luxurious hotel is operated by Russell Salvatore, known throughout the Buffalo area for his attention to detail and hospitality. Outside the hotel, Salvatore has created the Patriots and Heroes Park, with a number of memorials honoring those who have served our country. The park includes a 30-by-60-foot American flag, one of the largest free-flying flags in New York State. The upscale Russell's Steaks, Chops and More is located on the first floor. See *Dining Out.* $$.

Wyndham Gardens Buffalo Williamsville (716-276-9600), 5195 Main Street, Williamsville. This 120-room hotel is within walking distance of the Village of Williamsville and a short drive to downtown Buffalo. Amenities include a fitness center, indoor pool, and spa. $.

✱ Where to Eat

DINING OUT

AMHERST/SNYDER

Adam's Rib (716-839-3846; www.adamsribrestaurant.com), 4517 Main Street, Snyder. Monday–Saturday 4–10 PM. Established in 1968, this restaurant is known for prime rib and steak.

Grapevine (716-691-7799; www.grapevinerestaurant.com), 2545 Niagara Falls Boulevard, Amherst. Monday–Thursday 11:30 AM–10 PM, Friday and Saturday 11:30 AM–11 PM, Sunday 10 AM–9 PM. This restaurant, which has a large menu featuring seafood, beef, chicken, and pasta, is decorated with several large aquariums located throughout the restaurant.

Mulberrry Italian Ristorante (716-839-3663), 4548 Main Street, Snyder. Monday–Saturday 12 PM–12:30 AM. Enjoy pasta, homemade red sauce, and the huge meatballs that are found in their original Lackawanna location, along with pizza and other selections.

San Marco (716-839-5876; sanmarcobuffalony.com), 2082 Kensington Avenue, Amherst. Tuesday–Sunday 5:30 PM–closing. A small, elegant upscale restaurant that specializes in northern Italian cuisine, along with an extensive selection of Italian wines.

EAST AMHERST

Falletta's (716-741-7406; www.fallettas restaurant.com), 8255 Clarence Center Road, East Amherst. Tuesday–Thursday 5–9 PM, Friday–Saturday 5–10 PM, Sunday 3–8:30 PM. They have a large selection of Italian dishes to choose from, including pasta, veal, and chicken. They are known for their signature poppy seed dressing, which you can also buy by the bottle to take home.

Schnitzel & Co (716-689-3600; www.schnitzelandco.com), 9210 Transit Road, East Amherst. Monday–Thursday 11 AM–10 PM, Friday 11 AM–12;00 AM, Saturday 10:30 AM–12 AM, Sunday 10:30 AM–10 PM. This Swiss-German pub features 20 beers on tap, including German and local brews. The menu features traditional dishes like weiner schnitzel and sausages, along with American dishes like chicken pot pie and local favorite beef on weck.

Trattoria Aroma North French (716-688-8848; www.aromanorthfrench.com),

4840 North French, East Amherst. Lunch Tuesday–Friday 11:30 AM–2:30 PM, Dinner Monday–Thursday 5–9 PM, Friday–Saturday 5–10 PM, Sunday brunch 11 AM–2 PM, dinner 5–8 PM. Enjoy modern Italian cuisine and a variety of wines from Italy.

♀ **Yolo** (716-688-4479; www .yolobuffalony.com), 5841 Transit Road, East Amherst. Monday–Saturday 11:30 AM–10 PM, Sunday 11:30 AM–9 PM. Enjoy casual yet upscale American cuisine for lunch, brunch, dinner, and late night. Yes, it is named after the saying "You only live once."

Zoe (716-639-4550; www.thezoe restaurant.com), 5711 Transit Road, East Amherst. Monday–Saturday 6:30 AM–11 PM, Sunday 6:30 AM–10 PM. This Greek-American restaurant is known for its large portions of authentic Greek cuisine. They have a heated patio that is open all year.

GETZVILLE

⚓ ♿ ⚘ **Lebros** (716-688-0404; www .lebrosrestaurant.com), 330 Campbell Boulevard, Getzville. Open Monday–Thursday 11 AM–10 PM, Friday and Saturday 11 AM–11 PM, Sunday 4–9 PM. Enjoy Italian dining in a relaxed atmosphere, from traditional favorites to unique homemade pastas.

⚓ **Sean Patrick's** (716-636-1709; www.spatricks.com), 3480 Millersport Highway, Getzville. Monday–Thursday 11 AM–10 PM, Friday–Saturday 11 AM–11 PM, Sunday 12–9 PM. This popular casual fine-dining restaurant features an Irish atmosphere and an extensive menu, with items like filet mignon, pasta, and roast turkey, as well as a variety of sandwiches.

WILLIAMSVILLE

♀ **800 Maple** (716-688-5800; www .800maple.com), 800 Maple Road, Williamsville. Monday–Thursday 5–10 PM, Friday–Saturday 5–11 PM, Sunday brunch 10 AM–2 PM, dinner 5–9 PM. Very good American cuisine is served here with menu selections like steak and wood-fired pizza.

ENJOY ITALIAN CUISINE AT LEBROS IN GETZVILLE

Amaretto Italian Bistro (716-635-4750; www.amarettoitalianbistro.com), 7170 Transit Road, Williamsville. Tuesday–Saturday 5–10 PM. Enjoy upscale Italian cuisine in this recently enlarged restaurant.

Creekview Restaurant (716-632-9373; www.creekviewrestaurant.com), 5629 Main Street, Williamsville. Open for lunch Monday–Saturday 11:30 AM–4 PM, dinner Monday–Saturday 4–11 PM, Sunday 1–9 PM. Located in a historic older home overlooking Ellicott Creek, this restaurant features an American regional menu with dinner selections including steak, salmon, trout, lamb, and fresh haddock. A heated patio is open spring, summer, and fall for al fresco dining.

Cugino's (716-633-8432; www.cuginositalianrestaurant.com), 6011 Main Street Williamsville. Monday–Thursday 11 AM–9 PM, Friday and Saturday 11 AM–10 PM. Enjoy contemporary northern Italian dining with house-made pasta on the menu, along with a selection of wines and spirits. They also have an outdoor patio.

Eagle House (716-632-7669; www.eaglehouseonline.com), 5578 Main Street, Williamsville. Open Monday–Saturday 11 AM–10 PM, Sunday 12–9 PM. The Eagle House is one of the most well-known landmarks in the Village of Williamsville. This building has been in continuous service since 1827, from an inn and stagecoach stop to present-day fine dining. Menu selections include a variety of American cuisine, including fresh salmon, beef, Yankee pot roast, chicken, and low-fat specialties.

Eastern Pearl (716-204-8898; www.theeasternpearlrestaurant.com), 938 Maple Road, Williamsville. Monday–Thursday 11 AM–10 PM, Friday–Saturday 11 AM–11 PM, Sunday 12–10 PM. Enjoy upscale dining at this Chinese restaurant which features authentic Cantonese dishes on the menu.

Giancarlo's Sicilian Steakhouse and Pizzeria (716-650-5566; www.giancarlossteakhouse.com), 5110 Main Street, Williamsville. Monday–Saturday 11 AM–10 PM. An upscale Italian restaurant featuring Sicilian-style dishes, along with steak and brick-oven pizza.

The Irishman Pub and Eatery (716-631-3722; irishmanpub.com), 5601 Main Street, Williamsville. Monday–Thursday 11 AM–10 PM, Friday–Saturday 11 AM–11 PM, Sunday 10 AM–9 PM. This Irish-themed pub has dinner entrees like porterhouse and NY strip steak, along with Irish favorites, like Shepherd's pie and corned beef. Lunch selections include a corned beef reuben and an Irish pub burger, along with pizza and salads.

Milos (716-810-9489; www.milosonmain.com), 5877 Main Street, Williamsville. Daily 7 AM–11 PM. This very popular restaurant features classic Greek cuisine, an all-day breakfast, and American favorites. A second-floor banquet room is available.

Protocol (716-632-9556; www.protocolrestaurant.com), 6766 Transit Road, Williamsville. Monday–Thursday 11 AM–10 PM, Friday–Saturday 11 AM–11 PM. This restaurant has its seafood flown in fresh daily from one of Boston's finest seafood markets. They are also noted for ribs. Other menu choices include grilled meats, pasta, and poultry.

Rizotto Ristorante (716-204-4455; www.rizottoristorante.com), 930 Maple Road, Williamsville. Lunch Tuesday–Friday 11:30 AM–2:30 PM, dinner Tuesday–Friday 4:30–10 PM, Saturday 4:30–11 PM, Sunday 3:30–9 PM. Enjoy upscale dining with a menu featuring seafood, beef, and pasta. Live music is featured on Thursday evenings.

♉ **Russell's Steaks, Chops and More** (716-636-4900; www.salvatoresgrand.com), 6675 Transit Road. This is a place to celebrate special occasions and where you take someone when you want to impress them; the food and service are excellent. Enjoy steaks cooked to perfection, lobster, crab legs, rack of lamb, and more. You can also choose from their dining for two menu. See also *Lodging—Salvatore's Grand Hotel.*

Tavern at Windsor Park (716-689-6600; www.tavernatwindsorpark.com), 8444 Transit Road, Williamsville. Open daily at 11 AM. This British-style pub features traditional British fare like bangers and mash, fish and chips, and cottage pie, as well as American fare like pot roast, burgers, and sandwiches.

Wasabi (716-689-5888; www.wasabius .com), 100 Plaza Drive (Dash's Plaza) Williamsville. Monday–Thursday 11 AM–10:30 PM, Friday–Saturday 11 AM–11 PM, Sunday 12:30–10 PM. This Japanese restaurant offers a large selection of sushi, rolls, sashimi and more. They have close to 60 different rolls and also offer cooked menu items, like grilled chicken teriyaki and strip steak.

EATING OUT (See also *Breweries and Brewpubs*)

AMHERST

Black Forest Adler (716-564-2447) 2447 Niagara Falls Boulevard, Amherst. Wednesday–Sunday 4–8 PM. Authentic German cuisine prepared in the traditional style of the Black Forest region.

♦ & ♥ **Duff's** (716-834-6234; www .duffswings.com), 3651 Sheridan Drive, Amherst. Open Monday–Thursday 11 AM–11 PM, Friday and Saturday 11 AM–midnight, Sunday 12–10 PM. This small, casual restaurant is known for its chicken wings. It was opened in 1946 by Louise Duffney as a corner gin mill, but business took off when wings were introduced in 1969. Today over 12,000 pounds of Buffalo's favorite snack food are sold per week. Be advised: Medium is hot, medium hot is very hot, and hot is very, very hot! Besides wings, they also serve sandwiches, burgers, and salads. This is the original location; there are four others locally.

♦ & ♥ **Family Tree** (716-838-2233; thefamilytreerestaurant.com), 4346 North Bailey Avenue, Amherst. Sunday–Tuesday 7 AM–9:30 PM, Wednesday–Saturday 7 AM–10:30 PM. A reasonably priced Greek-American restaurant that features large portions of Greek specialties like souvlaki and pastitsio, along with seafood and ribs. They have an extensive breakfast menu and even have a special machine to make fresh-squeezed orange juice.

EAST AMHERST

Grover's Bar & Grill (716-636-1803), 9160 Transit Road, East Amherst. Open Monday–Saturday 11 AM–10 PM. This neighborhood tavern, located in a building said to once have been Grover Cleveland's hunting cabin, has one of the biggest and best tasting hamburgers around. It's very popular, so expect to wait for a table.

♦ & ♥ **Jonny C's New York Deli** (716-688-8400; www.jonnycs.com), 9350 Transit Road, East Amherst. Sunday 10 AM–7 PM, Monday–Saturday 10 AM–8:30 PM. The dining room of this New York–style deli is decorated with New York City photos and memorabilia. The menu includes an all-day breakfast, specialty wraps, burgers, salads, and of course, over 50 different deli sandwiches. You can even take the "big mouth" challenge. Eat the big mouth, an enormous sandwich with three pounds of meat, in 30 minutes or less and you get a t-shirt and your photo on their wall of fame.

Pautler's Drive-In (716-636-1690; www.pautlersdriveinofclarence.com), 6343 Transit Road, East Amherst. Open daily 11 AM–10 PM, shorter hours in fall and spring. Closed November–March. This casual family restaurant, originally established in 1958, serves up hot dogs, hamburgers, and more, along with a rather extensive ice cream menu.

GETZVILLE

Amherst Pizza & Ale House (716-625-7100; www.amherstpizzaandalehouse .com), 55 Crosspoint, Getzville. This busy sports bar has over 100 beers to choose from, including 20 on tap. The food menu features pizza, wings, appetizers, and salads.

DUFFS ON SHERIDAN DRIVE IS THE PLACE TO GO FOR WINGS IN THE NORTHTOWNS

✂ ♿ 🐾 **Nina's Custard** (716-636-0345), 2525 Millersport Highway, Getzville. Sunday–Thursday 11 AM–10 PM, Friday and Saturday 11 AM–11 PM. Menu selections in this casual restaurant include hot dogs, burgers, sweet potato fries, and chicken sandwiches, plus a large selection of ice cream treats.

WILLIAMSVILLE

♿ 🐾 ✂ **Anderson's Frozen Custard** (716-632-1416; www.andersonscustard.com), 6075 Main Street, Williamsville (several other locations throughout western New York). Monday–Saturday 11 AM–9 PM, Sunday 11 AM–8 PM. Specialties include beef on weck, oven-roasted turkey sandwiches, and a variety of ice cream treats.

Break 'n Eggs Creperie (716-634-EGGS) 5235 Main Street, Williamsville Tuesday–Sunday 7 AM–3 PM. Enjoy a variety of crepes, from savory to sweet, at this tiny restaurant that is always busy.

Deep South Taco (www.deepsouth taco.com) 6727 Main Street, Williamsville. Enjoy authentic Mexican cuisine at this suburban location of a popular restaurant chain that is also located on Ellicott Street and Hertel Avenue in Buffalo.

El Ranchito Mexican (716-906-3314; www.elranchitowny.com) 408 Evans, Williamsville. Monday–Thursday 11 AM–9:30 PM, Friday 11 AM–10 PM, Saturday

11:30 AM–10 PM, Sunday 11:30 AM–9:30 PM. Enjoy authentic Mexican cuisine at an affordable price.

Glen Park Tavern (716-626-9333; glenparktavernbuffalo.com), 5507 Main Street, Williamsville. Open Monday–Thursday 11:30 AM–10 PM, Friday and Saturday 11:30 AM–11 PM, Sunday 4–9 PM. Serving sandwiches, snacks, salads, pastas, and seafood in a pub atmosphere in a historic village building.

♿ ✂ **La Nova** (716-634-5151; www.lanova.com), 5151 Main Street, Williamsville. Sunday–Wednesday 10 AM–10 PM, Thursday 10 AM–11 PM, Friday–Saturday 10 AM–12 AM. This restaurant, along with its original Buffalo location, is the largest seller of chicken wings in the country. Choose from an array of specialty pizzas and several different flavors of chicken wings, including traditional Buffalo, BBQ, honey mustard, and raspberry.

Lloyd's Taco (716-289-0607; www.whereslloyd.com) 5933 Main Street, Williamsville. Daily 11 AM–2 AM. This is the second brick and mortar location for the very popular taco maker which has several food trucks and another location on Hertel Avenue in Buffalo.

♿ 🐾 **McPartlan's Corner** (716-632-9896), 669 Wehrle Drive, Williamsville. Open Sunday 10 AM–10 PM, Monday–Thursday and Saturday 10 AM–11 PM, Friday 10 AM–12 AM. A small, casual restaurant and neighborhood corner bar that has been popular since 1955 for its Friday night fish fry. While fish and seafood dominate the menu, they also serve sandwiches, liver and onions, pork chops, and other down-home favorites.

&. **Original Pancake House** (716-634-5515; www.originalpancakehouse.com), 5479 Main Street, Williamsville. Open daily 6:45 AM–9 PM. No matter when you come here, it's always busy, especially Sunday mornings, when Mass lets out at St. Peter and Paul's Church across the street. However, the food is worth the wait, so give your name to the hostess and get your taste buds ready. While pancakes and breakfast are the most popular meal here, lunch and dinner are also served.

Pairings Wine Bar (716-630-5951; www.pairingswinebar.com), 5893 Main Street, Williamsville. Monday–Thursday 3–11 PM, Friday–Saturday 3 PM–1 AM. This establishment offers an extensive wine list, served by the glass and by the bottle, along with a selection of beers and martinis. Food available includes appetizers, small plate entrees, paninis, flatbread pizza, and mac and cheese.

Rocco's Wood-fired Pizza (716-247-5272; www.roccoswoodfiredpizza .com), 5431 Transit Road, Williamsville. Monday–Thursday 11 AM–10 PM, Friday–Saturday 11 AM–11 PM, Sunday 12–9 PM. The menu features a variety of wood-fired pizzas, as well as steak, chicken, and pasta dishes.

Wok & Roll (716-631-8880; www .thewokandroll.com), 5467 Sheridan Drive, Williamsville. Tucked away in a suburban plaza, this restaurant features reasonably priced Chinese food in a nice setting.

✳ Entertainment

THEATERS &. **The Center for the Arts, University at Buffalo** (716-645-2787 or 716-645-6259; www.ubcfa.org),

Mainstage Theater, 103 Center for the Arts, University at Buffalo North Campus. This 250,000-square-foot modern building houses art, theater, media, and dance programs. Western New York's largest and most technically advanced performing arts venue has four theaters, three art galleries, and a screening room. Events include performances by world-renowned musicians and dance ensembles, distinguished speakers, and family entertainment.

&. **Katherine Cornell Theatre** (716-645-2038) on the University at Buffalo North Campus, Ellicott Complex, Amherst. This theater, which seats 400 in the round, is a venue for speakers, educational programs, stage productions, and more.

MusicalFare Theatre Company (716-839-8540; www.musicalfare.com), Daemen College, 4380 Main Street, Amherst. This professional musical theater company resides at Daemen College. Performances take place year-round at the theater.

Music Amherst Symphony (716-633-4606; www.amherstsymphony .com), Amherst Middle School, 55 Kings Highway, Snyder. For over 60 years, the Amherst Symphony has been a community cultural asset. Four concerts, free to the public, are held in the middle school auditorium during the symphony's season (October–March).

✳ Selective Shopping

ANTIQUES **J & M Antiques** (716-636-5874; www.jandmantiques.com), 6407 Transit Road, East Amherst. Open by appointment. Specializing in Victorian lighting and period furniture, plus professional lamp restoration.

Muleskinner Antiques (716-633-4077; www.muleskinnerantiques.com), 5548 Main Street Williamsville. Open Monday–Saturday 10 AM–5 PM. This shop, located in the historic village of Williamsville, is known for its high-end Americana items. They specialize in eighteenth- and nineteenth-century antiques, including folk art, weathervanes, furniture sporting original finishes, redware, stoneware, and picture frames.

ART GALLERIES **Vern Stein Fine Art** (716-626-5688; vernsteinartandframe .com), 5747 Main Street, Williamsville. A collection of art, from antique photos and paintings to contemporary works.

FARM MARKETS 🐾 **Badding Brothers Farm Market** (716-636-7824), 10830 Transit Road, East Amherst. Open seven days May–December, Monday–Saturday 9 AM–8 PM, Sunday 9 AM–7 PM. This family-owned and -operated farm offers in-season produce, annuals, and hanging baskets. In the fall they have a Scarecrow Village, along with pumpkins and other fall produce.

Farmers' Market at the Williamsville Mill, East Spring Street, Williamsville. Saturday 8 AM–1 PM, Mid-May–end of October.

Spoth's Farm Market (716-688-1110), 5757 Transit Road, East Amherst. Open May–December, Monday–Friday 8:30 AM–6 PM, Saturday–Sunday 8:30 AM–7 PM. Spoth's Farm Market has grown from a simple roadside stand to one of the largest and best-known farm markets in the East Amherst/Clarence area. They grow most of the produce on their 75-acre farm, located in Clarence Center.

SHOPPING MALLS **Boulevard Mall** (716-834-8600; www.boulevard-mall .com), 730 Alberta Drive (Maple Road at Niagara Falls Boulevard) Amherst. Open Monday–Saturday 10 AM–9 PM, Sunday 11 AM–6 PM. Anchor stores include JC Penney and Macy's, along with over 100 specialty shops.

Eastern Hills Mall (716-631-5191; www.shopeasternhills.com), 4545 Transit Road, Williamsville. Open Monday–Saturday 10 AM–9 PM, Sunday 11 AM–6 PM. Anchor stores include JC Penney, Bon Ton, and Sears, along with over 100 specialty shops.

SPOTH'S FARM MARKET IS THE BEST KNOWN FARM MARKET IN THE EAST AMHERST/CLAREN

SPECIAL SHOPS **Alethea's Chocolates** (716-633-8620; www.aletheas.com), 8301 Main Street, Williamsville. Monday–Saturday 10 AM–10 PM, Sunday 10 AM–9 PM. This gourmet chocolate shop features candies made fresh daily on premises. They are known for their sponge candy, a western New York delicacy. An ice cream parlor and dessert café is located adjacent to the candy shop.

BFLO Gallery & Gift Shop (716-616-9096; www.bfloshop.com), 4545 Transit Road, Williamsville (in Eastern Hills Mall). This is the largest Buffalo-themed retailer in western New York. Choose from jewelry, home decor, clothing, artwork, gifts, and more.

Carousel Clothing & Collectibles (716-634-5959), 6094 Main Street, Williamsville. Tuesday, Wednesday, Friday, Saturday 11 AM–5 PM, Thursday 11 AM–7 PM, Sunday 12–4 PM. This shop features antiques and collectibles, along with home decor, candles, primitives, and locally handcrafted items.

✐ **Clayton's Toys & Gifts** (716-633-1966; www.claytonstoystore.com), 5225 Main Street, Williamsville. Monday–Friday 10 AM–8 PM, Saturday 10 AM–5 PM, Sunday 11 AM–4 PM. This long-established store has a selection of unique toys, books, puppets, and lots more.

🔧 **Ed Young's Hardware** (716-632-3150; www.edyoungs.com), 5641 Main Street, Williamsville. Open Monday, Tuesday, Thursday, Friday 8 AM–9 PM, Wednesday and Saturday 8 AM–6 PM, Sunday 11 AM–4 PM. If you can't find a part at Ed Young's, it probably doesn't exist! This place has all sorts of tools, seasonal items, and hardware, along with a large gift shop.

Monarch (716-565-9333) 5454 Main Street, Williamsville. Monday–Friday 10 AM–6 PM, Saturday 11 AM–5 PM. This shop carries a large variety of reasonably priced costume jewelry, handbags, scarves, and other accessories.

New York International Style (716-639-7574; www.nyinternationalstyle.com), 6705 Transit Road, East Amherst.

Located in a bright pink house, this shop specializes in bridal and prom accessories, along with everyday apparel, jewelry, handbags, and shoes.

Oh Pour l'Amour du Chocolat (716-240-9815; www.ohpourlamourduchocolat.com), 4476 Main Street, Amherst. Monday–Thursday 10 AM–8:30 PM, Friday–Saturday 10 AM–9:30 PM, Sunday 11 AM–4 PM. They specialize in a variety of handmade artisan Parisian-style confections.

Port of Entry Square (716-689-8895), 635 Dodge Road, Getzville. Open Monday–Wednesday 10 AM–4:30 PM, Thursday–Saturday 11 AM–4:30 PM, Sunday 1–4:30 PM. Port of Entry Square complex is a collection of old barns and outbuildings from Getzville's early farming days that now houses a variety of shops. The buildings, dating back to the 1860s, once were part of a gristmill operation. The Port of Entry Store, housed in the former mill, features two floors of collectibles and antiques.

Premier Gourmet (716-877-3574; www.premiergourmet.com) 3904 Maple Road, Amherst. Monday–Thursday 9 AM–9 PM, Friday–Saturday 9 AM–9:30 PM, Sunday 12–6 PM. Rated one of the top fifty gourmet food stores in the country, this large shop has a variety of gourmet and local food items, including craft beers and buffalo-themed gift baskets. The adjacent Premier Wine and Spirits has a large selection of adult beverages to choose from, including locally produced wines.

Sarah's Vintage & Estate Jewelry (716-633-3738; www.sarahsvintage jewelry.com), 5459 Main Street, Williamsville. Tuesday–Saturday 11 AM–5 PM. Stop by Sarah's for vintage jewelry, evening bags, perfume bottles and silver flatware. Items range in price from $16 to $16,000.

Sweet Jenny's Ice Cream & Candy (716-631-2424; www.sweetjennys williamsville.com), 56 East Spring Street, Williamsville. Monday–Saturday 10 AM–9 PM, Sunday 11 AM–9 PM. Located in the historic Williamsville Water Mill, this shop features homemade candies and ice cream.

Tesori (716-626-3282), 5688 Main Street, Williamsville. Tuesday–Saturday 10 AM–6 PM. This unique shop, whose name means "treasure" in Italian, is located in the heart of Williamsville and carries a variety of items, both new and antique, including home decor, jewelry, artwork, furniture, and gift items.

Village Artisans (716-633-2384), 5550 Main Street, Williamsville. Monday–Friday 10 AM–6 PM, Thursday until 8 PM, Saturday 10 AM–5 PM. This shop offers a wide variety of handcrafted gifts. Choose from baby items, home decor, garden items, pottery, glassware, photography, painted furniture, and more.

✳ Special Events

July: **4th of July Fireworks**, University at Buffalo North Campus. Enjoy music and a fireworks display. **Old Home Days** Island Park (716-632-4120). A four-day festival featuring a parade, food, rides, children's activities, and nightly entertainment.

August: **Taste of Williamsville** Island Park, Family activities and food samplings from local restaurants. **Scottish Festival** (716-689-1440; www.bnhv.org), Buffalo Niagara Heritage Village. Highland games, dancers, and entertainment.

CLARENCE AND AKRON

Clarence, located about 12 miles east of Buffalo, is home to one of the largest variety of antiques-related businesses in the entire Northeast. Established in 1808, it is the oldest township in Erie County, so it's not surprising that it has managed to preserve many artifacts from the past.

Native American inhabitants referred to this area as Ta-Num-No-Ga-O, which means "place full of hickory bark." Main Street was once an Indian trail that ran along the Onondaga escarpment. In 1799, Joseph Ellicott—an agent for the Holland Land Company—offered lots for sale to any "proper man" who would build and operate taverns on them. The first settler to take advantage of this offer was Asa Ransom, a silversmith from Geneva. He erected a log house and tavern in the area now referred to as the "hollow," and he later added a sawmill and gristmill.

Today the town can be divided into six historic districts. Clarence Hollow, where Asa Ransom first settled, is now filled with antiques stores, restaurants, the historical society, and an upscale inn built on the property once owned by Ransom. The Hollow has been redesigned to appear as it did in the 1920s, with street lights resembling gaslights, decorative walkways, and over 200 trees and 400 shrubs. Harris Hill, about 4 miles west of the Hollow along Main Street, was a refuge for people from Buffalo who were displaced when their city was burned by the British during the War of 1812. The intersection of Main and Transit roads has been the town's center of commerce and travel ever since Joseph Ellicott laid out the county's main north-south "transit" line in 1800.

Wolcottsburg, which is still largely undeveloped farmland, was settled by German immigrants in the 1820s. The first movable carousel was built in Wolcottsburg for the carnival industry. Clarence Center, at Goodrich and Clarence Center Roads, was once the intersection of two Indian trails. The brick three-story building on the corner, now a gift shop, was built in 1872 by John Eshelman and operated as a dry-goods store for over 100 years.

The sixth historic area in the town, Swormville, sits on the border between Clarence and Amherst. This area was originally settled by Bavarian and French immigrants in the 1830s. Adam Schworm, who came to the area in the 1850s, built a store on Transit Road, and the community was dubbed Schwormville, from which its current name evolved. Rev. John Neumann, a missionary who was canonized a saint by the Catholic Church in 1977, founded St. Mary's parish. The brick church, completed in 1865, was built during the Civil War. The annual St. Mary's Church Picnic in July is locally famous for its chicken clam chowder.

The village of Akron, the central business district for the town of Newstead, is located in a predominately rural area. The first settlers, Asa Chapman and Peter Vandeventer, arrived in the area around 1801. Originally part of Batavia, Newstead was incorporated in 1823. The main occupation in the town's early days was farming. As the town grew, other businesses sprang up, including the cement industry, which turned Akron into a boomtown. The cement was produced by crushing, firing, and mixing local limestone with water. By the 1880s Akron was considered one of the most prosperous towns in Erie County. However, by the early 1900s all the local cement plants closed. Shortly after this point, gypsum was discovered in the area, and mining of the product began in 1905—but by the late 1940s many of these mines closed, too.

Today, one of Akron's best known businesses is Perry's Ice Cream, founded by Morton Perry. The business began as a home delivery dairy in 1918. In the 1930s the Akron High School cafeteria staff requested ice cream, and Morton complied by making the frozen confection using a family recipe. Soon they were delivering ice cream to local stores and restaurants, and today it's one of the best-known ice cream manufacturers in the state.

AREA CODE The area code is 716.

GUIDANCE **Akron Chamber of Commerce** (716-542-4050), 85 Main Street, Akron. Open Tuesday, Thursday and Friday 9 AM–12:30 PM.

    Clarence Chamber of Commerce (716-631-3888; www.clarence.org), 8975 Main Street, Clarence. Open Monday–Friday 9 AM–4:30 PM.

    Clarence Hollow Association (716-759-2345; www.clarencehollowassociation.org), 10490 Main Street, Clarence. They publish a brochure listing businesses, stores, and attractions in Clarence Hollow, along with a walking tour of the historic buildings in the area.

GETTING THERE *By air:* **Akron Airport** (716-542-4607). A small landing strip for private planes. See also *City of Buffalo—Getting There.*

    By bus: NFTA Metro bus from Buffalo stops at Transitown Plaza (Main and Transit).

    By car: Clarence and Akron are accessible from Route 5 (Main Street).

MEDICAL EMERGENCY Dial 911.

✳ To See

MUSEUMS AND HISTORIC HOMES **Clarence Historical Society Museum** (716-759-8575; www.clarencehistory.org), 10465 Main Street, Clarence. Open Wednesday

CLARENCE HISTORICAL SOCIETY MUSEUM

10 AM–1 PM, first and third Sundays of month 1–4 PM or by appointment. The building that houses the museum was built in 1843 as a church meeting house. The museum contains artifacts from area churches as well as an automotive display; Civil War, World War I, and World War II artifacts; and many other items. The centerpiece of the technology wing is the original red barn where the late Wilson Greatbatch, a local resident, invented the implantable heart pacemaker in the 1950s.

RICH-TWINN OCTAGON HOUSE IN AKRON

Rich-Twinn Octagon House (716-7022; www.newsteadhistoricalsociety.org), 145 Main Street, Akron. Open the first and third Sundays of the month 1–3 PM or by appointment. The Rich-Twinn House, built in 1849 by Charles B. Rich, is an example of Greek Revival architecture and a beautifully restored specimen of a mid-nineteenth-century architectural fad. The first floor features a receiving room, and a kitchen complete with a beehive oven, dumbwaiter, speaking tube, and pantry. A grand foyer with a curved staircase dominates the second floor, which features etched-glass doors and ornate plaster moldings. The nearby **Knight Sutton Museum** at 123 Main Street is also operated by the Newstead Historical Society, has information on local history. Open May–October, Wednesday 10 AM–1 PM, and first Sunday of the month 1–3 PM.

✳ To Do

FAMILY FUN ✐ **Great Pumpkin Farm** (716-759-2260; www.greatpumpkinfarm.com), 11199 Main Street, Clarence. Open seven days 10 AM–dusk, mid-September through Halloween. Admission charged first two weekends for festivals. Get your Halloween pumpkins and other fall decorating needs here. The World Pumpkin Weigh Off takes place the first weekend of October, with folks from all over the northeast hauling their gigantic gourds, some over 1,000 pounds, to Clarence for this competition. Halloween and fall activities take place each weekend, including hayrides, an amusement midway, and special events.

✐ **Kelkenberg Farm** (716-741-4862; www.kelkenbergfarm.com), 9270 Wolcott Road, Clarence Center. By reservation for group tours; call for public hours. This small family-operated farm tucked into the back roads of Akron is a great place for kids to learn about agriculture and farm life. Sheep, goats, pigs, and horses can be found in their barns, while pumpkins, cornstalks, and other fall decorating items can be found in the farm market.

GOLF **Arrowhead Golf Course** (716-542-4653; www.arrowheadgcwny.com), 12287 Clarence Center Road, Akron. An 18-hole, par-72 course with very few trees. Their Timberland Restaurant is open to the public.

Dande Farms Golf Course (716-542-2027; dandefarmsgolf.com), 13278 Carney Road, Akron. A semi-private, 18-hole, par-71 course.

Greenwood Golf Course (716-741-3395; www.greenwoodgolf.net), 8499 Northfield Road, Clarence Center. A 9-hole, par-35 public course with full bar and snack bar.

Links at Ivy Ridge (716-542-6342; www.thelinksativyridge.com), 12221 Main Road, Akron. An 18-hole, par 72 course featuring rolling hills and great scenery.

Rothland Golf Course (716-542-4325; www.rothlandsgolf.com), 12089 Clarence Center Road, Akron. A 27-hole (three 9-hole courses), par-72 (for 18 holes), privately owned, professionally managed golf course open to the public.

✳ Green Space

PARKS **Akron Falls Park** (716-542-2330), Route 93, Parkview Drive, Akron. A 285-acre Erie County Park that features walking and hiking trails, fishing, tennis courts, baseball diamonds, and picnic shelters. The park has a creek, a 40-foot waterfall, and lake. In winter, enjoy sledding, cross-country skiing, and ice skating on a pond. The park's creek, Murder Creek, is so named because legend has it that it is haunted by the ghosts of Ah-Weh-Gag and Gray Wolf, two Seneca lovers, and her father, Great Fire. The three were murdered by a white man named Sanders, who fell in love with Ah-Weh-Gag.

WALKING AND HIKING TRAILS **Akron Rail Trail** (716-542-4574). This 6.5-mile trail starts in Akron and continues through Newstead and Clarence. Enjoy walking, biking, and skating along with cross-country skiing and snowshoeing during the winter. Snowmobiling is allowed on the trail, except in the village of Akron.

Peanut Line Trail. This 7.5-mile trail, which runs from Main Street west to just past Shimerville Road, follows the rail bed of the old Canandaigua and Niagara Falls Railroad, which was known as the "Peanut Line."

West Shore Trail. This 5.25-mile trail begins at Main and Salt Roads in Clarence Hollow, following the former railroad lines of the New York, West Shore, and Buffalo Railroad, and continues into Akron. Another Clarence trail runs 3 miles from Clarence Town Park to Wehrle Drive.

✳ Lodging

INNS AND RESORTS **Asa Ransom House** (716-759-2315 or 800-841-2340; www.asaransom.com), 10529 Main Street, Clarence. This relaxing country inn is located on the site where Asa Ransom, a young silversmith, built the first gristmill in Erie County in 1803. The ruins of the mill can still be seen at the rear of the property. Part of this historic inn was built in 1853, with additions added in 1975 and 1993. The ten guest rooms, each with a private bath, are furnished with antiques and period reproductions. See *Dining Out*. $$.

ASA RANSOM HOUSE

✳ Where to Eat

DINING OUT **Asa Ransom House** (716-759-2315; www.asaransom.com), 10529 Main Street, Clarence. Open for dinner Tuesday–Sunday and for lunch on Wednesday; reservations strongly suggested. Afternoon tea offered by reservation only. The menu offers a selection of items that change seasonally, along with fresh rolls and muffins served with flavored butters. Desserts are homemade. See also *Lodging*.

The Hollow Bistro and Brew (716-759-7351; www.thehollowclarence.com), 10641 Main Street, Clarence. Monday–Saturday 11:30 AM–10 PM. Enjoy Asian and fusion cuisine in a circa-1804 building located in the "hollow" of Clarence. A jazz brunch is featured the first Saturday of the month.

Gertie's (716-741-1311; www.gertiesrestaurant.com), 6010 Goodrich Road, Clarence Center. Enjoy made from scratch comfort food in this cute little bistro in the heart of Clarence Center. All food is of excellent quality; be sure to save room for their house-made desserts. House specialties include French-style

GERTIE'S IN CLARENCE CENTER FEATURES MADE FROM SCRATCH COMFORT FOOD

quiche, along with sandwiches, wraps, and burgers.

Kennedy's Cove (716-759-8961; kennedyscove.com), 9800 Main Street, Clarence. Open Monday–Saturday 4–10 PM, Sunday 3–8 PM. Home of the famous blackened steak, they are noted for charbroiled steak and seafood.

Orazio's Restaurant (759-8888; www.orazios.com), 9415 Main Street, Clarence. Open Monday–Thursday 3–10 PM (closed Tuesday, except in December), Friday–Saturday 3–11 PM, Sunday 12–9 PM. A traditional Italian restaurant specializing in made-to-order pasta dishes with what has been deemed the best red sauce in the Buffalo area. Chef Orazio Ippolito's specialties include pasta con vodka and stuffed sirloin ala Orazio.

EATING OUT **Goodrich Coffee and Tea** (716-759-1791; www.goodrichcoffee.com), 9450 Main Street, Clarence. Monday–Thursday 6 AM–9 PM, Saturday 7 AM–10 PM, Sunday 8 AM–6 PM. A family-owned café serving gourmet coffees and teas as well as sandwiches, salads, and breakfast wraps.

Clarence Center Coffee Company and Café (716-741-8573; www.clarencecentercoffee.com), 9485 Clarence Center Road, Clarence Center. Opens Monday–Friday at 7 AM, Saturday and Sunday at 8 AM. This unique coffee café is located in the former Clarence Center post office, which dates back to 1829. In addition to coffees and specialty beverages, the café offers gourmet sandwiches, wraps, salads, and desserts. In warmer weather, sip your coffee on the wraparound porch.

& **Hayes Seafood House** (716-632-1772; www.hayesseafoodhouse.com), 8900 Main Street, Clarence. Open Tuesday–Thursday 11:30 AM–8 PM, Friday 11:30 AM–9 PM, Saturday 3–8 PM. Specialties include Maine lobster dinners, homemade chowder, grilled salmon, swordfish, tuna, and more.

Mardee's (716-741-3807), 9475 Maple Street (off Goodrich) Clarence Center.

Monday–Friday 7 AM–2 PM, Saturday 7 AM–noon, Sunday 8 AM–1 PM. Enjoy good homestyle cooking in a cute country café. Breakfast fare includes eggs, pancakes and the like, along with huge cinnamon rolls and LA cinnamon toast. The lunch menu includes specialty sandwiches, burgers and soups.

McDuffie's Bakery (716-759-8510; www.mcduffies.com), 9920 Main Street, Clarence. Monday–Friday 7 AM–6 PM, Saturday 7 AM–4 PM. They serve wraps, sandwiches, and soup. They are known for their Scottish shortbread cookies and baked goods, along with their pot pies, which are sold frozen to bake at home.

Murphy Brown's Craft Beer (716-407-3466; www.murphybrownscraftbeer.com), 9500 Main Street at Goodrich, Clarence. Monday–Thursday 4–11 PM, Friday 3–11 PM, Saturday 12–11 PM. Sample and purchase craft beers; a different selection is available each week, and enjoy a limited pub grub menu that includes items like Italian sausage sandwiches and pizza.

& **Ohlson's Bakery & Café** (716-626-7783; www.ohlsonsbakery.com), 8500 Sheridan Drive (at Harris Hill Road), Clarence. Open Monday 7:30 AM–6 PM, Tuesday–Friday 6:30 AM–6 PM, Saturday 7:30 AM–4 PM. This charming bakery features a European-style café that serves fresh Danish and muffins, egg sandwiches, freshly made café sandwiches, hot panini sandwiches, and quiche. They are known for their made-from-scratch baked goods, including pastries, cookies, coffee cake, cheesecake, and special-occasion cakes.

✳ Selective Shopping

ANTIQUES **Antiques at the Glencroft** (716-759-1720; www.glencroftantiques.com), 10210 Main Street, Clarence. Saturday–Sunday 12–4 PM or by appointment. They specialize in nineteenth- and twentieth-century antiques and art.

& **Antique World** (716-759-8538; www.antiqueworldmarket.com), 11111 Main Street, Clarence. Monday–Tuesday, Thursday–Friday 11 AM–5 PM, Saturday–Sunday 8 AM–5 PM; outdoor flea market Saturday–Sunday 8 AM–4 PM, April–October. The largest indoor and outdoor antiques market in New York State. Hundreds of dealers display their wares year-round indoors in several buildings, plus hundreds of outdoor dealers every Sunday during the summer.

& **Kelly Schultz Antiques** (716-759-2260; www.kellyschultzantiques.com), 10995 Main Street, Clarence (at Antique World). Daily 11 AM–5 PM, closed Wednesday. Choose from fine antiques and oriental rugs.

Premier Antique Center (716-759-0455), 11145 Main Street, Clarence (at Antique World). Monday–Friday 11 AM–5 PM (closed Wednesday), Saturday 9:30 AM–5 PM. This shop has an assortment of high-quality antiques.

Tschoppe Stained Glass (716-759-6010), 10830 Main Street, Clarence. Open Tuesday–Saturday 10 AM–5 PM, Sunday 12–5 PM. Antiques, along with window and lamp restoration.

FARM MARKETS **Clarence Hollow Farmers' Market** (www.clarencefarmersmarket.com), 10717 Main Street, Clarence. Saturdays 8 AM–1 PM, June–October. This market features local produce, baked goods, cheese, and more.

Greg's U-Pick (716-741-4239; www.gregsupick.com), 9270 Lapp Road, Clarence Center. A family-owned farm where you can pick strawberries, blueberries, and raspberries, as well as pumpkins in the fall. They also have a small farm market.

SPECIAL SHOPS **Smoke, Fire, and Spice** (716-759-4328; www.smokefireandspice.com), 10189 Main Street, Clarence. Wednesday–Thursday 10 AM–7 PM, Friday–Monday 11 AM–5 PM. This gourmet store specializes in the hot and spicy. They carry grills, BBQ accessories, Southwest-style giftware, and gourmet hot sauces, along with other hot and spicy delicacies.

Family Chocolate Shoppe (716-759-0658; www.familychocolateshop.com), 10295 Main Street, Clarence (George Courtyard). Open Monday–Friday 10 AM–6 PM, Saturday 10 AM–5 PM, Sunday 11 AM–4 PM. This shop has a large selection of candies, including Buffalo sponge candy and novelties like chocolate chicken wings.

☙ **The Perfect Gift** (716-741-0722; www.theperfectgiftbuffalo.com), 6000 Goodrich Road, Clarence Center. Monday–Friday 11 AM–6 PM, Saturday 10 AM–5 PM. This family-owned and -operated store is located in the historic Eshelman Building in the heart of Clarence Center. This three-story brick building was built in 1872, and a store was operated by the Eshelman family for nearly 100 years. The Perfect Gift carries quality home decor items, original artwork, hand-painted glassware, hand-made jewelry, greeting cards, seasonal gifts, and old-fashioned candy, as well as women's apparel, accessories, and shoes.

MAKING THE CHICKEN CLAM CHOWDER AT ST. MARY'S CHURCH PICNIC

Yours Truly (716-741-4500; www.yourstrulypaperie.com), 6045 Goodrich Road, Clarence Center. Tuesday–Friday 11 AM–6 PM, Saturday 10 AM–4 PM. Choose from a variety of stationery and gifts.

✳ Special Events

May and August: **Antique Expo** (716-759-8483; www.antiqueworldmarket.com), Antique World and Marketplace, Clarence. Over 800 dealers display their wares at these annual open-air shows.

July: **St. Mary's Church Picnic** (716-688-9380; stmaryswormville.org), 6919 Transit Road, Swormville. People come from miles around for their famous chicken clam chowder. Held annually on the third Sunday in July.

October: **World Pumpkin Weigh Off** (716-759-8483; www.greatpumpkinfarm.com), Great Pumpkin Farm, 11199 Main Street, Clarence. A competition for the biggest pumpkin in the country.

THE PERFECT GIFT IS LOCATED IN THE HISTORIC ESHELMAN BUILDING

LANCASTER, DEPEW, AND CHEEKTOWAGA

The first settlers arrived in the Lancaster area in 1803, building homes on Ellicott Creek in what is now Bowmansville. (Lancaster was part of the town of Clarence until 1833.) Many of the earlier settlers who followed came from New England and started businesses that included woodworking, tanning, milling, and slaughterhouses. In about 1830, German settlers, from both Pennsylvania and Germany, arrived in the region to set up farms.

Probably the most famous of the town's early industries was the glass factory, which produced bottles from 1849–1904. A new automated glass factory was built in 1907, which continued to operate until 1965.

The railway brought expansion and increased prosperity to the area in the 1890s. A small village grew around the shops erected by the New York Central Railroad near Transit Road. This village was named Depew, after Chauncey Depew, president of the New York Central & Hudson River Railroad.

The first inhabitants in the town now known as Cheektowaga were the Iroquois, who called the area *Ji-ik-do-wah-gah,* meaning "the land of the crab apple." The area was first settled by Appollos Hitchcock and his family in 1809. The town was officially incorporated in 1839, with Alexander Hitchcock, Appollos' son, elected the first supervisor.

Cheektowaga became a transportation center for the region, with four railroads by the end of the Civil War. In the 1920s an airport was constructed on Genesee Street, and in the 1950s the New York State Thruway cut across town.

While it remained semi-rural prior to World War II, Cheektowaga quickly developed after the war to become one of Buffalo's most populous suburbs, as well as a retail and business center.

AREA CODE The area code is 716.

GUIDANCE **Cheektowaga Chamber of Commerce** (716-684-5838; www.cheektowaga .org), 2875 Union Road, Suite 50, Appletree Business Park, Cheektowaga. Open Monday–Friday 8:30 AM–4 PM.
   Lancaster Chamber of Commerce (716-681-9755; www.wnychamber.com), 11 West Main Street, Lancaster.

GETTING THERE *By air:* **Buffalo Niagara International Airport** (716-630-6000; www .buffaloairport.com), 4200 Genesee Street, Buffalo. Served by most major airlines.
   By bus: **Niagara Frontier Transportation Authority** (716-855-7211; www.nfta.com), 181 Ellicott Street, Buffalo. Several routes run between these suburbs and downtown Buffalo, including two express routes.
   By car: Exits 51 and 52 off I-90 will take you into this area, as will exit 49 and then take Route 78 south.
   By Train: **Amtrak** (716-683-8440 or 800-872-7245; www.amtrak.com), 55 Dick Rd, Depew.

GETTING AROUND *By bus:* Several bus routes run from downtown Buffalo to these suburbs.

MEDICAL EMERGENCY Dial 911.

St. Joseph Hospital (716-891-2400; www.chsbuffalo.org), 2605 Harlem Road, Cheektowaga.

✳ To See

MUSEUMS AND HISTORIC HOMES **Cheektowaga Historical Museum** (716-684-6544), 3329 Broadway, Cheektowaga. Open 2–4 PM the first Sunday of every month.

Hull House (716-681-6451; www.hullfamilyhome.com), 5976 Genesee Street, Lancaster. See website or call for open times. Hull House, built in 1810 by Warren and Polly Hull, is the oldest stone house in Erie County. Mr. Hull was a Revolutionary War veteran who farmed about 360 acres in Lancaster. The Federal-style home is currently being restored.

Lancaster Historical Museum (716-681-7719; www.lancasternyhistoricalsociety .org), 40 Clark Street, Lancaster. Open Sunday 2–5 PM. This elegant home contains a collection of items made at the old Lancaster Glass Factory in addition to artifacts and memorabilia pertaining to the history of Lancaster. The historical society also operates the **Little Red School House**, William Street and Bowen Road, Lancaster, a one-room schoolhouse, constructed in 1868 from locally made bricks, featuring a pot-belly stove, single and double desks, a teacher's desk from the 1880s, and antique slates, toys, and books.

✳ To Do

AUTO RACING **Lancaster International Speedway** (716-759-6818; www.lancaster nationalspeedway.com), 57 Gunnville Road, Lancaster. Open Saturdays at 6 PM, Fridays at 7 PM. Admission vary according to event.

THE HULL HOUSE IS THE OLDEST STONE HOUSE IN ERIE COUNTY

FAMILY FUN ✐ **The "Airport Tunnel,"** Aero Drive at Youngs Road, Cheektowaga. Kids of all ages will get a kick out of driving under the runway of Buffalo Niagara International Airport. It's just a simple tunnel, but you get an almost surreal feeling if you approach the tunnel while an airliner is taxiing overhead on the runway.

GOLF **Walden Golf Range** (716-681-1670; waldengolfrange.com), 4011 Walden Avenue, Lancaster. A family-owned and -operated practice range since 1960, it is considered one of the best public driving ranges in western New York.

REINSTEIN WOODS NATURE PRESERVE

✳ Green Space

NATURE PRESERVES 🐾 ✏ ♿ **Reinstein Woods Nature Preserve** (716-683-5959; www
.dec.ny.gov/education/1837.html), 93 Honorine Drive, Depew. Trails open daily sun-
rise to sunset, environmental education center open Monday–Friday 9 AM–4:30 PM,
Saturday 1–4:30 PM. Special programs take place each month, see website for more
information. This 300-acre preserve has undisturbed ancient forests that look like
they did in prehistoric time, 19 ponds, marshes, and swamps. Marks are still visible
from the original Holland Land Survey in 1797. The land was purchased in 1932 by Dr.
Victor Reinstein, a doctor, attorney, and conservationist, for his own private sanctuary. The preserve is home to native western New York wildlife, including deer, beaver,
hawks, and woodpeckers.

PARKS **Cheektowaga Town Park** (716-895-7529), 2600 Harlem Road, Cheektowaga.
This 66.5-acre park has numerous picnic shelters, playground equipment, sports fields,
a swimming pool, and an open-air band shell. It is the site of many festivals throughout
the summer.
    Como Lake Park (716-683-5430), 2220 Como Park Boulevard, Lancaster. The third
largest Erie County Park, Como Lake is named after a famous tourist resort in Italy. The
park features a 4.5-acre man-made lake; used for ice skating in the winter. Other park
features include a stone lighthouse next to the lake and a circa-1928 lodge, along with
facilities for baseball, biking, fishing, hiking, picnicking, sledding, and cross-country
skiing.
    Stiglmeier Park, 810 Losson Rd, Cheektowaga. This 386-acre park is best known for
its wooden boardwalk walking trails that wind through the woods.
    Walden Pond Park (716-683-3949 or 716-684-3320), Walden Avenue and Ransom
Road, Lancaster. The 70-acre park has a playground, sports fields, walking trails, and
a scenic pond.

✻ Lodging

MOTELS AND HOTELS **The Delavan** (716-635-9000; www.salvatores.net), 6461 Transit Road, Lancaster. This luxurious 60-room boutique hotel and spa opened in 2016. Amenities include a full service spa and fitness center. The Delavan is adjacent to Salvatore's Italian Gardens—see *Dining Out.* $$$.

Garden Place Hotel (877-456-6036; www.salvatores.net), 6615 Transit Road, Williamsville. This luxurious hotel—a subsidiary of Salvatore's Italian Gardens restaurant—is almost always booked, so be sure to make reservations well in advance. Many of the 160 rooms and suites include king-sized beds and Jacuzzis. A continental breakfast is served in the beautifully decorated courtyard each morning. $$.

Millennium Airport Hotel (716-681-2400), 2040 Walden Avenue, Buffalo. This hotel offers 292 large guest rooms—many with balconies—as well as an indoor pool and an exercise facility. It is located adjacent to the Galleria Mall and I-90 and only 3 miles from the airport. $$.

There are numerous other national chain hotels located on Genesee Street near the airport and along Transit Road near the Thruway exit.

✻ Where to Eat

DINING OUT **Eddie Ryan's Restaurant** (716-651-0950; eddieryansbar.webs.com), 50 Central Avenue, Lancaster. Open Monday–Thursday 11 AM–11 PM, Friday 11 AM–midnight, Saturday 8 AM–2 AM, Sunday 8 AM–8 PM. This casual fine-dining establishment has an Irish theme. Specialties include Irish pot roast, potato pancakes, shepherd's pie, French onion soup, and the best fish fry in Lancaster.

&. **Ripa's Restaurant** (716-684-2418; www.ripas.com), 4218 Walden Avenue, Lancaster. Lunch Tuesday–Friday 11 AM–3 PM, Dinner Tuesday–Thursday 4–9 PM, Friday–Saturday 4–10 PM. Since 1955 Ripas has been serving high-quality food like grilled pork chops, charcoal-broiled fish, stuffed shrimp, steaks, and homemade pasta.

&. **Salvatore's Italian Gardens** (877-856-4097; www.salvatores.net), 6461 Transit Road, Lancaster. One of western New York's most elegant restaurants for over 40 years. Offered are such classic entrees as filet mignon and prime rib, as well as seafood and specialty pastas. The restaurant has several banquet rooms and they also operate the Delavan Hotel (on site) and the nearby Garden Place Hotel. See *Lodging.*

EATING OUT &. **Al-E-Oops** (716-681-0200; aleoops.com), 5389 Genesee Street, Lancaster. Monday–Thursday 3–10 PM, Friday 1–10 PM, Saturday 1–11 PM, Sunday 1–8:30 PM. Enjoy authentic hickory-smoked BBQ ribs, pork, and chicken along with smoked turkey and hickory-house ham in a casual homestyle atmosphere.

Broadway Deli (716-681-3100; www.bwaydeli.com), 5430 Broadway, Lancaster. Open Monday–Friday 11 AM–6 PM, Friday 11 AM–7 PM, Saturday 10 AM–4 PM. A family-owned New York–style deli and sandwich shop that features really good freshly made sandwiches, wraps, and paninis. House specialties include fresh, slow-roasted pork loin, roast beef, turkey breast, and corned beef. Eat in the small dining area or take out.

&. 🐾 **Charlie the Butcher** (716-633-8330; www.charliethebutcher.com), 1065 Wehrle Drive, Cheektowaga. Open Monday–Saturday 10 AM–10 PM, Sunday 11 AM–9 PM. When locals think of beef on weck, Charlie Roesch often comes to mind, because he is considered by many to be the food ambassador of western New York. This small vintage restaurant has indoor as well as outdoor seating. Often you'll see Charlie himself—wearing his trademark white hard hat and butcher's apron—behind the counter,

CHARLIE THE BUTCHER'S IS KNOWN FOR BEEF ON WECK

carving up his famous roast beef, smoked turkey, and other daily specials.

Smokin' Little Diner (716-683-9248; smokinlittlediner.somegreatbbq.com), 4870 Broadway, Depew. Sunday–Monday 7 AM–2 PM, Tuesday–Saturday 7 AM–9 PM. This quaint diner is one of the top barbecue destinations in the area, as well as a popular spot for breakfast.

Magruders (716-685-4400; www .magruders.org), 4995 Broadway, Depew. Sunday–Thursday 10 AM–11 PM, Friday–Saturday 11 AM–11:30 PM. This cozy restaurant offers good food at reasonable prices. Specialties include a soup and salad bar, famous half-pound burger and meatloaf dinner.

Thai House (716-601-7865; www .depewthaihouse.com), 5246 Transit Road, Depew. Monday–Saturday 11 AM–10 PM, Sunday 12–9 PM. This small restaurant doesn't look like much from the outside, but it is very nice inside and it has some of the best Thai and Burmese food in the area.

The Yelling Goat (716-683-0462; www.theyellinggoat.com), 205 Central Avenue, Lancaster. Sunday 12–9 PM, Monday–Thursday 11 AM–10 PM, Friday–Saturday 11 AM–11 PM. This popular bar and restaurant features a variety of menu choices, from sandwiches served with house-made fries, burgers, salads, and thin crust pizza to filet mignon, prime ribs, and salmon. During patio season you can even BYOD—that's bring your own dog, provided Fido is well behaved and on a leash.

✳ Entertainment

THEATERS **Lancaster Opera House** (716-683-1776; www.lancopera.org), 21 Central Avenue, Lancaster. Every small town and village in the country had a theater, or "opera house," at the turn of the twentieth century. Even though opera was rarely performed in them, these buildings were called opera houses rather than vaudeville theaters because it sounded more cultured to Victorian-era art patrons. Most of these structures had village offices located on the first floor and performance space on the second. Originally opened in 1897, the Lancaster Opera House hosted dances and recitals as well as musicals and traveling shows. After undergoing restoration during the late 1970s and early 1980s, the opera house is now a performing-arts center where visitors can enjoy a variety of entertainment.

✳ Selective Shopping

SHOPPING MALLS **The Walden Galleria** (716-681-7600; www.waldengalleria .com), 1 Walden Galleria Drive, Cheektowaga. Open Monday–Saturday 10 AM– 9 PM, Sunday 12–5 PM. The largest shopping mall in western New York features over 200 stores on two levels, including The Bon Ton, JC Penney, Macy's, and Lord & Taylor.

✳ Special Events

July: **Polish Festival** (716-686-3465), Cheektowaga Town Park. A 4-day event celebrating the area's Polish heritage.

LANCASTER OPERA HOUSE

SOUTHERN ERIE COUNTY

■

TOWN OF AURORA

East Aurora, Marilla, and Elma

ORCHARD PARK AND WEST SENECA

LAKE ERIE TOWNS

Hamburg, Blasdell, Eden, Angola, and Derby
(also North Collins)

SKI COUNTRY

Boston, Holland, Colden, Glenwood,
Springville, and West Falls

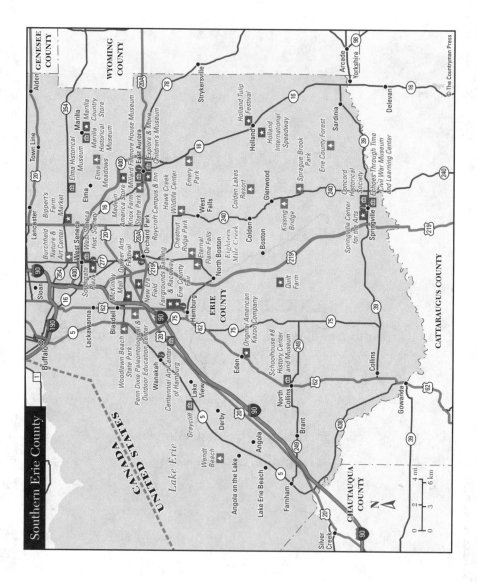

Southern Erie County

© The Countryman Press

INTRODUCTION

South of the City of Buffalo, generally referred to as the "Southtowns," is a mixture of residential areas, farmland, and rolling hills. Historic East Aurora, once home to President Millard Fillmore, is today the headquarters of Fisher-Price Toys. Nearby Orchard Park is the home of the Buffalo Bills. The shores of Lake Erie in Hamburg, Derby, and Angola boast several popular beaches, along with Graycliff, designed by noted architect Frank Lloyd Wright, which is open for tours. The southernmost portion of the county is ski country and a great place to view fall foliage.

TOWN OF AURORA

East Aurora, Marilla, and Elma

The Town of Aurora, located about 20 miles south of Buffalo, is a quaint town that's rich in history. The town's first settlers arrived in the early 1800s and many of them established farms. During the late nineteenth century the town was nationally known as a horse-breeding center and was home to the world's only 1-mile covered racetrack. One of the town's early settlers, Millard Fillmore, came to East Aurora in 1923 to study law and teach school. He went on to be the thirteenth president of the United States. The home he built here in 1825 has been designated a National Historic Landmark. East Aurora was the home of the Roycroft Arts and Crafts Movement, established by Elbert Hubbard in 1895. The village is also known as "Toy Town USA" since Fisher-Price Toys was founded here and remains the international headquarters for the toy company. Today East Aurora has many shops, restaurants, antiques stores, and museums, including the 14-building Roycroft Campus, a National Historic Landmark.

The nearby hamlet of Marilla, named after Marilla Rogers, the wife of an early settler, was established in 1853. The Marilla General Store, built in 1851, is still in business.

The town of Elma, officially formed in 1857, was named Elma in honor of a giant elm tree that once stood on the corner of Clinton and Bowen Roads. Elma was originally part of the Buffalo Creek Indian Reservation, which had several native villages located throughout its area.

AREA CODE The area code is 716.

GUIDANCE **Greater East Aurora Chamber of Commerce**, 652 Main Street, East Aurora 716-652-8444; www.eanycc.com. Open 8 AM–4:30 PM Monday–Friday.

GETTING THERE *By bus:* The NFTA Bus #70 is an express route between Buffalo and East Aurora.

By car: I-90 (New York State Thruway) to Route 400 (exit 54). East Aurora can also be reached via Routes 16 or 20A.

MEDICAL EMERGENCY Call 911.

✴ To See

MUSEUMS AND HISTORIC HOMES **Aurora Historical Society Museum** (716-652-7944; www.aurorahistoricalsociety.com), 300 Gleed Avenue, East Aurora. Open Wednesday 1–4 PM. This museum documents the history of the Town of Aurora, from Native American inhabitants to the present. On the building's main corridor are 15 murals, painted by Rix Jennings, son of a Roycroft artisan, that detail the town's history.

Elbert Hubbard Museum (716-652-4735; www.aurorahistoricalsociety.com), 363 Oakwood Avenue, East Aurora. Open June–October, Wednesday, Saturday, and Sunday 1–4 PM. In 1895 Elbert Hubbard acquired the Roycroft Press, which very rapidly became well known for its beautiful books. An interesting and sometimes controversial

MILLARD FILLMORE HOUSE MUSEUM

person, Hubbard published a pocket-sized magazine, *The Philistine*, which was filled with wit, wisdom, and irreverence. He was also the first printer to make use of color, white space, and endorsements in his advertising. This museum, formerly the home of a Roycroft artisan, is filled with artifacts belonging to Hubbard and his craftsmen, including rare books, furniture, and leatherworks. One of the Roycroft artists, W. W. Denslow, was the illustrator for the book *The Wizard of Oz*.

✍ ✪ **Millard Fillmore House Museum** (716-652-8875; www.aurorahistoricalsociety .com), 24 Shearer Avenue, East Aurora. Open June–October, Wednesday, Saturday, and Sunday 1–4 PM. Millard Fillmore, 13th President of the United States, built this home in 1825 for his new bride, Abigail, shortly after he began his law career in East Aurora. The tour of this National Historic Landmark begins in the stenciled living room and moves to the kitchen. Upstairs in the children's bedroom is a collection of toys and dolls from the 1800s. Some of the furnishings were owned by the Fillmore family.

Marilla Historical Museum (716-652-7608, town historian), 1810 Two Rod Road, Marilla. Tuesday 7–9 PM or by appointment. This museum has displays pertaining to the history of the Town of Marilla.

Elma Historical Museum (716-655-0046, www.elmanyhistory.com), 3011 Bowen Road, Elma. Open July–August the third Sunday of the month 1–4 PM; rest of year Thursday 1–4 PM or by appointment. This museum has information about the history of Elma.

❋ To Do

BREWERIES **42 North Brewery** (716-805-7500, www.42northbrewing.com), 25 Pine Street, East Aurora, Open Tuesday–Thursday 4 PM–11 PM, Friday 1 PM–12 AM, Saturday 12 PM–12 AM, Sunday 12–8 PM. The brewery is named after its location on the 42nd parallel. This establishment, which has 10 beers on tap, has an indoor game room as

ELBERT HUBBARD AND THE ROYCROFT ARTS AND CRAFTS MOVEMENT

I n 1892 Elbert Hubbard quit his job as a soap salesman in Buffalo and traveled to England, where he became acquainted with William Morris, father of the English Arts and Crafts movement. When he returned to the United States, he acquired a print shop in East Aurora and soon became well known for the beautiful books he produced. One published essay, *A Message to Garcia*, brought him international fame. Hubbard went on to develop a self-contained community of over 500 craftsmen, including furniture makers, metalsmiths, leathersmiths, and bookbinders. Items produced by the artisans were marked with the "Roycroft Mark," which signified that the work was of the highest quality.

Hubbard viewed the Roycroft as not merely a place but a state of mind. In 1905 the Roycroft Inn was opened to accommodate the thousands of people who journeyed there to learn about the Arts and Crafts movement. The community flourished until 1915, when, tragically, Hubbard and his wife perished on the *Lusitania*. The community continued on, under the leadership of his son, until 1938. The 14-building Roycroft Campus was designated a National Historic Landmark in 1986 and began going through extensive restorations and preservations during the 1990s.

well as outdoor beer garden. Their limited food menu includes small plate offerings of locally sourced foods, including Breadhive pretzels, meatballs, bruschetta, and a Cubano sandwich.

FAMILY FUN ✍ ♿ 🌳 **Explore & More Children's Museum** (716-655-5131; www .exploreandmore.org), 300 Gleed Avenue, East Aurora. Open Wednesday–Saturday 10 AM–5 PM, Sunday 12–5 PM; until 8 PM the first Friday of the month. This unique museum encourages children to touch the exhibits as they experiment, discover, play, and learn. The museum's fundamental philosophy is that play is essential for learning. The museum has educational workshops, activity days, and traveling exhibits for preschoolers through sixth graders. The museum is scheduled to move to Canalside in downtown Buffalo in late 2018.

GOLF 🏌 **Elma Meadows** (716-652-5475), 1711 Girdle Road, Elma. An 18-hole, par-72 course and driving range.

ICE SKATING **Healthy Zone Rink** (www.thinkrink.org), 41 Riley Street, East Aurora. A covered outdoor rink with 5,000 square foot warming lodge.

TOURS **Mason Winfield's Haunted History Ghost Walks** (716-655-6663; www .masonwinfield.com), 21 South Grove Street, Suite 240, East Aurora. See website for dates and times of tours.

✳ Green Space

NATURE PRESERVES **Hawk Creek Wildlife Rehabilitation Center** (716-652-8646; www.hawkcreek.org), 1963 Mill Road, West Falls. Hawk Creek is a wildlife center that specializes in birds of prey and mammals. The center focuses on preserving wildlife and the environment through rehabilitation, reproduction, research, and education.

Hawk Creek is the largest educational outreach facility in the state, and its educational programs include talks on owls, rare species, and unique mammals. The facility is only open to the public during special events and scheduled tours.

Sinking Ponds Wildlife Sanctuary, Pine Street Extension, East Aurora. Open daily, dawn to dusk. Free admission. A 70-acre area of woods and natural ponds that features walking trails and natural ponds for bird-watching.

PARKS **Aurora Town Park** (716-652-8866), South Street (at Olean Road), East Aurora. This three-acre park has a playground, picnic areas, and an outdoor pool.

Elma Meadows (716-652-5475), 1711 Girdle Road, Elma. Open daily, dawn to dusk. Free admission. This Erie County park includes picnic facilities, athletic fields, a decorative rock garden, and an 18-hole, par-72 golf course and driving range. Winter activities include cross-country skiing, sledding, and tobogganing.

Emery Park (716-652-1380), 2084 Emery Road (Route 200), South Wales. Open daily, dawn to dusk. Free admission. This park was established in 1925, when the parks commission purchased 175 acres from Josiah Emery. Today the park has 489 acres. Facilities include baseball diamonds, biking and hiking trails, and picnic tables, along with cross-country ski trails and downhill skiing with a T-bar.

Hamlin Park (716-652-8866), Prospect and South Grove Street, East Aurora. A 16-acre village park, located just a few blocks from the historic Roycroft Inn. Facilities include a large picnic area, playground, baseball fields, bandstand, tennis courts, and running track.

Knox Farm State Park (716-655-7200), 437 Buffalo Road (Seneca Street), East Aurora. This 633-acre park, formerly known as Ess Kay Farm, the estate of East Aurora's socially prominent Knox family, is a mixture of grasslands, woodlands, pastures, and ponds. Park activities include hiking, biking, horseback riding (by permit), and cross-country skiing. The park also has a number of farm animals used in educational programs. The visitor center has exhibits on nature, agriculture, and the farm's history.

✳ Lodging

INNS AND RESORTS **Hampton Inn and Suites** (716-655-3300 or 800-875-9440), 49 Olean Road, East Aurora. This inn features 80 deluxe guest rooms, including eight Jacuzzi suites with fireplaces. Amenities include an indoor heated pool, fitness center, and complimentary breakfast. $$.

○ **Roycroft Inn** (716-652-5552, www.roycroftinn.com), 40 South Grove Street, East Aurora. A designated National Historic Landmark inn built in 1905 and restored in 1995. The 22 unique guest suites have original and reproduction furnishings, along with modern amenities like Jacuzzi tubs, VCR TVs, and thick terry cloth robes. Each room has the name of a notable personality carved into the door, including Ralph Waldo Emerson, Henry David Thoreau, and Susan B. Anthony. $$.

ROYCROFT INN

✳ Where to Eat

DINING OUT **The Old Orchard Inn** (716-652-4664; www.oldorchardny.com), 2095 Blakeley Road, East Aurora. Tuesday–Thursday 4–8 PM, Friday–Saturday 4–9 PM, Sunday 12–8 PM. Also open for lunch during warmer months. This cozy restaurant, built in 1901 as a hunting lodge and converted to a tea-room in 1931, is located on 25 acres in the countryside. Home-cooked entrees include everything from chicken fricassee to surf and turf.

Rick's on Main (716-652-1253; www.ricksonmain.com), 687 Main Street, East Aurora. Lunch Monday–Friday 11 AM–2:30 PM, Saturday 12–3 PM. Dinner Monday–Thursday 5–10 PM, Friday–Saturday 5–11 PM. A contemporary restaurant, specializing in steaks and pasta, located in an older home right in the village.

The Roycroft Inn (716-652-5552; www.roycroftinn.com), 40 South Grove Street, East Aurora. The dining room is open for lunch Monday–Saturday 11:30 AM–3 PM; dinner Sunday 4:30-9 PM, Monday–Thursday 5–9 PM, Friday and Saturday 5–10 PM; Sunday brunch 10 AM–2 PM. The restaurant in the 1905 National Historic Landmark inn has a menu that features locally produced and seasonal ingredients. They are well known for their Sunday brunch buffet. During the warmer months guests can dine outdoors on the peristyle. The inn's more casual Craftsman Lounge, which serves soups, salads, and sandwiches, is open 3 PM–closing.

🍴 **Tony Rome's Globe Hotel & Restaurant** (716-652-4221; tonyromesea.com), 711 Main Street, East Aurora. Open Monday–Thursday 11 AM–10 PM, Friday–Saturday 11 AM–11 PM, Sunday 12–9 PM. Located in a historic 1824 hotel and stagecoach stop, this casual restaurant is East Aurora's oldest business operating in its original location—it was frequented by Millard Fillmore and Grover Cleveland. The building's exterior has changed little from the 1860s, while the interior also reflects its heritage, including exposed-beam ceilings in the dining room, tin ceilings in the bar, and an unusual twin fireplace. The restaurant is noted for its barbecue ribs. Other selections include steak, chicken, and fish fry seven days a week.

Yoshi (716-714-9372; www.yoshiea.com) 33 Elm Street, East Aurora. Tuesday–Friday 11:30 AM–2:30 PM and 4:30–9:30 PM, Saturday 12–10 PM. Enjoy authentic Japanese sushi, along with meat dishes, noodle dishes, craft beer, wine, and sake.

EATING OUT **189 Public House** (716-652-8189; www.oneeightynine.com), 189 Main Street, East Aurora. Tuesday–Thursday 11:30 AM–10 PM, Friday–Saturday 11:30 AM–12 AM, Sunday 12–11 PM. This bar and restaurant serves a variety of whiskeys, has a nano-brewery on-site and comfort food on the menu. Live music is featured on select evenings.

Arriba Tortilla (716-714-9176 www.arribatortilla.com), 40 Riley Street, East Aurora. Monday–Thursday 11:30 AM–9 PM, Friday–Saturday 11:30 AM–10 PM, Sunday 12–8 PM. Enjoy authentic Mexican cuisine, like their signature flatbreads, enchiladas, burritos, fajitas, and tacos, along with a tequila bar that features 90 varieties of tequila.

🍴 **Bar Bill Tavern** (716-652-7959; www.barbill.com), 185 Main Street, East Aurora. Monday–Saturday 8 AM–2 AM, Sunday 12 PM–2 AM. They do not accept credit cards. A popular neighborhood tavern that's an East Aurora institution. Specialties include beef on weck in three sizes and several varieties of super-jumbo chicken wings. *Buffalo Spree* magazine declared Bar Bill Tavern's wings Buffalo's best in 2015. They also offer five different kinds of French fries.

🍴 🍴 **Charlie's** (716-655-0282), 510 Main Street, East Aurora. Open Monday–Saturday 6 AM–8 PM, Sunday 7 AM–1 PM. This popular restaurant has been at this location for over 60 years. Menu selections include hearty fare like omelets and

French toast for breakfast, homemade soups and specialty burgers for lunch, and meat loaf and liver and onions for dinner. During the warmer months, the patio is *the* place to dine, with customers waiting an hour or more for a table.

Dy's Country Kitchen (716-655-4539), 11512 Bullis Road, Marilla. Daily 7 AM–2 PM. This rural café is noted for the area's best potato pancakes.

Elm Street Bakery (716-652-4720; www.elmstreetbakery.com), 72 Elm Street, East Aurora. Tuesday–Friday 7 AM–9 PM, Saturday 8 AM–9 PM, Sunday 9 AM–2 PM. Elm Street Bakery is known for artisan breads and pastries. The café has soups, sandwiches, and salads, with a market diner menu at 5 PM.

✐ ♿ ☙ **Iron Kettle Restaurant** (716-652-5310; www.ironkettlerestaurant .net), 1009 Olean Road (2 miles south of the village), East Aurora. Open daily 8 AM–8 PM. This large family restaurant features country decor and hospitality. You can dine in their bright and cheerful dining rooms, or eat outdoors on the screened patio in the warmer months. The menu features family favorites like sandwiches, wraps, salads, and pastas. Dinner selections include steaks, ribs, roast beef, pork chops, and a Friday fish fry.

McDuffies Bakery 718 Main Street, East Aurora. Monday–Friday 8 AM–6 PM, Saturday 8 AM–4 PM. They are noted for their pot pies and baked goods.

Taste (716-655-1874; www.tasteofea .com), 634 Main Street, East Aurora. Open Monday–Thursday 7 AM–10 PM, Friday 7 AM–11 PM, Saturday 8 AM–11 PM, Sunday 8 AM–10 PM. Located in the former Griggs & Ball building, this cozy café with brick walls and exposed ceilings offers hearty fare for breakfast, lunch, and dinner. Breakfast, which is served all day, includes selections like Belgian waffles and tiramisu French toast. All meals include fresh-baked scones, muffins, buns, or bagels. Some items on the menu reflect East Aurora's heritage. Try a *Millard Fill-me-more*, a chicken salad in a bistro blanket, or *Fish-for-a-price*, a real toy-town favorite.

Wallenwein's Hotel (716-652-9801), 641 Oakwood, East Aurora. Open Monday–Thursday 10 AM–12 AM, Friday and Saturday 10 AM–1 AM, Sunday 12 PM–12 AM. This turn-of-the-twentieth-century hotel is now a tavern and restaurant noted for chicken wings and a Friday fish fry. Enjoy your meal in the dining room or outdoors on the deck.

✳ Entertainment

THEATERS **Aurora Theater** (652-1660; theauroratheatre.com), 673 Main Street, East Aurora. Enjoy major motion pictures, along with independent and foreign films, in a 600-seat circa-1925 theater.

Aurora Players (716-687-6727; www .auroraplayers.org). This 70-year-old community theater group presents performances in the rustic Roycroft Pavilion in Hamlin Park. This historic pavilion seating 200 people was built by and for the Roycrofters and dedicated on July 4, 1903.

✳ Selective Shopping

ANTIQUES **Punkins Patch Antiques** (716-655-6235), 93 Elm Street, East Aurora. Open Wednesday–Saturday 11 AM–5 PM. An early 1900s mill building is now an antiques shop carrying a large selection of household accessories, glassware, silver, books, linens, furniture, tools, and Buffalo-related items.

Roycroft Campus Antiques (716-655-1565; www.roycroftantiques.com), 37 South Grove Street, East Aurora (Roycroft Campus). Open Monday–Saturday 10 AM–5 PM, Sunday 11 AM–4 PM. Located in the original Roycroft furniture building, this shop features antiques, collectibles, furniture, and original Roycroft items.

ART GALLERIES **Meibohm Fine Arts** (716-652-0940; www.meibohmfinearts

.com), 478 Main Street, East Aurora. Open Tuesday–Saturday 9:30 AM–5:30 PM. This family-owned and operated shop has been an East Aurora fixture since 1957. The Meibohm name has been known in western New York since 1901, when Carl Meibohm was the photographer at the Pan-Am Exposition. The store features a selection of artwork for collectors and home decorators, specializing in antique and vintage prints plus works by local artists.

FARM MARKETS ✐ **Bipperts Farm Market** (716-668-4328; bippertsfarms.com), 5220 Clinton Street (near Transit), Elma. Hours vary seasonally, closed January and February. For over 50 years, the Bippert family has been selling fresh produce grown on their 500-acre farm, along with fresh Angus beef raised on the farm. Their in-house bakery features baked goods made fresh daily, plus a variety of jams and jellies.

SPECIAL SHOPS **Aurora Popcorn Shop** (716-652-1660, theauroratheatre.com/aurora-popcorn-shop), 673 Main Street, East Aurora. Located inside the lobby of the Aurora Theater, this shop has a variety of gourmet popcorns.

Aurora Rails and Hobbies (716-652-5718; www.aurora-rails.com), 2268 Blakeley Road, East Aurora. Monday and Wednesday 8 AM–6 PM, Tuesday and Thursday 8 AM–7:30 PM, Friday 8 AM–5:30 PM. Model-railroad enthusiasts will enjoy this shop, which specializes in trains and accessories for all scales of model railroads.

The Bookworm (716-652-6554, www.eabookworm.com), 34 Elm Street, East Aurora. Monday–Thursday 10 AM–6 PM, Friday 10 AM–9 PM, Saturday 9 AM–4 PM. They carry a large selection of new and used books as well as gift items.

East Aurora Cooperative Market (www.eastaurora.coop), 591 Main Street, East Aurora. Daily 7 AM–9 PM. A retail food co-op.

East Aurora Flea Market at the East Aurora Auction and Events Center (716-655-7500; www.eastauroraevents.com), 11167 Big Tree Road, East Aurora. Saturday–Sunday 8:30 AM–4:30 PM. An 180,000-square-foot indoor and outdoor facility that features antiques, collectibles, produce, furniture, flea market items, and more.

Four Honey Bees Cottage (716-652-0292; fourhoneybeescottage.com), 306 Main Street, East Aurora. Monday–Saturday 10 AM–5 PM, Sunday 12–4 PM. This shop, located in a beautifully restored home, features a nicely displayed array of furniture and home decor items, including unique glassware, dishes, gifts, jewelry, and accessories.

✐ **Fisher-Price Toy Store** (716-687-3300; www.fisherpricetoystore.com), 636 Girard Avenue, East Aurora. Open Monday–Friday 10 AM–6 PM, Saturday 10 AM–5 PM. Located right in front of the Fisher-Price Toy Factory, this store has an extensive collection of Fisher-Price and Mattel items, including closeouts.

Head Over Heels in Love with Shoes (716-655-1811; www.headoverheelsea.com), 662 Main Street, East Aurora. Monday–Thursday 11 AM–6 PM, Friday 11 AM–7 PM, Saturday 10 AM–8 PM, Sunday 11 AM–5 PM. This shop features shoes, jewelry, clothing, accessories, and more. A connected shop, **Bella Casa**, has a variety of home decor items.

Marilla Country Store (716-655-1031; www.marillacountrystore.com), 1673 Two Rod Road (corner of Bullis Road) Marilla. Monday–Saturday 10 AM–7 PM, Sunday 10 AM–6 PM. This place has a little bit of everything, from hardware to gifts. Originally opened in 1851, the store still serves locals as a grocery and dry-goods store on the first floor. But climb up to the second floor to browse the area's largest selection of country decorating items. The building features the original floor, countertops, and gaslights. A museum located on the second floor has displays of inventory and store

THE MARILLA COUNTRY STORE HAS BEEN IN BUSINESS SINCE 1851

fixtures from the past as well as a Porter music box.

Muse Jar (716-655-1015, www.musejar .com), 17 Elm Street, East Aurora. A good place to get art supplies and sign up for drawing and painting workshops.

Made in America Store (716-652-4USA; www.saveourcountryfirst.com), 1000 West Maple Court, Elma. Founded in 2010 by Mark Andol, the store, which only sells merchandise made in America, has numerous locations in the Buffalo area, including this flagship store, located just off the 400 Expressway at the Maple Road exit. It has actually become a tourist destination for bus tour groups, who are attracted to the store's mission of preserving American jobs.

Roycroft Copper Shop Gallery (716-655-0261; www .roycroftcampuscorporation.com), 31 South Grove Street, East Aurora. Open daily 10 AM–5 PM. Located in the original copper shop on the Roycroft Campus, this shop is operated by the Roycroft Campus Corporation. The front room serves as a museum space, with original Roycroft printing presses and artifacts.

The middle of the section features unique handcrafted items, including some high-end furniture and glass items, made by local artisans as well as Roycroft artisans from all over the country. The back of the shop is set up as a meeting space, as classes and seminars are held here throughout the year.

Roycroft Artisans Schoolhouse Gallery (716-655-3229), 1054 Olean Road, East Aurora. Open Monday–Saturday 10 AM–4 PM. This shop, located in a circa-1850 former schoolhouse, features the work of Roycroft Renaissance artisans.

Upstairs Treasures (716-652-1146; www.upstairstreasures.com), 662 Main Street rear (Church Street entrance), East Aurora. Tuesday–Friday 11 AM–5 PM, Saturday 11 AM–6 PM. Gift items, including antiques, folk art, Mission furniture, quilts, and collectible dolls. Local crafters make many of the items, such as stained-glass lamps, folk art on wood and slate, and hand-knit sweaters.

✧ & ⬥ **Vidlers 5 & 10** (716-652-0481; www.vidlers5and10.com), 680–694 Main Street, East Aurora. Open Monday–Thursday, Saturday 9 AM–6 PM; Friday 9 AM–

VIDLER'S 5 & 10 IS ONE OF EAST AURORA'S MOST BELOVED LANDMARK

9 PM, Sunday 11 AM–5 PM. Look for the red-and-white awning on Main Street, and you'll find one of East Aurora's most beloved landmarks. Vidlers 5 & 10, housed in four connected 1890s-era buildings, has retained the atmosphere of an old-fashioned five-and-dime. They sell many interesting and hard-to-find items along with yarn, fabric, crafts, housewares, toys, books, candy, and cards. This business has been family-owned since 1930, when Robert Vidler Sr. opened the store in the midst of the Great Depression.

✳ Special Events

June: **Chamber Music Festival** (www.roycroftchambermusic.org), St. Matthias Church, 374 Main Street, East Aurora. Musicians from all over the US and Canada come to perform at this festival. **Roycroft Summer Festival** (www.ralaweb.com/our-shows), Roycroft Campus, East Aurora. An arts, crafts, and fine art show held the last full weekend of June.

August: **Wildlife and Renaissance Festival** (716-652-8646; www.hawkcreek.org), Hawk Creek Wildlife Center. An open house at the wildlife center features up-close encounters with hawks and other birds of prey.

December: **Roycroft Winter Festival** (www.ralaweb.com/our-shows), East Aurora Middle School. Craftsmen and artisans display their wares for holiday shopping during the first weekend of December.

ORCHARD PARK AND WEST SENECA

Orchard Park, founded by Quakers in the early 1800s, is a 40-square-mile town of rolling hills and wooded area dotted with lovely homes and many small businesses. The town's center is the village of Orchard Park, located at the "Four Corners" where Routes 277 and 20A intersect. It is a town for all seasons. In spring and summer, enjoy concerts at the Quaker Arts Pavilion. Come fall, get a start on your holiday shopping at the Quaker Arts Festival or cheer on the Buffalo Bills at New Era Stadium. In winter, head to Chestnut Ridge Park for tobogganing, skiing, and sledding. Nearby West Seneca is mainly residential, along with a large shopping plaza.

AREA CODE The area code is 716.

GUIDANCE **Orchard Park Chamber of Commerce** (716-662-3366; www.orchardpark chamber.com), 6524 East Quaker Road, Orchard Park.
    West Seneca Chamber of Commerce (716-674-4900; www.westseneca.org), 950 Union Road, #205, West Seneca.

GETTING THERE *By bus:* NFTA #72, an express route, travels between downtown Buffalo and Orchard Park. Bus #75 travels from downtown Buffalo to West Seneca.
    By car: Route 219, Orchard Park exit (Route 20A), Exit 55 off I-90 to West Seneca.

MEDICAL EMERGENCY Dial 911.
    Mercy Ambulatory Care Center (716-662-0500), 3669 Southwestern Boulevard, Orchard Park.

✳ To See

BREWERIES **Rusty Nickel Brewing** (716-608-6155; www.rustynickelbrewing.com/us), 4350 Seneca Street, West Seneca. A small-batch brewery located adjacent to the Ebenezer Ale House. See *Eating Out.*

MUSEUMS AND HISTORIC SITES **Firemen's Memorial Exhibit Center** (716-712-0413), 4141 Seneca Street, West Seneca. An exhibit about firefighting in western New York.
    Orchard Park Historical Society (716-662-2185), 4287 South Buffalo Street, Orchard Park. Call for hours. This circa-1870 brick Italianate architecture mansion was the home of Dr. Willard Jolls, a beloved country doctor who served Orchard Park and the surrounding communities. It currently houses the collections of the Orchard Park Historical Society.
    Quaker Meeting House (716-662-5749), 6924 East Quaker Street, Orchard Park. The Quaker Meeting House, constructed in 1820, is still a place of worship for the Quakers (Sunday service 11 AM). When it was built, a partition in the center separated the men from the women. The original hand-built wooden benches are still used today.

West Seneca Historical Society (716-674-4283; www.westsenecahistory.com), 919 Mill Road, West Seneca. Open Tuesday 10 AM–4 PM and on the first Sunday of the month 2–4 PM, or by appointment. Local history artifacts, including items from Seneca and other Native Americans and the Ebenezers, are displayed in an original 1850 Lower Ebenezer Society building.

✳ To Do

FAMILY FUN See *Green Space—Chestnut Ridge Park.*

GOLF **Bob-o-Link Golf Course** (716-662-4311; www.bobolinkgolf.com), 4085 Transit Road, Orchard Park. Open April–October. Driving range and 18-hole, par-3 golf course, which is lit at night.

✳ Green Space

NATURE PRESERVES *ə* **Charles E. Burchfield Nature and Art Center** (716-677-4843; www.burchfieldnac.org), 2001 Union Road at Clinton Street, West Seneca. Trails open daily dawn to dusk. This 29-acre nature preserve includes nature trails, gardens, a children's adventure area, and more. The visitor center building is currently under long-term repairs until 2018.

PARKS *ə* **Chestnut Ridge Park** (716-662-3290), 6121 Chestnut Ridge Road, Orchard Park. Chestnut Ridge, the largest park in Erie County, is popular year-round for a variety of activities. Winter activities include toboggan chutes, cross-country skiing, snowshoeing, sledding, and snowmobiling. In the warmer months Chestnut Ridge is a haven for picnickers, runners, and tennis players.

Yates Park (716-662-6450), South Buffalo Street, Orchard Park. This 51-acre town park located along Green Lake is technically for Orchard Park residents only. It includes picnic areas, boating access, swings, and hiking trails. An outdoor skateboard park is open spring, summer, and fall. In winter it becomes an ice skating rink.

WATERFALLS **Eternal Flame Falls.** Located in a secluded gorge within Chestnut Ridge Park, this 35-foot waterfall has three natural gas flames 3–9" long that flare out from the base of the waterfall. It can be reached via a short but challenging hike. For specific directions, contact the Orchard Park Chamber of Commerce or Chestnut Ridge Park.

NATURE ART ABOUNDS ON THE GROUNDS OF THE CHARLES E. BURCHFIELD NATURE & ART CENTER

TOBOGGAN CHUTES AT CHESTNUT RIDGE PARK

✳ Lodging

MOTELS AND HOTELS **Hampton Inn Buffalo South** (716-824-2030), 1750 Ridge Road, West Seneca. A five-story hotel with 105 guest rooms, five of them suites. Amenities include a small indoor pool and an exercise room. $$$.

✳ Where to Eat

DINING OUT **The Byrd House** (716-662-3909; www.thebyrdhouse.com), 4190 North Buffalo Street, Orchard Park. Enjoy pub food like burgers, wings, and a fish fry. They also have live music.

Connor's (716-674-9945; connorsofwestseneca.com), 3465 Seneca Street, West Seneca. Open Monday–Thursday 11 AM–10 PM, Friday–Saturday 11 AM–11 PM, Sunday 12–8 PM. The menu features a variety of items, from sandwiches to steak and seafood.

The Dove (716-823-6680; www.thedoveny.com), 3002 Abbott Road, Orchard Park. Open for lunch Monday–Friday 11:30 AM–2 PM, dinner Monday 5–8 PM, Tuesday–Saturday 5–9 PM. This restaurant specializes in upscale Italian food, with menu selections including veal piccata and eggplant parmigiana, as well as filet mignon.

Homegrown Bistro (716-725-3849, www.homegrownop.com), 4211 North Buffalo Street, Orchard Park. Monday 10 AM–3 PM, Tuesday–Sunday 8 AM–3 PM. Vegan sandwiches, including many gluten-free offerings, along with paninis and house-made sausages.

Mangia Ristorante & Caffé (716-9467; www.mangiaristorante.com), 4264 North Buffalo Road, Orchard Park. Lunch Monday–Saturday 11 AM–3 PM, dinner Monday–Thursday 4–10 PM, Friday–Saturday 4–11 PM. Mangia, meaning "eat" in Italian, is a fitting name for this elegant, brick-walled restaurant. Chose from pasta specialties, along with a lunch menu that includes salads, wraps, paninis, and more. Upstairs, enjoy cocktails in the upscale M Lounge.

Orchard Park Social Tap & Grille (www.opsocialtapandgrille.com), 4247 North Buffalo Street, Orchard Park. Open daily 4–10 PM. Brick-oven pizza, small plates, and more are features on the menu of this upscale sports bar.

HOMEGROWN BISTRO IN ORCHARD PARK OFFERS MANY VEGAN AND GLUTEN-FREE DISHES

Scharf's German Restaurant (716-895-7249, www.scharfsrest.com), 2683 Clinton Street, West Seneca. Open Tuesday–Sunday 4–9 PM, reservations requested. Enjoy German delicacies like sauerbraten, wiener schnitzel, and potato pancakes, along with German beers.

Schwabl's Restaurant (716-674-9821; www.schwabls.com), 789 Center Road, West Seneca. Open Monday–Saturday 11 AM–10:30 PM, Sunday 1–8:30 PM. This restaurant has been in business since 1837 and at its present location since 1942. It's best known for its beef on weck, but other menu selections include reasonably priced beef and seafood dishes and a daily fish fry.

EATING OUT **Cappelli's** (716-662-2290; www.cappellipizza.com), 3643 North Buffalo Road, Orchard Park. Open Monday–Thursday 10 AM–9:30 PM, Friday and Saturday 10 AM–10 PM, Sunday 2–9:30 PM. Since 1986 Gerard and Jodie Cappelli have been serving up pizza, subs, wings, and pasta to Orchard Park residents.

Danny's South Restaurant (716-649-1194; www.dannysrestaurant.com), 4300 Abbott Road, Orchard Park. Open Monday–Thursday 11 AM–11 PM, Friday and Saturday 11 AM–midnight, Sunday 10 AM–8 PM. A casual Irish-themed restaurant located near the stadium which serves a variety of food such as chicken, steaks, fresh seafood, and salads.

Duff's (716-674-7212), 3090 Orchard Park Road, Orchard Park. Open Monday–Thursday 11 AM–11 PM, Friday and Saturday 11 AM–midnight, Sunday 11 AM–10 PM. Chicken wings are the specialty of the house at this popular Southtowns branch of the original Duff's in Amherst.

Ebenezer Ale House (716-674-BEER; www.ebenezeralehouse.com), 4348 Seneca Street, West Seneca. Their extensive menu includes appetizers, wings, ribs, pizza, pasta, and burgers. There are 21 craft beers on tap, including some from the adjacent Rusty Nickel Brewing. See *Breweries*.

Great Lakes Station (716-675-5001), 1729 Union Road, West Seneca. Open seasonally April–September, Monday–Saturday 11 AM–11 PM, Sunday 12–11 PM. This is *the* place to come for ice cream in West Seneca. Housed in a bright-red train caboose, this stand serves up all sorts of ice cream treats, including cones, malts, shakes, and sundaes. Choose from hard ice cream or soft custard along with fruit slush and lemon ice. They have the only drive-up ice cream window in the area.

Kone King (716-675-8282; www .konekingwestseneca.com), 865 Center Road, West Seneca. A family-owned and operated creamery. Check their website for the flavor of the week.

LT's Olde Time Pizza and Subs (716-674-8202; www.ltspizzaandsubs.com), 1311 Union Road, West Seneca. Sunday–Thursday 9 AM–9 PM, Friday–Saturday 9 AM–10 PM. This casual eatery features generously sized, freshly made subs and pizza, including several specialty pizzas. They also have wraps, soups, salads, quesadillas, wings, and fingers.

Taffy's Hot Dog Stand (716-675-0264), 3261 Orchard Park Road, Orchard Park. Seasonally 11 AM–10 PM daily. In business over 60 years, this stand features 120 different flavors of milkshakes, along with burgers, subs, and hot dogs.

✳ Entertainment

MUSIC **Orchard Park Symphony Orchestra** (716-643-4000; opsymphony .org), September–March. Performances take place in the Orchard Park High School auditorium.

PROFESSIONAL SPORTS **Buffalo Bills Football** (716-648-1800 or tickets 877-BB-TICKS; www.buffalobills.com), New Era Stadium, One Bills Drive, Orchard Park. New Era Stadium features one of the largest Jumbotrons in the United States. Built in 1973, the facility can hold over 80,000 spectators.

✳ Selective Shopping

Major shopping areas include **Southgate Plaza** (716-674-5050; www.southgate plaza.com), Union Road and Seneca Street, West Seneca. Open Monday–Saturday 10 AM–9 PM, Sunday 12–5 PM.

FARM MARKETS **Orchard Park Farmers' & Artisan Market** (716-249-0641), 4050 North Buffalo Road, Orchard Park. Open Thursdays 3–7 PM, May–October.

SPECIAL SHOPS **Arthur's Home Furnishings** (716-662-2158; www.arthurs homefurnishings.com), 4288 South Buffalo Street, Orchard Park. Monday–Saturday 9 AM–6 PM. This business, which has furniture, accessories, and gifts, has been serving the village of Orchard Park since 1907.

Country Peddlers (716-675-4670, www .countrypeddlers.net), 1340 Orchard Park Road, West Seneca. Daily 7 AM–9 PM. This store features a deli, a bakery, produce, and even an ice cream shop.

Research & Design (716-662-0800, www.researchanddesign.com), 4109 North Buffalo Street, Orchard Park. Monday–Saturday 10:30 AM–6 PM (Thursday until 8 PM), Sunday 12–4 PM. Clothing and accessories can be found in this upscale shop which is located in an old barn.

Village Togs (716-662-0977), 4282 South Buffalo Street, Orchard Park. Monday–Saturday 10 AM–5 PM. This shop carries good quality ladies' clothing and jewelry.

✳ Special Events

February: **Winterfest** (chestnut ridgeconservancy.org), Chestnut Ridge Park, 6121 Chestnut Ridge Road, Orchard Park.

THE LATEST FASHIONS AND ACCESSORIES CAN BE FOUND AT RESEARCH AND DESIGN

July: **Quaker Days** (716-662-3366; www.orchardparkchamber.com), Orchard Park. This village-wide event includes sidewalk sales and a car show.

Sunday before Labor Day: **Classic Car Show** (716-674-5050; www.southgateplaza.com), Southgate Plaza, West Seneca.

September: **Quaker Arts Festival** (www.opjaycees.com), Orchard Park. Village-wide indoor and outdoor arts and crafts festival, featuring over 400 artists and craftsmen.

October: **Halloween Parade** (716-674-5050; www.southgateplaza.com), Southgate Plaza, West Seneca.

LAKE ERIE TOWNS

Hamburg, Blasdell, Eden, Angola,
and Derby (also North Collins)

Lake Erie and Erie County were named after the Erie Indians, who made their home in this area. The Hamburg Fairgrounds, site of the Erie County Fair, the largest county fair in the United States, was once the location of a Native American village. Eighteen Mile Creek, which runs through the town of Hamburg, is internationally famous for Devonian fossils found along its banks.

Hamburg is a 45-square-mile town incorporated in 1812. In those early days, a large number of wolves and panthers roamed the dense forests in the area. Prior to 1850 Hamburg included the towns of Orchard Park and West Seneca. A number of the earliest settlers to the town came from New England around 1803, followed in the 1830s by Germans, many of whom established farms.

The nearby town of Eden is best known for the Original American Kazoo Company. Established in 1916, the company is the only metal kazoo factory in the world. This working museum is still making kazoos using the same process and equipment as when the factory first opened.

The villages of Angola and Blasdell, located along Lake Erie, have several popular beaches. Farther south on Lake Erie's shores is Derby, home to the Frank Lloyd Wright–designed mansion Graycliff, which is open for tours.

AREA CODE The area code is 716.

GUIDANCE Hamburg Chamber of Commerce (716-649-7917; www.hamburg-chamber .org), 6122 South Park Avenue, Hamburg.

Hamburg Village Advisory Council (www.facebook.com/hamburgvbac)

  ♿ **Lake Erie Seaway Trail Visitors Center** (lakeerieseawaytrail.org), Route 5 (along Lake Erie) Hamburg. Memorial Day–Labor Day, hours vary. This visitor center, located in the former Wanakah Water Works, has Seaway Trail information. An observation deck overlooks Lake Erie.

GETTING THERE *By bus:* NFTA bus #30 travels between downtown Buffalo and Hamburg.

By car: The New York State Thruway (I-90) exit 57A will bring you into the area, as will Route 62.

MEDICAL EMERGENCY Dial 911.

❋ To See

ART MUSEUMS Centennial Art Center of Hamburg (716-649-3592), 3185 Amsdell Road, Hamburg. Call for current hours and classes. A nonprofit community art center that offers classes, workshops, lectures, and demonstrations.

BREWERIES AND WINERIES **Hamburg Brewing** (716-649-3249; www.hamburg brewing.com), 6553 Boston State Road, Hamburg. Monday–Tuesday 3–10 PM, Wednesday–Sunday 12–10 PM, Sunday 12–8 PM. Opened in 2013, this brewery has a taproom plus an outdoor dining patio with a limited menu that includes a few pizzas and sandwiches, along with over a dozen beers on tap. Live music is featured on Wednesday and Saturday.

Ten Thousand Vines Winery (716-646-9979, www.tenthousandvines.com), 8 South Buffalo Street, Hamburg. Located in a former firehouse by Hamburg's traffic circle, this winery offers tastings and sales of wines that are crafted in small batches. They also sell home winemaking supplies.

TEN THOUSAND VINES WINERY IN HAMBURG

MUSEUMS AND HISTORIC HOMES **Hamburg Historical Society** (716-648-6320; www.hamburghistoricalsociety.org), 5859 South Park Avenue, Hamburg. Open Saturday 12–3 PM or by appointment.

Graycliff (585-614-6195; graycliffestate.org), 6472 Old Lake Shore Road, Derby. A variety of tours of the house and grounds are offered, see website for descriptions. Built in 1927, this magnificent lakeside home, set on a 70-foot cliff overlooking Lake Erie, was the summer home of Darwin D. Martin, an executive at the Larkin Soap Company in Buffalo. Mr. Martin commissioned renowned architect Frank Lloyd Wright, who also

THE FRANK LLOYD WRIGHT DESIGNED GRAYCLIFF OVERLOOKS LAKE ERIE

designed Martin's house on Jewett Parkway in Buffalo, to design his summer retreat. Graycliff is referred to as a see-through house: It uses the first-story windows to frame the scenery on the Lake Erie side, and when standing on the front lawn of the house, one can look straight through to see the lake. Wright incorporated shapes he found in the surrounding landscape into his design. For example, diamond shapes found in the limestone along the lakeshore provided a motif repeated inside the home.

✐ ☂ **Original American Kazoo Company** (716-992-3960; www.edenkazoo.com), 8703 South Main Street, Eden. Monday–Thursday and Saturday 10 AM–5 PM, Friday 10 AM–7 PM. The Kazoo Capital of the World, Eden is home to the only metal kazoo factory in existence. Kazoos of all shapes and sizes are on permanent display at the museum, where you can learn the history of the kazoo and view kazoos being made on the original 1907 equipment. You can even make your own kazoo using a purchased form and a special press machine. The museum also has a large gift shop.

✽ To Do

FAMILY FUN Just Fun Family Entertainment Center (716-648-3222; www.justfun hamburgny.com), 6000 South Park Avenue, Hamburg. This fun center features an arcade, black light mini golf, bumper cars, and more.

GOLF 18 Mile Creek Golf Course (716-648-4410; www.townofhamburgny.com), 6374 Boston State Road, Hamburg. Open April–November. A public 18-hole, par-72 course.
    Eden Valley Golf Course (716-337-2190; www.edenvalleygolf.com), 10401 Sisson Highway (NY 75), Eden. Open April–November An 18-hole, par-73 public course with restaurant and full bar.
    Grandview Golf Course and Beachside Bar & Grill (716-549-4930), 444 Central Avenue, Angola. Open mid-February–November. A public 9-hole, par-36 course.

HORSE RACING ☂ Fairgrounds Gaming & Raceway (716-649-1280; www.the-fairgrounds.com/hamburg-gaming, www.buffaloraceway.com), 5600 McKinley Parkway, Hamburg. Open seven days 8 AM–4 AM, live harness racing January–July, Wednesday, Friday, and Saturday at 7:35 PM. The raceway's half-mile track was first used in 1868 during the county fair. Pari-mutuel harness racing began here in the 1940s. The grandstand and clubhouse, owned and operated by the Erie County Agricultural Society, can hold up to 10,000 racing fans. The clubhouse also features a 55,000-square-foot gaming floor that features close to 900 gaming machines.

✽ Green Space

BEACHES Bennett Beach, Bennett Road, off Route 5, Derby. This sand dune–lined beach is popular with swimmers, fishermen, and birdwatchers.
    Wendt Beach (716-947-5660), 7676 Old Lake Shore Road, Derby. This Erie County beach is located on Lake Erie at the mouth of Big Sister Creek. There is a bathhouse and snack bar near the beach. The 178-acre park has picnic areas, bike and nature trails, and sports fields. It is also a popular spot to view waterfowl and to fish.
    Woodlawn Beach State Park (716-826-1930), S-3585 Lake Shore Road, Blasdell. This park is known for its mile-long natural sand beach and its panoramic view of Lake Erie. During the summer months, visitors can swim, windsurf, play volleyball, and

SUNSET AT WOODLAWN BEACH STATE PARK

sunbathe. It is also a good place to bird-watch, especially during the migration seasons. The park also has a playground, hiking trails, visitor center, and nature exhibits.

NATURE PRESERVES ✤ **Penn Dixie Paleontological and Outdoor Education Center** (716-627-4560; www.penndixie.org), 4050 North Street, Hamburg. Open April–October, days and hours vary. Once a quarry, this 32-acre regional fossil site is owned and operated by the Hamburg Natural History Society, founded in 1993 to protect and promote education about natural resources. The site contains an abundance of 380-million-year-old fossils from the Devonian era. The public can visit the site to study and collect fossils and learn about local geology.

PARKS **Woodlawn Beach State Park** (716-826-1930), S-3585 Lake Shore Road, Blasdell. See *Beaches*.

✳ Lodging

INNS **Marienthal Country Inn** (716-337-0160, www.marienthalcountryinn.com), 5107 Langford Road, Eden. Enjoy a romantic getaway or a fun girl's weekend at this country inn located in a former church complex. The inn contains four beautifully decorated rooms, along with five bedrooms in the brick house. They offer a variety of art-related workshops and also have banquet facilities. $$.

MOTELS Several major chain motels are just off I-90 exits 56 and 57.

✳ Where to Eat

DINING OUT **Armor Inn** (716-202-1315; www.armorinn.com) 5381 Abbott Road,

Hamburg. Tuesday–Sunday for lunch and dinner; live music on Wednesday and Friday–Sunday. They serve burgers, sandwiches, wings, pizza, mac and cheese, and more.

Carte Blanche (716-649-2101; www.carteblanchehamburg.com), 61 Buffalo Street, Hamburg. Tuesday–Thursday 4–10 PM, Friday–Saturday 4–11 PM, Sunday brunch 10 AM–2 PM. Enjoy upscale dining in the heart of the village of Hamburg.

Daniel's Restaurant (716-648-6554; www.daniels-restaurant.com), 174 Buffalo Street Hamburg. Open Tuesday–Saturday at 5 PM. This intimate restaurant, located in a former residence, has been named one of the top 20 restaurants in western New York by the Buffalo News.

♿ **Ilio DiPaolo's** (716-825-3675; www.iliodipaolos.com), 3785 South Park Avenue, Blasdell. Open for lunch and dinner. Since 1965 this upscale yet casual restaurant has specialized in Italian-American cuisine, plus steaks, chops, and seafood. The walls are adorned with photos and other memorabilia documenting the pro-wrestling career of the late restaurant founder, Ilio DiPaolo. Popular menu selections include veal parmigiana, chicken cacciatore, and linguini with clam sauce.

Lucia's on the Lake (716-627-9752; www.luciasonthelake.com), 4151

ENJOY AUTHENTIC MEXICAN CUISINE AT COYOTE CAFE IN HAMBURG

Lakeshore Road, Hamburg. This restaurant, which has a great view of Lake Erie, is known for their stuffed hot banana peppers, along with seafood, steak, and burgers.

EATING OUT **2 Scoops Ice Cream** (716-863-5184; www.2scoopsicecream.com) 4626 Camp Road, Hamburg. The owners of this ice cream stand make their own soft-serve custard, including several creative flavors. They also have Perry's hard ice cream. You can enjoy your ice cream in homemade waffle cones and bowls.

Butera's Craft Beers and Craft Pizza (716-648-5017; www.buterasbrickoven.com), 32 Main Street, Hamburg. Monday–Thursday 11 AM–10 PM, Friday–Saturday 11 AM–11 PM, Sunday 12–10 PM. This restaurant specializes in handmade brick-oven pizza, as well as burgers and sandwiches.

♿ ⛇ ♿ **Comfort Zone Café** (716-648-5779; www.comfortzonecafe.com), 17 Main Street, Hamburg. Open Monday–Thursday 8 AM–10 PM, Friday–Saturday 8 AM–11 PM, Sunday 9 AM–9 PM. This bright, sunny restaurant with glass-topped tables and a view of Main Street features specialty coffees, teas, and desserts. Lunch and dinner specials—which include homemade soup, sandwiches, and entrees like spaghetti and salmon—are written on the board daily.

♿ **Connor's Hot Dogs** (716-549-1257; www.connorshotdogstand.com), 8905 Lakeshore Road, Angola. Open seasonally Sunday–Thursday 11 AM–10:00PM, Friday–Saturday 11 AM–11 PM. This popular hot dog stand has been family-owned and operated for over 70 years. Choose from hot dogs, burgers, and more, including fried bologna sandwiches, Italian sausage, ice cream, and milkshakes.

♿ **Coyote Café** (716-649-1837; www.thecoyotecafe.com), 36 Main Street, Hamburg. Open Monday 4–11 PM, Tuesday–Thursday 11 AM–9 PM, Friday and Saturday 11 AM–10 PM. Enjoy authentic Mexican cuisine, as well as American fare, in a large dining room with southwestern decor. Specialties include tequila-lime shrimp and pork tenderloin with raspberry glaze.

Dos Amigos (716-823-8247), 3800 Hoover Road, Blasdell. Tuesday–Thursday 4–10 PM. Enjoy waterfront views while dining on upscale tacos and regional Mexican fare, along with margaritas and custom cocktails.

East Eden Tavern & Smokehouse (716-575-4286; www.eastedentavern .com), 8163 East Eden Road, Eden. They specialize in barbecued pork, beef and chicken, along with steaks and country-style comfort food.

El Canelo (716-822-1220, www .elcanelo.com), 3670 McKinley Parkway, Hamburg. Monday–Thursday 11 AM–9:30 PM, Friday–Saturday 11 AM–10 PM, Sunday 12–8 PM. A small, very popular family-friendly, authentic Mexican restaurant. Some say they have the best Mexican cuisine in western New York.

⌀ **Fran-Ceil Custard** (www.franceil custard.com), 3411 South Park Avenue, Blasdell, Monday–Saturday 11 AM–11 PM, Sunday 12–10 PM. Established in the early 1950s, this seasonal custard stand also has hard ice cream, milkshakes, frozen yogurt, and more.

GRANGE COMMUNITY KITCHEN

Grange Community Kitchen (716-648-0022; www.grangecommunity kitchen.com), 22 Main Street, Hamburg. Tuesday–Thursday 7:30 AM–2:30 PM and 4:30–9 PM, Friday–Saturday 7:30 AM–2:30 PM and 4:30–10 PM. This neighborhood restaurant features locally sourced, seasonal ingredients.

Hoak's (716-627-7988 or 716-627-4570), S-4100 Lakeshore Road, Hamburg. Open daily 11 AM–11 PM. A landmark Hamburg restaurant since 1949, this casual lakeside eatery, which has a great view of the Buffalo skyline, specializes in fresh seafood seven days a week. They also have a great beef on weck.

J & M's West End Inn (716-649-9940; www.jandmwestendinn.com), 340 Union Street, Hamburg. They specialize in comfort food, along with beef on weck and burgers.

JP Fitzgerald's (716-649-4025; www .jpfitzgeralds.com), 4236 Clark Street, Hamburg. Monday–Saturday 11 AM–4 AM, Sunday 12 PM–4 AM. A popular, casual restaurant known for their reuben sandwiches and corned beef, which is served seven days a week.

Mammoser's Tavern & Restaurant (716-648-1390), 16 South Buffalo Street, Hamburg. Monday–Thursday11:30 AM–11 PM, Friday–Saturday 11:30 AM–12:30 AM Sunday 12–7 PM. This restaurant is noted for their hot wings, as well as for their 18 microbrews on tap. You can also purchase their sauces.

Mason's Grille 52 (716-649-7519; www.masonsgrille.com), 52 Main Street, Hamburg. A casual fine dining restaurant serving flatbreads, seafood, steak, and more.

The Public House on the Lake (716-627-5551; www.publichouseonthelake .com), 4914 Lakeshore Road, Hamburg. Enjoy a variety of appetizers and entrees with a great view of Lake Erie. Live music is featured on Friday and Saturday.

Rodney's (716-627-5166), 4179 Lakeshore Road, Hamburg. Sunday 12–10 PM, Monday–Saturday 11 AM–12 AM. This restaurant, located across the street from

Lake Erie, serves everything from sandwiches to surf and turf. They also have a Friday fish fry.

✤ **Super Freeze Drive-in** (716-947-5557), 6865 Erie Road, Derby. A '50s-style hamburger joint with references to the television show *Happy Days* on the menu and a replica of Mayberry's sheriff's car outside.

✤ ♿ ✤ **Tubby's Take Out** (716-549-1666), Route 5, Angola. Open seasonally May–August. A small hot dog and ice cream stand serving burgers, dogs, fries, and a variety of ice cream treats. A car cruise night is held Fridays at 6 PM. The adjacent convenience store and gas station, owned by the same family, is open daily 11 AM–11 PM.

✤ **Uncle Joe's Diner** (716-648-7154; www.unclejoesdiner.com), 4869 Southwestern Boulevard, Hamburg. Monday–Thursday 7 AM–10 PM, Friday 7 AM–11 PM, Saturday 6 AM–11 PM, Sunday 6 AM–10 PM. This very popular '50s-style restaurant has menu items that include classic diner food, like burgers and mac and cheese, as well as a fish fry served daily.

✤ ✤ **Water Valley Inn** (716-649-9691; watervalleyinn.com), 6656 Gowanda State Road, Hamburg. Open Tuesday–Friday 11 AM–9 AM, Saturday 12–9 PM, Sunday 12–8 PM. This historic inn dates back to the 1800s, when it served as a tavern and stagecoach stop. The walls of the inn are adorned with historic area photos and a working vintage 1930s bell system is used for calling your server to the table. While the ambiance is good, the food is even better. Menu selections include substantial entrees like steak, chops, seafood, and chicken to lighter fare, including sandwiches, burgers, and homemade soup. They do not accept credit cards.

✽ Selective Shopping

ANTIQUES **Antiques of Hamburg** (716-648-2341), 11 Buffalo Street, Hamburg. Open Monday–Saturday 10 AM–5 PM.

THE HAMBURG FARMER'S MARKET TAKES PLACE MAY THROUGH NOVEMBER

They carry a general line of antiques, including smalls, a category of reasonably priced decorative antiques, as well as glassware, furniture, and books.

FARM MARKETS **Hamburg Farmers' Market**, Saturday 7:30 AM–1 PM, May–November, in the Hamburg municipal parking lot, Union and Main Street, Hamburg.

Zittel's Country Market (716-649-3010; zittels.com), 4415 Southwestern Boulevard (Route 20), Hamburg. Hours vary seasonally, closed January–March. The Zittel family has been making their living growing crops for four generations, since 1898. The season starts out with spring flowers and plants grown in Zittel's Eden Valley greenhouses. Fresh produce is offered throughout the summer and early fall, along with fall decorating items. In December, choose from trees, wreaths, poinsettias, and more, including custom-made gift baskets.

SHOPPING MALLS ♿ **McKinley Mall** (716-824-0462), McKinley Parkway at Milestrip Road, Blasdell. Open Monday–Saturday 10 AM–9 PM, Sunday 11 AM–6 PM. One of western New York's best-kept secrets, this mall has numerous stores and a large food court. Anchor stores include JC Penney and Sears.

SPECIAL SHOPS **Expressions Floral & Gift Shoppe** (716-648-2110; shop expressions.com), 59 Main Street, Hamburg. Open Monday–Friday 8:30 AM–6 PM, Saturday 8:30 AM–5 PM, Sunday 10 AM–2 PM. This floral shop also carries a large selection of seasonal decorations and the wooden Hamburg Village Series, which features historic homes and buildings from the Hamburg area.

Snippets & Gems (716-649-0111, www.facebook.com/snippetsandgems), 31 Buffalo Street, Hamburg. Tuesday–Wednesday and Friday 11 AM–5 PM, Thursday 2–7 PM, Saturday 11 AM–2 PM. A boutique shop which features paintings, jewelry, home decor, antiques, and items made by local artisans.

Sweet Pea Bakery (716-202-1192 www.sweetpeabakerywny.com), 1 Buffalo Street, Hamburg. Monday–Wednesday 9 AM–3 PM, Thursday–Friday 9 AM–6 PM. This bakery features a variety of homemade desserts.

What a Woman Wants (716-649-2034, www.shopwhatawomanwants.com), 1 Buffalo Street, Hamburg. An accessory boutique carrying an array of jewelry, handbags, scarves, clothing, and shoes.

✳ Special Events

July: **Burgerfest** (www.hamburgburgerfest .com), along Main and Buffalo Streets, Hamburg. Celebrate the birth of the hamburger at this annual festival, which takes place the third Saturday of July. Although it's been hotly debated among some burger aficionados as to whether or not the first burger was actually created back in 1885 in this namesake town, it's a good excuse to party and chow down. Events include food vendors, a burger-eating contest, live entertainment, children's activities, a craft show, and a classic car show.

August: **Eden Corn Fest** (716-992-9141), American Legion Post 880, Legion Drive (off Route 62), Eden. Over 500,000 ears of corn are consumed at this four-day festival that pays homage to one of the area's favorite summer delicacies. Activities include rides, entertainment, a parade, and more.

Erie County Fair (www.ecfair.org), Hamburg. The largest county fair in the United States, the Erie County Fair celebrates the agricultural and historic legacy of Erie County. Enjoy amusement rides on the "mile-long midway," browse through barn upon barn of animal exhibits, catch some top-name musical entertainment, view historical displays, buy the latest items for your home, and, of course, consume mass quantities of delicious, and unfortunately fattening, fair food.

November/December: **Fairgrounds Festival of Lights** (716-649-3900; www .fairgroundsholiday.com). Holiday lights and more decorate the fairgrounds. It's one of the largest holiday light displays in the area.

SKI COUNTRY

Boston, Holland, Colden, Glenwood, Springville, and West Falls

This area well south of Buffalo is an area of natural beauty, a perfect destination when taking a drive "to the country." Holland, an area of rolling farmland along Cazenovia Creek, was settled in 1772, and many of the town's residents are descendants of those early settlers. Incorporated in 1818 when it separated from the town of Willink (today known as Aurora), Holland prospered through the middle of the 1800s, especially with the building of a plank road to Buffalo that allowed farm goods to be taken to market. After the Civil War, cheese making was one of the main industries in the area. Holland is probably best known in western New York for the annual tulip festival, heralding the coming of spring. This three-day event includes a parade, rides, and crafts, among other activities.

Formed from a portion of the town of Holland in 1827, Colden was named after Cadwallader Colden, a Scottish American who served as lieutenant governor of New York in the 1760s. The first pioneer to settle in Colden was Richard Buffum, who came from Rhode Island. His sawmill and the surrounding area was referred to as "Buffum's Mills." In the early days, the village had numerous taverns as well as cheese box and barrel factories, due to the large number of dairy farms. Other early industries included charcoal works and asheries, which used the area's abundant virgin forest to make products that could be sold to distillers and soap manufacturers.

Boston, Glenwood, Springville, and West Falls offer travelers places to dine, shop, and enjoy various recreational activities.

AREA CODE The area code is 716.

GUIDANCE **Colden Town Hall** (716-941-5012), Route 240, Colden. Open Monday–Friday 9 AM–5 PM.

Town of Holland (716-537-9443), 47 Pearl Street, Holland. Open Monday–Friday 9 AM–5 PM, Wednesday 4–9 PM.

Springville Area Chamber of Commerce (716-592-4746; www.springvillechamber .com), 23 North Buffalo Street, Springville.

GETTING THERE *By bus:* The NFTA bus #74, an express route, travels between downtown Buffalo and Boston.

By car: These towns can be reached via Route 219 or Route 240.

MEDICAL EMERGENCY Dial 911.

Bertrand Chaffee Hospital (716-592-2871; www.bertrandchaffee.com), 224 East Main Street, Springville.

✳ To See

MUSEUMS **Concord Historical Society** (www.townofconcordnyhistoricalsociety.org). They have several facilities including the **Concord Historical Library** (716-592-0094),

23 North Buffalo Street, Springville; **Concord Mercantile** (716-592-5546), 17 Franklin Street, Springville. Tuesday and Thursday 7–9 PM, Wednesday and Saturday 10 AM–2 PM. Historical displays in a 1900s general store; **Warner Museum** (716-592-0094), 98 Main Street, Springville. Saturdays April–October 10 AM–2 PM. Displays on area history and about football pioneer "Pop" Warner.

Echoes Through Time Civil War Museum and Learning Center (716-957-2740 or 716-870-0174; echoesthroughtime.org), 39 East Main Street, Springville. Saturday 12–5 PM, Sunday 1–5 PM. The only museum in western New York dedicated to the history of the Civil War.

Schoolhouse #8 History Center and Museum (716-337-3341, www.schoolhouse8 .info), Library Campus, 2101 School Street, North Collins. Free admission. Open Sunday 1–4 PM. An 1857 schoolhouse with period furnishings and memorabilia.

SCENIC DRIVES **Western New York Southtowns Scenic Byway** (www.wnyssb .org). This scenic drive takes you through a number of communities in southern Erie County, including Aurora, Boston, Colden, Concord, East Aurora, Orchard Park, and Springville.

CONCORD MERCANTILE IS PART OF THE CONCORD HISTORICAL SOCIETY

✳ To Do

ART CENTER Springville Center for Arts (716-592-9038, springvillearts.org/sca), 37 North Buffalo Street, Springville. Located in a former Baptist church, this art center has theater productions, concerts, art exhibits, and workshops.

AUTO RACING Holland International Speedway (716-537-2272; www.hollandspeedway.com), 2 North Main Street, Holland. Open Saturday nights April–September. One of the finest NASCAR sanctioned 3/8-mile short track racing facilities in the United States.

SPRINGVILLE CENTER FOR THE ARTS

GOLF Concord Crest Golf Course (716-592-7636; www.concordcrest.com), 9255 Genesee Road, East Concord. An 18-hole, par-72 public golf course.

    Holland Hills (716-537-2345; www.hollandhillscountryclub.com), 10438 Holland Glenwood Road, Glenwood. An 18-hole, par-71 public course. It has a restaurant, bar, and pro shop.

    Rolling Hills (716-496-5016; www.rollinghillspar3.com), 10739 Olean Road (Route 16), Chaffee. A 9-hole, par-3 course with snack bar.

SKIING Kissing Bridge (716-592-4963; www.kbski.com), 10296 State Road (Route 240), Glenwood. This family-friendly resort, which is within a one-hour drive from metro Buffalo, is located in the western New York "snowbelt." It has ten lifts and thirty-eight trails. They also offer skiing instructions for all ages and children's programs.

✳ Green Space

NATURE PRESERVES Erie County Forest (716-496-7410), Warner Gulf Road, East Concord. This is where Erie County's reforestation program began. There are two 1.75-mile yellow-blazed hiking trails. The easier trail, on the southern side of Genesee Road, has nature study stations along the trail, and in winter this path can be used for cross-country skiing and snowshoeing. For ambitious hikers, the more difficult trail covers rough terrain. There is also a Braille trail for the visually impaired. Wildlife in the area includes white-tailed deer, raccoon, fox, and mink. A working sawmill, open during special events, is located in the forest.

PARKS Sprague Brook Park (716-592-2804), 9674 Foote Road (Route 240), Glenwood. Activities include baseball, hiking, biking, fishing, camping (27 campsites), tennis, picnicking, and cross-country skiing and snowshoeing in winter.

✳ Lodging

Colden Lakes Resort (716-941-5530:
www.coldenlakes.com), 9504 Heath
Road, Colden. Open May 1–end of October. This camping resort offers numerous
leisure-time activities, including hiking
trails, volleyball, horseshoes, four lakes,
in-ground pool, grocery store, and snowmobile trails in winter. Camping facilities include a two-bedroom cabin and
140 campsites with water and electric.
$ A full-service restaurant offers a wide
variety of daily food and beverage specials. See also *Eating Out.*

NICK CHARLAP'S IS KNOWN FOR ICE CREAM

✳ Where to Eat

DINING OUT **Dog Bar** (716-652-5550),
Route 240, West Falls (about 6 miles south
of Orchard Park). Open Wednesday–
Saturday 4–12 PM. This circa-1845 restaurant features casual, fine dining in a
unique restaurant that's also a museum.
The bar, dedicated to man's best friend, is
best known for its lamb chops, garlic crou-
tons, and porterhouse steak, plus chicken
and seafood.

    Colden Lakes Resort Restaurant (716-
941-5530; www.coldenlakes.com), 9504
Heath Road, Colden. Open year-round,
hours vary according to season. This
bar/restaurant offers casual dining at
moderate prices. Enjoy everything from
pizza and wings to pasta and prime rib.
It is located at a camping resort. See
Lodging.

    ♭ **Colden Mill Restaurant** (716-
941-9357; thecoldenmill.com), 8348
Boston-Colden Road, Colden. Open
Tuesday–Thursday 4–9 PM, Friday–
Saturday 4–10 PM. An 1830 feed mill is
now a large country restaurant serving
steaks, fish fry, pasta, chicken pot pie,
and more.

    Raphael's (716-941-3112; www
.raphaelsitalian.com), 8936 Boston State
Road, Boston. Italian-American family
restaurant featuring old country recipes.

    Eating Out ✎ **George's Hot
Dogs** (716-648-0302), 5808 Herman
Hill Road (Route 77) North Boston. Cash only. Open early April–
mid-October 11 AM–8 PM. A seasonal,
family-friendly restaurant that has been
in business since 1967. They serve burgers, hot dogs, milkshakes, and more.
They have two outdoor playgrounds.

    ✎ ♭ ⚊ **Nick Charlap's** (716-312-
0592), 7264 Boston State Road, North
Boston. Hours vary seasonally. People
come from miles around for Charlap's
ice cream, which was started by Henry
Charlap in 1961 and is now operated by
his son, Nick. Charlap's has the feel of
an old-fashioned '50s ice cream parlor,
complete with a jukebox. On an average
summer day they sell over a thousand
cones, along with other goodies like
shakes and banana splits, as well as
hot dogs and hamburgers. You can also
purchase ice cream in containers to take
home.

✳ Selective Shopping

SPECIAL SHOPS **The Carousel Shop**
(716-592-3902), 38 East Main Street,
Springville. Choose from a selection of
Polish pottery and gift items.

SHOPPING ON EAST MAIN STREET IN SPRINGVILLE

Fresh Floral & Gift Company (716-592-5015; www.freshfloralandgifts.com), 23 East Main Street, Springville. In addition to a full-service floral shop, this store has jewelry, accessories, clothing, and gourmet food items.

Homewear (716-592-7012; www.hardwareandhomewear.com/folkart.php3), 52 East Main Street, Springville. This shop has the largest collection of folk art and primitive art in the Springville area.

Lulu Belle's (716-592-9123; www.lulubellesgifts.com), 35A East Main Street, Springville. Shop for clothing, accessories, jewelry, and home decor.

The Quilt Farm (716 941-3140; www.quiltfarm.net), 5623 South Feddick Road, Boston (Route 219 south to Rice Road exit; turn right at stop sign, and follow signs). Open Tuesday and Thursday 11 AM–7 PM, Wednesday, Friday, and Saturday 11 AM–5 PM. The largest quilt shop in western New York is located in a large red barn in the countryside. Choose from hundreds of bolts of fabric, patterns, threads, and other supplies. Quilting classes are offered in an upstairs room.

✳ Special Events

May: **Holland Tulip Festival** (town of Holland 716-537-9443), Main Street, Holland. This three-day festival celebrates the flower that originated in the "other" Holland. The festival features craft vendors, carnival rides, kids' activities, food vendors, and more.

CITY OF NIAGARA FALLS, NEW YORK

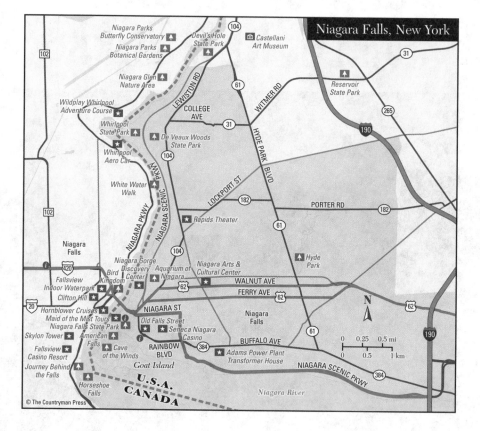

Niagara Falls, New York

CITY OF NIAGARA FALLS, NEW YORK

pproximately 900 waterfalls, both large and small, beautify western New York State, but the best known—both locally and worldwide—is, of course, Niagara Falls. One of the Seven Natural Wonders of the World, the falls draws tourists from around the globe to witness its splendor and awesome power. Niagara Falls is actually made up of three waterfalls: the Horseshoe or Canadian Falls, the American Falls, and the smaller Bridal Veil Falls. The first European to write an account of the falls was Father Louis Hennepin, a missionary who traveled to the area in 1678 with the explorer Robert de la Salle.

Shortly after the War of 1812, tourists began arriving in the area. In the early days, the falls were surrounded by factories and mills on privately owned land, with landowners often charging visitors a fee to view the falls. Fortunately, after landscape architect Frederick Law Olmsted, architect Henry H. Richardson, and attorney William Dorschmier visited the area in 1869, they decided to work toward preserving the area and returning it to its natural state.

By 1885 the property surrounding the falls had been purchased by New York State and was turned into the first state park in the United States, now known as the Niagara Falls State Park. The world's first railway suspension bridge, built over the Niagara Gorge, was opened in 1855. The 825-foot bridge was a prototype for the Brooklyn Bridge.

Niagara Falls is also known as the Honeymoon Capital of the World. Local legend has it that the first newlyweds, who honeymooned here in 1802, were Joseph Alston and his wife Theodosia Burr, daughter of Aaron Burr, Vice President of the United States. Napoleon Bonaparte's younger brother, Jerome, also honeymooned here with his wife, Elizabeth. Today the falls is still a popular spot to honeymoon or even get married.

Today Niagara Falls, both in New York and Canada (see *Southern Ontario—Niagara Falls, Ontario*) has a variety of attractions that appeal to visitors as well as locals, including tours, boat rides, nature areas, amusements, casinos, dining, shopping, and more.

AREA CODE The area code is 716.

GUIDANCE **Niagara USA Official Visitor's Center** (877-325-5787; www.niagara-usa .com) 10 Rainbow Boulevard, Niagara Falls. Daily 9 AM–5 PM, and until 7 PM in July and August.

&. **Niagara Falls State Park Visitors Center** (716-278-1796; www.niagarafallsstate park.com), 332 Prospect Street, Niagara Falls. The visitor center has information on the falls and the surrounding area.

GETTING THERE *By air:* See *Getting There—City of Buffalo.* A limited number of regularly scheduled flights, as well as charter and private flights fly out of the **Niagara Falls International Airport** (716-855-7300; www.niagarafallsairport.com), 2035 Niagara Falls Boulevard, Niagara Falls.

By bus: There are connecting routes to Niagara Falls from Buffalo; *see Getting There—City of Buffalo.*

By car: From the east, take I-90 to I-290 to I-190; cross over Grand Island, and follow the Niagara Falls exit (Niagara Scenic Parkway). From the south and west, take I-90 north to I-190, and follow above directions. From the north, take I-190 south or the Niagara Scenic Parkway. From Canada the main route into Niagara Falls, New York, is via the Rainbow Bridge.

By train: An **Amtrak** station is located at 825 Depot Avenue, Niagara Falls. (800-872-7245; www.amtrak.com).

GETTING AROUND *By car:* City streets are laid out in a grid pattern, with the main roads being Rainbow Boulevard, Main Street, and Niagara Street.

By bus: The **NFTA** (www.nfta.com) operates routes within the city as well as connecting routes to Buffalo and Lockport. Route 55T Metro Trolley serves downtown Niagara Falls, Pine Avenue, Niagara Falls Boulevard and the Niagara Falls airport. **Rural Niagara Transportation** (716-285-9357; www.niagaracounty.com/County-Information/Public-Transportation-Schedule). Transportation is provided from the rural communities of Niagara County to the cities of Niagara Falls, Lockport, and North Tonawanda.

By taxi: Taxicab companies include **LaSalle Cab** (716-284-8833) and **Blue United Cab** (716-285-3333).

By scenic trolley: This tram, which operates seasonally, stops at all points of interest in Niagara Falls State Park.

By Shuttle: **Discover Niagara Shuttle** (716-222-0729; www.discoverniagarashuttle .com), Mid-May–mid-October, Sunday–Thursday 9 AM–6:30 PM, Friday–Saturday 9 AM–midnight. Ride this free, hop-on, hop-off shuttle to visit 14 destinations between the Niagara Falls Visitors Center and Old Fort Niagara in Lewiston.

MEDICAL EMERGENCY Dial 911.

Niagara Falls Memorial Medical Center (716-278-4000; www.nfmmc.org), 621 10th Street, Niagara Falls.

✳ To See

Nightly Illumination of Niagara Falls. Hours vary according to season, generally from dusk until midnight or later. A visit to Niagara Falls is not complete unless you've experienced the nightly illumination of the falls. Huge spotlights aimed at the falls light them in various shades of blue, red, and green, with other colors to commemorate special events. Be sure to arrive well before dusk to get a prime viewing spot along the railings.

ART MUSEUMS **Niagara Arts and Cultural Center** (716-282-7530; www.thenacc .org), 1201 Pine Avenue, Niagara Falls. Monday–Friday 9 AM–5 PM, Saturday–Sunday 12–4 PM. This historic 1924 Classic Revival building, formerly Niagara Falls High School, is located less than a mile from the falls. This four-story 200,000-square-foot landmark is home to over seventy visual and performing artist's studios along with two theaters and two art galleries.

MUSEUMS AND HISTORIC HOMES ✍ ⅄ ↑ **Niagara Aerospace Museum** (716-297-1323; www.wnyaerospace.org), 9900 Porter Road, Niagara Falls. Wednesday–Sunday 11 AM–5 PM. Located in a former terminal building by the Niagara Falls International

Airport, This museum is dedicated to the thousands of western New Yorkers who contributed to the aviation and aerospace industry. Among the large collection is a Bell X-22A research aircraft, one of only two ever built, and a Bell Model 47 Helicopter, which was granted the world's first commercial helicopter license. Also on display are model planes and products made for the aviation industry in Buffalo.

♿ **Niagara Wax Museum of History** (716-285-1271; m.mainstreethub.com/niagarawaxmuseum), 363 Prospect Street, Niagara Falls. Hours vary seasonally. Exhibits include displays of daredevils' barrels as well as street scenes of Niagara's past, Native American villages, and more, all depicted in life-sized wax figures.

NIAGARA AEROSPACE MUSEUM

HISTORIC SITES ✪ **Adams Power Plant Transformer House**, Buffalo Avenue (near 15th Avenue and Portage Road), Niagara Falls. This little-known National Historic Landmark was the largest hydroelectric plant in the world when it was constructed in 1895. It is considered the birthplace of the modern power generating station. It is currently not open to the public, but you can see it from the street.

✳ To Do

BOAT EXCURSIONS **Maid of the Mist Tours** (716-284-8897; www.maidofthemist .com), 151 Buffalo Avenue, Niagara Falls. Mid-May to October, hours vary, call or see website. Since 1846, visitors, including movie stars, presidents, and kings, have been enjoying the *Maid of the Mist* boat tours, one of the oldest tourist attractions in North America. The ride originally started out as a ferry service across the Niagara Gorge between the United States and Canada. However, in 1848, after a new bridge across the gorge caused business to decline, the owner turned the operation into a sightseeing venture, which continues to this day. On this tour, visitors can see the falls from another perspective. Hooded rain ponchos are provided for the 30-minute cruise to the base of the American and Horseshoe (Canadian) Falls. Teddy Roosevelt commented, "The ride was the only way to fully realize the grandeur of the great falls of Niagara." See also *Niagara Falls, Ontario—Boat Excursions*.

CASINO GAMING **Seneca Niagara Casino** (716-299-1100 or 877-8-SENECA; www .senecaniagaracasino.com), 310 4th Street, Niagara Falls. Open 24 hours. Enjoy 2,900 reel-spinning slot machines and 100 table games along with fine dining and live entertainment at this casino operated by the Seneca Nation of Indians. Smoking is allowed in the casino; they also have a nonsmoking section. Several restaurants are part of the complex, as is a twenty-six-story hotel. Live entertainment is featured in the Bear's Den Showroom. See also *Dining Out* and *Lodging*. Note: You must be at least 21 to enter the casino.

VIEW OF NIAGARA FALLS FROM THE *MAID OF THE MIST*

CROSS-COUNTRY SKIING See *Green Space—Parks.*

FAMILY FUN ✦ ♿ ☂ **Aquarium of Niagara** (716-285-3575; www.aquariumofniagara .org), 701 Whirlpool Street, Niagara Falls. Open daily 9 AM–5 PM. During your self-guided tour you'll explore the undersea world, from the Great Lakes to coral reefs. The main exhibit is the new 3,500-square-foot, state-of-the-art living habitat for the aquarium's Humboldt Penguins. The Aquarium of Niagara is one of only 20 institutions in the country that have this type of penguin, which is native to Peru and Chile. In addition, the facility has over 1,500 species of aquatic animals, including sharks, piranhas, moray eels, and California sea lions in a two-floor tank, which allows for viewing the sea lion show from above, as well as below, the water.

HUMBOLDT PENGUINS AT THE AQUARIUM OF NIAGARA

Spirit of the Mist/Smokin' Joes Native Center (716-831-2585; www.sj nativecenter.com), 333 1st Street, Niagara Falls. Open seasonally. Featured in this complex is Native American history and artwork, a retail shop with native-made items, as well as Niagara Falls souvenirs. A coffee house and an events center are also located here.

♿ ✦ **Niagara Gorge Discovery Center** (716-278-1070; www.niagarafallsstatepark .com/attractions-and-tours/discovery -center-and-hiking-trails), off the Niagara Scenic Parkway near Main Street, Niagara Falls. Open seasonally May–October.

Virtual-reality exhibits, including the Gorge Cam, explore the history and geology of the Niagara Gorge. The Cataract Theater, with its 32-foot-diameter circular screen, offers a multimedia presentation of the Niagara Gorge. The building's exterior features a 26-foot climbing wall.

GOLF **Hyde Park Golf Course** (716-286-4956; www.hydeparkgolfclub.org), 4343 Porter Road (Route 62 and Robbins Drive; enter via Porter Road), Niagara Falls. This 18-hole, par-72 course features a restaurant, pro shop, and indoor driving range.

GUIDED TOURS **Bedore Tours, Inc.** (800-538-8433; www.bedoretours.com). Mailing address: 2968 Niagara Falls Boulevard, North Tonawanda. They offer a variety of tours of the Niagara Falls area, including attractions on both sides of the border.

Cave of the Winds (716-278-1730; www.niagarafallsstatepark.com/attractions-and -tours/cave-of-the-winds), on Goat Island. Open seasonally. The Cave of the Winds tours offers a unique view of the American Falls. Don a hooded rain poncho before descending the elevator down to the cave. When you emerge from the cave, you'll be able to walk along the catwalk that has been constructed near the base of the Bridal Veil Falls. Be prepared to get soaking wet; you'll only be an arm's length away from the thundering water.

CAVE OF THE WINDS TOUR

Gray Line of Niagara Falls (716-285-2113; www.graylineniagarafalls.com). This well-known tour company offers several tour packages of the Niagara Falls area, covering one or both sides of the border.

Helicopter Rides by Rainbow Air (716-284-2800; www.rainbowairinc.com), 454 Main Street, Niagara Falls. If you are a real thrill-seeker, why not view Niagara Falls from a different perspective? Get a bird's-eye view as you enjoy the beauty of the falls from the air.

Motherland Connexions (716-282-1028; www.motherlandconnextions.com). Fees and hours vary. The western New York area played a major role in the Underground Railroad—not an actual railway but a network of roads and safe houses used by slaves seeking freedom in the 1850s. Motherland Connexions provides an educational and enlightening experience. "Conductors" dressed in period clothing take groups to stops along the Underground Railroad in both western New York and southern Ontario.

Niagara Falls Walking Tours (716-222-2432; niagarawalkingtours.com). Choose from several private, small group walking tours offered by local author Joel Dombrowski.

Over the Falls Tours, Inc. (716-283-8900; www.overthefallstours.com). Tours of attractions in Niagara Falls on both sides of the border. They will pick up guests at local hotels.

WEDDING CHAPELS ⚭ **The Falls Wedding Chapel** (716-285-5570; www.fallswedding .com), 240 1st Street, Niagara Falls. By appointment. Weddings, including same-sex, as well as vow renewals, can be arranged in several locations, including at the brink of the falls, in a helicopter, at a local cathedral, or in their chapel at the Quality Hotel & Suites at the Falls. Wedding photographer, cake, and flowers available as additional options. See *Lodging*.

⚭ **Hanover House Bed & Breakfast** (716-278-1170; www.hanoverhousebb.com), 610 Buffalo Avenue, Niagara Falls. They offer traditional and "elopement" wedding packages, along with cake and buffet receptions after the ceremony. See *Lodging*.

⚭ **Niagara Weddings USA** (716-930-0107; www.niagaraweddingsusa.com), 751 Park Place, Niagara Falls. A full-service wedding chapel and wedding service located at the Butler House Bed & Breakfast. See *Lodging*.

⚭ **Rainbow House Bed & Breakfast and Wedding Chapel** (716-282-1135; www .rainbowhousebb.com/weddings), 423 Rainbow Boulevard South, Niagara Falls. This Victorian bed & breakfast is a romantic setting for small weddings. Outdoor weddings by the falls can also be arranged. See *Lodging*.

✴ Green Space

PARKS All parks are open dawn to dusk with free admission.

De Veaux Woods State Park (716-284-5778), 3180 De Veaux Woods Drive, Niagara Falls. This park, which connects to the Robert Moses Trail and Whirlpool State Park, includes two baseball diamonds and old-growth forest.

&. **Devil's Hole State Park** (716-278-1796), Niagara Scenic Parkway, Niagara Falls. This ominous-sounding park overlooking the lower whirlpool rapids was the scene of a massacre in 1763, in which British soldiers were pushed into the gorge by a group of warring Seneca Indians. The upper portion of this park has picnic areas. A hiking trail leads down the embankment 300 feet into the gorge, where visitors can get an up-close view of the rapids. It is a popular spot for fishing enthusiasts. While you're down in the gorge, look for a wide-mouthed, 50-foot long cave near the bottom. Legend has it that

GETTING MARRIED IN NEW YORK STATE

To get married in New York, a couple, heterosexual or same-sex, must obtain a marriage license at any city or town clerk's office. The Niagara Falls city clerk's office is located at 745 Main Street. Licenses are issued Monday–Friday 8 AM–3:30 AM, except legal holidays. Both parties must appear before the clerk and present one form of photo ID, such as a driver's license or passport. If either party is divorced, they must present a certified copy of their divorce decree. There is no blood test required, but there is a 24-hour waiting period between the issuing of the license and the wedding ceremony. The license is good for 60 days after issue. See also *Niagara Falls, Ontario—Wedding Chapels*.

this is the home of an evil spirit. Return to the rim of the gorge by continuing on the main hiking trail, which will lead you to the rim about 1 mile south of where you began.

& **Hyde Park** (716-286-4956), Route 62 and Robbins Drive, Niagara Falls. This park offers picnicking, swimming, bocce courts, volleyball, baseball, indoor ice skating, hiking and nature trails, tennis, fishing, and a golf course.

✪ & **Niagara Falls State Park** (716-278-1770 or 716-278-1796; www.niagarafallsstate park.com), Prospect Street, Niagara Falls. Open daily from dawn to nightly illumination of falls. Free admission; however, there is a parking fee if you park in their lot. America's oldest state park, established in 1885 and designed by noted landscape architect Frederick Law Olmsted, is made up of several small islands plus Prospect Point, which offers a great view of the falls. The park, a designated National Historic Landmark, includes access to the American Falls, Bridal Veil Falls, and Goat Island. Facilities include hiking and nature trails, fishing, picnic tables, and a restaurant. The visitor center offers information on park history as well as New York State information. Elevators in the observation deck take visitors to the *Maid of the Mist* boat ride. The Cave of the Wind Tour, located on Goat Island, takes visitors on a close-up tour of the falls.

Oppenheim County Park (716-439-7950; www.niagaracounty.com/parks/ Oppenheim-Park), 2713 Niagara Falls Boulevard, Niagara Falls. Facilities at this 92-acre county park include picnic shelters, fishing, and playgrounds.

Reservoir State Park (716-297-4484), Witmer Road and Military, Niagara Falls (near Lewiston). One of this popular park's most interesting and scenic aspects is that it overlooks the Robert Moses Power Plant Reservoir. Facilities in the park include four tennis courts, eight baseball diamonds, and a basketball court. The park also has picnic facilities and a playground in addition to nature trails for hiking and biking. Winter visitors can enjoy sledding and cross-country skiing.

Whirlpool State Park (716-285-7740), Niagara Rapids Boulevard (off the Niagara Scenic Parkway), Niagara Falls. This two-level park, located along a 90-degree turn in the Niagara River Gorge, overlooks the whirlpool that forms 3.5 miles downstream from the falls. From street level there are many spectacular overlooks to view the swirling rapids and the whirlpool. During the winter months many people also enjoy cross-country skiing here. Picnic areas and a playground are on this level. The lower level, which has nature trails and fishing access along the river, is accessible by walking down 300 feet of trails and steps.

WALKING AND HIKING TRAILS **Niagara Gorge Hiking Trails** (parks.ny.gov /parks/attachments/NiagaraFallsNiagaraGorgeTrailMap.pdf). Enjoy hiking a series of eight shorter trails that run parallel to the Niagara River Gorge from Niagara Falls to Lewiston. See website for descriptions and map or call 716-282-5154 for print brochure.

NIAGARA REGIONAL PARK INTERPRETIVE PROGRAMS

The New York State Office of Parks, Recreation, and Historic Preservation offers a selection of public programs throughout the year to educate the public about natural resources and regional history. Included are tours, hikes, walks, lectures, and outreach programs. A Niagara Gorge Trail System Hiking Patch can be earned by hiking several of the trails along the Niagara Gorge. For more information, contact Niagara Regional Park Interpretive Programs Office (716-278-1728 or 716-745-7848).

For additional trails, see *Parks*.

✳ Lodging

INNS AND RESORTS **Red Coach Inn** (716-282-1459 or 800-282-1459; www.redcoach.com), 2 Buffalo Avenue, Niagara Falls. The Red Coach Inn, modeled after the Old Bell Inn in Finedon, England, overlooks the upper rapids. It's only 500 yards from the brink; guests can hear the thundering rapids from their rooms. Accommodations include two-bedroom guest suites decorated with period antiques and reproductions. All suites have a private bath, a whirlpool tub, a small kitchen, a living room/dining room overlooking the rapids, a fireplace, and cable television. Several one-bedroom suites are also available, along with two standard guest rooms. $$$.

MOTELS AND HOTELS Hundreds of small, nondescript motels line Niagara Falls Boulevard (Route 62) from Amherst to Niagara Falls, quite a distance from the actual falls. In addition, numerous larger motor inns and chain hotels can

THE RED COACH INN OFFERS DINING AND LODGING OVERLOOKING THE UPPER RAPIDS OF NIAGARA FALLS

be found right in the Niagara Falls area. All of them provide clean, comfortable accommodations at fairly reasonable prices. My personal recommendation is to stay at a hotel that's within walking distance of the falls. Below are just a few.

Comfort Inn The Pointe (716-284-6835; www.comfortinnthepointe.com), 1 Prospect Point, Niagara Falls. This is the closest hotel to the falls. It's walking distance from many area attractions, including the *Maid of the Mist*, the Aquarium of Niagara, and the Seneca Niagara Casino. Amenities include a free deluxe continental breakfast, an exercise room, and Wi-Fi. $$$.

Courtyard by Marriott (716-284-2222) 900 Buffalo Avenue, Niagara Falls. Situated just a half-mile from the falls, this hotel is located in a building that once housed a chocolate factory in the early 1900s. $$.

Four Points Sheraton Hotel–Niagara Falls (716-299-0344), 7001 Buffalo Avenue, Niagara Falls. This hotel, just a short drive from the falls, has a nice view of the upper Niagara River and is family- and pet-friendly (additional fee for pets). It also has a fitness center, heated outdoor pool, and an on-site restaurant and lounge. $$.

The Giacomo (716-299-0200; www.thegiacomo.com), 222 1st Street, Niagara Falls. This boutique hotel, located in a 1929 art deco building listed on the National Register of Historic Places, offers luxurious rooms and suites, some with a fireplace or Jacuzzi tub. Included with your stay is a European style continental breakfast. $$$$.

Hampton Inn (716-285-6666), 501 Rainbow Boulevard, Niagara Falls. This hotel offers 100 rooms, including several deluxe king whirlpool rooms. Amenities include an indoor heated pool, fitness room, and a free continental breakfast buffet. It's about a half-mile walk to the falls. $$$.

☗ **Quality Hotel and Suites at the Falls** (716-282-1212; qualityniagarafalls.com), 240 1st Street, Niagara Falls. The hotel offers 211 spacious rooms, including two-room family suites and Jacuzzi suites. You can walk to the falls and the Seneca Niagara Casino; it is also pet-friendly. The on-site **Falls Wedding Chapel** is available for wedding ceremonies and vow renewals. See *Wedding Chapels.* $$.

Seneca Niagara Hotel (716-299-1100, 877-873-6322; www.senecaniagaracasino.com), 310 4th Street, Niagara Falls. At 360 feet tall, it is the region's tallest hotel. This 604-room hotel, located adjacent to the Seneca Niagara Casino, has pillow top beds and flat screen TVs among its amenities. There is an indoor heated pool along with several restaurants within the hotel. $$$$.

Sheraton at the Falls (716-285-3361), 300 3rd Street, Niagara Falls. This six-story hotel with 392 rooms is located across the street from the Seneca Niagara Casino. Amenities include an indoor heated pool and game arcade. $$$.

BED & BREAKFASTS **Butler House Bed & Breakfast** (716-930-0107; thebutlerhouse.com), 751 Park Place, Niagara Falls. Built in 1928, this B&B is located on a quiet street in the heart of the city of Niagara Falls. It features four bright and airy guest rooms, each with a private bath. The enclosed front porch offers privacy for guests. A homemade breakfast can be enjoyed in the dining room or outdoors on the covered veranda. They also offer wedding services through Niagara Weddings USA— see *Wedding Chapels.* $$$.

Hanover House Bed & Breakfast (716-278-1170; www.hanoverhousebb.com), 610 Buffalo Avenue, Niagara Falls. This Italianate-style mansion, within walking distance of the falls, was built in 1922 and retains many of the original features. The inn has four guest rooms, each with a private bath. Wedding services are also available. See *Wedding Chapels.* $$.

Park Place Bed & Breakfast (716-299-0189; www.parkplacebb.com), 740

Park Place, Niagara Falls. This 1913 Arts and Crafts Prairie-style home is on the National Register of Historic Places. The historic home features oak paneling, open spaces, and Steuben glass chandeliers in the den. Five uniquely decorated rooms, each with a private bath, are located on the second floor. $$.

Rainbow House Bed & Breakfast (716-282-1135 or 800-724-3536; www.rainbowhousebb.com), 423 Rainbow Boulevard, Niagara Falls. This Victorian home, built in 1895, has original woodwork and stained glass throughout. Each of the three guestrooms has a private bath, air-conditioning, and a ceiling fan. The Bridal Suite features a king-sized bed and a private porch with swing, while the Seaway Room has a nautical theme. The Garden Room has a hand-painted country mural, and the Country Room features a whimsical hand-painted mural in the bathroom. Call for room rates. Wedding services are also available. See *Wedding Chapels*.

✳ Where to Eat

DINING OUT **Como Restaurant** (716-285-9341; www.comorestaurant.com), 2220 Pine Avenue (Route 62A), Niagara Falls. Opens daily at 11:30 AM. This warm and inviting restaurant, located in Niagara Falls' Little Italy, has been in business since 1927. The menu features pasta and other Italian specialties.

Fortunas Restaurant (716-282-2252; www.fortunas.biz), 827 19th Street, Niagara Falls. Open Wednesday–Sunday for dinner; lunch also on Friday. One of the finest Italian restaurants in Niagara Falls, Fortuna's has been family-owned since 1945. Choose from homemade pasta entrees, specialty sauces, veal, seafood, and chicken plus steak and pork entrees.

La Cascata at the Seneca Niagara Casino (716-299-1100, 877-873-6322; www.senecaniagaracasino.com), 310 4th Street, Niagara Falls. Dinner

Wednesday–Sunday starting at 5 PM. This upscale restaurant offers both traditional and contemporary dining. La Cascata means "cascade" in Italian, aptly named as it is near the falls.

Red Coach Inn (716-282-1459; www.redcoach.com), 2 Buffalo Avenue, Niagara Falls. Open daily for breakfast, lunch, and dinner. The menu features Black Angus beef, pasta, and seafood, along with chicken and pork dishes. Warm yourself by the inn's natural stone fireplace during the winter months, or enjoy fine dining during warmer weather on their outdoor patio, which overlooks the rapids. See also *Lodging*.

Savor (716-210-2525; www.nfculinary.org), 28 Old Falls Street, Niagara Falls. Fine dining restaurant located in the Niagara Falls Culinary Institute. Foods are prepared by students at the institute.

&. **Top of the Falls Restaurant** (716-278-0340; www.topofthefallsrestaurant.com), Goat Island, Niagara Falls. Open late May–October 1, daily 11 AM–7 PM, Friday and Saturday until 10 PM. This upscale restaurant offers a magnificent view of Horseshoe Falls. It has outdoor seating as well as indoor tiered seating, so everyone gets a view of the falls. The menu features classic American fare, plus a kids' menu.

&. **The Western Door** at the Seneca Niagara Casino (716-299-1100, 877-873-6322; www.senecaniagaracasino.com), 310 4th Street, Niagara Falls. Open daily 5–11 PM. This nicely decorated, five-star steakhouse overlooking the casino's gaming floor features aged beef, including a 48-ounce porterhouse. They also have a selection of seafood as well as New York State wines and beers to go with your meal. Entree accompaniments, such as salad, potatoes, and other vegetables, are sold à la carte. However, the sides are quite large and will easily serve two people. See also *Casino Gaming*.

Wine on Third (716-285-9463; www.wineonthird.com), 501 3rd Street, Niagara Falls. Enjoy fine dining and tapas at the restaurant voted one of the best places to eat in Niagara Falls.

EATING OUT **Carmine's** (716-236-9195), 1701 Pine Avenue, Niagara Falls. Italian American restaurant known for large portions and homemade sauce located in the heart of Niagara Falls' Little Italy.

El Cubilete (716-297-4500; www .bestmexicanusa.com), 9400 Niagara Falls Boulevard, Niagara Falls. This restaurant has some of the best authentic Mexican food in western New York.

Frankie's Donuts and Pizza (716-285-7494; www.frankiesdonutsandpizza .com), 717 Portage Road, Niagara Falls. Open 24 hours. This local donut shop has some of the best donuts in the area. They also serve pizza, chicken wings, and sandwiches.

Griffon Pub (716-236-7474; www .thegriffonpub.com), 2470 Military Road, Niagara Falls. Enjoy pub food, including sandwiches and burgers. It's always very busy, so make reservations.

Judi's Lounge Bar & Grill (716-297-5759; www.judisbarandgrill.com), 2057 Military Road, Niagara Falls. Open daily 11 AM–2 AM. A casual restaurant known for chicken wings, homemade soups, and specialty sandwiches.

Legends Grill (716-299-0250; legendsbarnf.com), 240 Rainbow Boulevard (in the Quality Hotel & Suites), Niagara Falls. Daily 11 AM–10 PM. A reasonably priced family restaurant located within walking distance of the falls. Menu includes salads, burgers, sandwiches, pizza, and more.

♿ **Marketside Café** (716-282-0644), 712 East Market Street (City Market), Niagara Falls. Daily 7 AM–noon and also Friday dinner 5–7 PM. This is the place to go if you want the scoop on what's happening in town. You'll find early risers, politicians, farmers, and locals dining here. The food is very good, including homemade soup, desserts, and sandwiches.

♿ ☠ **Michael's Italian Restaurant** (716-282-4043; www

.michaelsniagarafalls.com), 3011 Pine Avenue, Niagara Falls. Daily 11 AM–9:30 PM; until 10 PM Friday and Saturday. You'll find this small, cozy restaurant right under the "Little Italy" sign that hangs over Pine Avenue. Entrees come in enormous portions, so be prepared to take home leftovers. Their extensive menu includes Michael's famous calzones, deep-fried Italian turnovers stuffed with ricotta and mozzarella, and the city's best eggplant parm, along with a selection of Italian and American fare, including pizza, wings, and a kids' menu.

Power City Eatery (716-289-0124: www.powercityeatery.com), 444 3rd Street, Niagara Falls. A breakfast and lunch restaurant that features made-from-scratch bagels and a variety of soups and sandwiches. Specialty sandwiches include house-cured smoked pastrami and corned beef, also cured in-house.

Taylor's Tap & Grill (716-216-6078; www.taylorstap.net), 2279 Niagara Falls Boulevard, Wheatfield. This bar and restaurant is noted for its made-from-scratch foods, including sandwiches, flatbreads, and soups, along with wings and specialty desserts. They have a

FRANKIES DONUTS NIAGARA FALLS, NY

full-service bar with craft cocktails and local beers on tap.

♦ ♂ ♿ **Twist o' the Mist** (716-285-0702), Rainbow Boulevard and Niagara Street (across from the Rainbow Bridge), Niagara Falls. Open seasonally. This casual eatery features hard ice cream and soft custard served from an ice cream cone–shaped building.

✳ Entertainment

THEATERS **Rapids Theater** (716-205-8925; www.rapidstheatre.com), 1711 Main Street, Niagara Falls. A circa-1921 theater that hosts concerts and other events.

OTHER ENTERTAINMENT VENUES **Old Falls Street** (716-278-2100; www.fallsstreet.com), 101 Old Falls Street, Niagara Falls. A three-block area between Niagara Falls State Park and the Seneca Niagara Casino where a number of festivals and events take place, including Taste of Niagara, craft shows, a Halloween parade, music, movies, and other events.

✳ Selective Shopping

SPECIAL STORES **Book Corner** (716-285-2928; www.fallsbookcorner.com), 1801 Main Street, Niagara Falls. Monday–Saturday 9 AM–5:30 PM, Thursday until 7 PM. This three-story bookstore, a Niagara Falls mainstay since 1927, serves as a beacon on a street with many boarded-up storefronts. They have one of the area's largest selections of books on Niagara Falls and western New York.

DiCamillo Bakery (www.dicamillo bakerybuffaloniagara.com). Five locations in the region: 811 Linwood (716-282-2341), 7927 Niagara Falls Boulevard (716-236-0111), 1700 Pine Avenue (716-284-8131), 535 Center Street in Lewiston (716-754-2218), and 5329 Main Street in Williamsville (716-635-6504). Open 7 AM–9 PM. DiCamillo's has been a local institution for over 80 years. Stop by to sample some of their crusty bread, pizzas, and cookies.

Fashion Outlets Niagara Falls (716-297-2022; www.fashionoutletsniagara .com), 1900 Military Road off Route 62, Niagara Falls. Monday–Saturday 10 AM–9 PM, Sunday 1–6 PM. Bargains galore can be found at hundreds of factory outlet stores.

Niagara Falls City Market, Pine Avenue at Market Street, Niagara Falls. Located in the heart of Niagara Falls' Little Italy, a farmers' market takes place here during the summer months.

Honeymoon Capital Souvenirs (716-285-6117), 16 Rainbow Boulevard, Niagara Falls. If you've traveled all the way to Niagara Falls, you'll probably want to bring back a little something to remember your trip. This store offers the city's largest selection of souvenirs and gifts.

Three Sisters Trading Post (716-284-3689; www.threesisterstradingpost .com), 454 Main Street, Niagara Falls. This family-owned rustic shop features a unique collection of home-decor items, handcrafted jewelry, and Native American art. They also have really cute stuffed animals, Niagara Falls souvenirs, country and primitive items, and nautical-themed gifts.

✳ Special Events

September: **Niagara Falls Blues Festival** (www.niagarafallsbluesfest.org), Old Falls Street, Niagara Falls. Enjoy live music and more in downtown Niagara Falls. **Taste of Niagara**, Old Falls Street, Niagara Falls. Enjoy foods from close to two dozen area restaurants.

NIAGARA COUNTY

■

NORTH OF THE FALLS
Lewiston, Youngstown, Sanborn, Ransomville, and Porter

NORTH TONAWANDA AND WHEATFIELD

LAKE ONTARIO SHORE
Wilson, Olcott, Burt, Newfane, and Barker

CANAL TOWNS
Lockport, Middleport, and Gasport

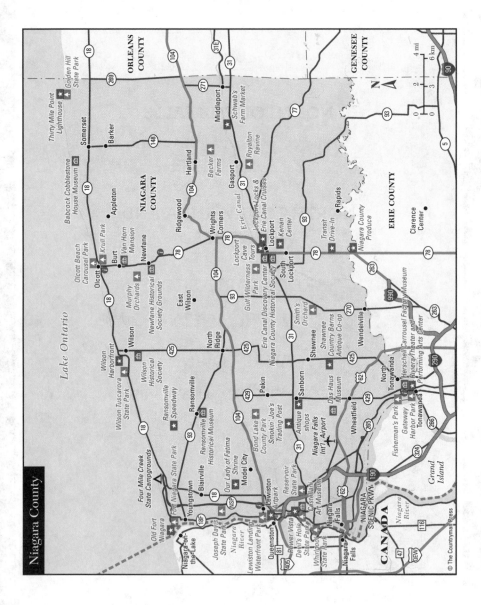

Niagara County

INTRODUCTION

While Niagara County's best-known tourist destination is, of course, Niagara Falls, there are many other interesting things to see and do here. Niagara County is home to the French Castle at Old Fort Niagara, the oldest building in the Great Lakes region. You can take a boat ride and "lock through" the double set of canal locks on the historic Erie Canal in Lockport. Sports fishermen will find an abundance of fish in Lake Ontario and the Niagara River as well as in creeks and streams.

Numerous parks are located throughout the county, including several along the Niagara Gorge and Lake Ontario. Our Lady of Fatima Shrine, located just north of Niagara Falls, was modeled after a shrine in Lisbon, Portugal, and attracts thousands of pilgrims each year.

Niagara County is one of the largest agricultural producers in the state, so you will see all types of farms dotting the countryside. In summer visitors can buy farm-fresh produce at roadside farm markets. It is also home to the Niagara Wine Trail, which has over two dozen wineries.

NORTH OF THE FALLS

Lewiston, Youngstown, Sanborn, Ransomville, and Porter

Established in 1798, Lewiston was named to honor Morgan Lewis, the third governor of New York. Lewiston was burned to the ground by the British in 1813, during the War of 1812. However, the town was rebuilt following the war; many of the homes constructed during this period are still standing. The village also played an important role in the Underground Railroad during the mid-1800s.

Today Lewiston's Center Street has numerous boutiques and restaurants. The village is also home to Artpark, a state park that offers an array of art and cultural events throughout the summer. Our Lady of Fatima Shrine, the second largest tourist attraction in Niagara County, attracts visitors from all over the world.

Youngstown, at the mouth of the Niagara River, is one of the most scenic spots in Niagara County. The village was named after John Young, who founded the village in 1811. Located only 12 miles from Niagara Falls, Youngstown is a popular spot to visit since it is relaxing yet not far from area attractions. It's also a popular spot for sports fishing, with anglers from as far away as Ohio and New Jersey coming for the salmon, trout, walleye, and steelhead. Of course, history is key in Youngstown; Fort Niagara, which has the oldest structure in the Great Lakes region, played an important role in many military battles, especially during the French and Indian War and the War of 1812.

The village of Sanborn was named after the Reverend E. C. Sanborn, a Methodist clergyman who arrived in this area in 1846. In the early days, the town had a sawmill, a gristmill, and one of the largest cheese manufacturing facilities in the state. Today the village, now part of the town of Lewiston, is home to several unique antique shops.

Ransomville was founded in 1817 by Gideon Curtiss and named after Jehial Ransom, who came here is 1826. He was the hamlet's first postmaster. Settlement of the Town of Porter, which was incorporated in 1812, began around 1801. It was named after Judge Augustus Porter, a land surveyor. Historically an agricultural region, in the past the area was known for its dairy farms and fruit industry.

AREA CODE The area code is 716.

GUIDANCE **Niagara River Region Visitors Center** (716-754-9500; www.niagarariver region.com) 895 Center Street, Lewiston.

   Lewiston Council on the Arts (716-754-0166; www.artcouncil.org). Many arts and cultural events take place in Lewiston throughout the year; see the website for a complete listing.

GETTING THERE *By car:* For Lewiston and Youngstown from Niagara Falls, take the Niagara Scenic Parkway. This area can also be reached from Route 104. The Sanborn and Ransomville area can be accessed via Routes 31, 104, 425, and 429.

MEDICAL EMERGENCY Dial 911.

SAILBOATS ON THE NIAGARA RIVER IN YOUNGSTOWN

Mount St. Mary's Hospital (716-297-4800; www.msmh.org), 5300 Military Road, Lewiston.

✳ To See

ART MUSEUMS ♿ **Castellani Art Museum** (716-286-8200; www.castellaniartmuseum .org), Niagara University Campus, Route 104, Lewiston. Open Tuesday–Saturday 11 AM–5 PM, Sunday 1–5 PM; closed holidays. Free admission. This museum, on the campus of Niagara University, has something for everyone, including over 5,000 pieces of mostly modern art as well as regional folk art and changing exhibits.

MUSEUMS AND HISTORIC HOMES
Das Haus (716-795-2890; dashausmuseum .org), 2549 Niagara Road, Bergholz. Open May–October, Sunday 2–4 PM. This 1843 log home and replica barn serves as the museum of the Historical Society of North German Settlements in western New York.

Lewiston Historical Museum (754-4214; www.historiclewiston.org), 469 Plain Street, Lewiston. Open Wednesday 1–4 PM. Displays on the history of Lewiston and the Niagara Frontier can be found in a circa-1836 church.

♿ **Native American Museum of Art** (716-297-0251) Smokin' Joe's, 2293

CASTELLANI ART MUSEUM AT NIAGARA UNIVERSITY

THE LEWISTON HISTORICAL MUSEUM IS LOCATED IN A 1836 CHURCH

Sanders Settlement Road, Sanborn. View artwork by internationally famous Native American sculptor Joseph Jacobs and other native artists, while learning about the history and culture of the Tuscarora Nation. The museum shop features Native American art, crafts, and books, along with gold jewelry. See also *Special Shops*.

Ransomville Historical Museum (716-791-4073), 3733 Ransomville Road, Ransomville. Open Saturdays 2–4 PM or by appointment. This museum has historical artifacts pertaining to the Ransomville area.

&. **Sanborn Historical Museum** (716-731-4708; www.sanbornhistory.org), 2822 Niagara Street, Sanborn. Open Sunday 2–4 PM April–November; December–March only open the first Sunday of month. This former schoolhouse houses artifacts from Sanborn's past, including numerous photos, a potbelly stove, a collection of German dolls, antique sewing items, and Tuscarora Indian Reservation history.

Sanborn-Lewiston Farm Museum (716-990-6909; www.sanbornhistory.org), 2660 Saunders Settlement Road, Sanborn. Open April–October, Wednesday 1–4 PM,

FREEDOM CROSSING MONUMENT IN LEWISTON LANDING PARK

Sundays 2–4 PM. This museum shows what farm life was like in the past. It has a farm kitchen and laundry, a barn with vintage equipment, and a smokehouse.

Town of Porter Historical Society (716-745-1271), 240 Lockport Street, 2nd Floor, Youngstown. Open Wednesday–Thursday 2–4 PM, Saturday 10 AM–2 PM. This museum focuses on the history of Youngstown and the Town of Porter.

HISTORIC SITES **Freedom Crossing Monument**. Located at the foot of Center Street at Water Street in Lewiston Landing Park, this monument depicts slaves crossing the Niagara River to freedom in Canada. There is also another bronze sculpture at the other end of town, at the corner of Center Street and Portage Road. The **Tuscarora Heroes Monument** depicts the Tuscarora Indians defending Lewiston against the 1813 British attack on the village.

Frontier House (716-754-2663), 460 Center Street, Lewiston. This Federal-style building, built between 1820 and 1824 with stone from the old Lewiston Stone Quarry, is listed on the National Register of Historic Places. Currently it is vacant, but in its day the Frontier House was a well-known stagecoach stop and was considered to be the finest hotel west of Albany. Many prominent people spent the night here, including James Fenimore Cooper, Charles Dickens, President Abraham Lincoln, and Thomas Edison.

✪ **Lewiston Portage Landing Site** at Artpark, 450 South 4th Street, Lewiston. This National Historic Landmark site along the Niagara River marks the spot where Native Americans and fur traders would land their vessels to portage the boats and goods to the upper landing above Niagara Falls, avoiding the lower rapids and the falls. An ancient Native American burial site is located just above the landing.

✏ ✪ **Old Fort Niagara** (716-745-7611; www.oldfortniagara.org), Fort Niagara State Park, Route 18F at the north end of the Niagara Scenic Parkway, Youngstown. Take a step back in time at Old Fort Niagara. Preserved as they stood in the 1700s, the fort's structures include the French Castle—the oldest building in the Great Lakes region. This National Historic Landmark fort, just minutes from Niagara Falls, was the site of many historic battles. The fort's costumed staff demonstrates eighteenth-century military life, including drills and musket and cannon firings. Re-enactments are held several times a year, and educational programs are offered to youth groups. Remnants of Fort Niagara's War of 1812 garrison flag, captured by the British is 1813 and acquired by the fort in the 1990s, is displayed in the visitor center.

THE FRENCH CASTLE AT OLD FORT NIAGARA

OUR LADY OF FATIMA SHRINE IN LEWISTON

LIGHTHOUSES **Old Fort Niagara Lighthouse** (716-745-7611; www.oldfortniagara.org), Fort Niagara State Park, Youngstown. Built in 1871 to mark the mouth of the Niagara River, the original tower was an octagon 50 feet high. Over the years it has gone through many renovations, including making it shorter and changing the roof of the work room to resemble a medieval castle. In 1900 alterations were made to make it more visible to passing ships. The lighthouse was in use until 1993.

RELIGIOUS SITES & **Our Lady of Fatima Shrine** (716-754-7489; www.fatimashrine.com), 1023 Swann Road, Lewiston. Open daily 9 AM–5 PM. During the Festival of the Lights November–January, open 9 AM–9 PM. Free admission. This shrine, operated by the Barnabite Fathers, is a place of natural beauty, art, prayer, and renewal for the thousands who visit it each year. Constructed in 1954, the shrine was modeled after the Fatima Shrine in Lisbon, Portugal. The focal point of the shrine is the basilica, a dome-shaped church 100 feet in diameter and 55 feet high, which depicts the Northern Hemisphere. A 13-foot statue of Our Lady of Fatima rests on the dome. The heart-shaped pond in front of the basilica is surrounded by a giant rosary. On the grounds of the 20-acre shrine are over 100 life-sized marble statues representing saints from every race and walk of life.

BREWERIES AND WINERIES There are a number of wineries, breweries, and cideries in this area that are part of the Niagara Wine Trail (niagarawinetrail.org).

A Gust of Sun Winery (716-731-4878; www.agustofsun.com), 4515 Baer Road, Ransomville. They have a variety of dry and sweet wines to choose from. A second location can be found in Spencerport in the Rochester area.

Long Cliff Winery (716-731-3316; www.longcliffwinery.com), 3617 Lower Mountain Road, Sanborn. Grapes for their wines, including Riesling, Pinot Gris, and Pinot Noir, are grown on their family farm on the Niagara Escarpment.

Midnight Run Winery (716-751-6200; www.midnightrunwines.com), 3301 Braley Road, Ransomville. Located in the peaceful countryside, just 20 minutes from Niagara Falls, they have a variety of wines from dry to specialty dessert wines.

See also *Breweries and Wineries* in *Lockport* and *Lake Ontario Shore*.

✳ To Do

AUTO RACING **Ransomville Speedway** (716-791-3602; www.ransomvillespeedway .com), 2315 Braley Road (off Ransomville Road), Ransomville. Open Friday nights May–September. A regional motorsport track.

BOATING AND SAILING With the abundance of water in the area, boating and sailing are very popular pastimes. One can launch a boat in Lewiston at the public ramp by **Lewiston Landing Waterfront Park** on South Water Street. In Youngstown there are two ramps located in **Fort Niagara State Park** as well as a public ramp located next to the **Youngstown Yacht Club** on Water Street.

Niagara Jet Adventures (716-745-7121; www.niagarajet.com), 555 Water Street, Youngstown. Enjoy white water boat tours on the lower Niagara River in climate-controlled boats.

Whirlpool Jet Boat Tours (888-438-4444; www.whirlpooljet.com), 115 South Water Street, Lewiston. Open May 1–end of October. Take a jet boat ride to the whirlpool through the world-famous Lower Niagara rapids for some great scenery and an exciting white water adventure. Choose either the wet-jet option (rain suits, ponchos, and life jackets are provided, but bring a change of clothes since you will get soaked during your adventure) or the jet dome ride (same exciting white water ride but in a fully enclosed boat).

CROSS-COUNTRY SKIING See **Bond Lake, Joseph Davis State Park, Reservoir State Park, Fort Niagara State Park** in *Green Space—Parks*.

GOLF **Shawnee Country Club** (716-731-5177), 6020 Townline Road, Sanborn. A public 9-hole, par-36 course with some memberships. Amenities include electric carts, a full bar, a restaurant, and banquet facilities.

FISHING The **Lower Niagara River** is a prime year-round fishing spot. From November through May steelhead are plentiful here, while lake trout are the catch of the day January through May. Brown trout can also be found in abundance during early winter and spring, and in spring the salmon fishing is phenomenal. Fishing licenses can be obtained at any town or county municipal clerk's office, Dick's Sporting Goods stores, Wal-Mart, and most bait and tackle shops. The Lower Niagara River offers many spots where anglers can fish from shore, including the following state parks: **Artpark, Devil's Hole, Fort Niagara, Joseph Davis,** and **Whirlpool.** Another fishing access site is the **Niagara Power Project Visitors Center Fishing Platform** (access road into the gorge near Niagara University)

FAMILY FUN ♿ ✎ **Power Vista–Niagara Power Project Visitors Center** (716-286-6661 or 800-NYPA-FUN; www.nypa.gov), 5777 Lewiston Road, Lewiston. Open 9 AM–5 PM year-round. Free admission. Exhibits on energy, electricity, and local history generate fun for the entire family. The "Power Vista," which overlooks the Niagara Gorge, attracts thousands of visitors yearly. Hands-on activities let visitors learn about electricity, get

THE POWER VISTA OVERLOOKS THE NIAGARA GORGE.

some helpful hints on energy efficiency, learn about hydropower in western New York history, and even send an electronic postcard over the Internet.

SCENIC DRIVES **Great Lakes Seaway Trail** (www.seawaytrail.com). Part of the trail follows Lake Road (Route 18) through Porter and Youngstown, River Road (Route 18 F) in Lewiston, and Route 104 and Main Street in Niagara Falls. The drive between Youngstown and Lewiston is very scenic, with the Niagara River on one side and large well-kept homes on the other.

SLEDDING See **Bond Lake County Park** in *Green Space—Parks*.

✳ Green Space

PARKS **Academy Park** (716-754-8272), 9th and Center Streets, Lewiston. This village green has a picnic area, recreational areas, and a baseball diamond.

Artpark State Park See *Theatres*.

Bond Lake County Park (716-731-3256), 2531 Lower Mountain Road, Lewiston. This park offers picnicking, boating, hiking trails, fishing, a nature center, and a 100-foot sledding hill in winter.

Constitution Park (716-745-7721), Main Street, Youngstown. This small park with a gazebo overlooks the Niagara River (steps lead down to boat docks), with a great view of Fort George in Niagara-on-the-Lake, Ontario.

Falkner Park (716-745-7721), 355 2nd Street, Youngstown. This large park has a playground, walkways, benches, and a picnic gazebo.

Fort Niagara State Park (716-745-7273), Route 18F, Youngstown. Open daily, dawn to dusk. Fort Niagara State Park offers breathtaking views of Lake Ontario; on a clear day you can see the skyline of Toronto, 24 miles across the lake. Some of the oak trees located in the 708-acre park are over 200 years old. Picnicking is popular here; over 500 picnic tables and five shelters are located within the park. There are also playgrounds, tennis courts, a wading pool, and an Olympic-sized swimming pool. The park's eighteen soccer fields are often used for regional and national competitions. In winter, visitors can cross-country ski, snowshoe, and sled. Historic Old Fort Niagara, located at the mouth of the Niagara River, offers visitors a glimpse of eighteenth-century military life (see *Historic Sites*). One of the area's best sunset vistas can be found on the hill overlooking Lake Ontario. See also *Lighthouses*.

Four Mile Creek State Campgrounds (716-745-3802 or 800-456-CAMP), Lake Road, Youngstown. Open for camping mid-April–mid-October. This park is used mainly for fishing, picnicking, and camping. There are 266 campsites, many with beautiful river views. Facilities include central shelters with flush toilets, showers, and laundry. Hiking trails follow densely wooded bluffs overlooking the lake. $

Hennepin Park (716-754-8271), 4th and Center Streets, Lewiston. This small park has a gazebo and several sitting areas.

Joseph Davis State Park (716-754-4596), 4143 Lower River Road, Lewiston. Open daily, dawn to dusk. Free admission. The terrain in this park along the lower Niagara River is flat, with fields, woodlands, and ponds. Facilities include a playground, a nature trail, and a 27-hole Frisbee disc golf course. Fishermen can either fish in the pond for largemouth bass or head down to the river for a variety of freshwater fish. During the winter months, park visitors enjoy cross-county skiing, snowshoeing, and snowmobiling.

Lewiston Landing Waterfront Park (716-754-8271), Water Street, Lewiston. Overlooking the Niagara River, this park is one of the most scenic spots in Lewiston. There's also a public boat launch.

Reservoir State Park (716-284-5778), Routes 265 and 31, Lewiston. Open daily, dawn to dusk. Free admission. Overlooking the Robert Moses Power Plant Reservoir, this park is one of the most used in Niagara County. Facilities include four tennis courts, eight baseball diamonds, a softball complex, picnic facilities, and open spaces for flying kites or model planes. It's a popular place to sled and cross-country ski during winter.

Veteran's Park (716-745-3061), 3rd Street, Youngstown. Facilities include baseball diamonds, tennis court and basketball courts, and picnic facilities.

WALKING AND HIKING TRAILS More information on the following trails can be obtained by calling the **New York State Office of Parks, Recreation and Historic Preservation** (716-278-1770).

Lewiston Branch Gorge Trail (in Artpark State Park). Starting at the edge of the Niagara Escarpment in Lewiston, this 2-mile round-trip hike offers upper and lower trail options, with the lower trail closer to the Niagara River.

HENNEPIN PARK, LEWISTON

Ongiara Trail (in Devil's Hole State Park). This 2.5-mile round-trip trail goes from the parking lot down stairs into the gorge near the Whirlpool and Devil's Hole Rapids.

Whirlpool Rapids Trail (Whirlpool State Park). A 3.25-mile round-trip trail that spans Whirlpool State Park and leads into the Niagara River Gorge. Choose between two paths, one at the river level and one at mid gorge.

Whirlpool Rim Trail (Whirlpool State Park). A 2.5-mile round-trip trail along the rim of the Niagara Gorge.

Upper Great Gorge Trail. This easy 2-mile round-trip trail starts at the Niagara Gorge Discovery Center and takes you into the gorge to the head of the rapids. The **Upper Great Gorge Rim Trail**, which also starts at the Niagara Gorge Discovery Center, is another easy 2-mile, round-trip hike, this one leading to the American Falls, Goat Island, and the Horseshoe Falls.

Lewiston River Walk. Along Route 18F between Lewiston and Youngstown. This paved, 6-foot-wide path offers scenic vistas of the Niagara River and the historic homes that line the parkway.

✳ Lodging

INNS AND RESORTS **Niagara Crossing Hotel & Spa** (716-754-9070; www.niagaracrossinghotelandspa.com) 100 Center Street, Lewiston. This upscale sixty-seven-room boutique hotel with full service spa overlooks the lower Niagara River. Rooms are decorated in Colonial and Federal style to reflect the area's heritage. Some rooms have fireplaces and/or whirlpools. $$.

MOTELS **Aartpark Hotel** (716-754-8295; www.aartparkhotel.com) 280 Portage

Road, Lewiston. This newly renovated hotel has family-friendly rooms, free Wi-Fi, and a continental breakfast. $$.

Riverside Motel (716-754-4101; riverside.vpweb.com), 160 South Water Street, Lewiston. Enjoy ten cozy, cottage-like rooms with a large front yard with outdoor seating and a view of the lower Niagara River. All rooms are decorated with country decor and include air conditioning and refrigerators. $$.

OTHER LODGING **Four Mile Creek State Campground.** See *Green Space—Parks.*

HENNEPIN PARK IN LEWISTON

✳ Where to Eat

DINING OUT 🖉 ♿ **Apple Granny** (716-754-2028; www.applegranny.com), 433 Center Street, Lewiston. Open Tuesday–Thursday 11 AM–9 PM, Friday and Saturday 11 AM–10 PM and Sunday 11 AM–8 PM. Enjoy casual dining at its finest in this circa-1830 building. This popular family restaurant serves perennial favorites like sandwiches and burgers, plus their specialty Granny's Awesome Blossom blooming onion. Dinner selections include prime rib, filet mignon, chicken, veal, Italian specialties, seafood, and Granny's famous beer-battered fish fry on Friday.

THE BRICKYARD PUB IN LEWISTON HAS GREAT BARBECUE

Brickyard Restaurant (716-754-7227; www.brickyardpub.com), 432 Center Street, Lewiston. Sunday 12–9 PM, Monday–Friday 11 AM–11 PM, Saturday 11 AM–12 AM, pub is open until 2 AM Sunday–Friday and until 3 AM on Saturday. This casual eatery and pub serves classic Southern BBQ, including ribs, chicken, and pulled pork. The adjacent Brickyard Brewing Company, which opened in summer 2017, is Lewiston's first craft brewery.

&. **Carmelo's** (716-754-2311; www.carmelos-restaurant.com), 425 Center Street, Lewiston. Tuesday–Thursday 5–9 PM, Friday and Saturday 5–9:30 PM. Contemporary cuisine is served in this 1838 building located in the heart of the historic district. Chef Carmelo Raimondi designs food that's as pleasing to the eye as it is to the palate.

Casa Antica (716-754-4904; www.casaanticarestaurant.com), 490 Center Street, Lewiston. Tuesday–Sunday 4–10 PM. Fine Italian cuisine is offered in this large white house with a dining room overlooking Center Street.

Center Cut Village Steakhouse (716-246-2023; www.thevillagesteakhouse.com), 453 Center Street, Lewiston. Opens daily at 5 PM. One of Lewiston's premier dining destinations, the menu features steak, chops, surf & turf, and more.

Griffon House, 810 Center Street, Lewiston. The menu features locally sourced ingredients, along with fifty taps of draft beer and custom cocktails. (To open August 2017.)

Water Street Landing (716-754-9200; www.waterstreetlanding.com), 115 South Water Street, Lewiston. Open daily for lunch 11:30 AM–12 AM. This riverside restaurant overlooks the Niagara River and the lower gorge and features a varied menu that includes steaks, chops, chicken, and seafood. In warmer weather dine outdoors on the patio overlooking the river and the Canadian shore.

EATING OUT **700 Center Street Juice Bistro and Café** (716-429-5466; www.700centerstreet.com), 700 Center Street, Lewiston. Monday–Saturday 8 AM–7 PM, Sunday 9 AM–4 PM. Enjoy a variety of smoothies, organic coffee, wraps, paninis, baked goods, and even wheatgrass shots.

DiCamillo Bakery (716-754-2218; www.dicamillobakery.com), 535 Center Street, Lewiston. Daily 6 AM–7 PM. They've been serving quality baked goods since 1920, including bread, rolls, donuts, bagels,

WATER STREET LANDING

pastries, and pizza. Two small tables are located in the front of the shop to eat in.

Gallo Coal Fire Kitchen (716-405-7596; www.gallocoalfirekitchen.com) 800 Center Street, Lewiston. Monday–Wednesday 4–9 PM, Thursday–Saturday 4–10 PM. Enjoy thin crust pizzas baked in a coal-fire oven at this restaurant located on the former site of Hustler's Tavern.

✦ **Hibbard's Custard** (716-754-4218; www.hibbardscustard.com), 105 Portage Road at Center Street, Lewiston (look for the blue-and-white awning). Open seasonally April–September, Sunday–Thursday 11 AM–9 PM, Friday–Saturday 11 AM–11 PM. Since 1939, Hibbard's has been serving its own homemade, original recipe soft-serve custard, along with shakes, floats, and hard ice cream.

✦ 🍴 ♿ **Hoover Dairy Restaurant** (716-731-3830), 6035 Ward Road, Sanborn. Monday–Friday 11 AM–8 PM, Saturday–Sunday 11 AM–6 PM. A casual restaurant serving burgers, sandwiches, ice cream, and milkshakes. You can purchase chocolate and strawberry milk, along with eggnog (seasonal) by bottle. Their dairy, which also supplies white milk, is located behind the restaurant on Hoover Road; it's open Monday–Friday 8:30 AM–6 PM, Saturday 8:30 AM–1 PM. Call 716-731-3822 for more info.

Johnston's Family Restaurant (716-791-3511), 2575 Academy Street, Ransomville. Open Sunday–Tuesday 6 AM–9 PM, Wednesday–Friday 6 AM–10 PM, Saturday 7 AM–10 PM. This restaurant has been family-owned and operated since Prohibition. The extensive menu features old-fashioned home cooking made with locally grown produce. Selections include homemade soups, salads served in an edible taco bowl, sandwich platters, steaks, seafood, ribs, and chicken.

✦ **Lewiston Silo** (716-754-9680; www.lewistonsilo.com), 115 North Water Street, Lewiston. Daily 10 AM–10 PM, May–September. Enjoy casual dining, including 30 flavors of hand-dipped ice cream, in a circular restaurant on the water's edge.

THE LEWISTON SILO RESTAURANT OVERLOOKS THE NIAGARA RIVER

♿ **Main Street Pizzeria Gas and Grill** (716-745-1130), 311 Main Street, Youngstown. Open Monday 3–9 PM, Sunday and Tuesday–Thursday 11 AM–9 PM, Friday–Saturday 11 AM–10 PM. A cute spot to stop for a quick bite to eat. It has a small, casual pizzeria restaurant and shop with groceries and other essentials that boaters may need, plus public rest rooms and a gas station.

Mug & Musket Tavern (716-745-9938), 418 Main Street, Youngstown. Wednesday–Thursday 4–10 PM, Friday–Saturday 12–10 PM, Sunday 12–9 PM. A casual restaurant featuring pub food and live music.

Ontario House/"The Jug" (716-219-4073), 358 Main Street, Youngstown. Enjoy dining in a circa-1845 hotel, restaurant, and tavern.

Orange Cat Coffee (716-754-2888), 703 Center Street, Lewiston. Monday–Friday 6 AM–6 PM, Saturday 8:30 AM–6 PM, Sunday 8:30 AM–3 PM. This restaurant features a variety of coffee beverages, along with a menu of strictly vegetarian selections.

Syros (716-754-1900; www.syrosrestaurant.com), 869 Cayuga Street, Lewiston. Monday–Saturday 7 AM–9 PM, Sunday 7 AM–8 PM. Greek-American food. Enjoy breakfast specials along with entrees like turkey, pot roast, and Greek specialties. They also have homemade soup, a Friday fish fry, and an outdoor patio.

The Spicey Pickle (716-754-2044), 463 Center Street, Lewiston. Open Monday–Saturday 11:30 AM–9 PM. Enjoy authentic Mexican cuisine at reasonable prices, including burritos, tacos, noodles, salads, and, of course, spicy pickles.

The Lewiston Stone House (716-754-7759; www.lewistonstonehouse.com), 755 Center Street, Lewiston. This wine bar with an outdoor patio is a popular place to enjoy wine slushies on a warm summer night. Live music is featured on select summer evenings. They also have a banquet room on the second floor.

Tin Pan Alley (716-754-4330; www.thetinpanalley.net), 775 Cayuga Street, Lewiston. Sunday 12–9 PM, Monday–Saturday 11 AM–10 PM. This casual restaurant and lounge is known for wings, ribs, and burgers.

The Village Bake Shoppe (716-754-2300; www.villagebakeshoppe.com), 419 Center Street, Lewiston. Open Monday–Saturday 7:30 AM–5:30 PM, Sunday 7:30 AM–3:30 PM; open in summer until 9 PM daily. A quaint shop featuring award-winning, from-scratch desserts, including pies, cookies, scones, coffee cakes, breads, and authentic Italian gelato. A few small tables are located in the front of the shop.

Vincenzo's Pizza House (716-754-7383; www.vincenzospizzahouse.com), 742 Center Street, Lewiston. Tuesday–Saturday 11 AM–10 PM, Sunday 12–10 PM. Enjoy specialty pizzas, subs, and wings.

🍴 ♿ 🐾 **Youngstown Village Diner** (716-745-9858; www.youngstownvillagediner.com), 425 Main Street, Youngstown. Open Monday–Thursday 6 AM–8 PM, Friday and Saturday 6 AM–2 PM, Sunday 6 AM–1:30 PM. Dine at the counter or at tables in this neat and clean restaurant overlooking the Niagara River. Enjoy salads, sandwiches, burgers, and wraps, plus breakfast and dinner specials that are posted on the blackboard.

✳ Entertainment

THEATERS ♿ **Artpark** (716-754-9000; www.artpark.net), 450 South 4th Street, Lewiston. Park open daily, dawn to dusk; theater performances July and August. Call or see website for schedule. Artpark is a 200-acre state park designed to bring the arts to the general public. Here, one can experience natural beauty as well as visual and performing arts during the summer season. Visitors can also picnic along the gorge or enjoy a hike on the scenic trails. Geologists believe that 10,000 years ago Niagara Falls, now 7 miles south of here, was located at this site, before the turbulent waters etched away at the gorge.

The Marble Orchard (716-754-0166; www.artcouncil.org), This unique theatrical performance, which started as

YOUNGSTOWN VILLAGE DINER

a tour of the village cemetery, features costumed actors portraying notable people from the area's past. Performance location and schedule varies.

✱ Selective Shopping

Note: A number of the shops are in buildings which date back to the early 1800s, some with several different levels, making wheelchair and stroller accessibility difficult.

ANTIQUES

LEWISTON

The Country Doctor Antiques and Gifts (716-754-0775), 549 Center Street, Lewiston. Open Monday–Saturday 10:30 AM–5:30 PM, Sunday 11 AM–5 PM. This shop features ten dealers that specialize in gifts, antique furniture, glassware, and jewelry.

Stimson's Antiques & Gifts (716-754-7815), 1727 Ridge Road (Route 104), Lewiston. Open 1–5 PM daily; winter, Friday and Saturday only. Located in a farmhouse basement, this shop has a nice selection of antiques and collectibles.

SANBORN/RANSOMVILLE

Hilltop Country Antiques Co-op and Gift Emporium (716-550-2945) 5154 Townline Road, Sanborn. Shop for antiques, primitives, memorabilia, and more at this shop, which has wide aisles that are easy to walk through.

Ransomville Antique Co-op (716-791-3930), 3596 Ransomville Road, Ransomville. Open Wednesday–Sunday 12–5 PM; January–April, Saturday and Sunday only. Three floors of antiques and collectibles are located in an 1877 church.

Sanborn Old General Store (716-731-4578; sanbornoldgeneralstore.yolasite .com), 5856 Buffalo Street (Route 429), Sanborn. Open Wednesday–Saturday 10 AM–5 PM, Sunday 11 AM–4 PM. This multi-dealer antiques and collectibles

co-op is located in the former LeVan Grocery & Hardware store, built in 1910. Choose from furniture, primitives, glassware, candles, and gifts.

&. **The Sanborn Mill Antiques** (716-731-2828), 5890 Ward Road (Route 429), Sanborn. Sunday 11 AM–5 PM, Monday–Tuesday 12–5 PM, Wednesday–Saturday 10 AM–5 PM. An antiques co-op and marketplace, located in a restored 1860 flour mill, features over 40 dealers dealing in antiques, collectibles, primitives, jewelry, gifts, glassware, military, coins, and more.

FARM MARKETS **Wagner's Farm Market** (716-731-4440; wagnersfarmmarket .com), 2672 Lockport Road, Sanborn. Open daily 9 AM–6 PM. Since 1967 the Wagner family has been offering a full range of produce from apples to zucchini as well as fresh baked goods, fresh and frozen meats, and gift baskets. The market's café restaurant features hot dogs, hamburgers, beef on weck, and more.

SPECIAL SHOPS **Canterbury Place** (716-754-4818), 547 Center Street, Lewiston. Open Tuesday–Saturday 10 AM–5 PM. A New England–style gift shop carrying a mix of romantic, traditional, and folk art accessories for the home, including Yankee Candles, Cats Village, and Williraye Studios.

Cheri Amour (716-754-8675; www .cheriamourgifts.com), 522 Center Street, Lewiston. Open Monday and Saturday 11 AM–5 PM, Tuesday–Friday 11 AM–5 PM. A French-inspired shop specializing in unique gifts and jewelry.

The Dory Trading Post (716-429-1167), 435 Main Street, Youngstown. Open Wednesday–Monday 9 AM–5 PM. This shop, located in a vintage building with exposed brick walls, is filled with a variety of art pieces and books, all created by local artists and authors.

The End of the Road Boutique (716-444-6109; www.theendoftheroad boutique.com), 335 Center Street,

THE DORY TRADING POST IN YOUNGSTOWN

Lewiston. This is the perfect place to shop for jewelry, scarves, handbags, and other accessories.

 ♿ **Smokin' Joe's Trading Post** (716-297-0251; www.smokinjoes.com), 2293 Sanders Settlement Road, Sanborn. Monday–Friday 8 AM–8 PM, Saturday 9 AM–8 PM, Sunday 9 AM–6 PM. Shopping at Smokin' Joe's is a unique experience. Since it's located on the Tuscarora Indian Reservation, which does not collect New York sales tax, it's best known for tax-free gas and cigarettes. But there's a whole lot more here. You can get groceries, gifts, jewelry, and even cigars. Located within the trading post is the **Museum of Native American Art.** See *Museums.*

You and Me (716-405-7692; www.shopyouandme.com), 467 Center Street, Lewiston. Choose from accessories, clothing, and jewelry in this small boutique shop.

✳ Special Events

June: **Strawberry Festival** (716-745-3369; www.stjohnsyoungstown.org), St. John's Episcopal Church, Main and Chestnut Streets, Youngstown. This annual festival, held in late June, features strawberry shortcake, crafts, a Chinese auction, and a flea market

July: **French and Indian War Encampment** (716-745-7611; www.oldfortniagara.org), Old Fort Niagara. This is Old Fort Niagara's largest annual event, the longest-running French and Indian War event in the world, with hundreds of re-enactors gathering at the fort to depict the war. **Tuscarora Nation Picnic** (www.tuscaroras.com), Tuscarora Nation, Lewiston. This event, the oldest field day in Niagara County, showcases the Tuscarora Nation's Native American culture.

August: **Lewiston Outdoor Fine Arts Festival and Chalkwalk Competition** (716-754-0166; www.artcouncil.org). A two-day event, ranked one of the top 100 attractions along the Seaway Trail, which showcases more than 150 artists from the United States and Canada. The festival's Chalkwalk is a popular art competition among area high schools. **Lewiston Jazz Festival** (716-754-9500; www.lewistonjazz.com). Music, antiques, vintage cars, and culinary samplings throughout the village.

September: **Niagara County Peach Festival** (716-754-9500). Lewiston Festivities include amusement rides, games of chance, Peach Queen Pageant, and, of course, peach-related food. **New York Power Authority's Wildlife Festival** Power Vista (716-286-6661; www.nypa.gov). A day of family fun, featuring live animals, music, art workshops, and more. **Youngstown Volunteer Field Days** (716-745-3335), Veteran's Park, Youngstown.

Family fun to celebrate the end of summer. Activities include a parade, car show, fireworks, and lawn mower racing.

October: **Frontier Fur Traders Weekend** (716-745-7611; www.oldfortniagara .org), Old Fort Niagara. Fort Niagara becomes a wilderness trading post once again as trappers and traders depict the early history of the fort. Re-enactors re-create the era when the fur trade dominated the region. **The Haunted Fortress,** also at Old Fort Niagara. Get up close and personal with some of the ghosts of the fort. **The Marble Orchard** (716-754-0166), Lewiston Village Cemetery. This annual event features stories about Lewiston's past and the Underground Railroad.

November–January: **Festival of Lights** (716-754-7489), Our Lady of Fatima Shrine. Enjoy 15 acres of religious-themed light displays.

December: **Castle by Candlelight** (716-745-7611), Old Fort Niagara. An annual holiday fund-raiser for the fort. **Christmas in the Village** (716-745-3061), Youngstown. Festivities include a Christmas play, musical entertainment, wagon rides, and Santa Claus. **Historic Lewiston Christmas Walk** (716-754-9500), Lewiston. This annual event offers visitors old-fashioned fun, including caroling, roasting chestnuts, sleigh rides, crafts shows, and a parade down Center Street.

NORTH TONAWANDA AND WHEATFIELD

Orth Tonawanda, incorporated as a Village in 1865 and as a City in 1897, is located on the Niagara County (north) side of the Erie Canal. The name came from Tonawanda Creek, which also has served as the Tonawanda's portion of the Erie Canal since 1825. In the Seneca language, *Tonawanda* means "swift running water."

Industrial development to the area began in 1825 once the Erie Canal was complete. Together with the neighboring Village of Tonawanda (Erie County), North Tonawanda was one of the largest lumber processing and distribution centers in the country. North Tonawanda was also home to the largest carousel manufacturer in the United States and the place where Randolph Wurlitzer first manufactured the Wurlitzer organ and jukebox. Many other industries of significance found their home in North Tonawanda. (See *Northern Erie County—Grand Island, Tonawanda, Kenmore* for more information and listings.)

The Town of Wheatfield was incorporated as a town in 1836, the last town to do so in Niagara County. Today most of the town is more rural in nature than some of the surrounding communities.

AREA CODE The area code is 716.

GUIDANCE **Chamber of Commerce of the Tonawandas** (716-692-5120; www.the-tonawandas.com), 254 Sweeney Street, North Tonawanda. Open Monday–Friday 8:30 AM–4:30 PM.

GETTING THERE *By bus:* NFTA buses #61 (North Tonawanda) and #79 (Tonawanda) offer express service to and from Buffalo.

By car: The major expressways running through the Tonawandas include the I-290 (Youngmann Memorial Highway) and Route 425 (Twin Cities Memorial Highway).

MEDICAL EMERGENCY Dial 911.

DeGraff Memorial Hospital (716-694-4500; www.kaleidahealth.org), 445 Tremont Street, North Tonawanda.

✳ To See

ART MUSEUMS **The Carnegie Art Center** (716-694-4400; www.carnegieartcenter .org), 240 Goundry Street, North Tonawanda. Open Thursday 6–9 PM and Saturday 12–3 PM. This building, originally a public library, was erected in 1903, one of many library buildings throughout the country built with funds donated by Andrew Carnegie. It was placed on the National Register of Historic Places in 1995. The arts center features contemporary art exhibits and special events as well as art education classes.

MUSEUMS AND HISTORIC HOMES & ♪ **Herschell Carrousel Factory Museum** (716-693-1885; carrouselmuseum.org), 180 Thompson Street, North Tonawanda. Open

HERSCHELL CARROUSEL FACTORY MUSEUM IN NORTH TONAWANDA

April–December, hours vary. The museum has a collection of carousel animals, exhibits on the early carousel industry, and the growth of "kiddie rides." The Allan Herschell Company, founded in 1915, manufactured over 2,000 hand-carved carousels at this factory. Seventy-one of the remaining 148 hand-carved carousels still in existence in the US were made by Allan Herschell. Watch wood carvers demonstrate how carousel horses are made, and ride on an antique 1916 hand-carved wooden carousel. Small children can also ride on a 1940s aluminum kiddie carousel. The gift shop is stocked with hundreds of carousel-themed items.

North Tonawanda History Museum (716-213-0554; www.nthistorymuseum.org), 54 Webster Street, North Tonawanda. Hours vary. This museum tells the story of North Tonawanda's ethnic and industrial heritage, including displays on the lumber industry.

Railroad Museum of the Niagara Frontier (716-694-9588; www.nfcnrhs.com), 111 Oliver Street, North Tonawanda. Open Saturdays 1–4 PM, June–August or by appointment. Donation. This museum is housed in a 1923 Erie Railroad station. It includes indoor exhibits as well as two locomotives, two cabooses, a boxcar, and an operating hand car.

HISTORIC ARCHITECTURE Take a walk down **Goundry Street** in **North Tonawanda** to get a glimpse of the mansions built by the lumber barons during Tonawanda's early days. They are private residences and not open for tours, but reportedly many of the homes have beautiful wood carvings and wainscoting. Pay special attention to **208 Goundry Street**, known as Kent Place. Considered one of the most beautiful mansions on the block, it was designed for Alexander Kent by Stanford White, the designer of Madison Square Garden and New York Central Terminal in New York City. The **US Post Office** on Goundry and Oliver Streets is listed on the National Register of Historic Sites.

✳ To Do

FAMILY FUN ✐ **Niagara Climbing Center** (716-695-1248; www.niagaraclimbingcenter .com), 1333 Strad Avenue, North Tonawanda. Folks of all ages can safely enjoy the sport of rock climbing, with safety lessons offered to first-time climbers. Climbers are strapped into a safety harness, so if you do slip, the only thing that's bruised is your ego.

FISHING The following parks are popular for fishing: **Fisherman's Park, Gratwick-Riverside Park, West Canal Marina**, and **Oppenheim County Park**. Fishing licenses can be obtained at any town or county municipal clerk's office, Dick's Sporting Goods stores, Wal-Mart, and most bait and tackle shops.

GOLF **Deerwood Golf Course** (716-695-8525), 1818 Sweeney Street, North Tonawanda, A public course with 27 holes (9-hole course, plus 18-hole course). It has a restaurant, a full bar, and a snack bar.

SKATING **Rainbow Rink** (716-693-1100; rainbowrink.com), 101 Oliver Street, North Tonawanda. Hours vary. The Rainbow Rink has been a North Tonawanda landmark since 1949. This family-run facility offers traditional skating along with a game zone and a bounce zone. Birthday skating parties can also be held here.

Green Space

PARKS **Fisherman's Park** (716-695-8520), River Road, North Tonawanda. This park, located along the Niagara River, offers two shelters, fishing, a band shell presenting Thursday evening concerts, and a nationally recognized monument to US Navy Seabees. There is also a US Marine Corps Memorial.

TONAWANDAS GATEWAY HARBOR

Gateway Harbor Park (716-695-8520, North Tonawanda; 716-743-8189, Tonawanda), Main and Webster Streets, Tonawanda/North Tonawanda. Gateway Harbor Park is a two-block park bordering the Erie Canal along Niagara Street in the City of Tonawanda and Sweeney Street in North Tonawanda. One of seven major harbors along the New York State Canal System, the park is the site of the annual Canal Fest each July. Docking facilities are equipped with electricity and water, and showers and rest rooms are available for boaters at the Harbor Master's Station on the Tonawanda side.

Gratwick-Riverside Park (716-695-8520), River Road, North Tonawanda. Open daily, dawn to dusk. Free admission. This 53-acre park has docking facilities, picnic shelters, nature areas, bird watching, nature trails, and fishing along the Niagara River. You can see the mist of Niagara Falls from here.

North Tonawanda Botanical Gardens, Sweeney Street at Robinson Road, North Tonawanda. This canal-side park features flowers, a gazebo, a boat launch, and walking paths.

West Canal Marina (716-439-7950), 4070 Tonawanda Creek Road, North Tonawanda. Find picnic shelters, fishing, a boat launch, and observation points.

WALKING, HIKING, AND BIKING TRAILS **Niagara River Walk and Bicycle Trail**. This 10-foot wide, 2-mile blacktop trail winds in and out of Gratwick Park, Fisherman's Park, and Gateway Harbor Park as well as the downtown business district. It connects with the **Buffalo and Erie County Riverwalk**. See also *Tonawanda—Walking, Hiking, and Biking Trails*.

✳ Where to Eat

DINING OUT **Canal Club 62 Tap & Eatery** (716-260-1824; www.canalclub62 .com), 62 Webster Street, North Tonawanda. Open Tuesday–Thursday 4–11 PM, Friday–Saturday 4 PM–12 AM, Sunday 4–9 PM. An upscale eatery that has a menu featuring salads, sandwiches, small plates, and entrees like short ribs and chicken piccata, along with draft beer and cocktails.

Remington Tavern & Seafood Exchange (716-362-2802; www .remingtontavern.com), 184 Sweeney Street, North Tonawanda. Located in a historic brick building that was once a trolley barn, this restaurant has a menu focusing on seafood as well as on beef and ribs. Live music is featured on Wednesdays and Mondays.

Webster's Bistro and Bar (716-264-4314; www.webstersbistro.com), 102 Webster Street, North Tonawanda. Tuesday–Thursday 4:30-9 PM, Friday–Saturday 4:30-10 PM. Dine in a neighborhood restaurant with the atmosphere of a French bistro. Menu items include steak au poivre, beef bourguiguon, chicken francaise, and crepes.

EATING OUT **Canalside Creamery** (716-695-2876), 82 Webster Street, North Tonawanda. Enjoy ice cream and gelato, along with a selection of sandwiches.

Crazy Jakes (716-693-9309), 26 Webster Street, North Tonawanda. This bar and restaurant has pub grub along with steaks and seafood. Live music is featured on the weekend. An outdoor patio is open during the warmer months.

🐷 🍴 **Country Cottage** (716-693-4911), 4072 Beach Ridge Road, Pendleton. Monday–Thursday, Saturday 8 AM–8 PM, Friday 8 AM–8:30 PM, Sunday 8 AM–2 PM. An area landmark since 1948, this cute country restaurant decorated with a pig theme features daily specials along with standbys like omelets and pancakes for breakfast, homemade soup, chili, salads, and sandwiches for lunch, and dinners like breaded pork chops and chicken and biscuits. Be sure to try the LA cinnamon bread, toasted and topped with cinnamon syrup.

THERE ARE A NUMBER OF SHOPS AND RESTAURANTS ALONG WEBSTER STREET IN NORTH TONAWANDA.

Dockside Bar and Grill (716-693-3600; www.docksident.com), 153 Sweeney Street, North Tonawanda. This casual restaurant, located beside the Erie Canal in a circa-1890 building, is known for its Friday fish frys. Boaters can dock right by the restaurant.

The Flavor Factory (716-389-0128; www.theflavorfactory.net), 31 Webster Street, North Tonawanda. Sunday–Thursday 11 AM–9 PM, Friday–Saturday 11 AM–10 PM. Enjoy ice cream, frozen yogurt, and smoothies. You can even build your own sundaes.

Hideaway Grille (716-694-2710; www.hideawaygrille.com) 399 Division Street, North Tonawanda. Lunch Monday–Friday 11:30 AM–3 PM, dinner Monday–Saturday 4 -10 PM. Their lunch menu features salads, wraps, paninis, and burgers, while the dinner menu has a variety of items including chicken, pasta, steak, seafood, and their ribs, which is their specialty. Prime rib is served on Saturday.

JP Dwyer's Irish Pub (716-692-4837; www.dwyerspub.com), 65 Webster Street, North Tonawanda. Open Monday–Thursday 4 PM–2 AM, Friday–Saturday 12 PM–3 AM, Sunday 12 PM–2 AM. This bar and restaurant serves traditional pub-style food. They are known for their fourteen different varieties of chicken wings. The restaurant, which has a cigar store Indian in the corner by the bar, is located adjacent to the Riviera Theater, about a block from the canal.

Lou's Restaurant (716-694-6025), 73 Webster Street, North Tonawanda. Tuesday–Friday 7 AM–7 PM, Saturday–Monday 7 AM–2 PM. A small, family-run restaurant which features homestyle cooking, daily specials, and homemade desserts. It is located right next door to the historic Riviera Theater and a short walk from the Erie Canal.

Panes Restaurant (716-692-7076; www.panesrestaurant.com), 984 Payne Avenue, North Tonawanda. Since 1959, Pane's has been the place to eat in North Tonawanda. The menu features salads, sandwiches, pasta, seafood, beef, chicken, pizza, wings, and more, along with their signature French onion soup.

The Shores Waterfront Restaurant (716-693-7971), 2 Detroit Street (Tonawanda Island), North Tonawanda.

Open seasonally May–October, daily 11 AM–9 PM, Friday and Saturday until midnight. Enjoy casual American cuisine, everything from sandwiches and burgers to steaks and seafood, with a great view of the Niagara River and Grand Island. Live bands are featured on the weekend.

Yummy Thai (716-694-1763; www.yummythairestaurant.com), 92 Webster Street, North Tonawanda. Sunday–Friday 11 AM–10 PM, Saturday 11 AM–11 PM. Enjoy authentic Thai cuisine in this cozy restaurant.

✲ Entertainment

Riviera Theater and Performing Arts Center (716-692-2413; www.riviera theatre.org), 67 Webster Street, North Tonawanda. This restored Italian Renaissance–style performing-arts venue was built in 1926 and is listed on the National Register of Historic Places. The theater's lobby boasts stained-glass windows, while a 15-foot-high French chandelier with stained-glass-light bulbs is suspended from the dome of the auditorium. Throughout the year the Riviera features plays, musical concerts, movies, and more, including a monthly American Theatre Organ concert on the 1926 "Mighty Wurlitzer" organ.

✲ Selective Shopping

For additional information on stores and other businesses in the North Tonawanda see www.ntmerchants.org.

ANTIQUES **Treasure Market** (716-694-1662), 38 Webster Street, North Tonawanda. Wednesday and Saturday–Sunday 10 AM–5 PM. This shop has a varied selection of antiques, including jewelry, toys, clothing, vintage magazines, postcards, and more.

Shawnee Country Barns Antique Co-op (716-731-1430; www.scbantiques.com), 6608 Shawnee Road (Route 425), Wheatfield. Open six days 10 AM–5 PM,

THE RIVIERA THEATER ON WEBSTER STREET IN NORTH TONAWANDA

SHAWNEE COUNTRY BARN ANTIQUE CO-OP

closed Wednesday. Over 70 dealers are housed in this restored 1912 barn. Browse through two floors of glassware, furniture, jewelry, toys, and country and primitive items.

ART GALLERIES River Art Gallery (716-260-1497; riverartgalleryandgifts .com), 83 Webster Street, North Tonawanda. Wednesday–Friday 11 AM–5 PM, Saturday 11 AM–5 PM. An art gallery featuring works by western New York and southern Ontario artists. In front is a shop which has artist-made goods, and in back is a gallery with changing exhibits. This bright pink building was once the office of the *Evening News*.

FARM MARKETS ♿ **North Tonawanda City Market** (716-693-3746), Payne Avenue (at Robinson Street), North Tonawanda. Open year-round Tuesday, Thursday, and Saturday 7 AM–1 PM. Established in 1908, this is the oldest farmers' market in Niagara County. While it is open year-round, the most popular time to visit is in the summer and early fall, when over seventy local farmers set up shop.

SPECIAL SHOPS **Gleam and Glimmer Glass** (716-213-0472 gleamglimmer.com), 34 Webster Street, North Tonawanda. This stained glass studio offers a variety of classes and also has glass items and gifts for sale.

Hip Gypsy (716-260-1313; hip -gypsy.com), 78 Webster Street, North Tonawanda. Tuesday–Wednesday, Saturday 11 AM–5 PM, Thursday 11 AM–8 PM,

THE HIP GYPSY IN NORTH TONAWANDA HAS UNIQUE FASHIONS AND MORE

Friday 11 AM–7 PM. This shop has a variety of unique fashions, jewelry, home decor, coffees, and teas.

Kissel Country Tin (716-692-0052), 7296 Schultz Road at Niagara Falls Boulevard, Wheatfield. Open Tuesday–Saturday 10 AM–5 PM, Sunday 12–4 PM. This rustic country store features painted items, country gifts, Americana, pottery, seasonal decorations, and candles, along with weaving supplies. Knitting, weaving, and felting classes are taught in the fiber studio at the rear of the store.

Martinville Soapworks (716-694-4822; martinsvillesoapworks.com), 88 Webster Street, North Tonawanda. Choose from a variety of homemade bath and body items.

Michele's Motif Boutique and Gift Shop (716-957-4900), 72 Webster Street, North Tonawanda. Open Monday–Saturday 10 AM–5:30 PM. This gift shop features a variety of items, including gifts, accessories, and jewelry. They also offer beading classes.

Muscoreil's Bakery (716-692-9081, 1-800-310-8766; www.muscoreils.com), 3960 Niagara Falls Boulevard, North Tonawanda. Open daily, hours vary. They are noted for their desserts, bakery items, and wedding cakes.

Platter's Chocolate Factory (716-693-5391; www.platterschocolates.com) 908 Niagara Falls Boulevard (Wurlitzer Building), North Tonawanda. Monday–Friday 7 AM–10 PM, Saturday 8 AM–10 PM,

WATCH CHOCOLATE BEING MADE AT PLATTER'S CHOCOLATE FACTORY IN NORTH TONAWANDA

Sunday 10 AM–10 PM. Watch them make chocolate in their factory, including their famous sponge candy and other assorted chocolates. They also have a café and ice cream shop.

✳ Special Events

July: **Canal Fest of the Tonawandas** (716-692-3292; www.canalfest.org), This eight-day festival is the largest of its kind along the Erie Canal. Events include parades, youth activities, midway rides, musical entertainment, tours of historical sites, gaming, lots of foods, an arts and crafts show, a car show, and much more.

LAKE ONTARIO SHORE
Wilson, Olcott, Burt, Newfane, and Barker

Most of this area's growth can be attributed to Reuben Wilson and his family, who came here from Canada in 1810. Reuben's son Luther developed the hamlet of Wilson in 1827, adding numerous buildings and additions to the village, including a cobblestone home built in 1844.The surrounding area is known as the fruit-growing region of Niagara County. Wilson is also known as a good fishing area, especially for trout, bass, and salmon. Popular with recreational boaters and fishermen, it has a small, protected boat harbor with a marina and docking facilities.

Visitors to Olcott will find a quaint lakeside village consisting of a huge park, a small beach, good fishing, and many small shops and restaurants. However, most visitors are unaware of the town's "golden era" from 1900 to 1937, when thousands of people flocked to the village each summer by steamship or trolley to stay in the 100-room hotel with a grand ballroom that featured acts such as Guy Lombardo, Louis Armstrong, and the Dorsey Brothers.

AREA CODE The area code is 716.

GUIDANCE Newfane Town Hall/Newfane Tourism (716-778-8531; www.olcott -newfane.com), 2896 Transit Road, Newfane. Open Monday–Friday 8:30 AM–4:30 PM. Maps, brochures, and other area information is also available at the **Red Caboose**, at the

THE RED CABOOSE IN OLCOTT BEACH CONTAINS LOCAL TOURISM INFORMATION

corner of Route 18 and 78 in Olcott Beach. The Red Caboose is open daily 9 AM–5 PM, end of April–beginning of November.

Village of Wilson (716-751-6764), 375 Lake Avenue, Wilson.

GETTING THERE *By car:* Take exit 49 off I-90 and head north on Route 78 (Transit Road) to Newfane and Olcott. Wilson, Burt, and Somerset are accessed from Route 18.

MEDICAL EMERGENCY Dial 911.

Eastern Niagara Hospital (716-778-5111; www.enhs.org), 2600 William Street, Newfane.

✳ To See

MUSEUMS AND HISTORIC HOMES **Babcock Cobblestone House Museum** (716-795-9948), 7449 Lake Road, Barker. Open Saturday and Sunday 1–4 PM, last Saturday in June through second Sunday of October. This two-story Greek Revival–style cobblestone house built in 1848 by farmer Jeptha Babcock represents the mid-to-late period of the Cobblestone era. One of the more interesting features of the home is the brick bread oven that was reconstructed in the restored kitchen. The house has been restored to reflect nineteenth-century life. The property is owned by New York State Electric and Gas Corporation, and the house is maintained and furnished by the Town of Somerset Historical Society.

Newfane Historical Society Grounds (716-778-6151), West Creek Road, Newfane. The grounds have eleven historical buildings that are open to the public during festivals and by appointment.

Van Horn Mansion (716-778-7197), 2165 Lockport-Olcott Road, Burt. Open Sunday 2–4 PM, summer only. This brick mansion was built in 1823 by James Van Horn,

VAN HORN MANSION

who built the first gristmill in Newfane in 1811. Maintained by the Newfane Historical Society since 1987, this home has been restored to its former grandeur. On your tour of the house and gardens, your guide will tell you many interesting tales about the home, such as that it has been rumored to have been a stop on the Underground Railroad. Many people also believe that the ghost of Malinda Van Horn, the young wife of James Jr., who died in childbirth, once roamed the grounds. In the late 1920s the remains of the Van Horn family were all moved from the family plot on the grounds to a local cemetery—except for Malinda, because they could not locate her grave. From that time until her remains were finally located in 1992, ghostly sightings and noises were observed in the mansion.

Wilson Historical Society (716-751-9883 or 716-751-9827, 716-751-9886; www .wilsonnewyork.com), 645 Lake Street, Wilson. Open Sunday 2–4 PM, April–December. A 1912 railroad station houses vintage cars and trucks. Local historical information is available.

THE THIRTY MILE POINT LIGHTHOUSE SHROUDED IN FOG

LIGHTHOUSES **Olcott Lighthouse**
Located at the end of Route 78 at Lake Ontario. This full-size replica of an 1873 lighthouse was dedicated in 2003.

Thirty Mile Point Lighthouse (716-795-3885 or 716-795-3117), Golden Hill State Park, Lower Lake Road, Barker. Tours Saturday and Sunday 2–4 PM, Memorial Day–Labor Day. Climb to the top of this 1875 lighthouse built of hand-carved stone for a spectacular view of Lake Ontario. The 60-foot lighthouse was built to warn ships of the rocky shoal and shifting sandbar in Lake Ontario; the site of at least five major shipwrecks prior to the construction of the lighthouse. The original navigational light, purchased from France, produced 600,000 candlepower and was the most powerful light on Lake Ontario. A rental suite is available in the lighthouse year-round. See *Other Lodging*.

BREWERIES AND WINERIES There are a number of wineries, breweries, and cideries in this area that are part of the Niagara Wine Trail (niagarawinetrail.org).

Blackbird Cider Works (716-795-3580; www.blackbirdciders.com), 8503 Lower Lake Road, Barker. Monday–Saturday 11 AM–5 PM, Sunday 12–5 PM. Producers of hard cider made from apples grown on their own orchards.

Black Willow Winery/Valhalla Meadery (716-439-1982; www.blackwillowwinery .com), 5565 West Lake, Burt. Open daily for tastings. This family-owned boutique winery also makes mead (honey wine) and sells artisanal olive oils and vinegars.

Chateau Niagara Winery (716-778-7888; www.chateauniagarawinery.com), 2466 West Creek Road, Newfane. Their specialties include Chardonnay, Riesling, and Gewürztraminer.

Live Edge Brewing Company (716-512-5414; www.livedgebrewingcompany.com) 2100 Coomer Road, Burt. Thursday 11 AM–8 PM, Friday–Saturday 11 AM–10 PM, Sunday–Monday 11 AM–8 PM. Enjoy craft brews along with a small menu featuring appetizers and salads in a rustic taproom. They are located next to Schulze Vineyards and Winery.

Marjim Manor (716-778-7001; www.marjimmanor.com), 7171 East Lake Road, Appleton. Open Monday–Saturday 10 AM–5 PM, Sunday 12–6 PM. This winery, which produces fruit wines, is operated by Margo Sue Bittner, one of only two women-owned wineries in the state. It is located in an 1834 mansion known as Appleton Hall. Each wine has a unique name, relating to the history of the home, which has several ghost stories associated with it.

Schulze Vineyards and Winery (716-778-8090; www.schulzewines.com), 2090 Coomer Road, Burt. Open Monday–Saturday 10 AM–6 PM, Sunday 12–6 PM. Ann and Martin Schulze specialize in sparkling wines, as well as several varieties of whites and reds.

Victorianbourg Wine Estates (www.victorianbourg.com), 4402 East Lake Road, Wilson. This winery specializes in European-style wines. They have a lovely rose garden with over 40 varieties of roses, all with the word "Victoria" in their name.

Woodcock Brothers Brewing company (716-333-4000; www.woodcockbrothers brewery.com), 638 Lake Street, Wilson. This is the first brewery in Niagara County to brew beer on-site and serve it in their restaurant. It is located in a historic old building that was once used for cold storage.

See also *Breweries and Wineries–Lockport* and *North of the Falls*.

THE PICTURESQUE WILSON PIER

FISHING/ANGLING IN NIAGARA AND ERIE COUNTIES

With its abundance of waterways, including Great Lakes Erie and Ontario, the Niagara River, and the Erie Canal, the Greater Niagara Region has a reputation for excellence among sports fishermen. Anglers can reel in trophy trout plus salmon, bass, walleye, and muskellunge, as well as other fish species. The Newfane/Olcott area is especially noted as a popular destination for fishing year-round. It's the ideal location for lake fishing from April to October, with its close proximity to the Niagara Bar and the ports of Wilson and Point Breeze. In September and October, salmon can be caught right from the Olcott Pier as they first enter Eighteen Mile Creek. From October to April, a popular fishing spot for a wide variety of fish is just north of the Burt Dam on Eighteen Mile Creek and a few miles south of Olcott.

Helpful resources include Western Lake Ontario Fishing Guide (www.olcottfishing.com), Niagara River Anglers (www.niagarariveranglers.com), Lake Ontario Counties (LOC) Fishing Derbies (1-888-REEL-2-IN; www.loc.org), which sponsors fishing derbies in the spring and fall, and Niagara County Fishing Hotline (716-433-5606). Fishing licenses can be obtained at any town or county municipal clerk's office, Dick's Sporting Goods store, Wal-Mart, or almost any bait and tackle shop.

❋ To Do

BOAT LAUNCHES AND MARINAS **Wilson Harborfront** (716-751-9202), 57 Harbor Street, Wilson. The harbor has a boat-launching facility and is a good spot to fish for trout, bass, and salmon.

FAMILY FUN ✿ **Olcott Beach Carousel Park** (716-778-8284; www.olcottbeachcarousel park.org), 5979 Main Street, Olcott. Open May–June, Saturday and Sunday 12–6 PM; July–August, open Wednesday–Sunday 12–6 PM, Saturday until 8 PM. Rides are only a quarter each. Enjoy a ride on a restored, historic 1928 Allen Herschell carousel and reminisce about a bygone era. Other vintage rides include a 1940s auto/fire truck kiddy ride, which originally operated at a former Olcott amusement park, as well as a 1940s kiddie skyfighter ride.

GOLF **Newfane Pro-Am Par 3** (716-778-8302), 2501 North Main Street (Route 78), Newfane. Open May–September. A 9-hole, par-27 course. Niagara County's only course lit for nighttime play. Fine food and legal beverages are served at Duffer's Restaurant and Tavern.

❋ Green Space

BEACHES **Olcott Beach**. See **Krull Park**. There is also a swimming beach at **Wilson-Tuscarora State Park**.

PARKS **Golden Hill State Park** (800-456-CAMP), 9691 Lower Lake Road, Barker.

OLCOTT BEACH CAROUSEL PARK

LAKE ONTARIO AT KRULL PARK/OLCOTT BEACH

Open daily, dawn to dusk. Popular with campers for its scenic location and with fishermen because of the excellent fishing on Lake Ontario, the park offers a variety of activities, including biking, picnicking, Frisbee golf, nature trails, playgrounds, and hiking. During the winter, visitors enjoy cross-country skiing, snowmobiling, and snowshoeing. Thirty Mile Point Lighthouse, built in 1875 of hand-carved stone, is located in the park. The lighthouse, recognized on a postage stamp in 1995, is open for tours Saturday and Sunday 2–4 PM, Memorial Day–Labor Day. See also *Lighthouses, Lodging*.

Keg Creek Rest Area, Route 18, between Olcott and Appleton. This roadside rest area has a few parking places and several picnic tables overlooking Keg Creek.

Krull Park/Olcott Beach (716-778-7711), Route 18, Olcott. Open daily, dawn to dusk. The 323-acre park, located along the southern shore of Lake Ontario, contains wooded and semi-woods areas as well as ample space for family and sporting activities. Looking toward Lake Ontario, one can observe sea ducks, diving ducks, and gulls. The spruce and pine portion of the park is a habitat for winter finches. Krull Park offers a wide variety of family activities, including fishing, boating, baseball fields, basketball courts, tennis courts, and soccer fields, as well as hiking trails, picnic facilities, a model plane airfield, and a small swimming beach. A replica of a pioneer log cabin that stood in the park from 1888–1957 was recently constructed in 2017.

Wilson-Tuscarora State Park (716-751-6361), 3371 Lake Road, Wilson. Open daily, dawn to dusk. Wilson-Tuscarora State Park has 395 acres of mature woods, open meadows, and marshland. Its 4 miles of hiking trails can also be used for snowshoeing and cross-country skiing during the winter months. The park has a boat launch located on a narrow strip of land referred to as "the island." Fishing, from either boats or shore, is very popular here. Other facilities include picnic areas, playgrounds, and a swimming beach.

✳ Lodging

Brookins Inn & Suites (716-870-6244; www.brookinsinn.com), 2697 Maple Avenue, Newfane. This bed & breakfast inn has two suites and three guest rooms. $$.

Lake Ontario Motel (716-778-5004; www.lakeontariomotel.com) 3330 Lockport-Olcott Road, Newfane. Stay in a nineteenth-century barn that has been converted to comfortable, modern motel. $.

Lighthouse Cottage Golden Hill State Park (716-795-3885 or 800-456-2267), 9691 Lower Lake Road Barker. The original lighthouse keepers' quarters in Thirty Mile Point lighthouse is a second-floor, three-bedroom apartment that sleeps up to six people, has a fully equipped kitchen, and offers a beautiful view of Lake Ontario. Minimum one-week rental during the summer season; two-day minimum stay during the rest of year. Note: The lighthouse is not handicapped accessible, and no smoking or pets are allowed. $$$.

✳ Where to Eat

DINING OUT **Mariner's Landing** (716-778-5535), 1540 Franklin Street, Olcott. Monday–Saturday 4–10 PM, Sunday 2–9 PM. A cozy seafood restaurant near Lake Ontario, located across the street from Krull Park. Entrees include broiled scallops, grilled salmon, filet mignon, chicken cordon bleu, and pasta dishes.

Sunset Bar & Grille (716-751-9141; sunsetgrillwilson.com), 3 O'Connell Island (off Route 18), Wilson. Open seasonally; daily for dinner June–August, weekends only September–October. Located along Wilson Harbor, this restaurant has a great view. Daily specials include prime rib and homestyle meals.

Wilson Boat House Restaurant (716-751-6060; www.wilsonboathouse.com), 57 Harbor Street, Wilson. Sunday–Thursday 11:30 AM–9 PM, Friday–Saturday 11:30 AM–10 PM. Shorter hours in spring, fall, and winter. This historic circa-1907 restaurant, located directly on the water, has one of the best views in town and the largest covered outdoor patio in the area.

EATING OUT 🐾 ♿ 🍦 **Baehr's Ice Cream Cottage** (716-778-9602), 7080 Lake Road (Route 18), Appleton. Open seasonally April–Labor Day, daily 12–9 PM. Choose from ice-cream treats like cones and milkshakes, as well as sundaes topped with fresh in-season fruit.

🐾 ♿ 🍦 **Barbara Ann's Carousel Concessions** (716-778-8284), 5976 Ontario Street, Olcott Beach (next to the Olcott Beach Carousel Park). Spring and fall, weekends only 12–6 PM; June–August, open seven days 12–6 PM. This take-out stand serves hot dogs, hamburgers, fries, and ice cream.

Cafora's (716-778-9069; www.caforasrestaurant.com), 2885 Main Street, Newfane. This has been a popular place for pasta and pizza since 1970.

🐾 ♿ 🍦 **Cameron's Lakeside Ice Cream Shoppe**, Ontario Street, Olcott Beach. A seasonal take-out shop in Lakeview Village Fair.

🐾 ♿ 🍦 **Gordie Harper's Bazaar** (716-778-8048), 3333 Lockport-Olcott Road,

GORDIE HARPER'S BAZAAR HAS A RESTARUANT, BAKERY, AND NUMEROUS SHOPS

Newfane. Open Sunday–Thursday 8 AM–8 PM, Friday–Saturday 8 AM–9 PM. A large, popular, country-style restaurant which features home-cooked favorites like pot roast, steaks, seafood, and chicken. There are also over sixty unique shops located in the complex. See also *Special Shops*.

Captain's Gallery (716-778-5580), 5885 Main Street, Olcott. Sunday–Tuesday 12–9 PM, Wednesday–Thursday 11 AM–9 PM, Friday–Saturday 11 AM–10 PM. Enjoy casual family dining one block from the lake. Menu includes wings, wraps, a kids menu, daily specials, and a Friday fish fry.

Park Place Restaurant (716-778-5537), Corner of Main and Franklin Streets, Olcott. Open daily at 6 AM. This restaurant, located across the street from Krull Park, is a good place to go for a quick meal and maybe catch up on all the local news, as the locals all seem to eat here. Choose from the usual breakfast fare, along with burgers, sandwiches, subs, chicken fingers, and ice cream.

✳ Selective Shopping

FARM MARKETS **Murphy Orchards** (716-778-7926; www.murphyorchards .com), 2402 McClew Road, Burt. Open seven days 8:30 AM–6 PM. May–November; Orchard Tea Room open Tuesday–Sunday 11 AM–4 PM. year-round. Take a drive out to rural Niagara County to pick your own fresh fruit and vegetables at this 65-acre farm that has been in continuous operation since the mid-1800s. (It was once a stop on the Underground Railroad; there's a secret room beneath the barn where slaves were once hidden.) The farm's Country Barn Store is stocked with jams, jellies, syrups, and vinegars, along with handcrafted items. See their website for various guided group tours.

SPECIAL SHOPS **Bye's Popcorn** (716-778-8218), Route 78, Olcott. Open March–November, hours vary seasonally. Enjoy freshly made gourmet popcorn and caramel corn at this roadside stand. An Olcott tradition since 1923.

MURPHY ORCHARDS HAS BEEN IN OPERATION SINCE THE MID-1800'S

♿ ✎ **Gordie Harper's Bazaar** (716-778-8048; www.gordieharpersbazaar.com), 3333 Lockport-Olcott Road, Newfane. Open Sunday–Thursday 8 AM–8 PM, Friday and Saturday 8 AM–9 PM. This large complex of over sixty unique shops just seems to go on and on. Find everything from collectibles, antiques, books, garden ornaments, and candies to florals and more, including a large selection of handcrafted items. Their bakery specializes in pies, pastries, cakes, and other goodies. Breakfast, lunch, and dinner are served in their country dining room. See *Where to Eat.*

♿ ✎ **Lakeview Village Fair** (716-778-8531), Route 78 and Ontario Street, Olcott. Open seasonally May–October (weekends only September–December). A charming village of retail specialty shops located on the south shore of Lake Ontario. There's a delightful view of the lake from the back walkway, and it's only a short stroll to Krull Park.

Shoppe on Main Street (716-778-5273; www.shoppeonmain.com), 2714 Main Street, Newfane. Tuesday–Sunday 10 AM–4 PM. This unique shop showcases and sells works handcrafted by local artisans in a century-old building. Items include paintings, jewelry, chocolate, books, pottery, and more.

♿ **Wilson Harborfront Shops** (www.wilsonboatyardmarina.com), 57 Harbor Street, Wilson. Of the several seasonal shops located along the harbor front, most are open seven days from the end of June–Labor Day and weekends only May–end of June, Labor Day–October.

❃ Special Events

March: **Polar Bear Swim** (716-778-5930), Olcott Beach. Watch brave souls venture into the frigid waters of Lake Ontario at this annual event, one of the oldest and largest polar bear swims in the country.

May: **Apple Blossom Festival** (716-778-6151), Newfane Historical Society Grounds. An annual festival featuring

THE SHOPPE ON MAIN IN NEWFANE SELLS LOCALLY HANDCRAFTED ITEMS

displays of local history and farm equipment, a flea market, and a Civil War encampment. **Somerset Old Fashioned Farm Festival** (716-795-9948), Babcock Cobblestone Museum, Barker. A festival featuring antique vehicles, period demonstrations, and horse-drawn wagon rides.

July: **Niagara Pirate Festival** (716-778-8531; www.olcott-newfane.com), Olcott Beach. Shiver me timbers, this is Olcott's largest event of the year. Events include a pirate water war, a Civil War encampment, a Scottish strongman competition, live music, fireworks, and a classic car show. **Old Olcott Days** (716-778-8531; www.olcott-newfane.com), Olcott Beach. Relive Olcott's "glory days" through historical exhibits and narrated trolley rides.

August: **Labor Day Car Show** (716-778-8531; www.olcott-newfane.com), Olcott Beach. One of the area's largest classic car shows.

October: **Apple Harvest Festival** (716-778-6151), Newfane Historical Society Grounds. Attractions include eleven historic buildings, apple-butter-making demonstrations, an antique car show, a petting zoo, and a Civil War encampment.

CANAL TOWNS

Lockport, Middleport, and Gasport

Settlement began in the Lockport area around 1802, after the Holland Land Company improved roads to the region, but settlers didn't flock in great numbers until Erie Canal construction began in 1817. Given the tools of the day, building the canal was truly an achievement. Since Lockport is located on the Niagara Escarpment—the same massive ridge of solid rock that Niagara Falls flows over—it was quite an engineering feat, build the canal so that boats could surmount the 59-foot-high escarpment. Lockport's claim to fame, the twin set of locks—referred to as the "flight of five"—was created after the rock was blasted through and removed. More than 1,200 laborers, many of them Irish immigrants, were needed to construct the Lockport portion of the canal. After completion of the canal, many choose to settle here. Although one set of the original locks was removed when the canal was modernized between 1908 and 1918, one set still remains today as a landmark. In fact, Lockport got its name from this impressive set of locks. Today the focal point of Lockport is still the canal, which serves as a recreational waterway from May through October. (The canal is drained in the winter months.) Another interesting bit of Lockport history: It was the first American city to have a fire hydrant system—designed by local inventor Birdsill Holly in 1863. Though far from a household name, Mr. Holly held more patents than anyone except Thomas Edison.

Middleport, located midway between Albion and Lockport, was a busy trade center during the canal's heyday. The town is the birthplace of Belva Lockwood (1830–1917), the first woman to practice law before the Supreme Court. Today it's a favorite docking spot for recreational boaters, offering electric and water hookups as well as shower and bathroom facilities. The tiny village of Gasport got its name from a gas spring that was discovered in the area shortly after the canal opened.

AREA CODE The area code is 716.

GUIDANCE **Erie Canal Discovery Center /Lockport Visitors Center** (716-439-0431; http://niagarahistory.org/discovery -center), 24 Church Street, Lockport. Open May–October daily 9 AM–5 PM, November–April Friday–Saturday 10 AM–3 PM. Admission charged for museum; no

MODERN LOCKS AND THE FLIGHT OF FIVE LOCKS IN THE ERIE CANAL IN LOCKPORT

charge to go in visitor center or gift shop. This state-of-the-art multi-media interactive museum takes you back to the early days of the Erie Canal. A 20-by-13-foot Raphael Beck mural depicts the opening of the canal.

Discover Lockport (www.discoverlockport.com).

GETTING THERE *By car:* Lockport is at the crossroads of Routes 78 and 31. Gasport and Middleport are found on Route 31.

By bus: The **NFTA** has routes between Lockport, Buffalo, and Niagara Falls.

MEDICAL EMERGENCY Dial 911.

Lockport Memorial Hospital (716-514-5700), 521 East Avenue, Lockport.

✳ To See

ART MUSEUMS **Kenan Center** (716-433-2617; www.kenancenter.org), 433 Locust Street, Lockport. Gallery open Monday–Friday 12–5 PM, Saturday–Sunday 2–5 PM. Free admission. This arts, education, and recreation center is located on 25 landscaped acres. The focal point of the campus is the 1800s brick Victorian Kenan House, home of philanthropist William Rand Kenan. Other buildings on the grounds include the carriage house, which now houses the 153-seat Taylor Theater, the Kenan Arena, site of special events and recreational programs, and the education building, which has an extensive art studio and classrooms on the second floor.

THE KENAN HOUSE AT THE KENAN CENTER

MUSEUMS AND HISTORIC HOMES **Niagara County Historical Society** (716-434-7433; www.niagarahistory.org), 215 Niagara Street, Lockport. Open Monday–Saturday 9 AM–5 PM. Visitors to Niagara County can learn about the region's history by visiting the six buildings in this museum complex. The 1864 Outwater Memorial Building features a Victorian parlor, toys, a Civil War room, changing exhibits, and a unique gift shop. Displayed in the 1835 Washington Hunt Building are surveying instruments used to lay out the villages of Lockport and Niagara Falls. The Pioneer and Transportation Building includes Native American artifacts and a replica pioneer cabin, as well as Erie Canal artifacts and early automotive transportation displays. Tools of many nineteenth-century trades are displayed in the Yates Farm Barn. Hille House contains an old-fashioned doctor's office, a business and industry exhibit, and more.

Col. William Bond House (716-434-7433), 143 Ontario Street, Lockport. Open April–December Thursday, Saturday, Sunday 1–5 PM. This circa-1824 house, part of the Niagara County Historical Society, is listed on the New York State and National Registers of Historic Places. It was the first brick house built in Lockport. Colonel Bond, a land speculator, came to Lockport to purchase land where he anticipated the Erie Canal locks would be built. The house, with twelve furnished rooms, is restored to reflect the period from 1820–1860.

Canal Museum (716-434-3140), Richmond Avenue (by the locks), Lockport. Open daily 9 AM–5 PM May–October. This small, one-room museum is located in a former powerhouse that served the Erie Canal's double locks at Lockport from its construction in 1918 until the mid-1950s. Displays include tools used in canal construction, photographs, and other canal memorabilia. A note of caution: This museum is located below street level and is accessible only by means of several flights of stairs. Railings are minimal, so it is not recommended to visit this site with small children or if you have trouble negotiating stairs.

Erie Canal Heritage Center (716-433-6155), 228 Market Street, Lockport. Only open for group tours of Lockport Locks & Erie Canal Cruises. This four-story stone building built in the 1840s once housed a flour mill that harnessed waterpower from the Erie Canal. The structure has been kept in its original condition and now houses canal-related exhibits and artifacts. See *Lockport—Boat Tours and Excursions*.

HISTORIC SITES **Belva Lockwood Memorial**, Griswold Street (3 miles south of Route 31), Middleport. This monument is dedicated to Middleport native Belva Lockwood, the first woman to practice law before the Supreme Court.

The Big Bridge, Lockport. Located by Locks 34 and 35, the "Big Bridge" built in 1914, is the widest bridge in the world, measuring 129 feet long and a whopping 399 feet wide. (By comparison, the George Washington Bridge in New York City is a mere 120 feet wide.)

Cold Spring Cemetery (716-434-3450), 4849 Cold Spring Road, Lockport. This historic 68-acre cemetery, incorporated in 1841, was the original burial ground of area Revolutionary War soldiers. There are many unique monuments throughout the cemetery. Cold Spring is the final resting place of several notable Niagara County residents, including inventor Birdsill Holly and Jessie Hawley, proponent of the Erie Canal System.

First Presbyterian Church (716-433-5905; www.1stpreslockport.org), 21 Church Street, Lockport (across from the Erie Canal Discover Center). Guided tours by appointment only or self-guided tour Sundays after 8:15 AM or 10:30 AM worship service; summer worship service at 9:30 AM only. This church, one of Lockport's hidden treasurers, has windows designed by Louis Comfort Tiffany.

BREWERIES AND WINERIES **Niagara Wine Trail** (www.Niagarawinetrail.org). The soil and climate of this area along the Niagara Escarpment are ideal for growing grapes to produce world-class wines. There are numerous wineries located in this region, as well as a few breweries.

Arrowhead Spring Winery (716-434-8030; arrowheadspringvineyards.com), 4746 Townline Road, Lockport. Friday–Monday 12–5 PM. This winery focuses on dry wines.

New York Beer Project (716-743-6927; www.nybeerproject.com), 6933 South Transit Road, Lockport. Open daily 11 AM–11 PM, until 1 AM Friday–Saturday. Enjoy brews and pub grub in a 17,000 square foot gastropub, taproom, and brewery, which opened in 2015.

Eveningside Vineyards (716-867-2415; www.eveningside.com), 4794 Lower Mountain Road, Cambria. Open Daily 12–6 PM, May–October, Saturday–Sunday 12–6 PM, December–March. Eveningside Vineyards is owned and operated by Randy and Karen Biehl. It is located in a small red barn behind their home. Their wines include Chardonnay, Riesling, rosé, and cabernet.

Flight of Five Winery (716-433-3360; www.flightoffivewinery.com), 2 Pine Street, Lockport. Lockport's urban winery, aptly named the Flight of Five Winery, overlooks the historic flight of five locks in the Erie Canal. The winery is located in Lockport's old city hall.

Freedom Run (716-433-4136; www.freedomrunwinery.com), 5138 Lower Mountain Rd., Lockport. Sunday–Wednesday 12–6 PM, Thursday–Saturday 10 AM–6 PM. Their large, light, and airy tasting room features unique hand-blown glass plates created by Florida artist Chuck Boux placed on the front of the tasting bar. Wines include their unique Manning Manor Reserve, a dry white wine made from Niagara grapes. Usually, wine made from the Niagara grape is a sweet wine.

Honeymoon Trail Winery (716-438-3255; www.honeymoontrailwinery.com), 4120 Ridge Road, Lockport. Monday–Saturday 10 AM–6 PM, Sunday 12–6 PM. Wines include *Honeymoon Sweet*, a sweet red wine made with Concord grapes and a semi-dry Cayuga White. Their best-seller, a Pink Catawba, is a semi-sweet wine.

Niagara Landing Wine Cellars (716-433-8405; www.niagaralanding.com), 4434 Van Dusen Road, Lockport. Open Monday–Saturday 10 AM–6 PM, Sunday 12–6 PM. This family-owned and operated winery, located amid vineyards dating back to the 1800s, features fine wines and original art in their tasting room and gift shop. They specialize in wines made from native Labrusca grapes and European vinifera varieties.

Spring Lake Winery (716-439-5253; www.springlakewinery.com), 7373 Rochester Rd. (Route 31), Lockport. January–April, Friday–Sunday 12–6 PM; May–December 12–6 PM daily. Three generations of the Varallo family are involved in the winery's operation. Some of their wines include a white syrah, merlot and gewürztraminer. The winery has a lovely spring-fed lake with walking trails on the grounds. You can even ride on the

SPRING LAKE WINERY, LOCKPORT

Vineyard Express Winery Train, which makes a stop at Spring Lake Winery (see winery website for details and dates).

Vizcarra Vineyards at Becker Farms (716-772-7815; www.beckerfarms.com), 3760 Quaker Road, Gasport. Open May–December 12–5 PM daily. This farm and farm market, operated by Oscar and Melinda Vizcarra, has been run by Melinda's family since 1894. Since 2004 the Vizcarras have made wine from their own fruits as well as from grapes purchased from other farms in western New York. They also have a brewery, **Becker Brewing**, along with a brewpub which serves foods made from locally sourced ingredients. See also *Family Fun*, and *Breweries and Wineries—Lake Ontario Shore* and *North of the Falls*.

✳ To Do

BOAT EXCURSIONS **Lockport Cave Tours and Underground Boat Ride** (716-438-0174; lockportcave.com), 5 Gooding Street, Lockport. Open May–October, hours vary seasonally. This 75-minute guided tour starts with viewing the Lockport locks, both the modern locks 34 and 35 and the remnants of the "Flight of Five," part of the canal in 1825. As you walk along the canal toward the "cave," you'll learn about Lockport's industrial heritage and also see the famous "upside-down bridge." The cave was originally a 2,400-foot water power tunnel used in the 1860s. Visitors take a walking tour through the cave then ride the longest underground boat ride in the United States.

Lockport Locks & Erie Canal Cruises (800-378-0352; www.lockportlocks.com), 210 Market Street, Lockport. Operating May–October; cruise times vary. Take a two-hour narrated trip down the historic Erie Canal. Your journey includes "locking through" the 50-foot locks 34 and 35, the only double set of locks on the entire canal. You will also have the opportunity to see the remnants of one set of the original "Flight of Five" locks, located north of the present-day locks. When the canal was built in 1825, the original locks allowed simultaneous travel in either direction; the modern locks have replaced one flight.

FAMILY FUN 🖋 **Becker Farms** (716-772-2211; www.beckerfarms.com), 3760 Quaker Road, Gasport. Open May–December. Becker Farms, a popular destination for local families, offers locally grown fruit and vegetables, homemade baked goods, and craft items. Fall is the most popular time to visit, when visitors can pick their own apples and pumpkins,

BECKER FARMS IN GASPORT IS A POPULAR FAMILY DESTINATION

get lost in a corn maze, and enjoy other family-oriented activities during their Pumpkin Fiesta. They also produce wine under the label Vizcarra Vineyards and have a brewery, Becker Brewing. See *Breweries and Wineries.*

Niagara Zipper (716-438-0174; www.niagarazipper.com), 5 Gooding Street, Lockport. Take a zipline ride 85 feet above the Erie Canal in downtown Lockport.

FISHING **Nelson Goehle Marina** (Widewaters) is a popular spot to fish. See *Marinas.*

GOLF **Niagara County Golf Course** (716-439-7954; www.niagaracounty.com/parks/ Golf-Course), 314 Davison Road, Lockport. A public 18-hole, par-72 course with full bar, snack bar, and restaurant.

Niagara Orleans Golf Club (716-735-9000; www.noccgolf.com), 8981 Telegraph Road off Route 31, Gasport. A semi-private 18-hole, par-71 course.

Oak Run Golf Club (716-434-8851; www.oakrungolf.com), 4185 Lake Avenue, Lockport. A semi-private 18-hole, par-72 course.

Willowbrook Golf Course & Restaurant (716-434-0111; willowbrookwny.com), 4200 Lake Avenue (Route 78) Lockport. An 18-hole, par-72 semi-private course and driving range with a full bar, snack bar, and restaurant.

MARINAS **The Nelson Goehle Marina at Widewaters**, Market Street, Lockport. This marina on the Erie Canal, named after a former superintendent of parks, is one of the most popular boating and fishing spots in town. It is located along the canal just east of Lockport.

SKATING ✐ **Rainbow Skateland Family Fun Center** (716-507-4381; rainbowskateland .com), 1109 Lincoln Avenue, Lockport. While skating on the large, modern, climate-controlled rink is, of course, the main attraction, there's plenty to do here for nonskaters, too, including an interactive laser tag game and video-game arcade.

✳ Green Space

NATURE PRESERVES **Gulf Wilderness Park** (716-433-1267), south side of West Jackson Street, near the 5900 block, Lockport. Open dawn to dusk. Free admission. The only full nature preserve on the Niagara Escarpment, this area is a true unspoiled wilderness. Four hiking trails traverse the wooded ravine. It is a great place to look for fossils and study rock formations as well as observe different wildflowers and plants. Indian Falls, which runs off the west branch of Eighteen Mile Creek, is located in the park.

PARKS **Niagara County Park** (716-439-7950), 314 Davison Road, Lockport. This park has picnic facilities, a golf course, and model airplane field.

Outwater Park (716-433-1267), Outwater Drive, Lockport. Open daily, dawn to dusk. Free admission. Visitors to this 48-acre park—named for Dr. Samuel Outwater, a successful Lockport physician who donated the land to the city—can enjoy picnicking, cross-country skiing, swimming, baseball, football, soccer, horseshoes, bocce, playgrounds, and hiking and nature trails. Located near the top of the Niagara Escarpment, the park also has a lovely rose garden. From the famous Outwater Park overview, one can see Lake Ontario and, on a clear day, the outline of the Toronto skyline.

Royalton Ravine (716-439-7950), Gasport Road, Gasport. Open daily, dawn to dusk. Free admission. Facilities include picnic shelters, baseball diamonds, and a nature trail with a suspension bridge and waterfalls.

WALKING, HIKING, AND BIKING **Trails Erie Canal Heritage Trail**. You could walk or bike all the way from downtown Lockport to Rochester and beyond along this paved trail along the north side of the Erie Canal. The trail follows the former towpath along the Erie Canal.

City of Lockport Walking and Biking Tour (canal towpath). For those who prefer a short trail, you can walk or bike the loop trail that runs on both sides of the canal from Locks 34 and 35 to Widewaters (at Goehle Widewaters Marina) and back. The 4-mile trail takes you on the north side of the canal past the modern locks, the historic "Flight of Five" locks, through Upson Park, up to Widewaters Marina, where you'll cross over the canal and return to downtown Lockport on the south side of the waterway.

✳ Lodging

MOTELS AND HOTELS ♿ **Lockport Inn & Suites** (716-434-5595, 877-465-4100; www.lockportinnandsuites.com), 315 South Transit Road, Lockport. This hotel has ninety modern rooms, including some Jacuzzi suites with fireplaces. Amenities include a swimming pool and in-room refrigerators and microwaves in all rooms. $$.

There are also several chain hotels represented in the Lockport area, including Hampton Inn, Best Western, and Quality Inn.

BED & BREAKFASTS **DeFlippo's Bed & Breakfast** (716-433-2913; www.deflippos .com), 326 West Avenue, Lockport. Open year-round. Innkeepers Jerry and Joan DeFlippo offer four uniquely decorated rooms. The Elvis Room is decorated with 1950s Elvis memorabilia, while the Lillian Bronson Room has its namesake's memorabilia. (Ms. Bronson was a character actress from the 1940s–1960s who hailed from Lockport.) The Garden Room features a queen-sized bed, while the antiques-decorated DeFlippo Room has a double bed and a pull-out sofa. The four rooms share two full baths. Rates include a continental breakfast. Call for rates. Dinner packages to their restaurant are also available. See *Dining Out*.

OTHER LODGING **Niagara County Camping Resort** (716-434-3991; www .niagaracamping.com), 7369 Wheeler Road, Lockport. Open May 15–October 15. A comfortable, clean, family-oriented RV park and campground located 2.5 miles from the canal. There are sixty-four sites, plus cabin rentals. $.

✳ Where to Eat

DINING OUT **Cammarata's** (716-433-5353; www.cammaratas.com) 6336 Robinson Road, Lockport. Established in 1975, this restaurant is known for steaks, seafood, and Italian specialties.

Danny Sheehan's Steak House (716-433-4666; dannysheehans.com), 491 West Avenue, Lockport. Tuesday–Thursday 4–9 PM, Friday and Saturday 4–10 PM, Sunday 3–9 PM. This restaurant has been popular for steaks for over four decades. The comfortable dining room features a mural of old downtown Lockport, while a deck and patio for outdoor dining is open during the warmer months.

DeFlippo's (716-433-2913; www .deflippos.com), 326 West Avenue, Lockport. Tuesday–Saturday 4–10 PM, Sunday 4–9 PM. The building housing this popular Italian restaurant was built in 1870 by carriage makers Brown and Bronson. They offer an extensive selection of Italian specialties, such as chicken parmigiana, baked lasagna, and a long list of pasta dishes, served amid a decor of Lockport and sports memorabilia. Other selections include surf and turf, strip steak, smoked chicken, and several low-fat choices. The Friday night fish fry is popular, so arrive early. See also *Lodging—Bed & Breakfasts*.

The Fieldstone Country Inn (716-625-6193; fieldstonecountryinn.com), 5986 South Transit Road, Lockport. Monday–Thursday 11 AM–9 PM, Friday 11 AM–10 PM, Saturday 12–10 PM, Sunday 12–8 PM. Specialties at this cozy country restaurant, constructed out of fieldstone, include prime rib and BBQ ribs.

Garlock's (716-433-5595; garlocksrestaurant.com), 35 South Transit Road, Lockport. Open Monday–Saturday 4:30–10 PM, Sunday 3:30–10 PM. This vintage restaurant, reminiscent of a 1950s-style lodge, has been the premier steak house in Lockport for over 60 years. The casual restaurant is filled with lots of unusual decorations, including a collection of model cars. While steak dominates the menu, other selections include chicken, pork, lamb, and an assortment of seafood.

The Shamus (716-433-9809; www.shamuslockport.com), 98 West Avenue, Lockport. Open for lunch Monday–Saturday 11 AM–4 PM, dinner Monday–Thursday 4:30–9 PM, Friday and Saturday 4:30–10 PM. Shamus, which is located in a 150-year-old building, has a reputation as one of the finest restaurants in Lockport, for both food and decor. Menu selections include fresh seafood, Angus beef, chicken, pork, and pasta. Choose from soups, salads, and sandwiches for lunch.

EATING OUT **Chiavetta's BBQ Takeout** (716-625-9503; www.chiavettas.com), 6100 Fisk Road, Lockport. Open daily 11 AM–6 PM. Enjoy their famous chicken ribs or pulled pork. Dine-in or take-out. Call ahead for catering.

EVERY DAY IS AN ICE CREAM DAY AT TASTY TREAT IN LOCKPORT

🍦 **Frey's Tasty Treat** (716-625-4068; freystastytreat.com), 6186 South Transit Road, Lockport. Open daily 11 AM–9 PM. March–October. Every day is an ice cream day at Tasty Treat. Enjoy sundaes, milkshakes, cones and more. You can also take home ice cream cakes and other treats.

🍦 **Lake Effect Ice Cream** (716-201-1643; www.lakeeffecticecream.com), 79 Canal Street, Lockport. Monday–Friday 4–9 PM, Saturday–Sunday 12–9 PM. Enjoy unique flavors of artisan ice cream at this ice cream parlor overlooking the Erie Canal.

♿ **One-Eyed Jack's Smokehouse Grill** (716-438-5414; oneeyedjacksbbq.com), 5983 South Transit Road (at Robinson Road), Lockport. Open Tuesday–Thursday 11 AM–9 PM, Friday–Saturday 11 AM–10 PM, Sunday 12–8 PM. The place to go for BBQ in Niagara County. Enjoy chicken, ribs, and pork, washed down with a variety of beers.

🍦♿ **Reid's Ice Cream** (716-433-2488), Lake Avenue (at Clinton Street), Lockport. Open seasonally. A long-standing Lockport institution, serving take-out hot dogs, ice cream, shakes, and more.

Tom's Diner (716-439-4283; www.tomsdinerinc.com), 11 Main Street, Lockport. Daily 7 AM–3 PM. Enjoy an all-day breakfast, along with homemade soups, sandwiches, and salads, including their signature super salads.

Wagner's (716-433-1200; wagnersrestaurant.com), 246 Park Avenue, Lockport. Open Tuesday–Friday opens at 11 AM, Saturday at 12 PM. A Lockport institution for over 50 years, noted for its beef on weck. Chicken wings are another specialty.

✳ Entertainment

THEATERS **Palace Theatre** (716-438-1130; www.lockportpalacetheatre.com), 2 East Avenue, Lockport. This historic theater in the heart of downtown Lockport is a beautiful example of a pre–World War II grand movie theater that has been restored to its original splendor. The Palace, which opened in 1925, was once part of the Schine chain of theaters. John Philip Sousa and his band performed here the year it opened. While first-run movies at reasonable prices are the daily fare, live performances are also held here.

Taylor Theater. See **Kenan Center**.

Transit Drive-In (716-625-8697; www.transitdrivein.com), 6655 South Transit Road, Lockport. A multiscreen theater complex, the largest drive-in theater in the state.

✳ Selective Shopping

ANTIQUES **Tattered Tulip** (716-438-5257), 4090 Lake Avenue (Route 78 just south of Route 104), Lockport. Open daily 11 AM–5 PM. Browse through 2,000 square feet of antique furniture,

YOU'LL FIND A NICE SELECTION OF ANTIQUES AND HOME DECOR ITEMS AT THE TATTERED TULIP

glassware, pottery, quilts, folk art, woven rugs, candles, garden decor, and more, displayed in a two-story, century-old barn.

ART GALLERIES **The Art 247** (716-404-9884; www.theart247.com), 247 Market Street, Lockport. Wednesday–Friday 10 AM–5 PM, Saturday–Sunday 11 AM–5 PM. This unique art center—in the historic Western Block and Tackle building on the banks of the Erie Canal—features several art galleries showcasing the work of Niagara County artists along with a gift shop with items made by local craftspeople, plus twenty working artist's studios.

FARM MARKETS **Becker Farm**. See *Family Fun*.

Niagara County Produce (716-639-0755; www.niagaraproduce.com), 8555 Transit Road (at Millersport), East Amherst. Open daily 8 AM–9 PM. This market on the border of Erie and Niagara Counties has been in operation for over 70 years. In season, choose from Niagara County crops—including apples, berries, and grapes—picked fresh daily. In the off-season enjoy apples and potatoes from cold storage as well as produce shipped in from other parts of the country. The market is also known for its full-service deli counter, featuring quality meats and freshly made sausage, as well as a small café. A second, smaller location is at 112 Chestnut Street in Lockport (716-478-0888).

Schwab's Farm Market (716-735-7570; www.schwabsfarm.com), 9035 Rochester Road, Gasport. Open year-round Monday–Saturday 8 AM–6 PM, Sunday 10 AM–4 PM. Choose from home-grown produce in-season, baked goods, deli meats, gift baskets, and locally made handcrafted items.

Smiths Orchard (716-625-4316; www.smithsorchard.com), 4960 Mapleton Road, Lockport. Open mid-September–end of November, Friday–Sunday 9 AM–5 PM. This is one of the best places in the area to purchase freshly made cider and freshly picked apples. You can also get apple cider slushies and freshly made apple cider donuts. If you want, you can go out in the orchard to pick your own apples.

SPECIAL SHOPS **Crafts and Creations** (716-434-2816), 1149 Lincoln Avenue, Lockport. Open Monday–Friday 9 AM–7 PM, Saturday 10 AM–5 PM, Sunday 12–4 PM. This large store carries a sizeable selection of crafting supplies, giftware, collectibles, and porcelain dolls.

Grimble's Hardware Store (716-434-1790), 18 West Main Street, Lockport. Open Monday–Saturday 9 AM–5 PM. An old-fashioned hardware store, complete with wooden floors and a popcorn machine up front—the place to go in Lockport for those hard-to-find gadgets. This store is one of Lockport's oldest businesses, established in 1920 and owned by the third generation of the same family.

Noah's Ark Books and Toys (716-434-4736), 20 Market Street, Lockport. Monday–Friday 10 AM–5 PM, Thursday 10 AM–6 PM, Saturday 10 AM–4 PM. This shop has a great selection of books and toys right in downtown Lockport.

Windsor Village Artisan and Antique Market (716-201-1489; www.windsorvillageshops.com), 43 Stevens Street, Lockport. Tuesday–Wednesday 11 AM–5 PM, Thursday–Friday 10 AM–6 PM, Saturday 10 AM–4 PM. This unique shop is a marketplace for local and regional goods and locally crafted items. There is a hands-on play area for kids, with ten historic exhibits of life on the Erie Canal in 1825. They also offer craft workshops for adults in basket weaving, painting, cross-stitch, and more.

✳ Special Events

May/June: **100 American Craftsmen Festival** (www.kenancenter.org), Kenan Center, Lockport. A juried arts-and-crafts

WINDSOR VILLAGE SHOP, LOCKPORT

show featuring artisans from all over the country.

July: **Niagara County Fair** (716-433-8839), Niagara County Fairgrounds, 4487 Lake Avenue (Route 78), Lockport. The Niagara County Fair is known as the "best little county fair in western New York." The fair's primary focus is on the achievements of youth involved in 4-H and other activities. Attractions include animal shows, crafts, live entertainment, midway rides, and vendors. The fair also features an antique tractor display and a car show.

September: **Johnny Appleseed Fest** (716-772-2211; www.beckerfarms.com), Becker Farms, Gasport. Celebrate the beginning of the apple harvest season with family-oriented activities such as apple picking, pony rides, musical entertainment, and more.

October: **Pumpkin Fiesta** (716-772-2211; www.beckerfarms.com), Becker Farms, Gasport. Old-fashioned fun for the entire family includes hayrides, corn maze, farm animals, pumpkin picking, and live entertainment.

SOUTHERN ONTARIO

FORT ERIE

NIAGARA FALLS, ONTARIO

NIAGARA-ON-THE-LAKE AND QUEENSTON

WELLAND CANAL CORRIDOR

St. Catharines/Port Dalhousie, Thorold, Welland, and Port Colborne

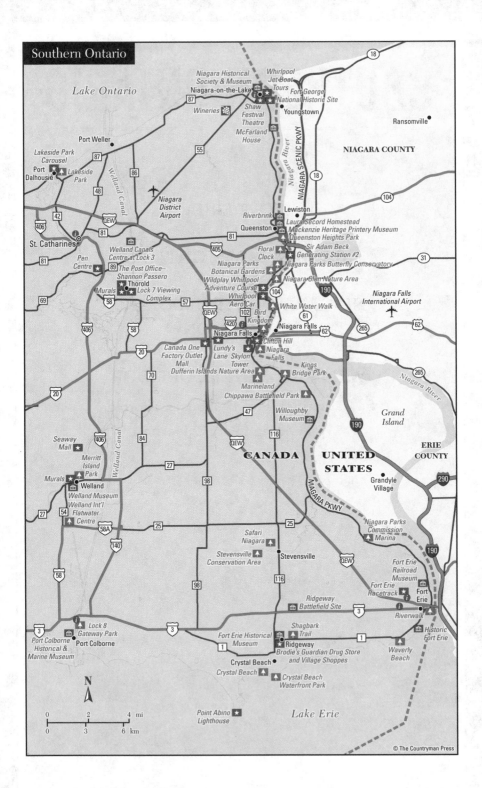

Southern Ontario

Lake Ontario

NIAGARA COUNTY

Ransomville

Niagara Historical Society & Museum
Niagara-on-the-Lake
Whirlpool Jet Boat Tours
Fort George National Historic Site
Youngstown
Shaw Festival Theatre
McFarland House
Wineries

Port Weller

Lakeside Park Carousel
Port Dalhousie
Lakeside Park

Niagara District Airport

St. Catharines

Pen Centre

Welland Canals Centre at Lock 3
The Post Office—Shannon Passero
Thorold
Lock 7 Viewing Complex
Murals

Niagara River

Lewiston

Riverbrink
Queenston
Laura Secord Homestead
Mackenzie Heritage Printery Museum
Queenston Heights Park

Floral Clock
Sir Adam Beck Generating Station #2
Niagara Parks Botanical Gardens
Niagara Parks Butterfly Conservatory
Wildplay Whirlpool Adventure Course
Niagara Glen Nature Area
Whirlpool Aero Car
White Water Walk
Bird Kingdom
Niagara Falls

NIAGARA SCENIC PKWY

Niagara Falls International Airport

Niagara Falls
Clifton Hill
Niagara Falls
Canada One Factory Outlet Mall
Lundy's Lane
Skylon Tower
Dufferin Islands Nature Area
Kings Bridge Park

Marineland
Chippawa Battlefield Park

Willoughby Museum

Grand Island

CANADA

UNITED STATES

ERIE COUNTY

Seaway Mall

Merritt Island Park

Murals
Welland
Welland Museum
Welland Int'l Flatwater Centre

Welland Canal

Grandyle Village

Niagara Parks Commission Marina

Safari Niagara

Stevensville Conservation Area
Stevensville

Fort Erie Railroad Museum
Fort Erie Racetrack
Fort Erie

NIAGARA PKWY

Niagara River

Ridgeway Battlefield Site

Lock 8 Gateway Park
Port Colborne Historical & Marine Museum
Port Colborne

Fort Erie Historical Museum
Ridgeway
Brodie's Guardian Drug Store and Village Shoppes

Shagbark Trail

Riverwalk
Historic Fort Erie

Waverly Beach

Crystal Beach
Crystal Beach
Crystal Beach Waterfront Park

Point Abino Lighthouse

Lake Erie

N

0   2   4 mi
0   3   6 km

© The Countryman Press

INTRODUCTION

A book about western New York would not be complete without a chapter focusing on our neighbors to the north in Canada. Southern Ontario is a vast area, though, with lots to see and do—a whole book could be written on the Niagara region alone! This chapter will highlight towns immediately across the border—Fort Erie, Niagara Falls, Queenston, and Niagara-on-the-Lake, as well as towns along the Welland Canal Corridor.

Crossing the Border: United States citizens age 16 and older are required to have a passport or enhanced license to cross the border into Canada. If you are traveling with children under 16, have a copy of their birth certificates and photo IDs if available. If both parents aren't traveling with a child, it's recommended that you have a note from the absent parent granting permission to bring the child across the border.

Frequent travelers to Canada can apply for the NEXUS program, designed to simplify border crossings for low-risk, pre-approved travelers. For more information, call 800-842-7647 or visit www.nexus.gc.ca.

When you approach the border crossing, stop your vehicle where instructed by the signs. Be prepared to answer the customs inspectors' questions with straight, no-nonsense answers; they take their jobs seriously, and joking around will delay your crossing. Questions they might ask include: Where were you born? Where are you going? What is the purpose of your visit? What are you bringing into Canada?

There are four border crossings from western New York to Canada: The Peace Bridge, from Buffalo, New York to Fort Erie, Ontario; the Rainbow Bridge from Niagara Falls, New York to Niagara Falls, Ontario; the Whirlpool Bridge, a NEXUS-only crossing, also goes between the two cities; and the Lewiston–Queenston Bridge, which crosses the border between Lewiston, New York and Queenston, Ontario. For up-to-date information on border traffic conditions, call the **Bridge Information Hotline** at 716-285-6322 (US) or 905-354-5641(Canada). You can also check online at www .niagarafallsbridges.com.

FORT ERIE

The area known today as the town of Fort Erie is made up of numerous communities, each with its own interesting history. While space doesn't permit discussing each one in depth, here is an overview of the area's rich past.

Archeologists suspect that the Fort Erie shore of the Niagara River near the Peace Bridge was home to an aboriginal flint manufacturing site over 9,000 years ago. Nearly a million artifacts have been discovered in the area in the past 10 years.

The area was first inhabited by the Chippawa and Mississauga tribes. European settlement began after the American Revolution in 1776, when Americans who remained loyal to Britain immigrated to Canada. One of the first settlers, William Dunbar, built a gristmill along the Niagara River in 1792. The area was named Bertie Township in 1793, honoring Willoughby Bertie, Fourth Earl of Abingdon. During the 1800s the township was divided into several different villages, including Crystal Beach and Fort Erie, named after the historic fort dating back to the French and Indian War. Several major battles of the War of 1812 were also fought in this region, along with the Irish Fenian Raid after the US Civil War.

The village of Crystal Beach was first settled in the late 1700s and remained agricultural until 1888, when John Rebstock started a religious assembly there. This assembly grew into Crystal Beach Amusement Park—at one point Canada's largest and most popular park—drawing summer visitors by steamship and trolley from both Buffalo and Toronto. The park closed in 1989, but many people from both sides of the border still have fond memories of the popular summertime destination. Today Crystal Beach, as well as nearby Ridgeway, is mainly residential, with a sprinkling of retail stores; there is still a beach at Crystal Beach.

The entire area saw economic growth when the railroad came to town in the mid-1800s and again in 1927, when the Peace Bridge opened. Today the Fort Erie area attracts visitors to several Asian restaurants, the historic old fort, and a Thoroughbred racetrack.

AREA CODE The area code is 905.

GUIDANCE ♿ **Economic Development & Tourism Corporation** (905-871-1332 or 888-270-9151; www.forteriecanada.com), 660 Garrison Road, Fort Erie, Ontario. You'll find local tourism information and brochures here.

♿ **Greater Fort Erie Chamber of Commerce** (905-871-3803; www.forteriechamber .com), 660 Garrison Road, Fort Erie, Ontario.

♿ **Ontario Information Center at "The Crossroads"** (905-871-3505), 350 Bertie Street, Fort Erie. Open daily 8:30 AM–5 PM. This large information center is located just off the Queen Elizabeth Way, a busy expressway known locally as the QEW.

Crystal Beach information, Friends of Crystal Beach (www.focb.net).

Ridgeway Information (www.ridgewayont.ca).

GETTING THERE *By air:* See *Getting There—City of Buffalo.*

By bus: **Greyhound** and **Coach Canada** both service the Fort Erie area. For information on both, contact **Robo Mart** (905-871-3738), 21 Princess Street, Fort Erie.

By car: The Peace Bridge is the main route from the United States into the Fort Erie area. From Buffalo, take the I-90 to I-190 and get off at the Peace Bridge/ Porter Avenue exit and cross the Peace Bridge. From other points in Canada (Niagara Falls, Niagara-on-the-Lake), take the Queen Elizabeth Way (QEW) to Fort Erie.

GETTING AROUND *By Bus*: The Niagara Regional Transit (905-980-6000; www .niagararegion.ca/transit) has bus routes between St. Catharines, Thorold, Niagara Falls, Welland, Port Colborne, and Fort Erie. Buses operate Monday–Saturday.

MEDICAL EMERGENCY **Douglas Memorial Hospital** (905-871-6600), 230 Bertie Street, Fort Erie, Ontario.

✳ To See

RIDGEWAY, ONTARIO

MUSEUMS **Historic Fort Erie** (905-871-0540; www.niagaraparks.com/niagara-falls-attractions/old-fort-erie.html), 350 Lakeshore Road, Fort Erie. Daily mid-May–August 10 AM–5 PM, September–October 10 AM–4 PM (until 5 PM Saturday–Sunday). Originally built in 1812 and reconstructed in the 1930s, this stone fort features period rooms and artifacts from the British Garrison of the War of 1812.

   ♿ **Fort Erie Historical Museum** (905-894-5322; www.forterie.ca/pages/Museum), 402 Ridge Road, Ridgeway. Open September–May Sunday–Friday 9 AM–5 PM. Located in the former Bertie Township Hall built in 1874, this museum features exhibits on the history and archeology of the region. The main exhibit highlights 4,000 years of the region's archaeology. Other exhibits include the Fenian Raids of the 1860s and Crystal Beach Amusement Park.

   Fort Erie LaFrance Association Museum (905-871-1271; www.forterielafrancefirefig htingmuseum.com), 1118 Concession Road, Fort Erie. Open by appointment only. This museum has some of the oldest working fire-fighting equipment in southern Ontario, including a 1904 Steamer, a 1917 Model T, a 1924 LaFrance, and a 1947 LaFrance.

   ☇ **Fort Erie Railroad Museum** (905-894-5322; www.forterie.ca/pages/Museum), 400 Central Avenue, Fort Erie. Open late May–early September 9 AM–5 PM. This museum showcasing numerous railroad exhibits is housed in the circa-1873 Ridgeway station. This station served that nearby community until 1975, when it was relocated to the museum grounds.

   ♿ **Mewinzha: A Journey Back in Time/The Bridge that Peace Built** (905-894-5322; www.museum.forterie.ca), 100 Queen Street, Fort Erie. Monday–Friday 9 AM–4 PM. Housed in the Buffalo & Fort Erie Public Bridge Authority Administrative Building are two small museums, one a display of archaeological artifacts found when the Peace

RE-ENACTORS AT HISTORIC FORT ERIE

Bridge was being built, the other a history of the building of the Peace Bridge. A large window overlooks the bridge and the Niagara River.

HISTORIC SITES **Ridgeway Battlefield Site** (905-894-5322), Highway #3 (Garrison Road) and Battlefield Park, east of Ridge Road, Ridgeway. This historic site commemorates the beginnings of the Battle of Ridgeway. A log house containing a small museum is on the site of the Fenian Raid of June 2, 1866.

LIGHTHOUSES ❂ **Point Abino Lighthouse** (905-871-1600, ext. 2431; www.forterie.ca/pages/PointAbinoLighthouse). Access by tour only, the 2nd and 4th Saturdays from June–September. Reservations recommended. This Classic Revival–style lighthouse was erected in 1917 due to navigational difficulties around Point Abino. The remains of many shipwrecks are below the waters off the point. It is the fifth-oldest remaining lighthouse on the Great Lakes and was dedicated as a National Historic Site in 1998.

✳ To Do

BREWERIES **Brimstone Brewing** (289-821-2738: www.brimstonebrewing.ca), 209 Ridge Road, Ridgeway. A craft brewery, located in a former church, with a tap room and restaurant. Live entertainment is featured on select evenings.

BOAT LAUNCHES AND MARINAS **Crystal Beach Waterfront Park and Boat Launch Ramp** (905-994-7825; www.forterie.ca/pages/WaterfrontParksandBeaches), End of Ridgeway Road), Crystal Beach. Open from May until mid-September. This waterfront park and boat launch offers a scenic view of Lake Erie, with Buffalo on the horizon. Park facilities include a picnic pavilion, washrooms, and plenty of parking.

Niagara Parks Commission Marina (905-871-4428), 2400 Niagara Parkway (about 5 miles north of the Peace Bridge), Fort Erie. The only public marina on the Canadian side of the Niagara River. Facilities include 135 seasonal docks, washrooms, showers, a snack bar, and a gift shop.

FAMILY FUN 🦒 **Safari Niagara** (1-866-367-9669; www.safariniagara.com), 2821 Stevensville Road, Stevensville. Open seasonally. A 150-acre, privately-owned nature park with over 1,000 animals.

GOLF **Fort Erie Golf Club** (905-991-8883; www.forteriegolfclub.com), 1640 Garrison Road, Fort Erie. A public, 18-hole, par-57 course with restaurant, pro shop, lessons, and driving range.

Rio Vista Golf Club (905-871-0921; www.golfriovista.com), Crooks Street and Bowen Road, Fort Erie. A semi-private 9-hole, par-36 course.

GAMING Fort Erie is known for its high-stakes bingo halls that regularly attract visitors from both sides of the border.

Delta Bingo Center (905-871-6440; deltabingo.com/our-locations/fort-erie), 427 Garrison Road, Fort Erie.

Golden Nugget Bingo (905-871-1277 or 888-739-6149; www.goldennugget.ca), 655 Garrison Road, Fort Erie.

HORSE RACING **Fort Erie Racetrack** (905-871-3200 or 800-295-3770; www.forterieracing.com), 230 Catherine Street, Fort Erie. Live Thoroughbred racing from April–mid-October. Racing takes place Sunday and Tuesday in June and July; Tuesday and Saturday August–mid-October. This 1897 track—host to one of the racing season's premier events, the Prince of Wales Stakes, the second leg of Canada's Triple Crown—is regarded as North America's most picturesque live Thoroughbred racetrack.

SCENIC DRIVES **Niagara River Parkway.** Fort Erie is the southern terminus of the 38-mile Niagara River Parkway, one of the most scenic drives in the world. The Fort Erie portion overlooks the Niagara River, the Peace Bridge, and Riverwalk Park.

SCENIC VISTAS For a great view of the Buffalo skyline, stop at the small parking area along **Lakeshore Drive between the Peace Bridge and Old Fort Erie.** Another scenic locale is the **Crystal Beach Waterfront Park,** which has views of both Buffalo and Point Abino.

✳ Green Space

BEACHES 🏖 **Crystal Beach/Bay Beach** (905-871-1600, ext. 2431) 4155 Erie Road, Crystal Beach. Free admission to beach; paid parking. Enjoy over 1,000 feet of well-maintained sand beach, which can get quite crowded on the weekends. It has a snack bar and washrooms, but no lifeguards.

🏖 **Crescent Beach,** on the Friendship Trail at the end of Crescent Road. A small beach, popular with families, that has 65 feet of beachfront.

Bernard Avenue Beach (Thunder Bay Beach), end of Bernard Avenue. A small, family-friendly beach.

Waverly Beach, end of Helena Street at Edgemere Road. A groomed, white-sand beach next to the site of the old Erie Amusement Park, which was a popular destination at the turn of the twentieth century.

NATURE PRESERVES **Shagbark Trail**, Corner of Dominion Road and Burleigh Road. This 64-acre wooded and meadowed park is popular with nature lovers.

Stevensville Conservation Area (905-788-3135), Main and Ott Roads, Stevensville. This 121-acre passive recreation area, under the auspices of the Niagara Conservation Authority, features Carolina forest, wetlands, a fishing pond, and a picnic area.

PARKS **Lions Sugar Bowl Park**, Gilmore Avenue at Central, Fort Erie. The park features a central fountain, playground, and municipal swimming pool. The park's bowl-like shape resembles a giant sugar bowl when it's filled with snow.

 ♿ **Mather Arch** (905-356-2241), 11 Niagara Parkway at the base of the Peace Bridge, Fort Erie. This structure was built in 1940 as a gateway for travelers arriving into Canada via the Peace Bridge. It was named after American inventor and manufacturer Alonzo Mather, who donated the land on which the arch is constructed. The park surrounding it consists of manicured lawns and two 165-foot-long flower beds.

Riverwalk, located just below the Peace Bridge at the intersection of Queen Street and Niagara Boulevard. This riverfront park features a sculpture commemorating the Underground Railroad, patios, outdoor cafés, and public seating. The park connects the Friendship Trail and the Niagara River Recreational Trail.

WALKING AND HIKING TRAILS **Friendship Trail**. The Fort Erie portion of the Niagara River Recreational Trail is popular for walking, jogging, cycling, and rollerblading, as well as cross-country skiing and snowshoeing in winter.

Niagara River Recreational Trail. A multi-use 38-mile trail system for walking, biking and in-line skating that runs parallel to the Niagara Parkway. The trail, mainly asphalt, was developed by the Niagara Parks Commission between 1986–1994.

Riverwalk. See *Parks*.

MATHER ARCH, FORT ERIE

✳ Lodging

INNS AND RESORTS ⅁ **Clarion Hotel & Conference Centre** (905-871-8333), 1485 Garrison Road, Fort Erie. Over a hundred quality guest rooms, some including fireplaces and whirlpools, are available in this hotel located in the Fort Erie Civic Centre. $$.

BED & BREAKFASTS **Friendship Trail Bed & Breakfast** (905-871-1424; www.friendshiptrailbandb.ca), 328 Kraft Road, Fort Erie. A bicycle-friendly inn with three guest rooms located by the Friendship Trail and the Niagara Circle Route. $$.

✳ Where to Eat

There are many places to eat in Fort Erie and the vicinity; here's just a sampling of what the area has to offer.

DINING OUT **Happy Jack's** (905-871-3970; www.happyjacksrestaurant.ca), 98 Niagara Boulevard, Fort Erie. Sunday–Thursday 11 AM–11 PM, Friday–Saturday 11 AM–midnight. Happy Jack's has been *the* place to go for Chinese food in the Fort Erie area since 1967. This large family-owned restaurant specializes in Cantonese and Peking-style food.

✐ ⅁ ⚘ **Green Acres Family Restaurant** (905-871-1212; www.greenacresrestaurant.ca), 1554 Garrison Road, Fort Erie. Open late February–December, Wednesday–Sunday 11:30 AM–8 PM. Since 1961 this restaurant has specialized in fish and chips, as well as ribs, roast beef, and chicken.

Ming Teh (905-871-7971; www.mingtehrestaurant.com), 126 Niagara Boulevard, Fort Erie. Tuesday–Sunday 11 AM–10 PM. This restaurant with exquisite Chinese decor is known for Peking duck and escargot, plus an extensive Mandarin and Szechwan menu.

Old Bank Bistro & Piano Bar (905-994-9222, www.oldbankbistro.com), 41 Jarvis Street, Fort Erie. Monday–Friday 11 AM–10 PM, Saturday 4–10 PM. Located in an old bank, this restaurant specializes in steak, seafood, pasta, and Greek dishes.

335 on the Ridge, (905-894-4229; www.335ontheridge.com), 335 Ridge Road, Ridgeway. Open daily for lunch and dinner. This upscale, yet casual café features specials like Chicken Milanese, lamb, pork chops, and steak, as well as gourmet pizza. Dine indoors or outside in the courtyard.

South Coast Cookhouse (905-894-7037), 423 Derby Road, Crystal Beach. Open daily 12–11 PM. A classy yet casual family-friendly restaurant and pub with burgers, sandwiches, pizza, and wings, along with a variety of entrees like ribs, steak, and pasta.

EATING OUT **Artemis Restaurant** (905-871-5344; artemisforterie.com), 199 Garrison Road, Fort Erie. Monday–Saturday 7 AM–9 PM, Sunday 7 AM–3 PM. This restaurant is noted for souvlaki and other Greek specialties.

Crystal Chandelier (905-894-9996; www.thecrystalchandelier.com), 3878 Erie Road, Crystal Beach. Wednesday–Sunday 3–10 PM. This restaurant and bar, which has many crystal chandeliers, has a menu that includes burgers and pizza, as well as seafood and steak. Live jazz entertainment is featured on the weekends.

Flying Squirrel Coffee Lounge (905-894-6590; www.flyingsquirrelcoffeelounge.com), 238 Ridge Road, Ridgeway. Monday–Saturday 8 AM–9 PM, Sunday 9 AM–4 PM. A cute little café that serves coffee, sandwiches, soups, salads, and desserts.

The Kitchen (905-894-2948; www.thekitchen.ca), 294 Ridge Road North, Ridgeway. Tuesday–Friday 10 AM–6 PM, Saturday 10 AM–3 PM; open Mondays in summer. Enjoy organic gourmet

ENJOY ORGANIC FARE AND MORE AT THE KITCHEN, LOCATED IN RIDGEWAY

sandwiches, grain bowls, soups, and baked goods at this cozy restaurant which has an upstairs dining room. Take out is available.

Maria's Downtown (905-321-1049) 301 Ridge Road North, Ridgeway. Enjoy homestyle diner food for breakfast and lunch.

🍴 **Sweet Dreams Ice Cream Parlor** (905-894-9573; www.sweetdreams online.ca), 367 Ridge Road North, Ridgeway. Hours vary seasonally. Enjoy twenty-eight flavors of hard ice cream, along with soft serve, milkshakes, and more. They also serve Stewart's Fried Chicken.

Trailside Bar & Grill (289-876-8000; www.trailsidebarandgrill.ca), 282 Ridge Road North, Ridgeway. Sunday and Tuesday 11:30 AM–11 PM, Wednesday–Thursday 11:30 AM–1 AM, Friday–Saturday 11:30 AM–2 AM. Enjoy gourmet burgers, wings, and more, including a Friday fish fry. Enjoy live music on Saturday evenings and patio dining during the summer.

✳ Selective Shopping

SPECIAL SHOPS

CRYSTAL BEACH

Crystal Beach Candy Company (905-871-7912; www.crystalbeachcandy.com). Order online and in select stores listed on the website. For those of you who still remember crossing the border to visit Crystal Beach Amusement Park, this is your source for the original Halls suckers and Crystal Beach sugar waffles you've been craving. They also sell a one-hour video, *One Last Ride*, which was filmed in 1989, on the last day the park was open.

RIDGEWAY

🍴 ♿ **Brodie's Guardian Drug Store and Village Shoppes** (905-894-2520), 315 Ridge Road North, Ridgeway. Open Monday–Saturday 9 AM–8 PM, Wednesday until 6 PM. Since 1902 Brodie's has been *the* place to shop in Ridgeway. The store is huge and just goes on and on. In addition to a full pharmacy and drugstore, you can find toys, shoes, household items, greeting cards, crafts, and more.

A Renaissance Woman Consignment Boutique (289-476-1084; www.arenaissancewoman.ca), 301 Ridge Road North, Ridgeway. Monday–Friday 11 AM–5 PM, Saturday 10 AM–4 PM. This upscale consignment boutique has a nice selection of items.

Lasting Impressions (905-894-2059), 327 Ridge Road North, Ridgeway. Monday–Saturday 10 AM–5 PM, Sunday 11 AM–4 PM. This shop has home and seasonal decor items, jewelry, fragrances, and accessories.

Lakeside Books and Art (289-876-9618; www.lakesidebooksandart.com), 341 Ridge Road North, Ridgeway. Daily 10 AM–5 PM. A cozy shop with books, antiques, toys, and more.

Schmittz & Gigglez Sweet Shop (289-968-7246) 300 Ridge Road North, Ridgeway. A cute candy shop carrying classic candies as well as European imports.

Three Ferrises (905-894-5557; www.threeferrisesboutique.com), 311 Ridge Road North, Ridgeway. A high-quality women's boutique shop named after the owner, her daughter, and her aunt, all named Ferris.

Unique Creations Artisan Outlet (289-321-0548; www.ucao.ca), 304 Ridge Road North, Ridgeway. This store carries handcrafted items made by over 125 artisans.

Work of Art Frame Shop (905-894-8588), 329 Ridge Road North, Ridgeway. Monday–Friday 10 AM–5 PM, Saturday 10 AM–2 PM. This frame shop also carries Crystal Beach prints, art postcards, local artwork, gift items, and home decor.

FORT ERIE

Peace Bridge Duty Free Shop (800-361-1302; www.dutyfree.ca). Located at the Peace Bridge on the Fort Erie side. Open 24 hours, seven days a week. Americans can spend up to $200 American duty free on every trip to Canada under 48 hours. The largest duty-free store in North America features exceptional prices on designer clothing, fragrances, china, and crystal, plus beer, alcoholic beverages, and cigarettes. Another duty-free shop is located at the **Queenston-Lewiston Bridge** (905-262-5363; www.dutytaxfree.com). Note that Americans that are in Canada for longer than 48 hours can bring back up to $800 American duty free.

✳ Special Events

July: **Friendship Festival** (905-871-6454; www.friendshipfestival.com), Mather Arch in Fort Erie and LaSalle Park in Buffalo. A multi-day event that includes concerts, amusement rides, crafts, children's activities, and fireworks celebrating the friendship between Canada and the United States. **Ridgeway Summer Festival** (905-894-1720; www.ridgewayont.ca), Ridgeway. An outdoor festival for the entire family which features foods, crafts, a car show, and entertainment.

December: **Spirit of Christmas and Dickens Style Open House** (905-894-1720; www.ridgewayont.ca), Ridgeway. Do your holiday shopping while sipping cider and listening to carols.

NIAGARA FALLS, ONTARIO

Niagara Falls, Ontario is probably one of the most unique cities in the world. It has seen massive commercial and tourism growth in the last several years while being the site of one of the Seven Natural Wonders of the World. The Niagara Falls area is definitely a study in contrasts. On the one hand, you have the thundering falls and the wild, scenic beauty of the lower gorge, yet just a few hundred feet away you have a bustling city that, in some aspects, rivals Las Vegas in its glitz. The city, which has about 80,000 permanent residents, attracts some 14 million visitors annually from around the world.

The history of the entire Niagara Peninsula goes back over 12,000 years, when native aboriginal people used the area as hunting and burial grounds. The name *Niagara* is a derivation of the Iroquoian word *Onguiaahra*, meaning "the strait." Many of the early European settlers in the region were British United Empire Loyalists, who left the United States after the Revolutionary War.

The city of Niagara Falls is actually a conglomeration of a number of different villages that eventually merged. These villages include Drummondville (named after Lt. General Gordon Drummond, who fought in the Battle of Lundy's Lane during the War of 1812), near present-day Portage Road and Lundy's Lane; Clifton, located in the vicinity of today's Skylon Tower; and Elgin, located near the Whirlpool Bridge. Clifton and Elgin merged in 1856, and the name was changed to the town of Niagara Falls in 1881. The same year, Drummondville changed its name to the village of Niagara Falls. The town and village later combined to make the city in 1904.

There are many attractions in the Niagara Falls area. Of course, you have the Falls and attractions connected to it, like the *Hornblower Niagara Cruises* and *Journey Behind the Falls*. Gardeners enjoy the Niagara Parks Botanical Gardens and Niagara Parks Butterfly Conservatory as well as the Floral Clock. If you have children in tow, be sure to visit Marineland and the Niagara Falls Bird Aviary, and take a walk along Clifton Hill.

AREA CODES The area codes are 905 and 289.

GUIDANCE **Niagara Falls Tourism Association** (905-356-6061 or 800-563-2557; www .niagarafallstourism.com), 5400 Robinson Street, Niagara Falls, Ontario. Open daily 9 AM–5 PM. The official tourism site of Niagara Falls.

Ontario Travel Information (905-358-3221), 5355 Stanley Avenue, Niagara Falls, Ontario. Open daily 8:30 AM–4:30 PM, until 8 PM in summer. This information center has Niagara region information as well as for the rest of Ontario.

Lundy's Lane Tourist Area (905-356-1161 or 866-551-LANE; www.lundyslane.com). Contact them for information on the Lundy's Lane business district, a 2-mile area of lodgings, restaurants, shops, and entertainment just west of the falls.

Tourism Partnership of Niagara (289-477-5344; www.visitniagaracanada.com).

City of Niagara Falls, Canada (905-356-7521; www.niagarafalls.ca).

GETTING THERE By air: See *Getting There—City of Buffalo.*

By bus: **City of Niagara Falls Bus Terminal** (905-356-1179), Corner of Bridge and Erie Streets, Niagara Falls, Ontario.

By car: The main entrance point from the United States is via the Rainbow Bridge. The Whirlpool Bridge is a NEXUS-only crossing.

GETTING AROUND *By car:* Traffic in the tourist area can be very congested, especially during the summer. It's best to park and walk. The main roads include Niagara Parkway/River Road, which runs along the gorge and river; Clifton Hill, Falls Boulevard, and Victoria Avenue, which are the main streets in the Clifton Hill area; and Fallsview Boulevard, which goes past most of the major hotels and the casino. Lundy's Lane has national chain hotels and restaurants located along it.

By bus: **Niagara Parks WEGO buses** (www.niagaraparks.com). Operates year-round. Park your car and ride all day around the falls tourist area in an air-conditioned bus. Choose from a 24- or 48-hour pass.

MEDICAL EMERGENCY **Greater Niagara General Hospital** (905-358-0171), 5546 Portage Road, Niagara Falls, Ontario.

✳ To See

Nightly Illumination of the Falls. Hours vary according to season, generally from dusk until midnight (10 PM January–March, 11 PM in April). A visit to Niagara Falls is not complete unless you've experienced the nightly illumination of the Falls. Huge spotlights light the falls in shades of blue, red, and green. Be sure to arrive well before dusk to get a prime viewing spot along the railings.

MUSEUMS AND HISTORIC HOMES **Niagara Falls History Museum** (905-358-5082; www.niagarafallsmuseums.ca), 5810 Ferry Street, Niagara Falls. Tuesday–Saturday 10 AM–5 PM, Thursday until 9 PM. This museum is housed in an 1874 building originally constructed as a town hall. On display are War of 1812 artifacts, information on the founding and development of Niagara Falls, and historical photos of the city. It is located on the site of the battle of Lundy's Lane, which took place July 25, 1814.

Willoughby Museum (905-295-4036; www.niagarafallsmuseums.ca), 9935 Niagara Parkway, Niagara Falls. Open May–August, Wednesday–Sunday 11 AM–5 PM. This museum, housed in a 1916 one-room schoolhouse, has historical treasures and artifacts from the towns of Willoughby and Chippawa.

ARCHITECTURE **Cham Shan Temple** (905-371-2678), 4303 River Road (across from the White Water Boardwalk, just north of the Whirlpool Bridge), Niagara Falls. Open daily 11 AM–5 PM June–September. Visitors can learn the basic principles of Buddhism and view artifacts on a 45-minute guided tour of this seven-level temple.

HISTORIC SITES **Chippawa Battlefield Park**, along the Niagara Parkway just south of Falls tourist area. A 300-acre site operated by the Niagara Parks Commission. It is the last remaining battlefield from the War of 1812.

✳ To Do

BOAT EXCURSIONS ♿ **Hornblower Niagara Cruises** (formerly *Maid of the Mist*), (905-643-4272; www.niagaracruises.com), 5920 Niagara Parkway, Niagara Falls.

Open seasonally mid-April–Labor Day. A variety of cruises are offered, call or see website for specifics. For over 150 years this boat excursion has been taking visitors on a journey close to the thundering waters of the Falls. This is considered a "must-do" when you visit the area. See also *Niagara Falls, New York—Boat Excursions*.

BREWERIES **Niagara Brewing Company** (www.niagarabrewingcompany.com), 4915-A Clifton Hill, Niagara Falls. Sunday 12–9 PM, Monday–Thursday 12–8 PM, Friday–Saturday 11 AM–1 AM. A brewery and restaurant located in the heart of Clifton Hill. Enjoy craft beers and pub food.

FAMILY FUN ✂ **Falls Incline Railway** (905-371-0254; www.niagaraparks.com), between Portage Road and the Niagara Parkway across from Horseshoe Falls, Niagara Falls. Operates late March–late October, daily schedule varies. Visitors can descend or ascend the escarpment to the falls area in an open-air car.

✂ **Fallsview Indoor Waterpark & Hotel Complex** (905-374-4444, 888-234-8413; www.fallsviewwaterpark.com), 5685 Falls Avenue, Niagara Falls. This 90,000 square foot waterpark, the largest hotel and indoor waterpark complex in North America, is accessible from three hotels: Sheraton on the Falls, Skyline Inn, and the Crowne Plaza Niagara Falls Fallsview. The Clifton Victoria Inn at the Falls is right behind the waterpark

✂ ♿ **Marineland** (905-356-2142; www.marinelandcanada.com), 7657 Portage Road, Niagara Falls. Open mid-May–October. This attraction features a marine mammal show, with whales, dolphins, and seals, and interactive animal displays. Visitors can touch the whales at the interactive whale habitats, Friendship Cove and Arctic Cove. The park also has amusement rides, including the Dragon Mountain steel roller coaster and the Sky Screamer, a 450-foot tower that propels riders skyward for a view of the falls.

FALLS INCLINE RAILWAY, NIAGARA FALLS, ONTARIO

✒ ⌕ **Niagara Falls Aviary: Birds of the Lost Kingdom** (905-356-8888; www.niagara fallsaviary.com), 5651 River Road, Niagara Falls. Open 9 AM–5 PM, longer hours in summer. Get up close with exotic and tropical birds and other creatures. Kids will enjoy seeing in person the colorful critters normally seen only on TV or in books, including poison dart frogs, toucans, and macaws. Visitors are permitted inside the lorikeet cage to mingle with and feed nectar to these tiny, friendly birds.

Niagara Fun Zone (905-357-1346; www.niagarafallsfunzone.com), 6455 Fallsview Boulevard, Niagara Falls. Enjoy 50,000 square feet of fun, including an arcade, laser tag, mini golf, and fun house.

Sir Adam Beck Generating Station #2 (1-877-642-7275), along the Niagara Parkway near Lewiston Queenston Bridge. Hours vary according to season. Forty-minute guided tours are offered of one of the largest hydroelectric plants in Ontario.

Table Rock Center (www.niagarafallstourism.com/play/falls-experiences/table-rock), 6650 Niagara Parkway, Niagara Falls. this facility has a welcome center where you can purchase tickets to area attractions, including *Journey Behind the Falls* (see *Guided Tours*) and *Niagara's Fury* (a 4-D show about the creation about the Falls). There are stores and a food court here, as well as the more upscale Elements on the Falls Restaurant (see *Dining Out*).

Wildplay Mistrider to the Falls (800-263-7073; www.wildplay.com/niagarafalls), 5847 Niagara Parkway, Niagara Falls. Take a ride on one of four ziplines that face the American and Canadian falls. Ride 2,200 feet at 40 mph along the edge of the Niagara Gorge.

Wildplay Whirlpool Adventure Course (www.wildplay.com/niagarafalls), Thompson Point, 3500 Niagara Parkway, Niagara Falls. Open daily 10 AM–6 PM mid-June–early September. Visitors to Niagara Falls have a new way to explore the Niagara Gorge and the whirlpool by making their way through a series of aerial obstacles of various difficulties. Three courses are featured: a kid's course, a classic course, and an extreme course.

FISHING **Niagara Fishing Adventures** (800-332-6865; www.niagarafishingadventures .com), found at variety of locations along the Niagara River. Fishing adventures along the Niagara Gorge. You will be provided with a fishing license, fishing tackle, and lunch after the excursion. Trout, salmon, and bass are the more popular catches.

GAMING Note: No one under 19 is permitted in the casinos.

⌕ **Casino Niagara** (905-374-3598 or 888-946-3255; www.casinoniagara.com), 5705 Falls Avenue, Niagara Falls. Open 24/7/365. This casino features 30 table games and 1,300 slot and video poker machines.

⌕ **Niagara Fallsview Casino Resort** (905-374-3598, 888-FALLSVU; www.fallsview casinoresort.com), 6380 Fallsview Boulevard, Niagara Falls. This large casino features 3,000 slot machines and over 130 gaming tables. The casino's Avalon Ballroom features top entertainers, including some Las Vegas headliners. A 30-story, 374-room hotel is at the center of the property, along with retail shops, restaurants, and a meeting space.

GOLF **Beechwood Golf & Country Club** (905-680-4653; www.beechwoodgolf.com), 4680 Thorold Towline Road, Niagara Falls. A semi-private 18-hole, par-71 course with restaurant and full bar.

Eagle Valley Golf Club (905-374-2110; www.golfeaglevalley.com), 2334 St. Paul Avenue, Niagara Falls. A public 18-hole, par-63 course. Amenities include a restaurant, full bar, club making, lessons, a driving range, and a health pro shop.

CLIFTON HILL

Clifton Hill (905-358-3676; www.cliftonhill.com) is a unique area in the heart of Niagara Falls. Part Las Vegas, part carnival midway, part Halloween, Clifton Hill's glitziness is in direct contrast with the natural wonder just a block away. While some visitors may find it chaotic and commercial, it does offer a refuge on a rainy day or a place to appease bored teenagers. The area is jam-packed with fast-food restaurants, amusements, shops, and other diversions. One of the most prominent attractions is the 175-foot-tall Niagara Skywheel, a ferris wheel which operates year-round with fully enclosed climate-controlled gondolas. Here is a sampling of Clifton Hill attractions:

Louis Tussaud's Waxworks (905-374-6601), 4915 Clifton Hill.

  ♿ Ripley's Believe-It-Or-Not! Museum (905-356-2238; www.ripleysniagara.com), 4960 Clifton Hill.

House of Frankenstein (905-357-9660), 4967 Clifton Hill.

Great Canadian Midway (905-358-3673), Clifton Hill. 70,000 square feet of family entertainment.

Dinosaur Park Miniature Golf (905-357-5911), 4960 Clifton Hill. Summer only.

Niagara Sky Wheel (905-358-4793; www.skywheel.ca) 4960 Clifton Hill. Open daily year-round.

CLIFTON HILL IN NIAGARA FALLS, ONTARIO HAS MANY ATTRACTIONS AND RESTAURANTS

Legends of the Niagara Golf Complex (905-295-9595 or 866-465-3642; www.niagaraparksgolf.com), 9233 Niagara Parkway, Niagara Falls. Two championship 18-hole courses plus a 9-hole putting course. Owned and operated by the Niagara Parks Commission, this course borders the historic grounds of the 1814 Battle of Chippawa site.

The Links of Niagara at Willodell (905-295-GOLF or 800-790-0912; www.thelinksofniagara.com), 10325 Willodell Road, Niagara Falls. A semi-private 18-hole, par-72 course with a restaurant, full bar, banquet facilities, lessons, pro shop, and practice facilities.

Niagara Falls Golf Club (905-358-5846; www.niagarafallsgolf.com), 6169 Garner Road, Niagara Falls. A semiprivate 18-hole, par-72 course with restaurant and full bar. This challenging course is designed for all levels of golfers.

Oak Hill Par 3 Golf Course (905-358-6418; www.niagaraparksgolf.com/oak-hall-par-3), 7516 Portage Road, Niagara Falls. A semiprivate 9-hole, par-35 course with a snack bar.

Oaklands Golf Course (905-295-6643; www.oaklandsgolfclub.ca), 8970 Stanley Street, Niagara Falls. A public 18-hole, par-72 course with restaurant and full bar.

THE NIAGARA FALLSVIEW CASINO RESORT AT NIGHT

Rolling Meadows Golf & Country Club (905-384-9894; www.rollingmeadows golf.ca), 12741 Montrose Road, Niagara Falls. A semi-private 18-hole, par-72 course with restaurant.

Whirlpool Public Golf Course (905-356-1140), 3351 Niagara Parkway, Niagara Falls. This 18-hole, par-72 course has been ranked one of the top public golf courses in Canada.

GUIDED TOURS **Double Deck Tours** (905-374-7423; www.doubledecktours.com). Tours run April–October; schedule varies according to season. This tour company offers four-hour tours of the Niagara Falls area on double-decker sightseeing buses. Three major attractions—*Hornblower Niagara Cruises, Journey Behind the Falls*, and *Whirlpool Aero Car*—are included.

& **Journey Behind the Falls** (877-642-7275; www.niagaraparks.com/niagara-falls -attractions/journey-behind-the-falls.html), 6650 Niagara Parkway, Niagara Falls. Open year-round. Tours begin at 9 AM; closing times vary throughout the year. This tour takes visitors down 100 feet through century-old tunnels to an observation platform near the base of the Horseshoe Falls. Rain ponchos are supplied.

Heritage Walking Tours Several self-guided walking tours brochures that highlight historical buildings in various sections of the city are available at Niagara Falls Tourism. These include the **downtown area** (near the Whirlpool Bridge), the **Drummond-ville area** (off Main Street and Lundy's Lane), and the **village of Chippawa** (just south of the falls near Marineland). See *Guidance*.

See Sight Tours (888-961-6584; www.seesight-tours.com), 5779 Desson Avenue, Niagara Falls. They provide guided motor coach tours of Niagara Falls Canada.

VIEW OF THE SKYLON TOWER, RAINBOW BRIDGE, AMERICAN FALLS AND THE NIAGARA FALLSVIEW CASINO RESORT

SCENIC DRIVES **Niagara Parkway** Winston Churchill called the Niagara Parkway "the prettiest Sunday afternoon drive in the world" when he visited Canada in 1943, and it's still true today. The 38-mile parkway, stretching from Fort Erie to Niagara-on-the-Lake, follows the curves of the Niagara River past stately mansions and well-manicured properties.

SCENIC VIEWS AND AIR TOURS **Air Tours Niagara** (289-668-4100; www.niagara airtours.com), Niagara District Airport, 468 Niagara Stone Road Niagara-on-the-Lake. Year-round 9 AM–sunset. They offer air tours of the entire Niagara region; sites include Niagara-on-the-Lake, the Welland Canal, and Niagara Falls.

   ♿ **Niagara Helicopters** (905-357-5672; www.niagarahelicopters.com), 3731 Victoria Avenue, Niagara Falls. Daily 9 AM–dusk, year-round, weather permitting. They've been offering a bird's-eye view of Niagara Falls since 1961.

   National Helicopters (800-491-3117; www.skywayhelicopters.com), Open year-round, 9 AM–sunset by reservation, weather permitting. A unique and comprehensive tour of Niagara Falls by helicopter.

   ♿ **Skylon Tower** (905-356-2651; www.skylon.com), 5200 Robinson Street, Niagara Falls. One of three yellow bug elevators will whisk you up to the top of the tower in 52 seconds. From the observation deck 775 feet above the Falls you can see almost 80 miles. You can even dine in one of two restaurants located in the tower, the Revolving Dining Room or the Summit Suite.

   Whirlpool Aero Car (905-371-0254) 3850 Niagara Parkway (3 miles downriver from the falls), Niagara Falls. Open daily 9 AM–5 PM, March–November, weather dependent; longer hours in summer. Take an open-air gondola ride across the gorge, suspended 250 feet over the Niagara Whirlpool. The car, which was built in 1913, is often referred to as the Spanish Aero Car. In operation since 1916, it was designed by Spanish engineer Leonardo Torres Quevedo.

WEDDING CHAPELS While there are numerous wedding chapels in the Niagara Falls area, most don't offer Las Vegas–style "quickie" weddings; reservations must be made in advance.

♂ **Niagara Fallsview Weddings** (905-356-1944; www.niagara-fallsview-weddings.com), 6732 Fallview Boulevard, Niagara Falls. Open by appointment. Niagara Falls' premier wedding and honeymoon service provider. Get married while overlooking the falls from the wedding chapel in the Tower Hotel.

♂ **Niagara Weddings** (905-374-3957; www.niagaraweddingscanada.com), 5669 Main Street, Niagara Falls. Open by appointment. They offer services seven days a week. Their specialty is elopements.

♂ **Occasions in Niagara** (905-357-7756 or 877-286-9436; www.occasionsniagara.com), 5368 Menzie Street, Niagara Falls. Open by appointment. A wedding-planning service.

THE WHIRLPOOL AEROCAR HAS BEEN IN OPERATION SINCE 1916

♂ **Two Hearts Wedding Chapel** (905-371-3204; www.twoheartsweddings.com), 5219 Victoria Avenue, Niagara Falls. Open by appointment. A small, dignified chapel that holds up to 60 guests.

♂ **Wedding Company of Niagara** (905-371-3695 or 877-6451-3111; www.weddingcompanyniagara.com), 6053 Franklin Avenue, Niagara Falls. Open by appointment. A full range of services for all denominations.

✳ Green Space

NATURE PRESERVES **Dufferin Island Nature Area** (905-371-0254; www.niagaraparks.com). Open daily, dawn to dusk. Located just south of the Falls, this area has trails that wind over eleven small islands connected by numerous bridges. A good place for picnicking, birding, and fishing.

Niagara Glen Nature Area See *Walking and Hiking Trails*.

GARDENS ♿ **Niagara Parks Botanical Gardens** (905-356-2241 or 877-642-7275; www.niagaraparks.com), 2565 Niagara Parkway, Niagara Falls. Open daily, dawn to dusk. Free admission. The 100-acre manicured gardens are maintained by students from the Niagara Parks School of Horticulture. The gardens are noted for their roses, along with their large collection of formal and informal gardens.

🦋 ♿ **Butterfly Conservatory** (905-356-2241 or 877-642-7275; www.niagaraparks.com), 2565 Niagara Parkway (in the Niagara Parks Botanical Gardens), Niagara Falls.

FLORAL CLOCK

Open daily 9 AM–5 PM. Get up close and personal with 2,000 tropical butterflies in this 11,000-square-foot, climate-controlled butterfly conservatory, the largest of its type in North America. Stroll along the 600-foot path that winds through the conservatory, and observe more than forty-five varieties of butterflies in all four stages of their life cycle.

    ♿ **Floral Clock.** Along the Niagara Parkway, just south of the Lewiston-Queenston Bridge. One of the world's largest working floral clocks, this horticultural attraction, built in 1950, is 40 feet in diameter and formed by 15,000 plants. It is designed, planted, and maintained by the Niagara Parks Commission.

    ♿ **Floral Showhouse** (905-356-2241 or 877-642-7275; www.niagaraparks.com), 7145 Niagara River Parkway, Niagara Falls. Open daily 9 AM–5 PM. The displays in this popular greenhouse change about eight times a year to celebrate the seasons or holidays. Plants from all over the world are featured, along with waterfalls, pools, tropical song birds, turtles, and fish.

    Oakes Garden Theatre (905-356-2241 or 877-642-7275; www.niagaraparks.com), River Road, Niagara Falls. Located at the base of Clifton Hill across from the American falls. Open daily, dawn to dusk. Free admission. This park, built in 1937 as an outdoor stage, is a blend of formal gardens and architecture, based on Greek amphitheaters.

PARKS Kings Bridge Park (905-356-2241 or 877-642-7275; www.niagaraparks.com), 7870 Niagara Parkway. Village of Chippawa. Parking is charged on summer weekends and holidays. The park has a picnic area, a playground, and a splash pad.

    Queen Victoria Park (905-358-5935 or 877-642-7272), Niagara Parkway across from the American Falls. Open daily, dawn to dusk. This 154-acre park, created in 1887, has manicured lawns and a variety of gardens. A popular restaurant in the park overlooks the falls.

WALKING AND HIKING TRAILS Bruce Trail (905-529-6821 or 800-665-HIKE; www .brucetrail.org). The trailhead is located near Brock's Monument in Queenston Park, Queenston. The Bruce Trail is Canada's oldest and longest footpath and provides the only public access to the Niagara Escarpment. This well-known Canadian trail goes from the Niagara Falls area to Tobermory in northern Ontario, near Georgian Bay and Lake Huron.

Niagara Glen Nature Area, Niagara Parkway, across from the Whirlpool Golf Course between Queenston and Niagara Falls. This nature area features hiking trails along the gorge. Many rare species of flora exist in this area, which is also an important birding area. Hikes through the area involve a change in elevation of over 200 feet. Niagara Glen has a large parking area, picnic tables and rest rooms. The Wildplay Whirlpool Adventure course is located here. See *Family Fun.*

Niagara River Recreational Trail (905-356-2241 or 877-642-7275; www.niagaraparks .com). This trail is located alongside the Niagara Parkway and the Niagara River from Fort Erie to Niagara-on-the-Lake.

  ﺏ **White Water Boardwalk** (905-356-2241 or 877-642-7275; www.niagaraparks.com), Niagara Parkway, Niagara Falls. Open daily 9 AM–5 PM mid-March–mid-November, with limited access in winter. About a mile and a half past the Whirlpool Bridge along the Niagara Parkway is the parking lot for the trail down into the gorge. This 1,000-foot boardwalk along the river's edge passes some of the strongest Class VI rapids in the world, past the swirling whirlpool.

✳ Lodging

Author's note: If you are planning to stay in the area, my advice is to splurge and stay at one of the hotels overlooking the falls. These hotels—primarily operated by major hotel chains—offer spectacular views of both the American and Canadian Falls. There are hundreds of accommodations in and around the Falls, which has the third-most hotel rooms in Canada. Space allows for just a small number of these accommodations to be highlighted in this book. For a complete list contact the **Niagara Falls Tourism Association** (905-356-6061 or 800-563-2557; www.niagarafallstourism.com).

HOTELS, INNS, AND RESORTS: OVER-LOOKING THE FALLS **Crowne Plaza Hotel** (905-374-4447, 800-263-7135; www .niagarafallscrowneplazahotel.com), 5685 Falls Avenue, Niagara Falls. This elegant 233-room hotel is connected to Casino Niagara by an indoor walkway. It offers spectacular falls-view rooms and suites, some with terraces overlooking the falls. Amenities include an indoor pool, whirlpool, and sauna. $$.

  Embassy Suites (905-356-3600 or 800-420-6980; www.embassysuites niagara.com), 6700 Fallsview Boulevard, Niagara Falls. This forty-two-story luxury hotel features 512 two-room suites, many overlooking the Falls. Amenities include an indoor pool, fitness center, and a complimentary breakfast. $$$$.

  ﺏ **Fallsview Casino Resort** (905-374-3598, 888-FALLSVU; www.fallsview casinoresort.com), 6380 Fallsview Boulevard, Niagara Falls. A 30-story, 374-room luxury hotel is at the center of the property, along with the casino, retail stores, an entertainment venue, restaurants, and a meeting center. $$$$.

  ﺏ **Hilton Niagara Falls** (905-354-7887 or 888-370-0700; www.niagarafalls .hilton.com), 6361 Fallsview Boulevard, Niagara Falls. This four-diamond, 516-room hotel features standard rooms as well as Jacuzzi suites, many with a fabulous view of the falls. The hotel's 10,000-square-foot indoor pool has the area's only spiraling three-story waterslide. Guest can enjoy fine dining in the water-themed rooftop restaurant, the Watermark. $$.

  ﺏ **Niagara Falls Marriott Falls-view** (905-357-7300, 888-501-8916; www.niagarafallsmarriott.com), 6740 Fallsview Boulevard, Niagara Falls. A four-diamond property located just 100 yards from the brink of the Falls, this

23-story, 427-room hotel features standard rooms plus Jacuzzi, loft, family, and fireplace suites. Many rooms have a falls view. Amenities include a 3,000-square-foot, full-service spa, indoor pool, fitness room, and arcade. $$$.

   ♿ **The Oakes Hotel** (905-356-4514 or 877-THE-OAKES; www.oakeshotel.com), 6546 Fallsview Boulevard, Niagara Falls. This 167-room hotel offers first-class accommodations overlooking the Horseshoe Falls. Many of the suites have fireplaces, Jacuzzis, and/or terraces. Hotel amenities include an indoor pool, exercise facilities, and room service. It is adjacent to the Fallsview Casino Resort. $$$.

   ♿ **Radisson Hotel & Suites Fallsview** (905-356-1944 or 800-333-3333; www.niagarafallsview.com), 6733 Fallsview Boulevard, Niagara Falls. This hotel offers 232 rooms, many with a view of the falls, Jacuzzi tubs, microwaves, and mini-fridges. They also have an indoor pool and fitness center. $$$.

   The Tower Hotel (905-356-1501; www.niagaratower.com), 6732 Fallsview Drive, Niagara Falls. This landmark boutique hotel, located in the former Minolta Tower offers forty-two guest rooms that feature wall-to-wall, floor-to-ceiling windows with views of either the falls or the city. $$$$.

   Marriott Fallsview (905-374-1077 or 800-618-9059; www.fallsview.com), 6755 Fallsview Boulevard, Niagara Falls. Over 400 luxury guest rooms and suites with great views of the falls are available at this thirty-two-story hotel. Amenities include an indoor pool, fitness center, fallsview terrace and observation deck. $$$.

   Sheraton on the Falls (905-374-4445 or 800-229-9961; www.sheratononthefalls.com), 5875 Falls Avenue, Niagara Falls. This hotel, directly across from the American Falls, offers 670 luxury rooms, suites, and bi-level suites, many with a great view of the Falls. Amenities include a spa and fitness center. It has indoor walkways to Casino

Niagara and the Fallsview Indoor Waterpark. $$.

OTHER HOTELS, INNS, AND RESORTS ♿ **Old Stone Inn Boutique Hotel** (800-263-6208; oldstoneinnhotel.com), 5425 Robinson Road, Niagara Falls. Just a 10-minute walk to the falls, this unique English-style country inn located in a former 1904 stone flour mill has 111 cozy guest rooms, some with Jacuzzis and fireplaces. Pet-friendly. See also *Dining Out—Flour Mill Restaurant*. $$$.

   🛏 ♿ **Americana Conference Resort and Spa** (905-356-8444 or 866-707-0030; www.americananiagara.com), 8444 Lundy's Lane, Niagara Falls. This 160-room hotel is the only full-service resort in Niagara Falls. Along with standard rooms, they offer family and two-room suites, Jacuzzi suites, and rooms with balconies. The Americana has a luxurious spa, as well as indoor and outdoor pools—one of which is a 25,000-square-foot water park with retractable roof—along with a fitness center, video arcade, and indoor and outdoor playgrounds. $$$.

   🛏 **Great Wolf Lodge** (905-354-4888 or 800-605-9653; www.greatwolf.com/niagara), 3950 Victoria Avenue, Niagara Falls. This 406-suite, four-story log-sided hotel with a Northwoods theme features a 100,000-square-foot waterpark that has thirteen watersides, ten pools, and a four-story tree house. They also have an outdoor mini golf course, along with kid's activities like story time, crafts, and an arcade. $$$$.

MOTELS Many nondescript national chain and family-owned motels are located throughout the city. While most don't offer a falls view, many are within walking distance to the cataracts, and in most cases these accommodations are moderately priced. There are also numerous hotels in the Lundy's Lane section of town, a short drive from the falls tourist area. **Lundy's Lane Tourism Information:** 866-551-LANE.

BED & BREAKFASTS Close to fifty bed & breakfast inns can be found in Niagara Falls, many in the area between the Whirlpool and Rainbow Bridges, about a 10-minute walk to the Falls. The inns located on River Road, many of them in Victorian-era homes, offer views of the gorge. For a complete list of bed & breakfast inns, contact **Niagara Falls Tourism** (see *Guidance*), or visit www.infoniagara.com/Bed-and-Breakfasts. Here is just a sampling:

Absolute Elegance Bed & Breakfast (905-353-8522; www.aebedandbreakfast.com), 6023 Culp Street, Niagara Falls. Choose from two elegant antiques-furnished guest rooms in this circa-1855 Queen Anne–style Victorian home. $$.

Ambiance by the Falls Bed & Breakfast (888-374-4314; www.ambiancebythefalls.com), 4467 John Street, Niagara Falls. This turn-of-the-twentieth-century home is a three-minute walk from the falls. It has three guest rooms with queen-sized beds and en suite baths. $$.

Danner House Bed & Breakfast (905-295-1805; www.dannerhouse.com), 12549 Niagara River Parkway, Niagara Falls. This historic stone home was built in 1805. Each of the three guest rooms has a private bath and waterfront view. An in-ground pool is available for guest use. $$.

Strathaird Bed & Breakfast (905-358-3421; www.strathairdinn.com), 4372 Simcoe Street, Niagara Falls. Each of the three guest rooms has a private bath. A full Scottish-style breakfast is served each morning. $$.

Orchard View Bed & Breakfast (905-357-4221; www.victoriancharmbb.com), 6028 Culp Street, Niagara Falls. This inn has four guest rooms with en suite baths in this 1889 Victorian home. Breakfast is served in a conservatory overlooking the gardens or in a screened gazebo. The inn is about a 15-minute walk to the falls. $$.

✳ Where to Eat

DINING OUT: OVERLOOKING THE FALLS Most of the hotels overlooking the falls have fine dining rooms located on their top floors—great food *and* a great view. Here are just a few of them.

Elements on the Falls Restaurant (905-354-3631), 6650 Niagara Parkway (at the Table Rock Center), Niagara Falls. This casual yet upscale restaurant has a bird's-eye view of the Canadian Horseshoe Falls. The menu features dishes such as veal tenderloin, salmon, and steak, as well as more casual fare like burgers and sandwiches.

Milestones on the Falls (905-358-4720; www.milestonesonthefalls.com), 6755 Fallsview Boulevard, Niagara Falls (at the Marriott Fallsview). Enjoy steak, seafood, and cocktails with a great view of the falls.

🐕 ♿ 🐾 **Queen Victoria Place Restaurant** (905-536-2217), across from the American Falls on the Niagara Parkway, Niagara Falls. Open seasonally May–October 11:30 AM–9 PM. This full-service restaurant, located in Queen Victoria Park and operated by the Niagara Parks Commission, offers an excellent view of the American and Canadian Falls.

Skylon Tower Revolving Dining Room (905-356-2651 or 877-840-0314; www.skylon.com), 5200 Robinson Road, Niagara Falls. Open for lunch 11:30 AM–3:30 PM, dinner 4:30–10 PM. Without a doubt, this 280-seat restaurant is one of the most romantic dining spots in the city. The award-winning continental cuisine, combined with the spectacular view from 775 feet above the , makes for a memorable evening. While romance is in the air in the evening, the restaurant, which makes a complete rotation each hour, is more family-oriented for lunch, complete with a children's menu. The **Summit Suite Dining Room**, also located in the Skylon Tower, is known for its buffet-style dining for breakfast, lunch, dinner, and Sunday brunch.

Watermark Restaurant at the Hilton Niagara Falls (905-353-7138; www.watermarkrestaurant.com) 6361 Fallsview Boulevard, Niagara Falls. Open daily for breakfast and dinner. Reservations required for dinner. This restaurant, on the 33rd floor of the Hilton Niagara Falls, 555 feet above the falls, has water-themed decor and a great view, along with wonderfully presented food.

Windows by Jamie Kennedy (866-374-4408; windowsbyjamiekennedy.com), 5875 Falls Avenue (in the Sheraton on the Falls), Niagara Falls. Located on the hotel's 13th floor, this upscale restaurant, with a great view of the Falls, has fresh and seasonal ingredients on the menu, along with an extensive wine list.

DINING OUT: OTHER NIAGARA FALLS RESTAURANTS

Ag Inspired Cuisine (289-292-0000; www.agcuisine.com), 5195 Magdalen Street, Niagara Falls. The farm to table menu features regional and seasonal ingredients.

🍴 ♿ **Betty's Restaurant** (905-295-4436; www.bettysrestaurant.com), 8921 Sodom Road, Niagara Falls (Chippewa). Daily 8 AM–8:30 PM. This large family restaurant has been popular for over 40 years. They specialize in seafood and are noted for their fish and chips. They have daily specials and a children's menu is available. Their coconut cream pie is out of this world!

Brasa Brazilian Steakhouse (905-353-7187; www.brasaniagara.com), 6361 Fallsview Boulevard (in the Hilton), Niagara Falls. Meats are cooked over an open fire and carved tableside.

Coco's Terrace Bar & Grill (905-356-1333; www.cocosniagarafalls.com), 5339 Murray Hill (at Holiday Inn by the Falls), Niagara Falls. The menu features wood-fired pizza, steaks, prime rib, and seafood.

Doc Magilligan's (905-374-0021; www.docmagilligans.com), 6400 Lundy's Lane, Niagara Falls. The only Irish pub

BETTY'S RESTAURANT IN NIAGARA FALLS, ONTARIO SPECIALIZES IN SEAFOOD

in Niagara Falls, it offers family dining, authentic Irish fare, and live entertainment on the weekend.

Falls Manor Resort and Restaurant (905-358-3211; www.fallsmanor.com), 7104 Lundy's Lane. Since 1953 this restaurant has been the original home of *broasted* chicken. It has also been voted the number one breakfast place in the Niagara region and is very popular with local people. In addition they have pet-friendly, affordable hotel rooms and cottages.

Flour Mill Restaurant (905-357-1234; www.oldstoneinnhotel.com), 5425 Robinson Road, Niagara Falls. Open daily 8 AM–10 PM for breakfast, lunch, and dinner. Fine dining is offered in a circa-1904 structure that once housed a flour mill. The dining room features stone walls, cathedral ceiling, and a wood-burning fireplace. Classic and regional cuisine using fresh ingredients is featured on their extensive menu. Overnight accommodations are available; see *Lodging— Old Stone Inn Boutique Hotel*.

Four Brothers Cucina (905-358-6951; www.fourbrothersniagara.com), 5283 Ferry Street, Niagara Falls. A family-owned restaurant since 1964 that features authentic Italian sauces and pastas made from scratch.

Remington's of Niagara (905-356-4410; www.remingtonsniagara.com), 5657 Victoria Avenue, Niagara Falls. Sunday–Thursday 4–10 PM, Friday–Saturday 4–10:30 PM. This restaurant, one of Niagara's premier steakhouses, uses the finest ingredients in their cooking. The upscale southwest decor was inspired by artist Frederic Remington. Dinner is accompanied by singing entertainment by the talented wait staff.

Twenty-One Club (888-325-5788; www.fallsviewcasinoresort.com), 6380 Fallsview Boulevard, Niagara Falls. Thursday–Monday 5–11 PM. This restaurant inside the Fallsview Casino Resort is known for steak and seafood.

EATING OUT Visitors will find hundreds of casual eateries in the Niagara Falls area, especially along Clifton Hill and Victoria Avenue. There are also many restaurants, both local and national chain establishments, along Lundy's Lane, a short drive from the tourist area. Below is just a sampling of what's available:

&. **Mick and Angelo's** (905-357-6543; www.mickandangelos.com), 7600 Lundy's Lane, Niagara Falls. Open 11 AM–1 AM daily. A popular restaurant and bar noted for homemade pasta, chicken, ribs, and steak.

&. 🐾 **Rainforest Café** (905-374-CAFÉ; niagarafallsrainforestcafe.com), 5875 Falls Avenue, Niagara Falls. Open daily 11 AM–11 PM, Friday and Saturday until midnight. A unique dining experience featuring an 80-foot-tall erupting volcano, a live shark exhibit, animatronic elephants and gorillas, and daily live animal encounters.

🐾 **Secret Garden Restaurant** (905-358-4588; www.secretgardenrestaurant .net), 5827 River Road, Niagara Falls. Open daily 8 AM–8 PM; closed in January. This affordable restaurant's dining room overlooks the American Falls. Outdoor patio dining is available in the summer, adjacent to Oakes Garden Theatre.

Swiss Chalet (www.swisschalet.com). Two locations in Niagara Falls: 6666 Lundy's Lane (905-356-1028) and 3770 Montrose Road (905-354-9660). This is a national chain in Canada, and it is very popular with folks in the Buffalo area. Swiss Chalet once had several locations in Buffalo, but all have closed and folks craving their chicken must make the trek across the border.

&. **Whirlpool Restaurant** (905-356-7221), 3351 Niagara Parkway (at the Whirlpool Golf Course), Niagara Falls. Open April–October. Pub fare and casual meals, along with Niagara region wines, are offered at this restaurant which overlooks the 18th hole.

✳ Entertainment

THEATERS 🎭 **Oh Canada Eh? Dinner Show** (800-467-2071; www.ohcanadaeh .com), 8585 Lundy's Lane, Niagara Falls. April–mid-October. A musical celebration of Canadian heritage, plus a family-style meal.

✳ Selective Shopping

SPECIAL SHOPS There are hundreds of stores in Niagara Falls, from inexpensive souvenir shops to exclusive boutiques with upscale items. You'll find numerous retailers on Falls Avenue. Even more shops are located along Victoria Avenue, Clifton Hill, Fallsview Boulevard, and on Lundy's Lane. The **Fallsview Casino Resort** includes 45 upscale retail shops. Major shopping centers include the **Canada One Factory Outlet Mall** (905-356-8989; www.canadaoneoutlets.com) on Lundy's Lane near the QEW Expressway, which has forty brand-name outlet stores, and the **Pen Centre** (905-687-6622; www.thepencentre.com), located in nearby St. Catharines, which has 180 stores.

The **Mount Carmel Gift Shop** (905-356-0047; www.carmelniagara.com), 7021 Stanley Avenue, Niagara Falls, is a religious gift shop specializing in European imports, statues, gold jewelry, rosaries, and crucifixes. They also have a retreat center for groups and individuals. **Souvenir City Headquarters** (905-357-1133; www.souvenircityheadquarters .com), 4199 River Road, Niagara Falls, offers the largest selection of souvenirs in the Niagara Falls area.

✳ Special Events

November–January: **Winter Festival of Lights** (905-356-6061 or 800-563-2557; www.wfol.com). For over 30 years the Niagara Falls area has been transforming into a winter wonderland of lights and color. Hundreds of displays light up the area along the Niagara Parkway and the falls. There are also weekly events, including live performances, parades, and fireworks.

WINTER FESTIVAL OF LIGHTS

NIAGARA-ON-THE-LAKE AND QUEENSTON

Both Niagara-on-the-Lake and Queenston were major battlefields during the War of 1812, when United States forces invaded Canada. The towns were destroyed at the end of that war, but they were quickly rebuilt, and many of these eighteenth- and nineteenth-century structures have been preserved. Niagara-on-the-Lake, originally called Onigahara, was Upper Canada's first capital, the site of the first sitting of the provincial legislature and the place where the first newspaper was published in Ontario.

Niagara-on-the-Lake, with its beautifully manicured gardens and historic Victorian properties, has been called the prettiest town in Canada. Visitors can enjoy museums, boutique shopping, fine dining, winery tours, and scenic vistas. The Old Town section along Queen Street features numerous specialty shops and restaurants. The cool nights and mild days in September and October make this region perfect for grape production and wine making.

The town is probably best known for the Shaw Festival, an internationally acclaimed theater season that features the works of George Bernard Shaw and his contemporaries.

If you are visiting during the summer, plan on arriving by 9 AM if you want to avoid crowds and get a decent place to park. A special note on accessibility: Since this is a town of historic structures, many of the stores and restaurants are not accessible to wheelchairs and strollers or have limited accessibility.

AREA CODES The area code is 905; some numbers have the 289 area code.

GUIDANCE Niagara-on-the-Lake Chamber of Commerce (905-468-1950; www.niagaraonthelake.com), 26 Queen Street (lower level). Open seven days 10 AM–7:30 PM. Located in the lower level of a historic 1847 courthouse, they have a large selection of brochures on attractions, accommodations, shopping, and dining.

GETTING THERE *By car:* Take I-190 to the Lewiston/Queenston Bridge. After passing through customs and toll, take the QEW to the first exit and follow the signs to the Niagara Parkway to Niagara-on-the-Lake, about 8 miles. Alternately,

STATUE OF GEORGE BERNARD SHAW ALONG QUEEN STREET IN NIAGARA-ON-THE-LAKE

cross the Peace Bridge from Buffalo or the Rainbow Bridge in Niagara Falls, and follow the scenic Niagara Parkway along the river.

MEDICAL EMERGENCY See *Niagara Falls, Ontario,* and *St. Catharines/Port Dalhousie* listings.

✳ To See

ART MUSEUMS Riverbrink (905-262-4477; www.riverbrink.org), 116 Queenston Street, Queenston. May–October, Monday–Saturday 10 AM–5 PM, November–April, Wednesday–Saturday 10 AM–5 PM. This gallery houses the collection of paintings, drawings, prints, sculpture, and decorative arts amassed by the late art collector Samuel E. Weir. The collection reflects Mr. Weir's interest in Canadian art and the history of the Niagara region.

Niagara Pumphouse Visual Arts Center (905-468-5455; www.niagarapumphouse.ca), 247 Ricardo Street, Niagara-on-the-Lake. Tuesday–Sunday 11 AM–4 PM. This arts center offers classes, exhibits, workshops, and lectures in a restored 1891 water-pumping station.

MUSEUMS AND HISTORIC HOMES Laura Secord Homestead (905-262-5676), 29 Queenston Street, Queenston. Open June–August 10 AM–4 PM daily. This restored homestead was the home of War of 1812 heroine Laura Secord, who journeyed 20 miles through the wilderness and the American lines to warn her husband and the British forces of an impending attack.

BROCK MONUMENT IN QUEENSTON HEIGHTS PARK

McFarland House (905-468-3322 or 877-NIA-PARK), 15927 Niagara Parkway, Niagara-on-the-Lake. Open May–Labor Day daily 11 AM–5 PM. This Georgian home is decorated in the gracious style of the 1840s. Built by John McFarland, it is one of the oldest homes in Niagara-on-the-Lake. Enjoy guided tours and teas in the finest fully licensed tea garden in Upper Canada.

Mackenzie Heritage Printery Museum (905-262-5676 or 877-NIA-PARK; www.mackenzieprintery.org), 1 Queenston Street, Queenston. Open June–August daily 10 AM–5 PM. This museum is located in the restored home of William Lyon Mackenzie, who published *The Colonial Advocate.*

Niagara Apothecary Museum (905-468-3845; www.ocpinfo.com/extra/apothecary/index.html), 5 Queen Street, Niagara-on-the-Lake. Open mid-May–Labor Day 12–6 PM daily. Free admission. Staffed by volunteers from the Ontario College of Pharmacists, this working museum takes you back in time to see how pharmacists worked over 100 years ago. The apothecary first opened its doors in the late 1860s.

 ♿ **Niagara Historical Society and Museum** (905-468-3912; www.niagara historical.museum), 43 Castlereagh Street, Niagara-on-the-Lake. Open May–October 10 AM–5 PM, rest of year 1–5 PM. The first building in Ontario designed and built to be a museum, this 1906 building has one of the finest collections of early Canadian artifacts in the country. The museum's interactive computer digitization program stores thousands of images from their archives.

❖ **The School of Restoration Arts at Willowbank Heritage Estates** (905-262-1239; www.willowbank.ca), 14487 Niagara Parkway, Queenston. Open daily June–August, by appointment rest of year. Constructed in 1834, Willowbank, named after the willow trees that once stood here, is one of the finest examples of Greek Revival architecture in North America. This National Historic Site was saved from the wrecking ball in 2001 and restored and is home to the school of restoration arts.

LIVING WATERS WAYSIDE CHAPEL ALONG THE NIAGARA PARKWAY

HISTORIC AND UNIQUE SITES ❖

Brock Monument, located in Queenston Heights Park. Open daily 10 AM–5 PM, May–Labor Day. This 185-foot monument honors Sir Isaac Brock, a British general killed at the Battle of Queenston Heights during the War of 1812. The memorial, a National Historic Site, was constructed between 1853–1856. Visitors can climb the 235 stairs to the top, visit the museum in the base of the monument, and take a guided tour of the battlefield.

    Cenotaph Clock Tower, also known as Memorial Clock Tower, Queen Street and King Streets. Probably the best known landmark of Niagara-on-the Lake, this clock tower was erected in 1922 as a memorial to fallen World War I townsmen.

    Fort Mississauga Ruins Niagara-on-the-Lake Golf Course, Niagara-on-the-Lake. Open daily, dawn to dusk. To reach this site, you take a walking trail through the Niagara-on-the-Lake Golf Course, so watch for stray balls. The tour of the remains of this fort is self-guided, with historical markers explaining the significance of the structure.

 ♿ **Fort George National Historic Park** (905-468-4257), Picton Street, Niagara-on-the-Lake. Open daily 10 AM–5 PM, April 1–October 31, November 1–March 31 by appointment. This 1796 British fort played a key role in the Niagara Frontier during the War of 1812. Costumed interpreters recreate the period leading up to the war.

⛏ **Living Waters Wayside Chapel**, 14908 Niagara Parkway, Niagara-on-the-Lake. This 10-by-10-foot mini chapel is one of the smallest chapels in the world. It is owned by the Christian Reform Church; contact them at 905-356-0832 to book weddings.

✳ To Do

BOAT EXCURSIONS **Niagara Sunset Cruises** (888-438-4444; www.niagarasunset cruises.com). Cruise down the Niagara River on the Niagara Belle, an authentic Mississippi-style sternwheeler. Lunch, dinner, and charter cruises are available.

   ᴛ **Whirlpool Jet Boat Tours** (905-468-4800 or 888-438-4444; www.whirlpooljet .com). Boats depart from 61 Melvill Street, Niagara-on-the-Lake, Ontario, and 115 South Water Street, Lewiston, New York. Journey into the whirlpool on specially designed jet boats and learn about the history, scenery, and white water of the Niagara River Gorge. If you opt for the open-boat tour, you will get wet despite wearing the full-length splash suit and wet boots provided, so bring a change of clothing. (See also *Boat Excursions* in *Niagara County—North of the Falls, Lewiston* and *Youngstown*.)

GOLF **Heritage Woods Golf Course** (905-685-9204; www.heritagewoodsgc.ca), 1140 Airport Road, Niagara-on-the-Lake. A semi-private 11-hole course.

   Niagara-on-the-Lake Golf Club (905-468-3271; www.notlgolf.com), 143 Front Street, Niagara-on-the-Lake. A semi-private, 9-hole, par-35 course, with a restaurant overlooking the Niagara River. The oldest golf course in North America, it overlooks Lake Ontario. The Fort Mississauga ruins are located adjacent to the course.

   Queenston Golf Club (905-262-4528), 269 Progressive Avenue (off Regional Road #81), Queenston. A public 9-hole, par-34 course with snack bar and full bar.

GUIDED TOURS **Grape & Wine Tours** (855-682-4920, 905-682-4920; www.grapeand winetours.com). This company offers a variety of tours through Niagara's wine country.

   Niagara Wine Tours International (905-468-1300, 800-680-7006; www .niagaraworldwinetours.com), 9 Queen Street, Niagara-on-the-Lake. Sip 'n Cycle bicycle tours, along with passenger van and coach tours through the Niagara wine region.

   Niagara-on-the-Lake Trolley Wine Country Tours (905-468-2195; www.vintage-hotels.com/niagara_wine_tours.php). Tours depart from various locations in Niagara-on-the-Lake. This two- to three-hour guided tour includes two tastings at selected area wineries, along with history and information about the region.

   Old Town Tours (1-888-492-3532, 289-292-3532; www.oldtowntours.ca), Seasonal April–October. Choose from three different walking tours of Niagara-on-the-Lake: Town Stroll, Gates and Gardens, or Saints and Sinner Graveyards.

   Sentineal Tours (905-468-4943; www.sentinealcarriages.ca), King Street, by the Prince of Wales Hotel, Niagara-on-the-Lake. Reservations recommended. Historic horse-drawn or vintage car tours through historic Old Town Niagara-on-the-Lake.

   Zoom Leisure Bicycle Tours and Rentals (866-811-6993; www.zoomleisure.com). Take a guided bicycle tour through Niagara's winery region while learning about the region's past and present. Rental bicycles are also available for you to explore the area on your own.

✳ Breweries and Wineries

THE WINERIES OF NIAGARA-ON-THE-LAKE (www.wineriesofniagaraonthelake .com). There are over two dozen wineries in the Niagara-on-the Lake area that welcome visitors to enjoy tours and tastings; see individual winery websites or call for specific tour times, as they change according to the season. Described below are just a few of the wineries.

The Ice House Winery (905-262-6161; www.theicehouse.ca), 14778 Niagara Parkway, Niagara-on-the-Lake. If you like icewine, this is the place to come. They offer a variety of icewines for tasting and even have icewine slushies.

♿ **Inniskillin Winery** (888-466-4754; www.inniskillin.com), Niagara Parkway at Line 3, Niagara-on-the-Lake. This winery is named after the famous Inniskillin Fusiliers, an Irish regiment that served in the War of 1812. The winery's historic Brae Burn barn was built in the 1920s from a design influenced by the work of Frank Lloyd Wright. Inniskillin was granted a winery license in 1997, the first wine producer in Ontario to be given a license since 1929. They offer many premium wines, including merlot, pinot noir, chardonnay, and icewine.

♿ **Jackson-Triggs Niagara Estate Winery** (1-866-589-4637; www.jacksontriggs winery.com), 2145 Niagara Stone Road, Niagara-on-the-Lake. This state-of-the-art winery is a blend of modern winemaking technology and traditional skills. Be sure to visit their tasting gallery, where wines are skillfully paired with food. They also have a 500-seat open-air amphitheater used for summer musical entertainment.

Joseph's Estate Wines (905-468-1259; www.josephsestatewines.com), 1811 Niagara Stone Road, Niagara-on-the-Lake. Founded by Joseph Pohorly in 1992, this winery offers unique wines like pinot gris, a white wine with fruit aromas, along with a selection of reds, rose, and icewines.

♿ **Konzelmann Estate Winery** (905-935-2866; www.konzelmannwines.com), 1096 Lakeshore Road, Niagara-on-the-Lake. This winery offers breathtaking views of Lake Ontario. Herbert Konzelmann, a native of Germany, introduced German winemaking and vineyard techniques to the Niagara region. The craft has been practiced on his mother's side of the family since 1521. The winery has won many national and international awards, including the Winemaker of the Year Award.

THE VINEYARDS AT KONZELMANN ESTATE WINERY OVERLOOK LAKE ONTARIO

Lailey Vineyard (905-468-0503; www.laileywinery.com), 15940 Niagara Parkway, Niagara-on-the-Lake. The Lailey family has been growing premium wine grapes since 1970 and are known for producing wines with fruit characteristics. Their wines include chardonnay, Riesling, sauvignon blanc, and icewines.

Niagara Teaching College Winery (905-641-2252; www.nctwinery.ca), 135 Taylor Road, Niagara-on-the-Lake. This is the Niagara region's only educational winery; a brewery and the Niagara College Canadian Food & Wine Institute are also located here.

& **Peller Estate Winery** (905-468-4678 or 888-673-5537; www.peller.com), 290 John Street East, Niagara-on-the-Lake. Explore the vineyards as well as their underground barrel aging cellar when you take a tour of this award-wining winery located on 40 picturesque acres. Enjoy a meal at their winery restaurant.

& **Pillitteri Estates Winery** (905-468-3147; www.pillitteri.com), 1696 Niagara Stone Road, Niagara-on-the-Lake. The grapes used to make their wines are grown on the family's 53-acre farm. The Italian *carretto*, or cart, depicted on their label reflects their Italian heritage. This family heirloom, which was brought from Sicily, is displayed in the winery's tasting room.

Ravine Vineyards (905-262-8463; www.ravinevineyard.com), 1366 York Road, St. Davids. Located on a farm more than 100 years old, it is one of the few wineries in the Niagara region that farms biodynamically, which is similar to organic farming. The winery restaurant bakes its own bread, grows organic vegetables, and even raises its own pigs.

Reif Estate Winery (905-468-7738; www.reifwinery.com), 15608 Niagara Parkway, Niagara-on-the-Lake. This winery and wine boutique, surrounded by 135 acres of vineyards, is located on the Niagara Parkway overlooking the Niagara River. Reif Estate

RAVINE VINEYARD RESTAURANT IN ST. DAVIDS OFFERS ORGANIC VEGETABLES AND MORE

Winery produces outstanding wines, using winemaking techniques passed down over thirteen generations.

Riverview Estate Winery (905-262-0636; www.riverviewcellars.com), 15376 Niagara Parkway, Niagara-on-the-Lake. A family-run winery that produces small batches of wine.

♿ **Strewn Estate Winery** (905-468-1229; www.strewnwinery.com), 1339 Lakeshore Road, Niagara-on-the-Lake. Customized tours and tastings are offered at this winery housed in a unique building that once was a canning factory. They have a winery cooking school. Lunches and dinners are served in their restaurant, Oliv Tapas Bar and Restaurant (www.olivtapasnotl.com).

SAMPLE A FLIGHT OF BEER AT THE EXCHANGE BREWERY

Sunnybrook Farm Estate Winery (905-468-1122; www.sunnybrookwine.com), 1425 Lakeshore Road, Niagara-on-the-Lake. This winery specializes in wines made from fruits other than grapes, including peaches and strawberries.

BREWERIES While the Niagara Peninsula is best known for their wineries, there are a number of craft breweries springing up all over the region.

The Exchange Brewery (905-468-9888; www.exchangebrewery.com), 7 Queen Street, Niagara-on-the-Lake. This craft brewery and tasting room is located among shops and restaurants along Queen Street. Sample a flight of beers; they have a variety to choose from, including IPA, porter, sour, and more. A limited food menu is available.

Niagara College Teaching Brewery (905-641-2252; www.niagaracollegebeer.ca), 135 Taylor Road, Niagara-on-the-Lake. This is the first and only fully licensed teaching brewery in Canada.

Niagara Oast House Brewers (www.oasthousebrewers.ca), 2017 Niagara Stone Road, Niagara-on-the-Lake. This craft brewery, located in a barn, offers a variety of farmhouse-style beers. They have tours, tasting, food, and special events.

Silversmith Brewing (905-468-8447; www.silversmithbrewing.com) 1523 Niagara Stone Road, Niagara-on-the-Lake. Enjoy handcrafted beers, food, tours, and live musical entertainment.

✲ Green Space

PARKS **Queenston Heights Park** (905-356-2241), Niagara Parkway (just north of the Lewiston-Queenston Bridge), Queenston. Open daily, dawn to dusk. This park includes a picnic area, formal gardens, a tennis court, a wading pool, and hiking trails. The Brock Monument is located in the park, along with an upscale restaurant. See also *Historic Sites* and *Where to Eat*.

Queen's Royal Park (905-468-4362), Front and King Streets, Niagara-on-the-Lake. This park on the banks of the Niagara River has a panoramic view of the river, Lake Ontario, and Old Fort Niagara across the river in Youngstown, New York. The park's

gazebo was built for the Stephen King movie *The Dead Zone* and was donated to the town by the film company.

Simcoe Park (905-468-4362), Picton and King Streets, Niagara-on-the-Lake. Open daily, dawn to dusk. A small picturesque public park with a playground, a wading pool, and an outdoor stage.

✳ Lodging

Over three hundred accommodation properties are in and around Niagara-on-the-Lake, from five-star resorts to bed & breakfast inns to small cottages. Though it would obviously be impossible for one person to visit and describe them all for this book, I would like to note that Niagara-on-the-Lake has a reputation for quality accommodations, so you won't find a bad room here. The **Niagara-on-the-Lake Chamber of Commerce** (905-468-1950; www.niagaraonthelake .com) offers an accommodation booking service as well as brochures on the properties. Reservations should be made well in advance, especially during the theater season, April–November. I recommend

the booklet published by the **Shaw Festival** (800-511-SHAW; www.shawfest.com), which lists all lodging, with brief descriptions and prices. Below are a few of Niagara-on-the-Lake's accommodations.

INNS AND RESORTS **Olde Angel Inn** (905-468-3411; www.angel-inn.com), 224 Regent Street, Niagara-on-the-Lake. The Olde Angel Inn, established 1789, the oldest operating inn in Canada, has an English-style pub and five guest rooms. See also *Eating Out*. $$.

Harbour House Hotel (905-468-4683, 866-277-6677; www.harbourhouse hotel.ca), 85 Melville Street, Niagara-on-the-Lake. This four-diamond boutique offers luxurious accommodations that include king-size beds, with 300 thread count linens, fireplaces, whirlpool tubs, and flat screen TVs. A gourmet breakfast is served each morning. $$$$.

Moffat Inn (905-468-4116; www .moffatinn.com), 60 Picton Street, Niagara-on-the-Lake. This charming inn, located in Old Town, offers 22 unique rooms plus a luxury suite. All have private baths, some have fireplaces. It is a historic building without elevators. $$$.

Oban Inn (905-468-2165, 888-669-5566; www.obaninn.ca), 160 Front Street, Niagara-on-the-Lake. This four-diamond, full-service inn was built in 1824 as the home of a Captain Duncan Milloy of Oban, Scotland. The original structure was destroyed by fire in 1992 and rebuilt the following year. Surrounded by beautiful English-style gardens, the inn has 26 luxurious guest rooms, many with a view of the lake. $$$$.

Pillar and Post (905-468-2123 or 888-669-5566; www.vintageinns.com), 48 John Street, Niagara-on-the-Lake. This

GUEST ROOM AT THE PRINCE OF WALES HOTEL

two-story, 123-room luxury brick hotel was built in 1862 as a canning factory and converted into an inn and restaurant in 1969. Amenities include indoor and outdoor pools, fitness center, European spa, and world-class dining. $$$.

Prince of Wales Hotel (905-468-3246 or 888-669-5566; www.vintageinns.com), 6 Picton Street, Niagara-on-the-Lake. One of the finest heritage hotels in the world, the Prince of Wales offers personalized service, award-wining cuisine, and an exclusive European spa. Built in 1864, the hotel offers 114 individually appointed guest rooms. $$$$.

&. **Queen's Landing** (905-468-2195 or 888-669-5566; www.vintageinns.com), 155 Byron Street, Niagara-on-the-Lake. This four-diamond Georgian-style mansion offering 144 luxurious guestrooms—some with fireplaces and whirlpool baths—is situated close to the Niagara River. Amenities include an indoor pool, sauna, outdoor gardens, a patio, and fine dining. $$$$.

Riverbend Inn & Vineyards (905-468-8866, 888-955-5553; www.riverbend inn.ca), 16104 Niagara River Parkway, Niagara-on-the-Lake. This secluded country inn with elegant Georgian decor offers twenty-two guestrooms with queen and double beds. Some rooms have working fireplaces and five have

THE MOFFAT INN, NIAGARA-ON-THE-LAKE

balconies overlooking the vineyards. Enjoy fine dining in their restaurant. $$$.

Shaw Club Hotel (800-511-7070; www .niagarasfinest.com/shaw), 92 Picton Street, Niagara-on-the-Lake (across from the Shaw Festival Theatre). This hotel features well-appointed guest rooms with king-size feather top beds, Egyptian cotton linens, and oversize showers. $$$.

South Landing Inn (905-262-4634; www.southlandinginn.com), 21 Front Street South, Queenston. This historic country inn overlooking the Niagara River was built by Thomas Dickson in the 1800s to accommodate travelers following the portage route around Niagara Falls. There are six guest rooms with private baths in the original inn. The South Landing Annex, built in 1987, offers eighteen additional rooms, including four with balconies. Breakfast is available in the inn's café for a nominal charge. $$.

& **White Oaks Royal Niagara Spa Resort and Conference Center** (905-688-2550 or 800-263-5766; www .whiteoaksresort.com), 253 Taylor Road, Niagara-on-the-Lake. Niagara's only four-diamond, five-star resort has 220 elegant, oversized guest rooms. Amenities include a private fitness and racquet club, preferred rates at the Royal Niagara Golf Course, and a luxurious spa. Fine

QUEEN'S LANDING (OUTSIDE VIEW)

dining is available at the four-diamond Liv restaurant. $$$.

124 Hotel & Spa (1-855-988-4552, 905-468-4522; www.124queen.com), 124 Queen Street, Niagara-on-the-Lake. This luxury hotel and spa has a variety of accommodations from deluxe rooms to three-bedroom villas. $$$$.

Charles Inn (905-468-4588; www .charlesinn.ca), 209 Queen Street, Niagara-on-the-Lake. This historic Victorian inn with twelve guest rooms has balconies overlooking the Niagara-on-the-Lake Golf Course and their landscaped yard. See also *Dining Out—Hob Nob Restaurant*. $$$$.

Hotel Dallavalle (905-468-3263; www .hoteldallavalle.com), 142 Queen Street, Niagara-on-the-Lake. This newly renovated hotel, located just steps away from Queen Street shops, has ten large guest rooms and an in-house restaurant, Bella Vista Ristorante. $$$.

BED & BREAKFASTS With so many properties to choose from, it would be impossible to visit and rate each one. Below are some associations that can be of assistance, as well as a description of a few bed & breakfast inns.

The Niagara-on-the-Lake Bed & Breakfast Association (905-468-0123; www

GUEST ROOM AT THE WHITE OAKS ROYAL NIAGARA SPA RESORT & CONFERENCE CENTER

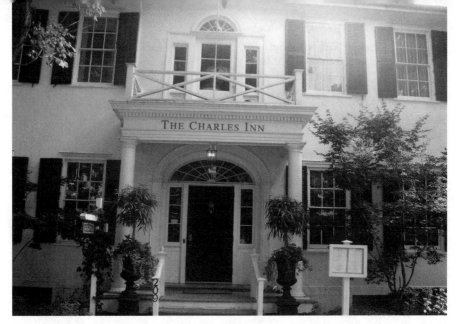

THE CHARLES INN IN NIAGARA-ON-THE-LAKE HAS 12 COZY GUEST ROOMS

.bookyourstay.ca). Members maintain high standards and follow a strict code of ethics. Over 150 properties are listed on this site. Reservations can be made online.

Bed & Breakfast Niagara (www .bedandbreakfast.com/niagara-on-the-lake-ontario.html). The official bed & breakfast and cottage directory for Niagara-on-the-Lake and the Niagara region.

Cycle & Stay Niagara (www .cycleandstayniagara.com). This website has information about bicycle-friendly accommodations throughout the Niagara region.

Everheart Country Manor Bed & Breakfast (905-262-5444 or 866-284-0544; www.everheart.ca), 137 Queenston Street, Queenston. This circa-1905 restored, asymmetrical Queen Anne Victorian-style home, located on a quiet side street, has three large, luxurious suites. Amenities include an indoor pool and a delicious made to order breakfast. $$.

Grand Victorian Bed & Breakfast (905-468-0997; www.grandvictorian.ca), 15608 Niagara Parkway, Niagara-on-the-Lake. This 1860s mansion, located adjacent to Reif Estate Winery has six large guestrooms, some with river views. The inn has a large veranda with wicker furniture to relax on. $$.

Old Bank House Bed & Breakfast (877-468-7136; www.oldbankhouse.com), 10 Front Street, Niagara-on-the-Lake. Nine rooms and suites are available in this former Bank of Canada building that overlooks Queens Royal Park, the Niagara River, and Lake Ontario. $$.

✳ Where to Eat

Here are just a few of the many restaurants that can be found in Niagara-on-the-Lake.

DINING OUT **Bella Vita Ristorante** (905-468-3263; www.hoteldallavalle .com), 142 Queen Street, Niagara-on-the-Lake. This restaurant features authentic Italian cuisine and an extensive wine list.

Benchmark Restaurant at Niagara College Canadian Food and Wine Institute (905-641-2242; www .ncbenchmark.ca), 135 Taylor Road, Niagara-on-the-Lake. Enjoy local and seasonal food, along with wine and beer created by students at the college.

Escabeche (905-468-3246; www.vintage-hotels.com/princeofwales), 6 Picton Street (in the Prince of Wales Hotel), Niagara-on-the-Lake. Five-diamond service is offered in this exquisite dining room, which features contemporary Canadian cuisine on the menu.

Hob Nob Restaurant at the Charles Inn (905-468-4588; www.hobnobrestaurant.ca), 209 Queen Street, Niagara-on-the-Lake. Dine in a Four-Diamond restaurant located in the circa-1832 Charles Inn. Dinner is served daily, as well as small plate menus, afternoon tea, wine pairing menu, weekend breakfast; see website for menus and hours.

Liv (905-688-2032, ext. 5248 or 800-263-5766; www.whiteoaksresort.com), 253 Taylor Road, Niagara-on-the-Lake. (in the White Oaks Resort) Open daily for breakfast 7 AM–11 AM and dinner 5–10 PM. This four-diamond restaurant mixes a variety of world flavors and cooking styles. Dinner selections include oven-roasted rack of lamb, grilled prime tenderloins, and grilled sea scallops. All desserts are baked on site by their own pastry chef.

Niagara's Finest Thai (905-468-1224 or 844-333-8421; www.niagarasfinestthai.com/home), 88 Picton Street, Niagara-on-the-Lake. Monday–Thursday 11 AM–9:30 PM, Friday–Saturday 11 AM–10 PM. Enjoy generous portions of authentic Thai cuisine, like the chef's signature Pad Thai. Be sure to make a reservation, as it can be busy at times.

& **The Oban Inn** (1-888-669-5566; www.oban.com), 160 Front Street, Niagara-on-the-Lake. Open daily for lunch and dinner. The dining room features large windows overlooking English-style gardens. The dinner menu features items like beef tenderloin and oven roasted cod, along with burgers and sandwiches on the lunch menu.

& **Peller Estates Winery Restaurant** (1-888-673-5537; www.peller.com), 290 John Street East, Niagara-on-the-Lake. Open daily for lunch 12–3 PM, dinner 5–9 PM. This upscale restaurant offers elegant regional wine-country cuisine, paired with Peller's award-winning wines. Dine indoors or out, weather permitting. Reservations strongly suggested.

Shaw Café & Wine Bar (905-468-4772; www.shawcafe.ca), 92 Queen Street, Niagara-on-the-Lake. This restaurant has a really cute dining patio which is very popular during the summer months. Lunch selections include their signature turkey club, while the dinner menu features dishes like roasted pork tenderloin and steak.

Treadwell Farm to Table Cuisine (905-934-9797; www.treadwellcuisine.com), 114 Queen Street, Niagara-on-the-Lake. Located next the 124 Hotel and Spa, this upscale yet casual restaurant features locally sourced foods and wines.

Zee's Grill (905-468-5715; www.zees.ca), 92 Picton Street, Niagara-on-the-Lake. This bistro and bar, which is open for breakfast, lunch, and dinner, is located right across the street from the Shaw Festival Theater. During the warmer months you can dine outdoors on the covered patio.

QUEENSTON

& **Queenston Heights Restaurant** (905-262-4274), Queenston Heights Park, Niagara Parkway, Queenston. Open seasonally May–October, hours vary. This elegant restaurant offers a breathtaking view of the Niagara Gorge. Dine on unique Niagara cuisine selections either indoors or out on the patio.

EATING OUT ✿ **Avondale Dairy Bar** (905-687-7403; www.avondaledairybar.com), 461 Stewart Road, Niagara-on-the-Lake. Since 1955 they have been known for their made-to-order milkshakes as well as other ice cream treats.

Bistro Six-One (905-468-2532; www.bistrosixone.com), 61–63 Queen Street, Niagara-on-the-Lake. A casual

QUEENSTON HEIGHTS RESTAURANT

restaurant known for its wood-fired pizzas and pasta.

Corks Wine Bar & Eatery (289-868-9527; www.corksniagara.com), 19 Queen Street, Niagara-on-the-Lake. Enjoy pub fare, like fish and chips, either indoors or outside on the large covered porch. They have over 30 local wines by glass and almost two dozen beers on tap.

The Irish Harp Pub (905-468-4443; www.theirishharppub.com), 245 King Street, Niagara-on-the-Lake. Enjoy a wee bit of Ireland at the authentic Irish pub. The menu features traditional Irish fare, like corned beef and cabbage and Irish stew, along with sandwiches, burgers, and steaks. There is live entertainment on weekends and there are three guest rooms furnished with Irish imports for overnight accommodations.

The Clubhouse Restaurant (905-468-3424; notlgolf.com/dining), 43 Front Street, Niagara-on-the-Lake. Open seasonally for breakfast, lunch, and dinner. This restaurant overlooks the Niagara-on the-Lake golf course, the oldest golf course in North America, circa 1875.

The Grill at the Epicurean (905-468-3408), 84 Queen Street, Niagara-on-the-Lake. Open daily 5:30–9 PM; also open for lunch in summer. A cafeteria-style

gourmet deli by day, a trendy French bistro with full table service at night. The lunch menu includes gourmet sandwiches, salads, quiche, and meat pies, while the dinner menu features grilled salmon, braised lamb shank, and roast chicken.

The Olde Angel Inn (905-468-3411; www.angel-inn.com), 224 Regent Street, Niagara-on-the-Lake. Open 11 AM–1 AM daily. This historic inn features a lively English pub that has a menu featuring traditional English and Irish pub fare, including their award-winning fish and chips.

🐾 ✍ **Stagecoach Family Restaurant** (905-468-3133) 45 Queen Street, Niagara-on-the-Lake. Opens at 7 AM daily; closing times vary. This family restaurant has the most reasonably priced breakfast in town, plus sandwiches and burgers on the lunch menu.

✳ Entertainment

THEATERS **Shaw Festival** (905-468-2172 or 800-511-7429; www.shawfest.com), 10 Queen's Parade, Niagara-on-the-Lake. Niagara-on-the-Lake is probably best known for the Shaw Festival, the only theater company specializing exclusively in plays either by George Bernard Shaw or those written about his era. It is North America's foremost theater organization. The season runs April–early November, with performances in three different theaters. See below:

Court House Theatre, 26 Queen Street, Niagara-on-the-Lake. This 1840 National Historic site is where the Shaw Festival began in 1962. It has a 327-seat auditorium with a thrust stage.

Festival Theatre, 10 Queen's Parade, Niagara-on-the-Lake. This 869-seat venue is the flagship theatre of the festival.

Jackie Maxwell Studio Theatre, 10 Queen's Parade, Niagara-on-the-Lake. Located next to the Festival Theatre, this 200-seat theatre, named after long-time Shaw Festival Director Jackie Maxwell, is the smallest of the four theatres.

Royal George Theatre, 83 Queen Street, Niagara-on-the-Lake. This 328-seat theater was built in 1913 as the Kitchener and used to entertain troops stationed in the area during World War I, then later used as a silent film house. In the 1980s it was purchased by the Shaw Festival and renovated to resemble an Edwardian opera house.

✳ Selective Shopping

A high concentration of shops and boutiques can be found along Queen Street, as well as some shops on the outskirts of town. There are many shops, including clothing stores and franchise establishments, which will not be reviewed here. Described below is just a sampling of what the town has to offer.

ANTIQUES **Lakeshore Antique & Treasures** (905-646-1965; www.lakeshore antiques.ca), 855 Lakeshore Road, Niagara-on-the-Lake. Open year-round 10 AM–5 PM. A 6,000-square-foot multi-dealer shop, carrying everything from pre-Victorian to retro to country, located just west of historic Niagara-on-the-Lake.

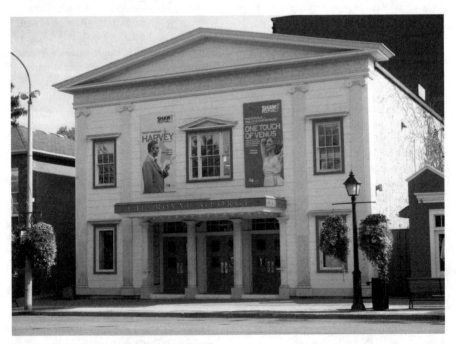

THE ROYAL GEORGE THEATER IN NIAGARA-ON-THE-LAKE

ART GALLERIES **Niagara Image Gallery** (800-667-8525; www.romancecollection.com), 1627 Niagara Stone Road, Virgil. Tuesday–Sunday 10 AM–5 PM. This gallery features the work of Trisha Romance, Tanya Jean Peterson, Jordan Morrison, and Alex Coville.

FARM MARKETS ✂ ♿ **Kurtz Orchards Country Market** (905-448-2937), 16006 Niagara Parkway, Niagara-on-the-Lake. Open seasonally. This large farm market has a bounty of in-season produce along with jams and preserves, maple syrup, honey, fresh-baked goods, Canadian crafts, and more.

SPECIAL SHOPS **The Shawp** (800-511-7429, ext. 2276), 10 Queens Parade, in the Festival Theatre. Open year-round. This shop has a mix of books, home accessories, and handcrafted items. They also stock scripts for the current season's plays, posters, and Shaw Festival clothing.

Butterfly Gallery (905-468-9063), 92 Queen Street, Niagara-on-the-Lake. Daily 10 AM–5 PM. They carry fashions, accessories, and jewelry with a butterfly theme.

Cecile's (905-468-0066; www.cecilehouse.com), 113 Queen Street, Niagara-on-the-Lake. This French-inspired shop has items for the home, gourmet coffees, French-milled soaps and more. The adjacent shop, C3 for Her, has jewelry, scarves, and accessories.

Chocolate F/X (905-684-2626 or 1-866-360-1660; www.chocolatefx.ca), 335 Four Mile Creek Road, St. Davids (Niagara-on-the-Lake). Open daily 10 AM–6 AM. This shop offers a large amount of chocolates that are handmade in the adjacent factory. Tours are available, with a free sample at the end.

Greaves (905-468-3608 or 800-515-9939; www.greavesjams.com), 55 Queen Street, Niagara-on-the-Lake. Daily 10 AM–5 PM, 9:30 AM–8 PM in summer. Since 1927 Greaves has been making jams, jellies, marmalades, and condiments. This

ENJOY CANDY SAMPLES AT CHOCOLATE F/X

shop carries their products, along with teas and other gourmet food items.

Irish Design (800-268-9064; www.irishdesign.com), 75 Queen Street, Niagara-on-the-Lake. Monday–Friday 10 AM–5 PM, Saturday 9:30 AM–6 PM, Sunday 10 AM–5:30 PM. This shop specializes in Irish imports, including clothing, jewelry, kilts, sweaters, music, and more.

Just Christmas (905-468-4500; www.justchristmas.ca), 36 Queen Street, Niagara-on-the-Lake. Daily 10 AM–5 PM; longer hours in summer. Established in 1985, this year-round Christmas shop has over 5,000 Christmas items to choose from.

Kennedy's (905-468-3238), 43 Queen Street, Niagara-on-the-Lake. Daily 9 AM–9 PM. Here you can find inexpensive Canadian souvenirs, film, and drug store items, as well as ice cream, hot dogs, and coffee.

IT'S CHRISTMAS YEAR-ROUND AT JUST CHRISTMAS IN NIAGARA-ON-THE-LAKE

✐ **Maple Leaf Fudge** (905-468-2211; www.mapleleaffudge.com), 114 Queen Street, Niagara-on-the-Lake. They offer 25 varieties of quality fudge, old-fashioned candies, brittles, maple products, and other candies and gift items.

Niagara Home Bakery (905-468-3431), 66 Queen Street, Niagara-on-the-Lake. Open Tuesday–Sunday 9 AM–6 PM. This bakery, established in 1915, features homemade scones, cookies and pastries, along with tea biscuits, Scotch meat pies, jams, jellies, teas, and mustards.

Outlet Collection at Niagara, (905-687-6777; www.outletcollectionniagara .com), 300 Taylor Road, Niagara-on-the-Lake. Monday–Saturday 10 AM–9 AM, Sunday 10 AM–6 PM. Opened in 2014, it is Canada's largest open-air outlet mall, with over 100 stores.

The Owl and the Pussycat (905-468-3081), 16 Queen Street, Niagara-on-the-Lake. This shop carries locally designed high-quality women's clothing and accessories.

Victoria's Teas and Coffee (888-550-8327; www.victoriasteas.com), 108 Queen Street, Niagara-on-the-Lake. Choose from a variety of teas and coffees from around the world, along with teapots and other accessories.

Serendipity the Little French Shop (905-468-8881; www .tableclothsgalore.ca), 106C Queen Street. A boutique shop with French table linens, fine giftware, and jewelry.

✳ Special Events

Here is just a sampling of the annual events that take place in Niagara-on-the-Lake.

January: **Niagara Icewine Festival** (905-688-0212; www.niagara icewinefestival.com). This 10-day festival, which takes place throughout the Niagara Peninsula, celebrates Ontario icewine, which is produced during December, January, and February. The grapes are pressed while frozen, producing a sweet concentrated juice used to make icewine. The festival features gourmet dinners, tours, tastings, and other special events.

August: **Peach Harvest** Festival (Niagara-on-the-Lake Chamber of Commerce, 905-468-1950; www .niagaraonthelake.com for details). Enjoy music and street performers along Queen Street, as well as peach baked goods and beverages.

September: **Niagara Grape & Wine Festival** (905-688-0212; www.grapeand wine.com). From Niagara-on-the-Lake to St. Catharines. This internationally acclaimed wine festival takes place during the last 10 days of September.

Events include dinners, live entertainment, wine tastings and seminars, and artisan shows.

October: **Ghost Tours** (905-468-6621; www.friendsoffortgeorge.ca), Fort George, Niagara-on-the-Lake. Explore Fort George by candlelight as you learn about its history and hear accounts of real-life encounters at the fort with the spirits and phantoms that lurk there. Purchase tickets well in advance; they do sell out.

December: **Candlelight Stroll** (Niagara-on-the-Lake Chamber of Commerce, 905-468-1950; www .niagaraonthelake.com for details). Take a guided stroll through the historic town of Niagara-on-the-Lake.

NIAGARA ICEWINE FESTIVAL

WELLAND CANAL CORRIDOR

St. Catharines/Port Dalhousie, Thorold, Welland, and Port Colborne

The Welland Canal Corridor is possibly one of the most unique attractions you'll find in this region. It is an engineering marvel that attracts people from all over the world to see it in operation from April to December. The 27-mile shipping route, which connects Lake Ontario to Lake Erie, allows ships, including "lakers," which sail the Great Lakes, and "salties," ocean-going vessels which hail from all over the world, to proceed inland around Niagara Falls to the other Great Lakes. Cruise ships, barges, and pleasure crafts are also permitted to use the canal. The ships bypass Niagara Falls and navigate the Niagara Escarpment through a series of eight locks; it takes a ship between eight to ten hours to travel the entire canal.

✳ History of the Canal

If you look at a map of the United States and Canada, you can see that ships from the Atlantic Ocean can travel inland through the St. Lawrence Seaway into Lake Ontario. However, at the turn of the nineteenth century, the furthest inland they could proceed was the lower Niagara River; as Niagara Falls presented a barrier to the remaining four Great Lakes.

The Welland Canal Company, founded by William Hamilton Merritt, began the construction of the first Welland Canal between Lake Ontario and Lake Erie in 1824. It took five years to dig it by hand, connecting a series of creeks and rivers. It had thirty-nine small locks with wooden gates. Once it opened in 1829, ships were able to sail the rest of the Great Lakes region.

Over time, ships got bigger and the canal had to be enlarged to accommodate them. It was rebuilt three times, in 1845, 1887, and in 1932. The last major construction project on the canal was over 40 years ago; when a new channel was dug to bypass the downtown section of the city of Welland.

AREA CODES The area codes are 905 and 289.

GUIDANCE **Niagara's Welland Canal** (www.niagarawellandcanal.com). Website with history, brochures, maps and more.
   Welland Canal (www.wellandcanal.com/transit.htm).
   St. Catharines Tourism (905-984-9882 or 800-305-5134; www.stcatharines.ca), 50 Church St., St. Catharines.
   Port Dalhousie Business Association (905-937-4783).
   Thorold Tourism (www.thoroldtourism.ca).
   Thorold Business Improvement Area (www.thoroldbia.com).
   City of Welland (905-735-1700; www.welland.ca), 60 East Main Street, Welland.

SHIP ON LAKE ONTARIO NEAR PORT DALHOUSIE

Port Colborne City Hall (905-835-2900; www.city.portcolborne.on.ca), 66 Charlotte St., Port Colborne. Visitor Center is located at 76 Main Street.

GETTING THERE For St. Catharines and Thorold, cross over the Lewiston-Queenston Bridge and take Highway 405 to the Queen Elizabeth Way. For Thorold and the lock viewing complexes, exit at Glendale Ave. There are several St. Catharines exits; for Port Dalhousie take exit 47. For Port Colborne and Welland, cross over the Peace Bridge and take Highway 3 to Port Colborne; for Welland, take West Side Road north from Port Colborne.

MEDICAL EMERGENCY **Welland County General Hospital** (905-732-6111), 65 Third Street, Welland.
   Niagara Health System (905-378-4647), 1200 Fourth Avenue, St. Catharines.
   Urgent Care Center (905-378-4647), 260 Sugarloaf Street, Port Colborne.

St. Catharines is the largest city in the Niagara region and the sixth largest urban area in Canada, with a population of 130,000. Because of its large size, this book will not go into detail about the entire city; we will only discuss the areas by the canal.

The terminus of the first three Welland Canals was located several miles west of the present-day terminus of Port Weller on Lake Ontario, in the Old Port Dalhousie section of St. Catharines. Although Port Dalhousie is not technically on today's canal, it's a great place to visit, as it has restaurants, shops, a large beach, and an antique carrousel that you can ride for only five cents.

From Port Dalhousie, head east on Lakeshore Rd. to Bunting Road, which connects to the Welland Canals Parkway, a scenic route that follows the canal. While you really can't pull over here, you will get your first glimpse of the canal as you drive, and

SHIP IN LOCK 7 IN THOROLD

perhaps see a freighter or two. A recreational hiking and biking trail also runs parallel to the canal.

Continue on the parkway to the Welland Canals Center at Lock 3. The observation deck here is the best place to view the ships on the canal. Check the posting of the daily ship schedule to see when a ship will be passing through the lock. You may want to call ahead (1-800-305-5134) before leaving home, so you can time your visit to coincide when a ship is in the lock. Some days only one or two navigate the canal, while on others, there may be a dozen or more ships.

Thorold, referred to as "the place where ships climb the mountain," is the most unique site along the canal. It is here that ships must pass through locks 4, 5, and 6, a set of three twinned locks, which allow them to climb (or descend) the Niagara Escarpment, the same ridge of rock that Niagara Falls flows over. You can view ships in the canal at the Lock 7 Viewing complex, and then head into historic downtown Thorold for dining and shopping.

MURAL IN WELLAND

The city of Welland is located right on the canal; as a matter of fact, until 1973, when a by-pass channel was built, ships sailed right through downtown Welland. The old section of the canal is now used as a recreational waterway for flatwater sports such as canoeing, rowing, kayaking, water polo, stand up paddling, and open water swimming. The **Welland International Flatwater Centre** (www .wifc.ca) hosts major international sporting events

The movie *A Christmas Story* was filmed in part in St. Catharines in 1983 at the Victoria public school on Niagara Street (now a women's shelter). Other scenes were filmed in Toronto, Ontario, and in Cleveland, Ohio. A display about the movie at the St. Catharines Museum features several items donated by the production company, including a Red Ryder BB Gun, Ralphie's eye glasses, and a script from the movie.

A CHRISTMAS STORY EXHIBIT AT THE ST. CATHARINES MUSEUM

One of the most striking features of Welland is the over two dozen murals depicting scenes from Welland's past which are painted on buildings throughout the downtown area. Back in 1986, the city hired artists from all over Canada to create the murals as a way to beautify and revive the downtown area. Most of these murals are concentrated along King Street, East Main Street, and Division Street, although a few can be found in the outskirts along Niagara Street. All of those in the downtown area are relatively close to each other; you could park the car and walk if it's a nice day. Descriptions of murals and a map can be found at wellandmurals.ca/murals.htm.

Port Colborne is the southern terminus of the Welland Canal. You can view the canal from both the Welland Canal Lock 8 Park and the historic West Street promenade, which has six blocks of shops and restaurants.

✳ To See

ST. CATHARINES/PORT DALHOUSIE

MUSEUMS ♿ ✎ ☺ **Welland Canals Centre at Lock 3** (905-984-8880, 800-305-5134), 1932 Welland Canals Parkway, St. Catharines. Open daily 9 AM–5 PM, April–December. The St. Catharines Museum is open year-round (weekends only in winter). An elevated viewing platform gives visitors a bird's-eye view of the ships as they enter and exit the lock. This complex also has two museums, the St. Catharines Museum, which focuses on local and canal history and the Lacrosse Hall of Fame and Museum.

SHOPS AND RESTAURANTS ALONG WEST STREET IN PORT COLBORNE

THOROLD

Heritage Thorold (905-227-6613; www.heritagethorold.com/designatedproperties .html). Follow link for walking tour brochure of heritage buildings in Thorold.

Thorold Murals (www.thoroldmurals.com). Murals throughout the city depict the history of Thorold and the four Welland Canals.

SIGN AT THE WELLAND CANALS CENTER AT LOCK 3

WELLAND

MUSEUMS AND HERITAGE SITES **Heritage Site Guide Panels**, Canal Terrace, King Street by East Main Street Bridge. These panels, which explain buildings, industries, canal structures and bridges, are located on a terrace that overlooks the recreational waterway which was the main channel of the canal prior to 1972. Note that the East Main Street Bridge, also known as Welland Bridge number 13, is lit up at night with bright LED lights; special events are commemorated with different colors.

Welland Museum (905-732-2215; www .wellandmuseum.ca), 140 King Street, Welland. Tuesday–Saturday 10 AM–4 PM. Located in a former Carnegie library building, this museum has exhibits focusing on Welland's history as well as interactive exhibits geared toward children.

PORT COLBORNE

MUSEUMS AND OTHER SITES **Port Colborne Historical and Marine Museum Heritage Village** (905-834-7604; portcolborne.ca/page/museum), 280 King Street, Port Colborne. Open May–December. This museum features several historical buildings, including Anabella's Tea Room, which serves an afternoon tea June–September.

Shrinking mill. Take a drive east on Lakeshore Road from Cement Plant Road. When you look ahead toward the curve in the road you will see a mill. As you drive toward it, it seems to get smaller, rather than larger. It's an optical illusion caused by the interplay of the water, trees, and light, which throws off your perspective.

DOWNTOWN THOROLD

WELLAND MUSEUM, WELLAND

✷ To Do

ST. CATHARINES/PORT DALHOUSIE

BREWERIES **Lock Street Brewing** (www.lockstreet.ca), 15 Lock Street, Port Dalhousie. Monday–Saturday 11 AM–9 PM, Sunday 11 AM–6 PM. A microbrewery specializing in artisanal beers.

FAMILY FUN 🐾 ♪ **Lakeside Park Carousel**, Lakeside Park, 1 Lakeport Road, Port Dalhousie. Open late May–mid-October, hours vary. This Looff Carousel, which has sixty-eight animals and four chariots, was carved between 1898 and 1905 in Brooklyn, New York. It was brought to St. Catharines in 1921. Rides are only five cents.

THOROLD

Lock 7 Viewing Complex (905-680-9477; www.thorold.com/content/lock-7-viewing-complex), 50 Chapel Street South, Thorold. The Lock 7 Viewing Complex is a good spot to watch the ships. Be sure to visit the legendary "kissing rock" located by the complex. Sailor Charles Snelgrove started the tradition of kissing the ladies he met in port at the rock before he set sail. Soon other sailors were bringing their ladies to the rock; it was considered bad luck to leave Lock 7 without visiting the kissing rock.

KISSING ROCK, THOROLD

✷ Green Space

ST. CATHARINES/PORT DALHOUSIE

PARKS **Lakeside Park**, 1 Lakeport Road, Port Dalhousie. This park has 1,500 feet of beachfront on Lake Ontario, a playground, concessions, picnic pavilion, and carousel. See also *Family Fun*.

WALKING AND HIKING TRAILS **Waterfront Trail** (www.waterfronttrail.org). This is a 1,600 km trail (approximately 1,000 miles) along the Canadian Shoreline. Part of it goes through the Niagara region.

Greater Niagara Circle Route (www.regional.niagara.on.ca). This route connects the Welland Canals Trail, Waterfront Trail, and Friendship Trail (Fort Erie). See website for maps.

Welland Canals Trail. A multiuse trail from Lakeshore Road to Thorold; it will eventually go to Port Colborne.

LOCK 8 GATEWAY PARK, PORT COLBORNE

WELLAND

PARKS **Chippawa Park**, 128 Fitch Street and First Avenue, Welland. This large park features a large variety of roses, which bloom in June.

Merritt Park, 115 King Street, Welland. This park, which overlooks the recreational waterway, contains the Welland Canal Memorial Monument as well as a 750-seat amphitheater, the site of summer concerts.

Merritt Island Park, located on an island between the recreational waterway (old canal) and the Welland River, has a 4.2-km (2.6-mile) hiking/walking trail and a playground.

PORT COLBORNE

PARKS **Lock 8 Gateway Park**, 113 Mellanby Avenue, Port Colborne. Lock 8 is a regulating lock, which raises or lowers ships only a few feet, depending on the water level of Lake Erie. The lock is 1,380 feet long, one of the longest canal locks in the world. The park surrounding the lock has an elevated viewing platform.

✳ Lodging

THOROLD

Keefer Mansion (905-680-9581; www.keefermansion.com), 14 St. Davids Street West, Thorold. This 9,000-square-foot 1886 mansion is a heritage boutique inn with three guest rooms, all with private baths. The entire inn can also be rented for weddings. $$.

Inn at Lock 7 (905-227-6177 or 1-877-465-6257; www.innatlock7.com), 24 Chapel Street South, Thorold. After a full day of sightseeing, it is time to pull up a chair on the lawn at the Inn at Lock 7 and watch ships from around the world proceed through the lock. The twenty-four-guestroom inn, just down the street from the viewing complex, is the only inn in the region where one can view the ships as they pass through the canal. $$.

PORT COLBORNE

Canalside Inn (905-834-6090; www .canalside.ca), 232 West Street, Port Colborne. Two studio suites, which overlook the canal, are available for nightly or weekly accommodations. Call for prices. See also *Where to Eat* and *Selective Shopping*.

✳ Where to Eat

ST. CATHARINES/PORT DALHOUSIE

Acqua Restaurant and Bar (289-362-1222), 1 Lock Street, Port Dalhousie. Enjoy Italian and Mediterranean cuisine at this large restaurant just a block from the beach.

Balzac's Coffee (905-397-8648; www .balzacs.com), 9 Lock Street, Port Dalhousie. Open 7 AM–7 PM. Located in a 1907 building that was once a bank, this two-story coffee shop, which also has several other locations in Ontario, is a popular place to enjoy coffee and other beverages. They have an outdoor patio to enjoy in summer.

Oasis Lakeside Pita (905-938-8080), 48 Lakeport Road, Port Dalhousie. A popular place for pitas and ice cream.

THOROLD

Donnelly's Pub (905-227-1947), 54 Front Street, Thorold. Daily 11:30 AM–11 PM. This Irish pub features a weekly Friday fish fry.

On the Front Café & Eatery (905-397-4734), 30 Front Street, Thorold. Enjoy fair-trade coffee, baked goods, sandwiches, and ice cream, along with beer and wine.

Cosmo's Diner (905-680-6692), 26 Front Street, Thorold. Tuesday–Sunday 8 AM–3 PM. Stuffed French toast is one of the specialties at this '50s-style diner, along with traditional breakfast fare and burgers.

The Karma Kameleon Gastro Pub (905-227-2233; www.karmakameleonpub .com), 1 Front Street North, Thorold. Tuesday–Saturday 11 AM–9 PM. Menu items include gourmet sandwiches and burgers, paninis, wraps, lobster grilled cheese, and Southern fried chicken with buttermilk waffles.

Sweetest Addiction (905-680-2121), 32 Front Street, Thorold. Monday–Saturday 10 AM–5 PM. Choose from a variety of cupcakes to eat in or take out, including some that are gluten-free and vegan. You can also order specialty cakes.

PORT COLBORNE

Bremfield's (289-836-9863 www .bremfields.blogspot.com), 91 Main Street West, Port Colborne. Enjoy lunch, coffee, and desserts at this café, which also has a florist and antiques.

Canalside Restaurant (905-834-6090; www.canalside.ca) 232 West Street, Port Colborne. Opens daily at 11:30 AM. This casual restaurant has an open-air patio with a view of the canal. They also have an adjacent kitchen store and two hotel suites for overnight accommodations.

Jay the Pie Guy Café and Bakery (289-407-4474) 174 West Street, Port Colborne. Daily 10 AM–7 PM. Enjoy made from scratch meat pies, pot pies, and fruit pies.

Lotus Gardens (905-835-2552: lotus garden.letseat.at/menu), 182 West Street, Port Colborne. Tuesday–Sunday 3:30–9 PM. Good Chinese food and a view of the canal.

Smokin' Buddha (905-834-6000; www.thesmokinbuddha.com), 265 King Street, Port Colborne. Located in a former train station, this very popular restaurant serves a variety of cuisines, with an emphasis on Thai and Asian. Reservations suggested.

WALTER'S RESTAURANT IN PORT COLBORNE IS KNOWN FOR SEAFOOD

Walter's & Neptune's Restaurant & Tavern (905-835-1791), 258 West Street, Port Colborne. Open 11:30 AM–9 PM. A family-friendly restaurant with good food, especially known for its fish and chips. You can see the canal from the windows.

WELLAND

The Black Sheep Lounge (905-735-0666), 64 Niagara Street, Welland. Tuesday–Sunday; hours vary. Enjoy specialty coffees, along with lunch and dinner made with organic and locally sourced ingredients.

Don Marco's Italian Eatery (905-714-4417; www.donmarcos.ca), 248 Wellington Street, Welland. A small restaurant serving fresh, homemade traditional Italian fare.

Matteo's (905-732-2111), 125 East Main Street, Welland. An Italian restaurant featuring wood-fired pizza and pasta dishes; reservations a must.

M.T. Bellie's Tap & Grillhouse (905-788-9474; www.mtbellies.com), 871 Niagara Street, Welland. A family-friendly, casual restaurant located near the Seaway Mall.

✳ Entertainment

PORT COLBORNE

Showboat Festival Theatre (905-834-0833; www.showboattheatre.ca), 296 Fielden Avenue, Port Colborne. Theater season is June–August.

✳ Selective Shopping

ST. CATHARINES/PORT DALHOUSIE

Ausmosis (905-646-7873; www.ausmosis.ca), 15 Lock Street, Port Dalhousie. This shop carries surfing apparel. They are the makers of the only Canadian-designed and -manufactured surfboards and stand-up paddleboards.

Lock & Main Marketplace, located at Lock and Main Streets in Port Dalhousie. This building contains several different shops and restaurants.

THOROLD

Figg Street Company (289-786-0012), 40 Front Street, Thorold. Monday–Saturday 10 AM–5 PM; Thursday–Friday until 6 PM. This shop has a variety of stationary, fine papers, art prints, soaps, books, and gift items. They also offer classes and workshops.

The Post Office–Shannon Passero (905-397-7578; www.shannonpassero.com), 18 Front Street, Thorold. Monday–Wednesday, Saturday 10 AM–6 PM, Thursday–Friday 10 AM–8 PM. Located in a former post office building, this unique 6,500-square-foot specialty boutique features clothing, accessories, jewelry, and household items. Some of the

THE POST OFFICE—SHANNON PASSERO IS A 6,500-SQUARE-FOOT BOUTIQUE SHOP

clothing items, which are eco-conscious, are designed by the store's owner, Shannon Passero, an internationally known designer who was born and raised in nearby Welland. The store also has a gallery space featuring the work of local artists.

WELLAND

Seaway Mall (905-735-0694; www .seawaymall.com), 800 Niagara Street, Welland. This mall has over ninety stores and other services.

PORT COLBORNE

Canalside Kitchen Store (905-834-6090; www.canalside.ca), 232 West Street, Port Colborne. Thursday–Saturday 11:30 AM–10 PM. This shop has kitchen products, gadgets, spices, and gift items.

⚭ **Candy Safari** (905-401-9439; www .candysafari.com), 238 West Street, Port Colborne. Choose from nostalgic and retro candies, British candies, and ice cream.

Crew's Quarters (905-834-5921), 192 West Street, Port Colborne. Shop for unique and unusual nautical items, books, souvenirs, and gift items.

Glam Girl (905-834-1437), 220 West Street, Port Colborne. A boutique shop with clothing, jewelry, shoes, and accessories.

Grants Gifts (905-834-1459), 226 West Street, Port Colborne. They carry home décor and art.

Harmony on West (905-834-2288: www.harmonyonwest.ca), 264 West Street, Port Colborne. Tuesday–Saturday 11 AM–5 PM. Browse through a selection of natural bath, home, and baby products.

The Honey Bee Store (289-836-8138; www.thehoneybeestore.ca), 216 West Street, Port Colborne. Tuesday–Saturday 10 AM–5 PM, Sunday 12–4 PM. Choose from a large selection of unpasteurized honey and other honey products, along with tea, teapots, maple syrup, skin care items, and candies.

Picket Fence Gift Shop (905-835-2002) 230 West Street, Port Colborne.

Monday–Saturday 10 AM–5 PM, Sunday 12–4 PM. This shop has home decor and giftware.

Serendipities (905-834-1446; www.serendipitiesboutique.com), 162 West Street, Port Colborne. Tuesday–Saturday 11 AM–5 PM, Sunday 12:30–4 PM. A boutique shop which specializes in women's clothing and accessories.

Something Else (289-836-9893), 244 West Street, Port Colborne. Monday–Saturday 11 AM–5 PM, Sunday 12–4 PM. Browse through handmade fashions and accessories, as well as art and home decor items.

✳ Special Events

WELLAND

Welland Rose Festival (905-732-7673; www.wellandrosefestival.on.ca).

Welland is known as the "Rose City." Their annual Rose Festival is held in June in Chippawa Park, which has one of the finest rose gardens in Ontario. The festival, which focuses on Welland's history and culture, includes a parade, musical entertainment, arts and crafts, sporting events, and of course, a rose show.

PORT COLBORNE

August: **Canal Days Marine Heritage Festival** (portcolborne.com/page/canal_days). A four-day celebration of area history and canal heritage. It is Port Colborne's signature event, with over 300,000 people attending over the four days. Activities are family-friendly and include historical displays, a car show, live musical entertainment, food, and more.

OVERVIEW OF NEARBY COUNTIES

GENESEE

ORLEANS

WYOMING

CHAUTAUQUA

CATTARAUGUS

ALLEGANY

INTRODUCTION

A book about Buffalo Niagara would not be complete without mentioning the other counties in the Greater Niagara region. Here is a brief overview of the six other counties in the region.

GENESEE COUNTY

Genesee County, established in 1802, is located in the center of western New York, midway between Buffalo and Rochester. Batavia is the county seat, and it was from the Holland Land Office in Batavia that early settlers bought three million acres of western New York land in the early 1800s. The name Genesee comes from the Seneca word *Gen-nis-he-yo*, which translates to "beautiful valley" or "pleasant banks."

Today the county is agricultural in nature, and a couple of the main crops are onions and potatoes. There are many unique places to visit in Genesee County, no matter what your interests. History buffs won't want to miss the Jell-O Museum in LeRoy, while nature lovers will enjoy the pristine beauty of the Bergen Swamp, a National Natural

LEARN ABOUT THE HISTORY OF GENESEE COUNTY AT THE HOLLAND LAND OFFICE MUSEUM

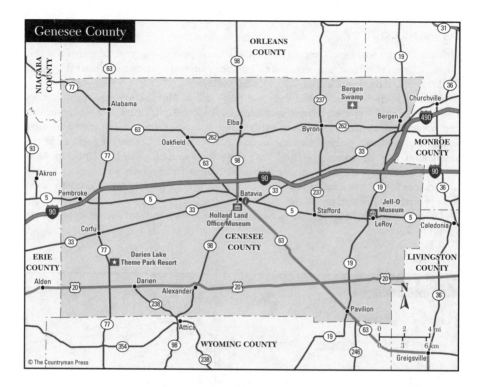

History Landmark, in the northern part of the county. Of course, families and thrill seekers alike will enjoy Darien Lake Theme Park Resort.

Genesee County Chamber of Commerce (1-800-622-2686; www.geneseeny.com), 8276 Park Road, Batavia. Open year-round Monday–Friday 8:30 AM–4:30 PM.

ORLEANS COUNTY

Orleans County was incorporated in 1825, the same year as the completion of the Erie Canal. During that time, numerous small villages sprang up along and near the canal. Still thriving today are Medina, Albion, and Holley.

History buffs will enjoy the railroad museum in Medina and the world's only museum for cobblestones, located just north of Albion. Agriculture is the number-one industry in the county, so visitors can stop at numerous roadside stands and farm markets to get fresh-picked produce in-season. Recreational boating is popular on the Erie Canal, Oak Orchard River, and Lake Ontario. If sport fishing is your thing, Lake Ontario is noted for its giant salmon, along with brown and steelhead trout.

Orleans is a rather small county, only 23 miles across, permitting visitors to cover a lot of territory in one day.

Orleans County Tourism (800-724-0314; www.orleanscountytourism.com), 14016 Route 31, Albion.

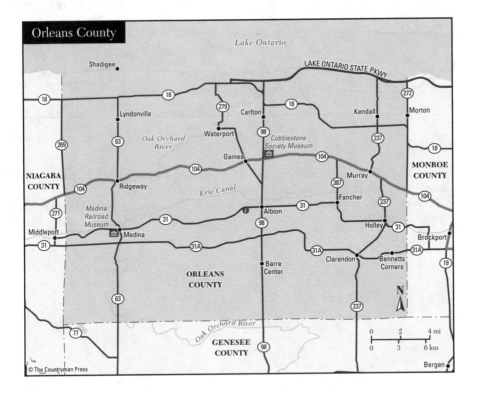

WYOMING COUNTY

Wyoming County has a little bit of everything for the traveler. If you're looking for a place of scenic beauty, Wyoming County is bordered on the east by Letchworth State Park, the "Grand Canyon of the East," with its 600-foot-deep gorge. Nature lovers will also enjoy the pristine beauty of Beaver Meadow Audubon Center.

History buffs will enjoy taking a ride on the vintage steam engine Arcade & Attica Railroad, visiting the historic village of Wyoming—still lit by its original gaslights—or touring some of the area's many museums.

Prior to pioneer settlement in 1802, the area was used by the Seneca Nation as hunting and fishing ground. The first settlers came from New England, while later settlers were European immigrants attracted to various industries. Irish and German settlers arrived in the 1830s to farm the land. Then in the late 1880s, the salt, stone cutting, and railroad industries employed Italian immigrants, while the textile mills attracted many Polish émigrés.

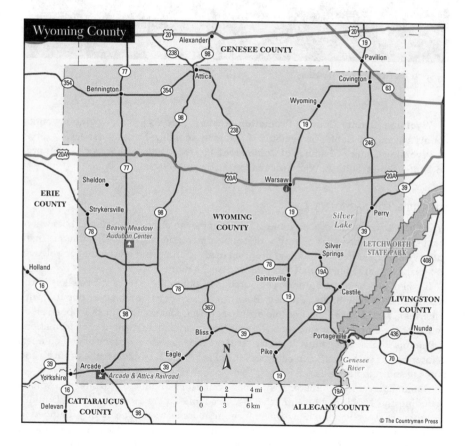

THE GORGE AT LETCHWORTH STATE PARK

Wyoming County Tourist Promotion Agency (800-839-3910, www.gowyoming countyny.com), 36 Center Street, Suite A, Warsaw. Monday–Friday 9 AM–5 PM.

Wyoming County Chamber of Commerce (585-786-0307; www.wycochamber.org), 36 Center Street, Suite A, Warsaw. Monday–Friday 9 AM–5 PM.

CHAUTAUQUA COUNTY

When you hear the word "Chautauqua," what comes to mind? The lake with its waterfront activities? The entire county with its many attractions? Or the Chautauqua Institution, which has offered a summer program in art, culture, and recreation for well over 100 years. Chautauqua is all of this plus a whole lot more.

If you enjoy the great outdoors, Chautauqua County has a total of five lakes in the county—Erie, Chautauqua, Findley, Bear, and Cassadaga—which are popular with fishermen, recreational boaters, and swimmers. Tour Chautauqua Lake by boat, enjoy nature at the Jamestown Audubon Nature Center, or explore ancient rock formations at Panama Rocks. The county boasts over 150 parks as well as dozens of golf courses. Winter-sports enthusiasts can enjoy skiing at Peek 'n Peak, or explore the county's 400 miles of snowmobile trails.

Chautauqua is rich in history, with many museums and historical sites to explore, including the McClurg Museum, the 1891 Fredonia Opera House, and the Dunkirk Lighthouse, as well as the Lucy-Desi Museum in Jamestown. The county, founded in 1808, was named after Lake Chautauqua, which comes from the Native American word *Jad-da'gwah*, which, loosely translated, means "bag tied in the middle," referring to the shape of the lake. The county is noted for its many bed & breakfast inns, plus a large concentration of antiques shops.

If you want intellectual stimulation, spend some time at the Chautauqua Institution, which offers theater, entertainment, lectures, seminars, and more during its nine-week summer season.

Chautauqua County Tourism (716-357-4569 or 800-242-4569; www.tourchautauqua.com), PO Box 1441, Chautauqua Institution Main Gate, 1 Massey Avenue (off Route 394), Chautauqua. Open daily 9 AM–5 PM, year-round.

 ♿ **Chautauqua County Chamber of Commerce** (716-484-1101; www.chautauquachamber.org), 512 Falconer Street, Jamestown.

THE ATHENAEUM HOTEL AT THE CHAUTAUQUA INSTITUTION

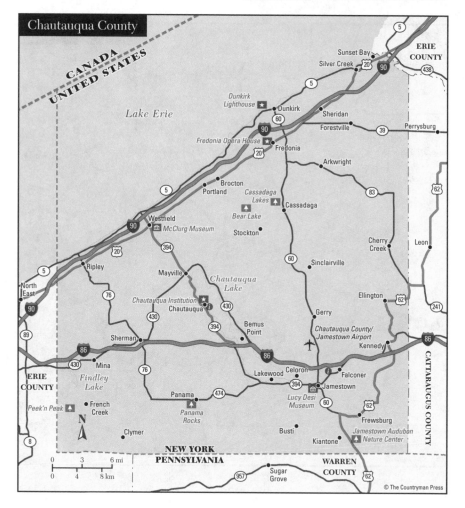

CATTARAUGUS COUNTY

Cattaraugus County offers visitors vacation variety. Known as the Enchanted Mountains, Cattaraugus County is the heart of western New York's ski country, and Ellicottville, proclaimed the "Aspen of the East," is in the central part of the county. The Zoar Valley in the northern part of the county has some of the largest old-growth forests in the United States and is a popular spot for wilderness hiking and white water rafting. Salamanca, in the southern portion of the county, is the only city in the United States located entirely on a tribal reservation, and while in Salamanca, visitors can enjoy Allegany State Park, at 65,000 acres New York's largest state park. Nearby Olean was once one of the largest oil producers in the world. There is also a large Amish community in both Cattaraugus and Chautauqua counties; you can visit their shops for quilts, baked goods, furniture, and more.

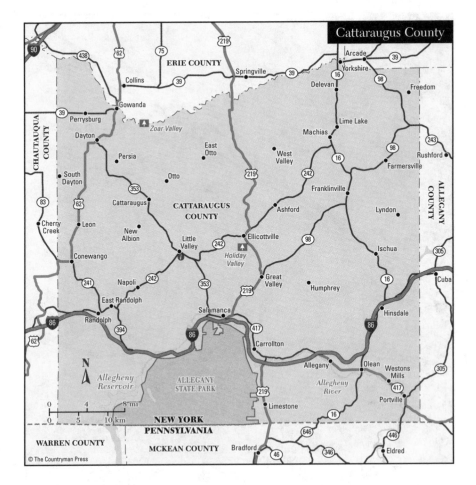

EXPLORE ROCK CITY PARK JUST SOUTH OF OLEAN

Cattaraugus County was formed in 1808, and the first country seat was the village of Ellicottville, due to its geographic location at the center of the county. In 1868 the county seat was moved to its present location, the town of Little Valley.

Cattaraugus County Department of Economic Development, Planning, and Tourism (800-331-0543; www.enchantedmountains.info), 303 Court Street, Little Valley. Open Monday–Friday 8 AM–5 PM.

ALLEGANY COUNTY

While most of New York was settled during the 1800s, Allegany County remained a wilderness area, so it isn't as highly developed as the rest of the state. Visitors will find an abundance of small villages and towns throughout the county, many retaining their Victorian charm of days gone by.

Allegany County is rich in rural heritage and scenic beauty. No matter what your interest—antiquing, hiking, skiing, hunting, or just enjoying nature—you'll be able to indulge it in Allegany County.

Love nature? Allegany County has lakes and streams, woodland trails, wildlife areas, equestrian farms, and more.

THE HISTORIC POST OFFICE IN ANGELICA, ALLEGANY COUNTY

There are twenty-three state forests, totaling over 46,000 acres. The county is also an angler's paradise, with trout and bass found in the Genesee River and Allen and Rushford Lakes. Cuba Lake is known for its perch and bass fishing. Deer hunters will be thrilled to know that Allegany has more bucks per square mile than any other county in the state.

Incidentally, in case you're wondering, confusion abounds on the spelling of the county's name. While the county, village, and tribal reservation spell their names "Allegany," the river, reservoir, and mountain range all spell it "Allegheny." No one seems to know why the spelling is different. Either way, it's a translation from the original Seneca language meaning "land of beautiful water."

Allegany County Tourism (585-268-7612; www.alleganyco.com), 7 Court Street, Belmont.

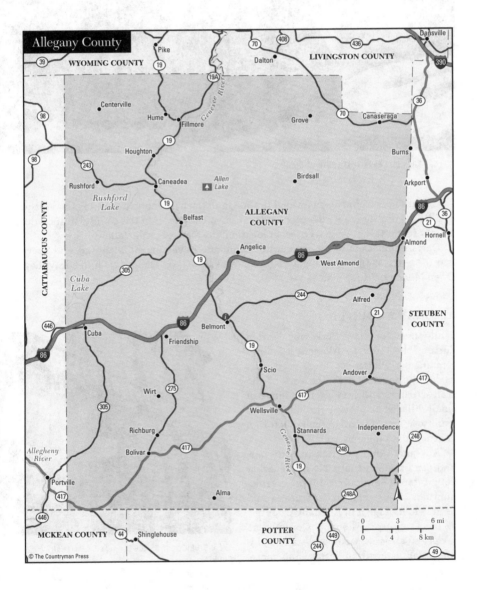

INDEX

Italics indicate illustrations.

A

Aartpark Hotel, 180
Absolute Elegance Bed & Breakfast, 237
Academy Park, 178
Acqua Restaurant and Bar, 266
Activities
    in Amherst, 97–98, 100
    in Aurora, 127–128
    in Buffalo, 50, 50–56, 51, 53, 55, 56, 59
    in Canal Towns, 208, 208–209, 210
    in Clarence and Akron, 112–113
    in Fort Erie, 220–221, 222
    in Grand Island, 89–91, 92
    in Lake Erie Towns, 143
    in Lake Ontario Shore, 199
    in Niagara Falls, New York, 159–162, 160, 163
    in Niagara Falls, Ontario, 227–233, 228, 230, 231, 232, 234–235
    in Niagara-on-the-Lake and Queenston, 244
    in North of the Falls, 177–180, 178
    in North Tonawanda and Wheatfield, 188–189, 190
    in Orchard Park and West Seneca, 136
    in St. Catharines/Port Dalhousie, 264
    in ski country, 151, 151
    in Thorold, 264
    in Welland Canal Corridor, 264
Adams Mark, 60
Adams Power Plant Transformer House, 159
Adam's Rib, 101
Adler, Dakmar, 45
Adrian's Custard & Beef, 93
Adventure Calls, 28
Adventure Landing, 90
African American Cultural Center/Paul Robeson Theatre, 76
African American historical and cultural sites, 21
Ag Inspired Cuisine, 238
Agricultural fairs, 19
Airports and air service, 15
"Airport Tunnel," 118
Air Tours Niagara, 232
Akron. *See also* Clarence and Akron
    airport in, 111
Akron Falls, 25, 113
Akron Rail Trail, 113
Albion, 204, 274
Albright, John J., 40
Albright-Knox Art Gallery, 18, 18, 37, 40, 57
Al-E-Oops, 120

Alethea's Chocolates, 108
Allegany County, 279, 279–280, 280
Allegany Reservation, 17
Allen, Lewis, 37, 89
Allen Burger Venture, 68
Allendale Theater, 76
Allen Lake, 280
Allen Street Hardware Company, 68
Allen Street Poutine, 68
Allentown, 37
    art festival in, 37, 82
Alleyway Theatre, 76
Alston, Joseph, 157
Amaretto Italian Bistro, 103
Ambiance by the Falls Bed & Breakfast, 237
Americana Conference Resort and Spa, 236
American Falls, 157, 161, 163, 232
American Revolution, 96
Amherst, 96–109
    activities in, 97–100
    antiques in, 106–107
    art galleries/museums in, 97, 107
    breweries and brewpubs in, 97–98
    eating in, 101–106
    entertainment in, 106
    farm markets in, 107
    getting there, 97
    golf in, 98
    green space in, 98–100
    lodging in, 100–101
    marinas in, 98
    medical care in, 97
    museums and historic sites in, 97
    parks in, 99
    shopping in, 106–109
    sightseeing in, 97
    special events in, 109
    waterfalls in, 100
Amherst, Jeffrey, 96
Amherst Canalway Trail, 100
Amherst Marine Center, 98
Amherst Pizza & Ale House, 104
Amherst/Snyder, eating in, 101
Amherst State Park, 99
Amici, 93
Amtrak, 15, 39, 117, 158
Amusement parks, 25
    in Grand Island, 89–90, 90
Anchor Bar, 65
Anchor Marine, 91
Anderson Gallery, 40
Anderson's, 20

Anderson's Frozen Custard, 105
Angola, 125. *See also* Lake Erie Towns
Anna Grace, 80
Antique Expo, 116
The Antique Lamp, 77, *78*
Antique Man, 77
Antiques
  in Amherst, 106–107
  in Aurora, 131
  in Buffalo, 77–78
  in Canal Towns, *212*, 212–213
  in Clarence and Akron, 115
  in Lake Erie Towns, 147
  in Niagara-on-the-Lake and Queenston, 254
  in North of the Falls, 184
  in North Tonawanda and Wheatfield,
    192–193
Antiques Allentown, 77
Antiques at the Glencroft, 115
Antiques of Hamburg, 147
Antique World, 115
Apple Blossom Festival, 203
Apple Granny, 180
Apple Harvest Festival, 203
Apples, 19
Aquarium of Niagara, *25*, 25–26, 160, *160*
Aquariums, 25–26
Architecture, 28
  in Buffalo, *44*, 44–46
  in Niagara Falls, Ontario, 227
  in North Tonawanda and Wheatfield, 188
Arctic Cove, 228
Armor Inn, 144–145
Arriba Tortilla, 130
Arrowhead Golf Course, 112
Arrowhead Spring Winery, 207
The Art 247, 18, 213
Art associations and councils, 18
Art deco architecture, *44*
Art Dialogue Gallery, 40
Artemis Restaurant, 223
Art galleries/museums, 18, *18*
  in Amherst, 97, 107
  in Aurora, 131–132
  in Buffalo, 40–41, *41*, 78
  in Canal Towns, 205, 213
  in Lake Erie Towns, 141
  in Niagara Falls, New York, 158–159, *159*
  in Niagara-on-the-Lake and Queenston,
    242, 255
  in North of the Falls, 173, *173*
  in North Tonawanda and Wheatfield, 187,
    193
Arthur's Home Furnishings, 139
Artpark State Park, 177, 178, 183
Arts Service Initiative of WNY, 18
Ashbury Hall/Babeville, 76
Ashkers Juice Bar, 68, *68*
Athenaeum Hotel, *277*
Attic to Basement Repeats, 95
Audubon Golf Course, 98
Aurora, 126–134
  activities in, 127–128

antiques in, 131
art galleries in, 131–132
breweries in, 127–128
eating in, 130–131
entertainment in, 131
farm markets in, 132
getting there, 126
golf in, 128
green space in, 128–129
lodging in, 129
medical care in, 126
museums and historic homes in, 126–127,
  127
nature preserves in, 128–129
parks in, 129
shopping in, 131–134, *133*
sightseeing in, 126–128, *127*, *128*
special events in, 134
theaters in, 131
Aurora Historical Society Museum, 126
Aurora Players, 131
Aurora Popcorn Shop, 132
Aurora Rails and Hobbies, 132
Aurora Theater, 131
Aurora Town Park, 129
Ausmosis, 267
Auto racing
  in North of the Falls, 177
  in ski country, 151
Aviation museums, 21
Avondale Dairy Bar, 252

B
Babcock Cobblestone House Museum, 196
Backroads and Byways of Upstate New York,
  30
Badding Brothers Farm Market, 107
Baehr's Ice Cream Cottage, 201
Bailey Campus to Amherst Campus, 100
Baker, Howard H., Company ship chandlery, 47
Baker, Nelson, 38, 49
Balzac's Coffee, 266
Barbara Ann's Carousel Concessions, 201
Bar Bill Tavern, 130
Barker. *See* Lake Ontario Shore
Barton House, 42
Bassett Park, 99
Batavia, 110
Bay Beach, 22
Beaches, 22
  in Buffalo, 56
  in Fort Erie, 221
  in Lake Erie Towns, 143–144, *144*
  in Lake Ontario Shore, 199
The Beach House, 93
Beaver Island State Park, 22, 90, 91
Beaver Meadow Audubon Center, 275
Beck, Sir Adam, Generating Station #2, 229
Becker Brewing, 208
Becker Farms, *208*, 208–209, 213
Bed & Breakfast Niagara, 251
Bedore Tours, Inc., 161
Beechwood Golf & Country Club, 229

Beer, 19–20. *See also* Breweries and wineries
Bella Casa, 132
Bella Vita Ristorante, 251
Bellie, M. T., Tap & Grillhouse, 267
Bellissimo, Frank and Theresa's, Anchor Bar, 21
Benchmark Restaurant, 251–252
Benjamin's Art Gallery, 78
Bennett Beach, 22, 143
Bergen Swamp, 272
Bernard Avenue Beach (Thunder Bay Beach), 221
Bertha's Diner, 70–71, *71*
Bertie, Willoughby, 218
Bertie Township, 218
Betty's, 68
Betty's Restaurant, 238, *238*
BFLO Gallery & Gift Shop, 108
Bicycling, 26. *See also* Activities
The Big Bridge, 206
Big Ditch Brewery, 51
Big Orbit Art Gallery, 40
Big Tree Treaty (1797), 17
Bijou Grille, 65
Billy Club, 68
Biltmore Estate, 25
Bipperts Farm Market, 132
Bird Island, 53, 59
Bistro Six-One, 252–253
Blackbird Cider Works, 197
Blackbird Sweets, 70
Black Button Distillery, 51
Black Forest Adler, 104
Black Rock Canal, 59
Black Rock Historical Society, 46
Black Rock Locks and Canal, 50
The Black Sheep, 74, 267
Black Squirrel Distillery, 51
The Blackthorn, 75
Black Willow Minery, 197
Blaisdell. *See* Lake Erie Towns
Blue Mountain Coffees, 80
Blue United Cab, 158
Blue Water Marina, 91
Blueways and Greenways Intermodal Depot, 92
Blush Boutique, 80
Boating, 26
   in Amherst, 98
   in Buffalo, 50, *50, 51,* 55–56
   in Canal Towns, 208, 209
   in Fort Erie, 220–221
   in Grand Island, 91
   in Lake Ontario Shore, 199
   in Niagara Falls, New York, 159, *160*
   in Niagara Falls, Ontario, 227–228
   in Niagara-on-the-Lake and Queenston, 244
   in North of the Falls, 177
Bob & John's La Hacienda, 71
Bob-o-Link Golf Course, 136
Bonaparte, Elizabeth, 157
Bonaparte, Jerome, 157
Bonaparte, Napoleon, 157
Bond, Col. William, House, 206

Bond Lake County Park, 178
Book Corner, 168
The Bookworm, 132
Boulevard Mall, 107
Bowmansville, 117
Brasa Brazilian Steakhouse, 238
Bread Hive Bakery, 74
Break'n Eggs Creperie, 105
Bremfield's, 266
Breweries and wineries
   in Amherst, 97–98
   in Aurora, 127–128
   in Buffalo, 51–52, *53*
   in Canal Towns, 207–208
   in Fort Erie, 220
   in Lake Erie Towns, 142
   in Lake Ontario Shore, 197–198
   in Niagara Falls, Ontario, 228
   in Niagara-on-the-Lake and Queenston, 244–247, *245, 246, 247*
   in North of the Falls, 176–177
   in Orchard Park and West Seneca, 135
Brickyard Brewing Company, 181
Brickyard Restaurant, 181, *181*
Bridal Veil Falls, 157, 163
Brighton Park Golf Course, 91
Brimstone Brewing, 220
Broadway Deli, 120
Broadway Market, 79–80, *80*
Brock Monument, *242,* 243
Broderick Park, 29
Brodie's Guardian Drug Store and Village Shoppes, 224–225
Brookins Inn & Suites, 201
Brown, Murphy, Craft Beer, 115
Brown, William Wells, 43
Bruce Trail, 234–235
Bryncliff Resort, 28
Buckhorn Island State Park, 22, 91
Buffalo, 15, *32, 33*–84
   activities in, *50,* 50–56, *51, 53, 55, 56*
   airport in, 17
   antiques in, 77–78
   architecture in, *44,* 44–46
   art museums and galleries in, 40–41, *41,* 78
   beaches and pools in, 56
   boating in, 50, *50, 51*
   bookstores in, 78
   breweries, distilleries, and wineries in, 51–52, *53*
   casinos in, 52
   cemeteries in, 56
   East Side, 38
   eating in, 62–75
   Elmwood Village, 36
   entertainments in, 76–77
   farm markets in, 78–79
   fishing in, 53
   gardens in, 56
   getting there and getting around in, 39–40
   golf in, 53–54
   green space in, 56–59
   guide tours in, 54–55

Buffalo (*continued*)
history of, 34–35
ice skating in, 55, *56*
Larkinville, 36, *37*
lighthouses in, *49*, 49–50
lodging in, 59–61
marinas in, 55–56
medical care in, 40
museums and historic sites in, 37–38, 42, *42*, 43, 46–49
nature preserves in, 56–57
public library in, 41
shopping in, 77–82
sightseeing in, 40–50, *41*, *42*, *43*, *44*, *46*, *47*, *48*, *49*, *50*
South Buffalo/Lackawanna, 38–39
special events in, 82–84
University District, 38
walking and hiking trails in, 59
Waterfront/Inner Harbor, 35–36
Waterfront/Outer Harbor, 36
West Side/Black Rock, 38
Buffalo, University of
Art Gallery, 40, 97
Center for the Arts, 106
Medical School, 35
Buffalo and Erie County Botanical Gardens, 22, 56, *57*
Buffalo and Erie County Naval and Military Park, 21, 46–47, *47*
Buffalo and Erie County Public Library, 41
Buffalo and Erie County Riverwalk, 92, 190
Buffalo Antiques, 77
Buffalo Arts Studio, 40–41
Buffalo Bandits Lacrosse, 77
Buffalo Big Print, 78
Buffalo Bills (football), 28, 77, 125, 135, 139
Buffalo Bisons (baseball), 28, 77
Buffalo Bites Food Tours, 54
Buffalo Brewery District, 51
Buffalo Brewing Company, 51
Buffalo Brew Pub, 97
Buffalo Chamber Music Society, 75–76
Buffalo Chop House, 62
Buffalo City Hall Observation Deck, 52–53
Buffalo Creek Indian Reservation, 126
Buffalo Distilling, 51
Buffalo Double Decker Bus Tours, 54
Buffalo Fire Historical Museum, 47
Buffalo Harbor Cruises, 26, 50, 54
Buffalo Harbor Kayak, 50
Buffalo Harbor Museum, 47
Buffalo Harbor State Park, 36, 58
Buffalo History Museum, 21, 24, *37*, 37–38, 42, 57, 84
Buffalo History Tours, 54
Buffalo International Film Festival, 84
Buffalo Irish Center, 39
Buffalo Irish Festival, 84
Buffalo Lighthouse, 36, 50, 57
Buffalo Main Light, 28, *29*, *49*, 49–50
Buffalo Marriott Harborcenter, 61
Buffalo Museum of Science, 47, 58

Buffalo Naval Park, 67
Buffalo News "Gusto" section, 30
Buffalo Niagara Brewers Association, 51
Buffalo Niagara Heritage Village, 97
Buffalo Niagara International Airport, 39, 117
Buffalo Niagara Marriott, 100
Buffalo Olmstead Parks Conservancy, 58
Buffalo Pedal Tours, 54
Buffalo Philharmonic Orchestra, 45, 76
Buffalo Place, 39
Buffalo Proper, 62
Buffalo Psychiatric Center, 45
Buffalo Religious Arts Center, 47
Buffalo River, grain elevators on, *46*
Buffalo Riverfest Park, 59, *59*
Buffalo River History Tours, 54
Buffalo River Keeper Tours, 54
Buffalo Riverworks, 36, *36*, 50
Buffalo Sabres (hockey), 28, 77
Buffalo's Polonia, 38
Buffalo Spree, 30
Buffalo Tiki Tours, 50
Buffalo Touring Company, 54
Buffalo Transportation Pierce-Arrow Museum, 47–48, *48*
Buffalo Vibe/Buffalo Citybration, 30
Buffalo wings, 21
Buffalo Zoo, 53, *53*, 57
Bunshaft, Gordon, 40
Burchfield, Charles E., Nature and Art Center, 136, *136*
Burchfield-Penney Art Center, 18, 38, 41, *41*
Burgerfest, 148
Burning Buffalo Bar & Grille, 71
Burr, Aaron, 157
Burr, Theodosia, 157
Burt. *See* Lake Ontario Shore
Bus service, 15
Butera's Craft Beers and Craft Pizza, 145
Butler House Bed & Breakfast, 165
Butterfly Conservatory, 233–234
Butterfly Gallery, 255
Bye's Popcorn, 202
Byrd House, 137

C
Cabaret, 62
Café on the Avenue, 71
Cafora's, 201
Cameron's Lakeside Ice Cream Shoppe, 201
Cammarata's, 210
Camping, 26
Canada One Factory Outlet Mall, 240
Canadian customs, 15
Canadian Falls, 157
Canal Club 62 Tap & Eatery, 190
Canal Days Marine Heritage Festival, 269
Canal Fest of the Tonawandas, 95, 194
Canal Museum, 206
Canalside, 35
Canalside Creamery, 190
Canalside Inn, 266
Canalside Kitchen Store, 268

Canalside Restaurant, 266
Canal Towns, 204–214
  activities in, *208,* 208–209
  antiques in, *212,* 212–213
  art galleries/museums in, 205, 213
  boating in, 208, 209
  breweries and wineries in, 207–208
  eating in, 210–212, *211*
  entertainment in, 212
  farm markets in, 213
  fishing in, 209
  getting there, 205
  golf in, 209
  green space in, 209–210
  historic sites in, 206
  lodging in, 210
  medical care in, 205
  museums and historic homes in, 206
  nature preserves in, 209
  shopping in, 212–213
  sightseeing in, *205,* 205–208, *207*
  special events in, 213–214
  theaters in, 212
Candlelight Stroll, 257
Candy Safari, 268
Canterbury Place, 184
Cantina Loco, 68
Cappelli, Gerard, 138
Cappelli, Jodie, 138
Cappelli's, 138
Captain's Gallery, 202
Carl Stone, 77
Carmelo's, 181
Carmine's, 167
The Carnegie Art Center, 187
Carousel Clothing & Collectibles, 108
The Carousel Shop, 152
Carte Blanche, 145
Cary, George, 42
Casa Antica, 181
Casa Azul, 65
Casino Niagara, 16, 229
Casinos, *15,* 15–16
  in Buffalo, 52
  in Fort Erie, 221
  in Niagara Falls, New York, 159
  in Niagara Falls, Ontario, 229
Castellani Art Museum, 18, 173, *173*
Castle by Candlelight, 186
Cathedral Park, 59
Cats Like Us, 95
Cattaraugus County, *278,* 278–279
Cattaraugus Creek, 28
Cattaraugus Reservation, 17
Cave of the Winds, 161, *161*
Cayuga Seneca Canal, 27
Cazenovia Creek, 57
Cazenovia Golf Course, 53–54
Cazenovia Park, 54, 57
Cecelia's, 68–69
Cecile's, 255
Cemeteries in Buffalo, 56
Cenotaph Clock Tower, 243

Centennial Art Center of Hamburg, 141
Center Cut Village Steakhouse, 181
Central Park, 25
Central Terminal, 44, *44*
CEPA Gallery, 41
Chamber Music Festival, 134
Champlain Canal, 27
Cham Shan Temple, 227
Chanel, Coco, 62
Chapman, Asa, 110
Charles Inn, 250, *251,* 252
Charlie's, 130–131
Charlie's Boatyard, 65
  restaurant at, 56
Charlie the Butcher, 120–121, *121*
Chateau Buffalo, 52
Chateau Niagara Winery, 197
Chautauqua County, 276–277, *277*
Chautauqua Lake, 276
Chautauqua-Lake Erie Wine Trail, 20
Cheektowaga, 96, 117. *See also* Lancaster,
    Depew, and Cheektowaga
  town park in, 119
Chefs, 65
Cheri Amour, 184
Chestnut Ridge Park, 135, 136, *137*
Chiavetta's BBQ Takeout, 211
Chiavetta's Chicken, 22
Chicken wings, 21, 22
Chillibration, 82
"Chinaman's Light," 49
Chippawa, 218
Chippawa Battlefield Park, 227
Chippawa Park, 265
The Chocolate Bar, 65
Chocolate F/X, 255, *255*
Chris's NY Sandwich Company, 65
Christmas in the Village, 186
Churchill, Winston, 25, 232
Civil Rights movement, 42
Civil War, 218
Clarence and Akron, 34, 87, 110–117
  activities in, 112–113
  antiques in, 115
  eating in, *114,* 114–115
  events in, 116, *116*
  farm markets in, 115
  getting there, 111
  golf in, 112–113
  green space in, 113
  historic homes in, *111,* 111–112
  lodging in, 113, *113*
  medical care in, 111
  museums in, *111,* 111–112
  parks in, 113
  shopping in, 115–116
  sightseeing in, 111–112
Clarence Center, 110, 116, *116*
  Coffee Company and Café in, 114
Clarence Historical Society Museum, *111,*
    111–112
Clarence Hollow, 110, *111*
  farmers' market in, 115

Clarion Hotel & Conference Centre, 223
Classic Car Show, 140
Clayton's Toys & Gifts, 108
Clearfield Recreation Center, 99
Cleveland, Grover, 37, 89
Cleveland, Grover, Park, 98
Clifton Hill, 230, *230*
Clifton Victoria Inn at the Falls, 228
Clinton-Bailey Market, 78–79
The Clubhouse Restaurant, 253
Coach Canada, 218
Coco Bar and Bistro, 62
Coco's Terrace Bar & Grill, 238
Coit, George, 43
Colden. *See* Ski country
Colden Lakes Resort, 152
Colden Mill Restaurant, 152
Colden Town Hall, 149
Cold Spring Cemetery, 206
Cole's, 69
Colored Musicians Club, 43
Colter Bay Grill, 69
Colt House, 43
Comfort Inn The Pointe, 165
Comfort Zone Café, 145
Community Beer Works, 52
Como Lake Park, 119
Como Restaurant, 166
Concord Crest Golf Course, 151
Concord Historical Library, 149–150
Concord Historical Museum, *150*
Concord Historical Society, 149–150
Concord Mercantile, 150
Cone Five Pottery, 80, *81*
Conley Interiors, 80
Connor's, 137
Connor's Hot Dogs, 145
Constitution Park, 178
Consumer Beverages Craft Cruiser, 54
Corks Wine Bar & Eatery, 253
Cornell, Katherine, Theatre, 106
Corner of Clark and Kent Streets, 38, *38*
Cosmo's Diner, 266
Country Cottage, 190
The Country Doctor Antiques and Gifts, 184
Country Peddlers, 139
Court House Theatre, 254
Courtyard by Marriott, 60, 165
Coyote Café, *145*, 145–146
Crafts and Creations, 213
Cravings, 71
Crazy Jakes, 190
Creekwater Restaurant, 103
Crescent Beach, 22, 221
Crew's Quarters, 268
Crowne Plaza Hotels, 228, 235
Crystal Beach, 22, 218, 221
    amusement park at, 218
    waterfront park at, 220, 221
Crystal Beach Candy Company, 224
Crystal Chandelier, 223
Cuba Lake, 280
Cugino's, 103

Curly's Grill, 75
Curtain Up!, 84
Curtiss, Harlow, building, 60
Curtiss Hotel, 60, *61*
Cycle & Stay Niagara, 251
Czolgosz, Leon, 24

D
Daily Planet Coffee, 71, *71*
Daisies Café, 75
Dande Farms Golf Course, 113
Daniel's Restaurant, 145
Danner House Bed & Breakfast, 237
Danny's South Restaurant, 138
The Dapper Goose, 64
Darien Lake Theme Park Resort, 273
Dart, Joseph, 34
Das Haus, 173
Davidson House, 42
Davis, Joseph, State Park, 177, 179
Deep South Taco, 65, 71, 105
Deerwood Golf Course, 189
DeFlippo's, 210–211
The Delavan, 120
Delaware Park, 37, 54, 57
Delta Bingo Center, 221
Depew, 15. *See also* Lancaster, Depew, and
    Cheektowaga
Depew, Chauncey, 117
Derby, 125. *See also* Lake Erie Towns
De Veaux Woods State Park, 162
Devil's Hole State Park, 162, 177
DiCamillo Bakery, 168, 181–182
Dick and Jenny's Bake and Brew, 93
Dinosaur Bar-B-Que, 65–66
Discover Niagara Shuttle, 158
Dockside Bar and Grill, 191
Doc Magilligan's, 238–239
Dog Bar, 152
Dog Ears Bookstore and Café, 82
Dolci Bakery, 80
Dombrowski, Joel, 54
Donnelly's Pub, 266
Donut Kraze, 93
Dorschmier, William, 157
Dory Trading Post, 184, *185*
Dos Amigos, 146
Double Deck Tours, 231
Doubletree Club, 60
Douglass, Frederick, 43
The Dove, 137
Downtown Buffalo Country Market, 79
Dufferin Island Nature Area, 233
Duffs, 21, 104, *105*, 138
Dunkirk Lighthouse, 276
Dyngus Day Celebrations, 38, 82
Dy's Country Kitchen, 131

E
Eagle House, 103
Eagle Valley Golf Club, 229
East Amherst, 96
    eating in, 101–102, 104

East Aurora Cooperative Market, 132
East Aurora Flea Market, 132
East Eden Tavern & Smokehouse, 146
Eastern Hills Mall, 107
Eastern Pearl, 103
Eating
    in Amherst, 101–106
    in Aurora, 130–131
    in Buffalo, 62–75
    in Canal Towns, 210–212, 211
    in Clarence and Akron, 114, 114–115
    in Fort Erie, 223–224, 224
    in Grand Island, Tonawanda and Kenmore,
        93–95
    in Lake Erie Towns, 144–147, 145, 146
    in Lake Ontario Shore, 201, 201–202
    in Niagara Falls, New York, 166–168, 167
    in Niagara Falls, Ontario, 237–239, 238
    in Niagara-on-the-Lake and Queenston,
        251–253, 253
    in North of the Falls, 180–183, 181, 182, 183
    in North Tonawanda and Wheatfield,
        190–192
    in Orchard Park and West Seneca, 137–139,
        138
    in Port Colborne, 266–267
    in St. Catharines/Port Dalhousie, 266
    in ski country, 152, 152
    in Thorold, 266
    in Welland, 267
    in Welland Canal Corridor, 266–267
Ebenezer Ale House, 138–139
Eberhardt, Louis Phillip Adolph, 88
Echoes Through Time Civil War Museum and
    Learning Center, 150
Eden, 141. See also Lake Erie Towns
    corn fest in, 148
Eden Valley Golf Course, 143
Edward M. Cotter (fireboat), 43, 43
Eggertsville, 96
Eighteen Mile Creek, 141, 199
18 Mile Creek Golf Course, 143
800 Maple, 102
El Buen Amigo, 78
El Canelo, 146
El Cubilete, 167
"Electric Building," 44
Elements on the Falls Restaurant, 237
"Elevator Alley," 34
Elevator Alley Kayak, 50
Ellicott, Benjamin, 96
Ellicott, Joseph, 34, 44, 96, 110
Ellicott Creek, 96, 117
Ellicott Creek Bike Path, 100
Ellicott Creek Park, 91
Ellicott Square Building, 44
Ellicottville, 28, 278
Elma, 126
Elma Historical Museum, 127
Elma Meadows, 128, 129
Elm Street Bakery, 131
El Museo Francisco Oller y Diego Rivera, 78
Elmwood Avenue Festival of the Arts, 83–84

Elmwood Village, 36
Elmwood Village Farmers' Market, 79
Embassy Suites, 60, 235
Emergencies, 16
Emery, Josiah, 129
Emery Park, 129
Empire pass, 22
Enchanted Mountains, 278
Encore, 62
End of the Road Boutique, 184–185
English Arts and Crafts movement, 128
Entertainment
    in Amherst, 106
    in Aurora, 131
    in Buffalo, 76–77
    in Canal Towns, 212
    in Niagara Falls, New York, 168
    in Niagara Falls, Ontario, 240
    in Niagara-on-the-Lake and Queenston,
        253–254, 254
    in North of the Falls, 183–184
    in North Tonawanda and Wheatfield, 192
    in Orchard Park and West Seneca, 139
    in Port Colborne, 267
    in Welland Canal Corridor, 267
Erie Basin Marina, 50, 55–56, 59
Erie Canal, 23, 27, 27, 34, 88, 96, 274
Erie Canal Discovery Center, 204–205
Erie Canal Heritage Center, 206
Erie Community College City Campus, 45
Erie County Fair, 19, 19, 141, 148
Erie County Forest, 151
Erie County Medical Center, 40
Erie Indians, 141
Escabeche, 252
Eshelman, John, 110
Ess Kay Farm, 129
Eternal Flame Falls, 136
Evangola, 22
Eveningside Vineyards, 207
Everheart Country Manor Bed & Breakfast, 251
Everything Elmwood, 81
Exchange Brewery, 247, 247
Explore Buffalo, 54
Explore & More Children's Museum, 128
Expo Food Market, 66
Expressions Floral & Gift Shoppe, 148

F
Fables Café, 66
Fairgrounds Festival of Lights, 148
Fairgrounds Gaming & Raceway, 143
Falkner Park, 178
Falletta's, 101
Fall foliage, 28
Fallingwater, 23
Falls Incline Railway, 228, 228
Falls Manor Resort, 239
Fallsview Casino Resort, 235, 240
Fallsview Indoor Waterpark & Hotel Complex,
    228
Falls Wedding Chapel, 162, 165
Family Chocolate Shoppe, 116

Family fun. *See* Activities
Family Tree, 104
Fantasy Island, 25, 89–90, *90*
Farm markets, 20
  in Amherst, 107
  in Aurora, 132
  in Buffalo, 78–79
  in Canal Towns, 213
  in Clarence and Akron, 115
  in Lake Erie Towns, 147, *147*
  in Lake Ontario Shore, 202, *202*
  in Niagara-on-the-Lake and Queenston, 255
  in North of the Falls, 184
  in North Tonawanda and Wheatfield, 193–194
  in Orchard Park and West Seneca, 139
Fashion Outlets of Niagara Falls, 168
Fat Bob's Smokehouse, 69
Fellheimer, Alfred, 44
Fens, 25
Fern & Arrow, 81
Festival of Lights, 186
Festival Theatre, 254
Fieldstone Country Inn, 211
Figg Street Company, 267
Filling Station, 67
Fillmore, Millard, 125, 126
  house museum of, 127, *127*
Firemen's Memorial Exhibit Center, 135
First Buffalo River Marina, 56
First Night Buffalo, 84
First Presbyterian Church, 206
Fisherman's Park, 189
Fisher-Price Toys, 126, 132
Fish fry, 20
Fishing, 26–27
  in Buffalo, 53
  in Canal Towns, 209
  in Niagara and Erie Counties, 199
  in Niagara Falls, Ontario, 229
  in North of the Falls, 177
  in North Tonawanda and Wheatfield, 189
Five Points Bakery and Toast Café, 74
The Flavor Factory, 191
Flight of Five Winery, 207
Floral Clock, 234, *234*
Floral Showhouse, 234
Flour Mill Restaurant, 239
Fly Buffalo Aerial Photo Tours, 54
Flying Bison Brewery, 52
Flying Squirrel Coffee Lounge, 223
Forest Lawn Cemetery & Garden Mausoleums, 56
Forever Young magazine, 30
Forgotten Buffalo Tours, 54
Fort Erie, 25, 28, 29, 218–225
  activities in, 220–222
  beaches in, 221
  boating in, 220–221
  breweries in, 220
  eating in, 223–224, *224*
  gaming in, 221

getting there and getting around in, 218–219
  golf in, 221
  green space in, 221–222
  horse racing in, 221
  lighthouses in, 220
  lodging in, 223
  medical care in, 219
  museums in, 219–220, *220*
  parks in, 222
  scenic drives in, 221
  shopping in, 224–225
  sightseeing in, 219–220
  special events in, 225
Fort Erie Historical Museum, 219
Fort Erie LaFrance Association Museum, 219
Fort Erie Racetrack, 221
Fort Erie Railroad Museum, 219
Fort George, 28
Fort George National Historic Park, 243
Fort Mississauga Ruins, 243
Fort Niagara Light, 28
Fort Niagara State Park, 177, 178
Forts, 28
Fortunas Restaurant, 166
42 North Brewery, 127–128
Foundry Suites Hotel, 60–61
Four Brothers Cucina, 239
Four Honey Bees Cottage, 132
Four Mile Creek State Campgrounds, 178, 180
Four Points Sheraton Hotel-Niagara Falls, 165
4th of July Fireworks, 109
Fran-Ceil Custard, 146
Frankie Primo's +39, 66
Frankie's Donuts and Pizza, 167, *167*
Franks Sunny Italy, 71
Fredonia Opera House, 276
Freedom Crossing Monument, *174*, 175
Freedom Run, 207
French and Indian War, 185, 218
French Castle, 13
Fresh Floral & Gift Company, 153
Frey's Tasty Treat, 211, *211*
Friendship Cove, 228
Friendship Festival, 82, 225
Friendship Trail, 222
Friendship Trail Bed & Breakfast, 223
Frontier Fur Traders Weekend, 186
Frontier House, 175
Front Park, 58

G
Gabriel's Gate, 69
Gahlen's, 22
Gallagher Beach, 36, 58
Gallo Coal Fire Kitchen, 182
Garden Place Hotel, 120
Gardens, 22
  in Buffalo, 56
  in Niagara Falls, Ontario, 233–234
Garden Walk, 83
Garlock's, 211
Garrison Park, 99

Gasport, 204. *See also* Canal Towns
Gates Vascular Institute, 35, 40
Gateway Harbor Park, 91, *92*, 190
Gatur's Fast and Tasty, 69
Genesee County, *272*, 272–273, *273*
Genesee River, 28, 34, 280
George's Hot Dogs, 152
Gertie's, 114, *114*
Getzville, 96
   eating in, 102, 104–105
Ghost Tours, 257
Giacobbi's Cucina Citta, 68
The Giacomo, 165
Giancarlo's Sicilian Steakhouse and Pizzeria,
   103
Glam Girl, 268
Gleam and Glimmer Glass, 193
Glen Falls, 25, 96, *99*, 100
Glen Oak Golf Course, 98
Glen Park, 99
Glen Park Tavern, 105
Globe Market, 80, 81
Goat Island, 161, 163
Golden Hill State Park, 28, 199–200
Golden Nugget Bingo, 221
Golden Park Program, 22
Golf, 27
   in Amherst, 98
   in Aurora, 128
   in Buffalo, 53–54
   in Canal Towns, 209
   in Clarence and Akron, 112–113
   in Fort Erie, 221
   in Grand Island, Tonawanda and Kenmore,
     90–91
   in Lake Erie Towns, 143
   in Lake Ontario Shore, 199
   in Niagara Falls, New York, 161
   in Niagara Falls, Ontario, 229–231
   in Niagara-on-the-Lake and Queenston, 244
   in North of the Falls, 177
   in North Tonawanda and Wheatfield, 189
   in Orchard Park and West Seneca, 136
   in ski country, 151
Goodrich Coffee and Tea, 114
Gordie Harper's Bazaar, *201*, 201–202, 203
Gothic City, 78
Goundry Street in North Tonawanda, 188
Grain Elevators on Buffalo River, *55*
Gramma Mora's, 71–72, *72*
Grand Island, Tonawanda and Kenmore,
   88–95, 91, 158
   activities in, 89–92, *90*
   eating in, 93–95
   family fun in, 90
   getting there, 89
   golf in, 90–91
   green space in, 91–92
   lodging in, 93
   marinas in, 91
   medical care in, 89
   nature preserves in, 91
   parks in, 91–92

shopping in, 95
   sightseeing in, 89
   special events in, 95
Grand Island Historical Society, 89
Grand Lady, 26, 50
Grand Victorian Bed & Breakfast, 251
Grandview Golf Course and Beachside Bar &
   Grill, 143
Grange Community Kitchen, 146, *146*
Grants Gifts, 268
Grapevine, 101
Grape & Wine Tours, 244
Gratwick-Riverside Park, 189, 190
Graycliff, 125, 141, *142*, 142–143
Graycliff Derby, 21–22
Gray Line of Niagara Falls, 161
Great Baehre Swamp Conservation Area/Billy
   Wilson Park, 98
Greater Niagara Circle Route, 264
Great Lakes Seaway Trail, 23–24, 178
Great Lakes Station, 139
Great Pumpkin Farm, 112
Great Wolf Lodge, 236
Greaves, 255
Green, Edward B., 40, 61
Green Acres Family Restaurant, 223
Green Lake, 136
Green spaces
   in Amherst, 98–100
   in Aurora, 128–129
   in Buffalo, 56–59
   in Canal Towns, 209–210
   in Clarence and Akron, 113
   in Fort Erie, 221–222
   in Grand Island, Tonawanda and Kenmore,
     91–92
   in Lake Erie Towns, 143–144, *144*
   in Lake Ontario Shore, 199–200
   in Niagara Falls, New York, 162–163
   in Niagara Falls, Ontario, 233–235, *234*
   in Niagara-on-the-Lake and Queenston,
     247–248
   in North of the Falls, 178–180, *179*
   in North Tonawanda and Wheatfield,
     189–190
   in Orchard Park and West Seneca, 136, *136*,
     137
   in Port Colborne, 265
   in St. Catharines/Port Dalhousie, 264–265
   in ski country, 151
   in Welland, 264–265
Greenwood Golf Course, 113
Greg's U-Pick, 115
Greyhound Lines, 39, 218
Greystone, 62
Griffon House, 181
Griffon Pub, 167
The Grill at the Epicurean, 253
Grimble's Hardware Store, 213
Grindhaus Café, 69
Grover's Bar & Grill, 104
Guggenheim Museum, 23
Gulf Wilderness Park, 209

Gunderlach, Jeffrey, 40
A Gust of Sun Winery, 176
Gypsy Parlor, 74

H
Halloween Parade, 140
Hallwalls Contemporary Arts Center, 18, 41
Hamburg, 125, 141. *See also* Lake Erie Towns
    fairgrounds in, 141
    farmers' market in, 147, *147*
Hamburg Brewing, 142
Hamburg Natural History Society, 144
Hamlin Park, 129
Hampton Inns, 61, 100–101, 129, 137, 165
Handicapped accessible, 16
Hanover House Bed & Breakfast, 162, 165
Happy Jack's, 223
Harborcenter, 35
Harbour House Hotel, 248–249
Harmony on West, 268
Harris Hill, 110
The Hatch, 67
The Haunted Fortress, 186
Hawk Creek Wildlife Rehabilitation Center,
    128–129
Hayes Seafood House, 114
Head Over Heels in Love with Shoes, 132
Healthy Scratch, 67
Healthy Zone Rink, 128
Heath, William R., House, 42
Helicopter Rides by Rainbow Air, 162
Hennepin, Louis, 157
Hennepin Park, 178, *179, 180*
Heritage Site Guide Panels, 262
Heritage Thorold, 262
Heritage Walking Tours, 231
Heritage Woods Golf Course, 244
Herschell, Allan, 188
Herschell Carrousel Factory Museum, 187–188,
    188
Her Story Boutique, 81
Hibbard's Custard, 182
Hideaway Grille, 191
Hilltop Country Antiques Co-op and Gift
    Emporium, 184
Hilton Garden Inn, 61
Hilton Niagara Falls, 235
Hip Gypsy, 193–194, *194*
Historical Society of the Tonawandas, 89
Historic Buffalo River Tours of Industrial
    Heritage Committee, Inc., 54
Historic Fort Erie, 219, *220*
Historic Lewiston Christmas Walk, 186
Historic sites. *See* Sightseeing
Hitchcock, Alexander, 117
Hitchcock, Appollos, 117
Hoak's, 146
Hob Nob Restaurant, 252
Holiday Valley, 28
Holland, 149. *See also* Ski country
Holland Hills Golf Course, 151
Holland International Speedway, 151
Holland Land Company, 96, 110, 204

Holland Land Office Museum, 272, *272*
Holland Land Purchase, 17, 34
Holland Land Survey, 119
Holland Tulip Festival, 153
Holley, 274
Hollow Bistro and Brew, 114
Homegrown Bistro, 137, *138*
Homewear, 153
The Honey Bee Store, 268
Honeymoon Capital Souvenirs, 168
Honeymoon Trail Winery, 207
Hoover Dairy Restaurant, 182
Hornblower Niagara Cruises, 26, 227–228
Horse racing
    in Fort Erie, 221
    in Lake Erie Towns, 143
Horseshoe Falls, 157
Horton, Tim, 20
Hotel at the Lafayette, 61
Hotel Dallavalle, 250
Hotel Henry Urban Resort Conference Center, 61
Hotels. *See* Lodging
Hubbard, Elbert, 126, 128
Hubbard, Elbert, Museum, 126–127
Hudson River, 27
Hull, Polly, 118
Hull, Warren, 118
Hull House, 118, *118*
Humbrodt Park, 58
Hunting, 27
Hutch's, 62
Hyatt Place Buffalo Amherst, 101
Hyatt Regency, 61
Hyde Park, 163
    golf course at, 161
Hydraulic Hearth, 63

I
Ice at Canalside, 55, *56*
Ice House Winery, 245
Ilio DiPaolo's, 145
India Gate, 69
Indian Falls, 25
Inn at Lock 7, 265–266
Inn Buffalo, *16*, 59
Inniskillin Winery, 245
Inter-Campus Bikeway, 100
Ippolito, Orazio, 114
Irish Classical Theater, 76
Irish Design, 255
The Irish Harp Pub, 253
The Irishman Pub and Eatery, 103
Iron Island Museum, 48–49
Iron Kettle Restaurant, 131
Iroquois Nations, 16
Island Fun Center, 90
Island Park, 99
Isle View Park, 91–92
Italian Heritage Festival, 82–83

J
Jackson-Triggs Niagara Estate Winery, 245
Jacobs, Joseph, 174

Jamestown, 276
Jamestown Audubon Nature Center, 276
Janie's Emporium, 95
Jay the Pie Guy Café and Bakery, 266
Jell-O Museum, 272
Jerk's Ice Cream, 66
Jim's Steak Out, 69
JJ's Casa di Pizza, 66
J & M Antiques, 106
J & M's West End Inn, 146
Joe's Deli, 72
John and Mary's, 20
Johnny Appleseed Fest, 214
Johnston's Family Restaurant, 182
Jolls, Willard, 135
Jonny C's New York Deli, 104
Journey Behind the Falls, 231
JP Dwyer's Irish Pub, 191
JP Fitzgerald's, 146
Judi's Lounge Bar & Grill, 167
Juneteenth Festival, 82
Just Christmas, 255, *256*
Just Fries, 66
Just Fun Family Entertainment Center, 143

K
The Karma Kameleon Gastro Pub, 266
Karpeles Manuscript Library Museum, 48
Kavinoky Theatre, 76
Keefer Mansion, 265
Keeley, Patrick, 45
Keg Creek Rest Area, 200
Kelkenberg Farm, 112
Kelly's Country Store, 95
Kenan Center, 18, 205, *205*, 212
Kenmore, 88
Kennedy's, 255
Kennedy's Cove, 114
Kent, Alexander, 188
Kent Place, 188
King, Martin Luther, Jr., Park, 58
King Condrells, 95
Kings Bridge Park, 234
Kissel Country Tin, 194
Kissing Bridge, 28, 151
Kissing Rock, 264, *264*
The Kitchen, 223–224, *224*
*Kleinhans Music Hall, 45, 76
*Kleinhan's Music Hall, 38
Knox, Seymour H., Jr., 40
Knox Farm State Park, 129
KOA Kamping Kabins and Kampsites, 93
Ko-Ed Candies, 82
Kone King, 139
Konzelmann Estate Winery, 245, *245*
Kostas Restaurant, 72
Krull Park, 199, 200, *200*
Kuni's, 69
Kurtz Orchards Country Market, 255

L
Labatt Blue beer, 36
Labor Day Car Show, 203

La Cascata, 166
Lackawanna, 38, 39
Lady of Victory Basilica, 28
Lagerhaus 95, 66
Lailey Vineyard, 246
Lait Cru Brasserie, 74
Lake, Darien, Theme Park Resort, 25
Lake Effect Diner, 73
Lake Effect Ice Cream, 211
Lake-effect snow, 17
Lake Erie, 17, 24, 33, 34
Lake Erie towns, 141–148
    activities in, 143
    antiques in, 147
    art museums in, 141
    beaches in, 143–144, *144*
    breweries and wineries in, 142
    eating in, 144–147, *145, 146*
    farm markets in, 147, *147*
    getting there, 141
    golf in, 143
    green space in, 143–144, *144*
    horse racing in, 143
    lodging in, 144
    medical care in, 141
    museums and historic homes in, 142–143
    parks in, 144
    shopping in, 147–148
    sightseeing in, 141–143
    special events in, 148
Lake Kirsty, 53, 57
Lake Ontario, 24, 171, 274
Lake Ontario Counties (LOC) Fishing Derbies,
    199
Lake Ontario Motel, 201
Lake Ontario Shore, 195–203
    beaches in, 199
    boating in, 199
    breweries and wineries in, 197–198
    eating in, *201*, 201–202
    family fun in, 199
    farm markets in, 202, *202*
    getting there, 196
    golf in, 199
    green space in, 199–200
    lighthouses in, 197, *197*
    lodging in, 201
    medical care in, 196
    museums and historic homes in, 196–197
    parks in, 199–200
    shopping in, *201*, 201–203, *203*
    sightseeing in, *196*, 196–198, *197, 198*
    special events in, 203
Lakeshore Antique & Treasures, 254
Lakeside Books and Art, 225
Lakeside Park, 264
Lakeview Village Fair, 203
Lakeward Spirits Craft Distillery, 52
Lancaster, Depew, and Cheektowaga, 117–122
    activities in, 118
    auto racing in, 118
    eating in, 120–121, *121*
    entertainment in, 121–122, *122*

Lancaster, Depew, and Cheektowaga (*continued*)
    family fun in, 118
    getting there and getting around in, 117, 118
    golf in, 118
    green space in, 119, *119*
    lodging in, 120
    medical care in, 118
    museums and historic homes in, 118
    nature preserves in, 119
    parks in, 119
    shopping in, 122
    sightseeing in, 118, *118*
    special events in, 122
    theaters in, 121–122, *122*
Lancaster Historical Museum, 118
Lancaster International Speedway, 118
Lancaster Opera House, 121, *122*
La Nova Pizzeria, 21, 75, 105
Larkin Soap Company, 36
Larkin Square, 36
Larkinville, 36, *37*
La Salle, Robert, 157
LaSalle Cab, 158
LaSalle Park, 59
LaserTron, 98
Lasting Impressions, 225
La Tavola Trattoria, 72
Lebros, 102, *102*
Left Bank, 64
Legends Grill, 167
Legends of the Niagara Golf Complex, 230
Lehigh Valley Railroad Path, 100
Lenox Grill, 66
LeRoy, 272
Letchworth State Park, 28, 275, *276*
Lewiston, 29. *See also* North of the Falls
Lewiston Branch Gorge Trail, 179
Lewiston Council on the Arts, 172
Lewiston Historical Museum, 173, *174*
Lewiston Jazz Festival, 185
Lewiston Landing Waterfront Park, *174*, 177, 179
Lewiston Outdoor Fine Arts Festival and
    Chalkwalk Competition, 185
Lewiston Portage Landing Site, 175
Lewiston River Walk, 180
Lewiston Silo, 182, *182*
The Lewiston Stone House, 183
Lewiston Stone Quarry, 175
Lexingtron Co-op Market, 81
Liberty Hound, 67
Lighthouse Cottage, 201
Lighthouses, 28
    in Buffalo, *49*, 49–50
    in Fort Erie, 220
    in Lake Ontario Shore, 197, *197*
    in North of the Falls, 176
Light Rail Rapid Transit System, 40
Lincoln Park, 92
Lincoln Parkway, 38
Ling Ling, 93
Links at Ivy Ridge, 113
The Links of Niagara at Willodell, 230
Linwood Historic Preservation District, 59–60

Lions Sugar Bowl Park, 222
"Little Italy," 37
Little Red School House, 118
Liv, 252
Live Edge Brewing Company, 198
Living Waters Wayside Chapel, 243, *243*
Lloyd's Churn, 72
Lloyd's Taco Factory, 72, 105
Local lingo, 16
Lock 8 Gateway, Port Colborne, 265, *265*
Lockhouse Distillery, 52
Lock & Main Marketplace, 267
Lockport, 204, 210, 212. *See also* Canal Towns
Lockport Cave and Underground Boat Ride,
    26, 208
Lockport Inn & Suites, 210
Lockport Locks & Erie Canal Cruises, 26, 208
Lock Street Brewing, 264
Lock 7 Viewing Complex, 264
Lockwood, Belva, 204
Lodging
    in Amherst, 100–101
    in Aurora, 129
    in Buffalo, 59–61
    in Canal Towns, 210
    in Clarence and Akron, 113, *113*
    in Fort Erie, 223
    in Grand Island, Tonawanda and Kenmore,
        93
    in Lake Erie Towns, 144
    in Lake Ontario Shore, 201
    in Niagara Falls, New York, 164–166.*164*
    in Niagara Falls, Ontario, 235–237
    in Niagara-on-the-Lake and Queenston,
        248–251
    in North of the Falls, 180
    in Orchard Park and West Seneca, 137
    in Port Colborne, 266
    rates for, 16
    in ski country, 152
    in Thorold, 265–266
    in Welland Canal Corridor, 265–266
Long, Benjamin, 89
Long, Mary, 89
Long Cliff Winery, 176
Long Homestead, 89
Lotus Gardens, 266
Lou's Restaurant, 191
Lower Niagara River, 177
LT's Olde Time Pizza and Subs, 139
Lucia's on the Lake, 145
Lucy-Desi Museum, 276
Lulu Belle's, 153

M
Mackenzie Heritage Printery Museum, 242
Macs on Hertel, 72
Macy Casino, 64
Made in America Store, 133
Magruders, 121
Mahony, Brian, 62
The Mahony, 62
Maid of the Mist, 26, *26*, 159, *160*, 163

Main Street Pizzeria Gas and Grill, 182
Mammoser's Tavern & Restaurant, 146
Mangia Restaurant & Caffé, 137
Mansion on Delaware Avenue, 59, 60
Maple Leaf Fudge, 256
Maple sugaring, 20
Maple Weekend, 20
The Marble Orchard, 183–184, 186
Marble & Rye, 25–26, 62
Marco, Don, Italian Eatery, 267
Marco's Italian Deli, 73
Mardee's, 114–115
Mardi Gras Festival, 82
Maria's Downtown, 224
Marienthal Country Inn, 144
Marilla, 126
    country store in, 132–133, *133*
    general store in, 126
Marilla Historical Museum, 127
Marineland, 25, 26, 228
Mariner's Landing, 201
Marjim Manor, 198
Mark, Mitchell, 44
Marketside Café, 167
Marriott Fallsview, 236
Martin, Darwin D., 42, 142–143
    house of, 21, 38, 42, *42*
Martinville Soapworks, 194
Mason's Grille, 146
Mather Arch, 222, *222*
Matteo's, 267
Maxwell, Jackie, Studio Theatre, 254
McClurg Museum, 276
McDuffies Bakery, 131
McDuffie's Bakery, 115
McFarland, John, 242
McFarland House, 242
McKinley, William, 24, 34
    assassination of, 43
McKinley Mall, 147–148
McPartlan's Corner, 105–106
Medina, 274
Meibohm Fine Arts, 131–132
Melting Point, 69
Memorial Clock Tower, 243
Mercy Ambulatory Care Center, 135
Merge, 69
Merritt, William Hamilton, 258
Merritt Park, 265
Mes Que, 72–73
Mess Hall, 75
Mewinzha: A Journey Back in Time/The
    Bridge that Peace Built, 219–220
Mezza, 69
Michael's Italian Restaurant, 167
Michele's Motif Boutique and Gift Shop, 194
Michigan Avenue Baptist Church, 42
Michigan Street Baptist Church, 29, 43
Mick & Angelo's, 239
Middleport, 204. *See also* Canal Towns
Midnight Run Winery, 177
Midtown Kitchen mou, 70
Milestones on the Falls, 237

Millennium Airport Hotel, 120
Mills, Williams, 96
Milos, 103
Ming Teh, 223
Miss Buffalo, 54
Miss Buffalo II, 50
Mississauga, 218
Mississippi Mudds, 94, *94*
Modern Nostalgia, 80
Moffatt Inn, 249, *249*
Monarch, 108
Mondays, 17
Moondance Catamaran, 50
Mooney's Sports Bar & Grill, 94
Moor Pat, 98
Morgulis, Michael, Studio-Local Color Gallery,
    78
Morris, William, 128
Motherland Connexions, 29, 55, 162
Mother's, 70
Mount Carmel Gift Shop, 240
Mug & Musket Tavern, 182
Mulberry Italian Ristorante, 75, *75*, 101
The Mulberry Tree, 95
Muleskinner Antiques, 106–107
Murder Creek, 113
Murphy Orchards, 29, 202, *202*
Muscoreil's Bakery, 194
Muse Jar, 133
Muse Restaurant, 40
Museum of Disability History, 97
Museum of Native American Art, 185
Museums and historic sites, 21–22, 219–220,
    220
    in Amherst, 97
    in Aurora, 126–127, *127*
    in Buffalo, 42, *42*, 46–49
    in Canal Towns, 206
    in Clarence and Akron, *111*, 111–112
    in Fort Erie, 219–220, *220*
    in Lake Erie Towns, 142–143
    in Lake Ontario Shore, 196–197
    in Niagara Falls, New York, 158–159, *159*
    in Niagara Falls, Ontario, 227
    in Niagara-on-the-Lake and Queenston,
        242–243
    in North of the Falls, 173–174
    North Tonawanda and Wheatfield, 187–188
    Orchard Park and West Seneca, 135–136
    in St. Catharines/Port Dalhousie, 262
    in ski country, 149–150
    in Welland Canal Corridor, 263
MusicalFare Theatre Company, 106
Music Amherst Symphony, 106
Mythos, 70

N
NAACP, 21, 35
Nash, J. Edward, 42
Nash House Museum, 42
National Buffalo Wing Festival, 83, *83*, 84
National Helicopters, 232
National Historic Landmark Richardson, 61

National historic landmarks, 22
National Register of Historic Places, 22, 25
National Scenic Byway, 24
Native American culture, 16–17
Native American Museum of Art, 173–174
Nature, 22–25
Nature preserves, 22
   in Aurora, 128–129
   in Buffalo, 56–57
   in Canal Towns, 209
   in Fort Erie, 222
   in Grand Island, Tonawanda and Kenmore,
     91
   in Lake Erie Towns, 144
   in Niagara Falls, Ontario, 233
   in Orchard Park and West Seneca, 136, *136*
   in ski country, 151
Nelson Goehle Marina, 209
Neo Gift Studio, 81
Neumann, John, 110
New Era Cap, 79
New Era Stadium, 135
Newfane. *See* Lake Ontario Shore
Newfane Historical Society Grounds, 196
Newfane Pro-Am Par 3, 199
Newfane Town Hall/Newfane Tourism,
   195–196
New Moon Café, 73
New Phoenix Theatre, 76
Newstead, 110
New York Beer Project, 207
New York Central & Hudson River Railroad,
   117
New York Central Railroad, 117
New York International Style, 108
New York Power Authority's Wildlife Festival,
   185
New York State Canal System, 27
New York State Parks, 22
Niagara Aerospace Museum, 21, *21*, 158–159,
   159
Niagara Apothecary Museum, 242–243
Niagara Arts and Cultural Center, 18, 158
Niagara Brewing Company, 228
Niagara Climbing Center, 188–189
Niagara College Teaching Brewery, 247
Niagara County, *170*, 171–214
Niagara County Camping Resort, 210
Niagara County Fair, 214
Niagara County Golf Course, 209
Niagara County Historical Society, 206
Niagara County Park, 209
Niagara County Peach Festival, 185
Niagara County Produce, 213
Niagara County Wine Trail, 20
Niagara Crossing Hotel & Spa, 180
Niagara Distillery, 52
Niagara Escarpment, 23, 25, 204
Niagara Falls, Canada, 226
Niagara Falls, New York, 13, 15, 23, 25, 34, *156*,
   157–168, 204
   activities in, 159–162, *160*
   art museums in, 158–159, *159*

boat excursions in, 159, *160*
casino gaming in, 159
eating in, 166–168, *167*
entertainment in, 168
family fun in, *160*, 160–161
getting there and getting around in,
   157–158
golf in, 161
green space in, 162–163
guided tours in, 161–162
lodging in, 164–166.*164*
medical care in, 158
museums and historic sites in, 158–159, *159*
nightly illumination of, 158
parks in, 162–163
shopping in, 168
sightseeing in, 158–159
special events in, 168
theaters in, 168
walking and hiking trails in, 163
wedding chapels in, 162, *163*
Niagara Falls, Ontario, 226–240
   activities in, 227–235, *228*, *230*, *231*, *232*
   architecture in, 227
   boating in, 227–228
   breweries in, 228
   eating in, 237–239, *238*
   entertainment in, 240
   fishing in, 229
   gaming in, 229
   gardens in, 233–234
   getting there and getting around in, 227
   golf in, 229–231
   green spaces in, 233–235, *234*
   guided tours in, 231
   lodging in, 235–237
   medical care in, 227
   museums and historic sites in, 227
   nature preserves in, 233
   nightly illumination of, 227
   parks in, 234
   shopping in, 240
   sightseeing in, 227, 232–233
   special events in, 240, *240*
   theaters in, 240
   wedding chapels in, 233
Niagara Falls Aviary: Birds of the Lost Kingdom, 229
Niagara Falls Blues Festival, 168
Niagara Falls Bus Terminal, 227
Niagara Falls City Market, 168
Niagara Falls Golf Club, 230
Niagara Falls History Museum, 227
Niagara Falls International Airport, 15, 157
Niagara Falls Marriott Fallsview, 235–236
Niagara Falls Memorial Medical Center, 158
Niagara Falls State Park, 157, 163
Niagara Falls Tourism, 226, 235, 237
Niagara Fallsview Casino Resort, *15*, 16, 229,
   231, *232*
Niagara Fallsview Weddings, 233
Niagara Falls Walking Tours, 162
Niagara Fishing Adventures, 229

Niagara Frontier Transportation Authority, 15, 39–40, 117
Niagara Fun Zone, 229
Niagara Glen Nature Area, 233, 235
Niagara Gorge, 160–161, 171
Niagara Gorge Hiking Trails, 163
Niagara Grape & Wine Festival, 257
Niagara Helicopters, 232
Niagara Historical Society, 22, 243
Niagara Home Bakery, 256
Niagara Icewine Festival, 256–257, *257*
Niagara Image Gallery, 255
Niagara Jet Adventures, 177
Niagara Landing Wine Cellars, 207
Niagara Mohawk Power Building, 44
Niagara Movement, 21, 35
Niagara Oast House Brewers, 247
Niagara-on-the-Lake and Queenston, 13, 20, 25, 232, 241–257
    activities in, 244
    antiques in, 254
    art galleries and museums in, 242, 255
    boat excursions in, 244
    breweries and wineries in, 244–247, *245, 246, 247*
    eating in, 251–253, *253*
    entertainment in, 253–254, *254*
    farm markets in, 255
    getting there, 241–242
    golf in, 244
    green space in, 247–248
    guided tours in, 244
    lodging in, 248–251
    medical care in, 242
    museums and historic homes in, 242–243
    parks in, 247–248
    shopping in, 254–256
    sightseeing in, 242, 242–243, *243*
    special events in, 256–257
    theaters in, 253–254
Niagara-on-the-Lake Trolley Wine Country Tours, 244
Niagara Orleans Golf Club, 209
Niagara Parks Botanical Gardens, 22, 233
Niagara Parks Commission Marina, 220–221
Niagara Parks WEGO buses, 227
Niagara Parkway, 13, 25, 232
Niagara Pirate Festival, 203
NiagaraPumphouseVisualArtsCenter, 242
Niagara Regional Park Interpretive Programs, 164
Niagara Reservation State Park, 25
Niagara River, 24, 29, 34, 59, 218
Niagara River Parkway, 221
Niagara River Recreational Trail, 222, 235
Niagara River Walk and Bicycle Trail, 92, 190
Niagara's Finest Thai, 252
Niagara Square, *33*
Niagara Sunset Cruises, 244
Niagara's Welland Canal, 258
Niagara Teaching College Winery, 246
Niagara Wax Museum of History, 159
Niagara Weddings Canada, 233

Niagara Weddings USA, 162
Niagara Wine Tours International, 244
Niagara Wine Trail, 171, 207
Niagara Zipper, 209
Niawanda Park, 92
Nick Charlap's, 152, *152*
Nickel City Cheese & Mercantile, 74
Nightly Illumination of the Falls, 227
Nina Freudenheim Gallery, 78
Nina's Custard, 105
Noah's Ark Books and Toys, 213
North Collins. *See* Lake Erie Towns
Northern Erie County, *86,* 87–122
North Forest Park and Pool, 100
North of the Falls, 172–186
    activities in, 177–180, *178*
    antiques in, 184
    art museums in, 173, *173*
    auto racing in, 177
    boating and sailing in, 177
    breweries and wineries in, 176–177
    eating in, 180–183, *181, 182, 183*
    entertainment in, 183–184
    farm markets in, 184
    fishing in, 177
    getting there, 172
    golf in, 177
    green spaces in, 178–180, *179*
    historic sites in, 175
    lighthouses in, 176
    lodging in, 180
    medical care in, 172–173
    museums and historical sites in, 173–174
    parks in, 178–179
    scenic drives in, 178
    shopping in, 184–185, *185*
    sightseeing in, *173,* 173–177, *174, 175, 176*
    special events in, 185–186
    theaters in, 183–184
North Park Florist, 80
North Tonawanda and Wheatfield, 88, 187–194
    activities in, 188–189, 190
    antiques in, 192–193
    architecture in, 188
    art galleries and museums in, 187, 193
    eating in, 190–192
    entertainment in, 192
    farm markets in, 193–194
    fishing in, 189
    getting there, 187
    golf in, 189
    green spaces in, 189–190
    medical care in, 187
    museums and historic homes in, 187–188
    parks in, 189–190
    shopping in, *192,* 192–194, *193, 194*
    sightseeing in, 187–188, *188*
    special events in, 194
North Tonawanda Botanical Gardens, 190
North Tonawanda City Market, 193
North Tonawanda History Museum, 188
Northtown Center, 98

Northtowns, 87
Nottingham Terrace, 38

O

Oakes Garden Theatre, 234
The Oakes Hotel, 236
Oak Hill Par 3 Golf Course, 230
Oaklands Golf Course, 230
Oak Orchard River, 274
Oak Run Golf Club, 209
Oakwood Golf Course, 98
Oasis Lakeside Pita, 266
Oban Inn, 249
The Oban Inn, 252
Occasions in Niagara, 233
Oh Canada Eh? Dinner Show, 240
Ohlson's Bakery & Café, 115
Oh Pour L'Amour du Chocolat, 108
Oil Springs Reservation, 17
Olcott, 195. See also Lake Ontario Shore
Olcott Beach, 22, 195, 199, 200, 200
Olcott Beach Carousel Park, 199, 199, 201
Olcott Lighthouse, 197
Old Bank Bistro & Piano Bar, 223
Old Bank House Bed & Breakfast, 251
Old County Hall, 45
Olde Angel Inn, 248
The Olde Angel Inn, 253
Old Editions Book Shop & Café, 78
Old Falls Street, 168
Old First Ward Brewing and Gene McCarthy's,
    52
Old Fort Erie, 28, 50
Old Fort Niagara, 28, 171, 175, 175
Old Fort Niagara Lighthouse, 176
Old Home Days, 99
Old Home Days Island Park, 109
Old Man River, 94, 94
Old Olcott Days, 203
The Old Orchard Inn, 130
Old Stone Inn Boutique Hotel, 236
Old Town Tours, 244
Oliver's, 64
Olmstead, Frederick Law, 13, 25, 33, 45, 57, 58,
    157, 163
Olmstead Parks, 57–58
Olmsted Crescent, 38
Onandaga Escarpment, 25
One-Eyed Jack's Smokehouse Grill, 211
100 Acres: The Kitchens at Hotel Henry, 64
100 American Craftsmen Festival, 213–214
189 Public House, 130
124 Hotel & Spa, 250
Ongiara Trail, 180
Onigahara, 241
Ontario House/"The Jug," 182
On the Front Café & Eatery, 266
Open Air Autobus Tours, 55
Oppenheim County Park, 163, 189
Orange Cat Coffee, 182
Orazio's Restaurant, 114
Orchard Park and West Seneca, 125, 135–140, 141
    activities in, 136

breweries in, 135
    eating in, 137–139, 138
    entertainment in, 139
    farm markets in, 139
    getting there, 135
    golf in, 136
    green space in, 136, 136, 137
    lodging in, 137
    medical care in, 135
    museums and historic sites, 135–136
    nature preserves in, 136, 136
    parks in, 136
    professional sports in, 139
    shopping in, 139
    sightseeing in, 135–136
    special events in, 139–140
    waterfalls in, 136
Orchard Park Farmers' & Artisan Market, 139
Orchard Park Historical Society, 135
Orchard Park Social Tap & Grille, 137–138
Orchard Park Symphony Orchestra, 139
Orchard View Bed & Breakfast, 237
Original American Kazoo Company, 141, 143
Original Pancake House, 106
Orleans County, 274, 274
Oscar's Bed & Breakfast, 59–60
Osteria 166, 66
Oswego Canal, 27
Our Lady of Fatima Shrine, 28–29, 171, 176,
    176
Our Lady of Victory National Shrine and
    Basilica, 38, 48, 48
Outdoors and family fun, 25–28
Outer Harbor, 36
Outlet Collection at Niagara, 256
Outwater Park, 209
Over the Falls Tours, Inc., 162
The Owl and the Pussycat, 256

P

Paddock Chevrolet Golf Dome, 91
Pairings Wine Bar, 106
Palace Theatre, 212
Panama Rocks, 276
Pan-American Exposition, 24, 34, 43
Pan American Grill and Brewery, 66
Panes Restaurant, 191
Panorama on 7, 63
Pano's, 70
Papaya, 62
Park Place Bed & Breakfast, 165–166
Park Place Restaurant, 202
Parks, 23. See also Activities
    in Amherst, 99
    in Aurora, 129
    in Canal Towns, 209–210
    in Clarence and Akron, 113
    in Fort Erie, 222
    in Grand Island, Tonawanda and Kenmore,
        91–92
    in Lake Erie Towns, 144
    in Lake Ontario Shore, 199–200
    in Niagara Falls, New York, 162–163

in Niagara Falls, Ontario, 234
in Niagara-on-the-Lake and Queenston, 247–248
in North of the Falls, 178–179
in North Tonawanda and Wheatfield, 189–190
in Orchard Park and West Seneca, 136
in St. Catharines/Port Dalhousie, 264
in ski country, 151
Parkside Candy, 73
Parkside District, 38
Parkside House Bed & Breakfast, 60
Parkside Meadow, 73
Patina 250, 62, *63*
Paula's Donuts, 94
Pautler's Drive-In, 104
Peace Bridge, 39, 50, 218, 220
    duty free shop at, 225
Peach Harvest Festival, 257
Peanut Line Trail, 113
Pearl Street Grill & Brewery, 66
Peek'n Peak, 28
*Peller Estates Winery Restaurant, 252
*Peller Estate Winery, 246
Pen Centre, 240
Penn Dixie Paleontological Site, 22, 144
The Perfect Gift, 116, *116*
Perry, Morton, 111
Perry's Ice Cream, 111
Picket Fence Gift Shop, 268–269
Pillar and Post, 249
Pillitteri Estates Winery, 246
Pizza Amore, 94
Pizza Plant, 67
The Place, 70
Platter's Chocolate Factory, 194, *194*
Plyer, Lee, 48
Point Abino Lighthouse, 220
Polar Bear Swim, 203
Polish Festival, 122
Polonia Trail, 55
Port Abino Lighthouse, 28
Port Colborne, 261
    eating in, 266–267
    entertainment in, 267
    green spaces in, 265
    lodging in, 266
    shopping in, 268–269
    sightseeing in, 263
    special events in, 269
Port Colborne Historical and Marine Museum Heritage Village, 263
Port Dalhousie, 258, 259–260
Porter. *See* North of the Falls
Porter Historical Society, 175
Port of Entry Square, 108
Port Weller, 259
The Post Office-Shannon Passero, 267–268, *268*
Power City Eatery, 167
Prairie Style buildings, 23
Premier Antique Center, 115
Premier Gourmet, 108

Preservation Buffalo Niagara/Buffalo Tours, 54
Preservation Coalition, 54
Prince of Wales Hotel, 249, *249*
Prospect Point, 163
Protocol, 103
Prudential Building (Guaranty Building), 45
The Public House, 73, 146
Pumpkin Fiesta, 214
Punkins Patch Antiques, 131

Q
Quaker Arts Festival, 135, 140
Quaker Arts Pavilion, 135
Quaker Days, 140
Quaker Meeting House, 135
Quakers, 135
Quality Hotel and Suites at the Falls, 165
Queen City Bike Ferry, 50, *51*
Queen City Roller Girls, 36
Queen's Landing, 249, *250*
Queen's Royal Park, 247–248, *248*
Queenston. *See* Niagara-on-the-Lake and Queenston
Queenston Golf Club, 244
Queenston Heights Park, 247
Queenston Heights Restaurant, 252, *253*
Queenston-Lewiston Bridge, 225
Queen Victoria Park, 234
Queen Victoria Place Restaurant, 237
The Quilt Farm, 153

R
Raclettes, 66
Radisson Hotels, 93, 236
Rail Barons Model Train Exhibit, 84
Railroad Museum of the Niagara Frontier, 188
Raimondi, Carmelo, 181
Rainbow Bridge, *232*
Rainbow House Bed & Breakfast, 166
    and Wedding Chapel, 162
Rainbow Rink, 189
Rainbow Skateland Family Fun Center, 209
Rainforest Café, 239
Ransom, Asa, 110
Ransom, Asa, House, 113, *113*, 114
Ransomville. *See* North of the Falls
Ransomville Antique Co-op, 184
Ransomville Historical Museum, 174
Ransomville Speedway, 177
Raphael's, 152
Rapids Theater, 168
Ravine Vineyards, 246, *246*
Rebstock, John, 218
Red Caboose, 195, *195*
Red Coach Inn, 164, *164*, 166
Reddy Bike Share, 39, *39*
Reid's Ice Cream, 211–212
Reid's on Elmwood, 94
Reif Estate Winery, 246–247
Reikart House, 101
Reinstein, Victor, 119

Reinstein Woods Nature Preserve, 22, 119, *119*
Religious sites, 28–29
Remington's of Niagara, 239
Remington Tavern & Seafood Exchange, 190
A Renaissance Woman Consignment Boutique, 225
Research & Design, 139, *140*
Reservoir State Park, 163, 179
Restaurants, 20–21. *See also* Eating
Resurgence Brewing Company, 52
Rich, Charles B., 112
Richardson, Henry Hobson, 13, 28, 33, 44, 45, 157
Rich-Twinn Octagon House, 112, *112*
Rick's on Main, 130
Ridgeway, 218, 219
Ridgeway, Ontario, *219*
Ridgeway Battlefield Site, 220
Ridgeway Summer Festival, 225
Rio Vista Golf Club, 221
Ripa's Restaurant, 120
Ristorante Lombardo, 64
River Art Gallery, 193
Riverbend Inn & Vineyards, 249–250
Riverbrink, 242
River Grill, 94
River Lea Farm House, 89, 91
River Oaks Marina, 91
Riverside Motel, 180
Riverside Park, 58
Riverstone Grill, 93
Riverview Estate Winery, 247
Riverwalk, 222
Riverwalk Bike Path, 59
Riverworks Brewery, 52
Riviera Theater and Performing Arts Center, 192, *192*
Rizotto Ristorante, 103
R & L Lounge, 75
Road Less Traveled Productions, 76
Robo Mart, 218
Rocco's Wood-fired Pizza, 106
Rock City Park, *279*
Rockwell Hall, 76–77
Rodney's, 146–147
Roesch, Charlie, 120
Rogers, Marilla, 126
Rolling Hills Golf Course, 151
Rolling Meadows Golf & Country Club, 231
Rome, Tony, Globe Hotel & Restaurant, 130
Romeo's & Juliet's Bakery Café, 73
Roosevelt, Theodore, 24, 34
Roosevelt, Theodore, Inaugural National Historic Site, 21, *24*, 43, 84
Roost, 74
Roswell Park Cancer Institute, 35, 60
Rotary Rink at Fountain Plaza, 55
Rothland Golf Course, 113
Route 104, 24–25
Royal George Theatre, 254, *255*
Royalton Ravine, 210
Roycroft Artisans Schoolhouse Gallery, 133
Roycroft Arts and Crafts Movement, 126, 128

Roycroft Campus Antiques, 131
Roycroft Copper Shop Gallery, 133
Roycroft Festivals, 134
Roycroft Inn, 129, *129*, 130
Ru Pierogi Restaurant, 74
Rural Niagara Transportation, 158
Rushford Lake, 280
Russell's Steaks, Chops and More, 103
Rusty Nickel Brewing, 135, 139
Ryan, Eddie, Restaurant, 120

S
Saarinen, Eero, 45
Saarinen, Eliel, 45
Safari Niagara, 221
Safe Harbor Marina, 53, 56
Saigon Bangkok, 93
Saigon Café, 63, *63*
St. Catharines/Port Dalhousie, 259, *261*
   activities in, 264
   eating in, 266
   green space in, 264–265
   museums in, 262
   parks in, 264
   sightseeing in, 258, 262, *262*
   walking and hiking trails in, 264
St. Francis Xavier Church, 47
St. Joseph Roman Catholic Cathedral, 45
St. Lawrence River, 24
St. Lawrence Seaway, 258
St. Louis Church, 45
St. Mary's Church Picnic, 110, 116, *116*
St. Mary's parish, 110
St. Patrick's Day Parade, 82
St. Paul's Episcopal Cathedral, 29, 45, 59
Salamanca, 278
Salvatore's Grand Hotel, 101
Salvatore's Italian Gardens, 120
Sanborn. *See* North of the Falls
Sanborn Historical Museum, 174
Sanborn-Lewiston Farm Museum, 174–175
The Sanborn Mill Antiques, 184
Sanborn Old General Store, 184
Sandoro, James T., 48
San Marco, 101
Santasieros, 74
Sarah's Vintage & Estate Jewelry, 108
Sato, 63–64
Sato Brewpub, 66–67
Sato Ramen, 73
Savor, 166
Scenic highways, 23–24
Scharf's German Restaurant, 138
Schmitzz & Gigglez Sweet Shop, 225
Schnitzel & Co., 101
Schoolhouse #8 History Center and Museum, 150
The School of Restoration Arts, 243
Schultz, Kelly, Antiques, 115
Schulze Vineyards and Winery, 198
Schwabl's Restaurant, 138
Schwab's Farm Market, 213
Schworm, Adam, 110

Scoops Ice Cream, 145
Scottish Festival, 109
Seabar, 63
Sean Patrick's, 102
Sear Steakhouse, 63
Seaton, Mary, Room, 76
Seaway Mall, 268
The Second Reader, 77–78
Secord, Laura, Homestead, 242
Secret Garden Restaurant, 239
Seneca Allegany Casino, 16
Seneca Buffalo Creek Casino, 16, 52
Seneca Indians, 88
Seneca Nation, 16
Seneca Niagara Casino, 15–16, 159
Seneca Niagara Hotel, 165
Sentineal Tours, 244
Serendipities, 269
Serendipity the Little French Shop, 256
700 Center Street Juice Bistro and Café, 181
Shagbark Trail, 222
Shakespeare in Delaware Park, 77
The Shamus, 211
Shango, 65
Shark Girl, 35, 36
Shaw Café & Wine Bar, 252
Shaw Club Hotel, 250
Shaw Festival, 248, 253–254
Shawnee Country Barns Antique, 192–193,
    193
Shawnee Country Club, 177
The Shawp, 255
Shea's Performing Arts Center, 77
Sheehan, Danny, Steak House, 210
Sheraton at the Falls, 165
Sheraton on the Falls, 228, 236
Sheridan Park Golf Course, 91
Shoppe on Main Street, 203, 203
Shopping, 29
    in Amherst, 106–109
    in Aurora, 131–134, 133
    in Buffalo, 77–82
    in Canal Towns, 212–213
    in Clarence and Akron, 115–116
    in Fort Erie, 224–225
    in Grand Island, Tonawanda and Kenmore,
        95
    in Lake Erie Towns, 147, 148
    in Lake Ontario Shore, 201, 201–202,
        202–203, 203
    in Niagara Falls, New York, 168
    in Niagara Falls, Ontario, 240
    in Niagara-on-the-Lake and Queenston,
        254–256
    in North of the Falls, 184–185, 185
    in North Tonawanda and Wheatfield, 192,
        192–194, 193, 194
    in Orchard Park and West Seneca, 139
    in Port Colborne, 268–269
    in ski country, 152–153, 153
    in Thorold, 267–268, 268
    in Welland, 268
    in Welland Canal Corridor, 267–269

The Shores Waterfront Restaurant, 191–192
Showboat Festival Theatre, 267
Shrinking mill, 263
Sightseeing
    in Amherst, 97
    in Angelica, 279
    in Aurora, 126–127, 127
    in Buffalo, 40–50, 41, 42, 43, 44, 46, 47, 48,
        49, 50
    in Canal Towns, 205, 205–208, 207
    in Clarence and Akron, 111, 111–112
    in Fort Erie, 219–220
    in Grand Island, Tonawanda and Kenmore,
        89
    in Lake Erie Towns, 141–143
    in Lake Ontario Shore, 196, 196–198, 197,
        198
    in Niagara Falls, New York, 158–159
    in Niagara Falls, Ontario, 227
    in Niagara-on-the-Lake and Queenston,
        242, 242–243, 243
    in North of the Falls, 173, 173–177, 174, 175,
        176
    in North Tonawanda and Wheatfield,
        187–188, 188
    in Orchard Park and West Seneca, 135–136
    in Port Colborne, 263
    in St. Catharines/Port Dalhousie, 262, 262
    in ski country, 149–150, 150
    in Thorold, 262, 263
    in Welland, 262, 263, 263
Sights to see, 28
Sight Tours, 231
Silo City, 46
Silversmith Brewing, 247
Simcoe Park, 248
Sinatra's, 93
Sinking Ponds Wildlife Sanctuary, 129
Six Mile Creek Marine, 91
16 Food and Sport, 67
Skating
    in Canal Towns, 209
    in North Tonawanda and Wheatfield, 189
Ski country, 149–153
    activities in, 151, 151
    art center in, 151
    auto racing in, 151
    eating in, 152, 152
    getting there, 149
    golf in, 151
    green space in, 151
    lodging in, 152
    medical care in, 149
    museums in, 149–150
    natural preserves in, 151
    parks in, 151
    scenic drives in, 150
    shopping in, 152–153, 153
    sightseeing in, 149–150, 150
    special events in, 153
Skiing, 28
    in ski country, 151
Skyline Inn, 228

Skylon Tower, 232, *232*
  revolving dining room at, 237
Sky Screamer, 228
Smiths Orchard, 213
Smoke, Fire, and Spice, 115–116
Smoke on the Water, 94–95
Smokin' Buddha, 266
Smoking, 17
Smokin' Joe's Trading Post, 185
Smokin' Little Diner, 121
Snippets & Gems, 148
Snowmobiling, 28
Snowshoeing, 28
Snyder, 96
Soho Burger Bar, 67
Somerset Old Fashioned Farm Festival, 203
Something Else, 269
Sophia's, 95
Sousa, John Philip, 212
South Coast Cookhouse, 223
Southern Erie County, *124*, 125–153
Southern Ontario, *216*, 217–240
Southgate Plaza, 139
South Landing Inn, 250
South Park, 54, 58
Southtowns, 125
Souvenir City Headquarters, 240
Special events
  in Amherst, 109
  in Aurora, 134
  in Buffalo, 82–84
  in Canal Towns, 213–214
  in Fort Erie, 225
  in Grand Island, Tonawanda and Kenmore,
    95
  in Lake Erie Towns, 148
  in Lake Ontario Shore, 203
  in Niagara Falls, New York, 168
  in Niagara Falls, Ontario, 240, *240*
  in Niagara-on-the-Lake and Queenston,
    256–257
  in North of the Falls, 185–186
  in North Tonawanda and Wheatfield, 194
  in Orchard Park and West Seneca, 139–140
  in Port Colborne, 269
  in ski country, 153
  in Welland, 269
The Spicey Pickle, 183
Spirit of Buffalo, 50
Spirit of Christmas and Dickens Style Open
  House, 225
Spirit of the Mist/Smokin' Joes Native Center,
  160
Spirits, 19–20
Spoiled Rotten, 81
Sports, 28
Spoth's Farm Market, 107, *107*
Sprague Brook Park, 151
Spring Lake Winery, *207*, 207–208
Springville. *See* Ski country
Springville Center for Arts, 151, *151*
Stagecoach Family Restaurant, 253

Steel Plant Museum, 48
The Steer, 73–74
Stein, Vern, Fine Art, 107
Step Out Buffalo, 30
Stevensville Conservation Area, 222
Steve's Ox and Pig Roast, 75
Stiglmeier Park, 119
Stimson's Antiques & Gifts, 184
Strathaird Bed & Breakfast, 237
Strawberry Festival, 185
Strewn Estate Winery, 247
Sullivan, Louis, 13, 28, 33, 44, 45
Summit Suite Dining Room, 237–238
Sundays, 17
Sunnybrook Farm Estate Winery, 247
Sunset Bar & Grille, 201
Sunset Bay, 22
Super Freeze Drive, 147
Sutton, Knight, Museum, 112
Swannie House, 67
Swan Street Diner, 67–68
Sweet Dreams Ice Cream Parlor, 224
Sweetest Addiction, 266
Sweet Jenny's Ice Cream and Candy, 97, 108–109
Sweet Pea Bakery, 148
Sweet Temptations du Jour, 70
Swiss Chalet, 20–21, 239
Switson's Beef & Keg, 95
Swormville, 96, 110
Syros, 182–183

T
Table Rock Center, 229
Taffy's Hot Dog Stand, 139
Talking Leaves Books, 78
Ta-Num-No-Ga-O, 110
Tappo, 67
Tara Gift Shoppe, 82
Taste, 131
Taste of Buffalo, 83
Taste of Niagara, 168
Taste of Siam, 70
Taste of Williamsville, 99, 109
Tattered Tulip, *212*, 212–213
Tavern at Windsor Park, 104
Taylor, James Knox, 45
Taylor's Tap & Grill, 167
Taylor Theater, 212
Ted's Hot Dogs, 20
Templeton Landing, 63
Tempo, 63
Ten Thousand Vines Winery, 142, *142*
The Terrace at Delaware Park, 64
Tesori, 109
Tewksbury Lodge, 59, *59*
Thai House, 121
Theaters, 18–19
  in Amherst, 106
  in Aurora, 131
  in Canal Towns, 212
  in Niagara Falls, New York, 168
  in Niagara Falls, Ontario, 240

in Niagara-on-the-Lake and Queenston, 253–254
in North of the Falls, 183–184
Theatre of Youth Company, 76
Thin Ice Gift Shop, 81, *81*
Thin Man Microbrewery/Restaurant, 52, *53*
Thirsty Buffalo, 70
31 Club, 62
Thirty Mile Point Lighthouse, 28, 197, *197*, 200, 201
Thompson, John, 96
Thorold, 260, *260, 263*
  activities in, 264
  business improvement area in, 258
  eating in, 266
  lodging in, 265–266
  murals in, 262
  shopping in, 267–268, *268*
  sightseeing in, 258, 262, *263*
Three Ferrises, 225
335 on the Ridge, 223
Three Sisters Trading Post, 168
Thunder Bay, 22
Thunder Bay Beach, 221
Tifft Nature Preserve, 22, *23*, 53, 56–57
Tillou, Dana, Fine Arts, 77
Timberland Restaurant, 112
Times Beach Nature Preserve, 36, 57
Tim Horton's, 20, *20*
Tin Pan Alley, 183
Tokyo Shanghai Bistro, 70
Tommyrotter Distillery, 52
Tom's Diner, 212
Tonawanda, 88
Tonawanda Aquatic and Fitness Center, 90
Tonawanda Creek, 25
  bike path at, 100
Tonawanda-Kenmore Historical Society, 89
Tonawanda Rails to Trails, 92
Tonawanda Reservation, 17
Tonawandas Gateway Harbor, *189*
Top of the Falls Restaurant, 166
Tourism, 15. *See also* Sightseeing
Toutant, 67
The Tower Hotel, 236
Towne Restaurant, 70
Trails Erie Canal Heritage Trail, 210
Trailside Bar & Grill, 224
Transit Drive-In, 212
Trattoria Aroma, 64, 101–102
Treadwell Farm to Table Cuisine, 252
Treasure Market, 192
The Treehouse, 81
Tschoppe Stained Glass, 115
Tubby's Take Out, 147
Turkey Trot, 84
Tuscarora Heroes Monument, 175
Tuscarora Nation Picnic, 185
Tuscarora Reservation, 17
12 Gates Brewing Company, 97
Twenty-One Club, 239
"The Twin Cities," 88

Twist o' the Mist, 168
208 Goundry Street, 188
Two Hearts Wedding Chapel, 233

U
Ujima Theatre Company, 77
Ulrich's Tavern, 67
Uncle Joe's Diner, 147
Underground Railroad, 21, 29, 34–35, 43, 55
Unique Creations Artisan Outlet, 225
Upjohn, Richard, 45
Upper Great Gorge Rim Trail, 180
Upstairs Treasures, 133
USS *Croaker,* 46
USS *Little Rock,* 46, 50
*USS *Sullivans,* 46–47, 50

V
Valhalla Meadery, 197
Vandeventer, Peter, 110
Van Horn, James, 196–197
Van Horn, Malinda, 197
Van Horn Mansion, *196,* 196–197
Varysburg, 28
Vaux, Calvert, 25, 58
Vera Pizzeria, 70
Veteran's Park, 179
Victorianbourg Wine Estates, 198
Victorian Christmas, 84
Victoria's Teas and Coffee, 256
Vidler, Robert, Sr., 134
Vidlers 5 & 10, 133–134, *134*
Viking Lobster Company, 64, *64*
Village Artisans, 109
The Village Bake Shoppe, 183
Village Designs, 82
Village Togs, 139
Vincenzo's Pizza House, 183
Vinos, 70
Vizcarra Vineyards, 208

W
Wagner, Stewart, 44
Wagner's, 212
Wagner's Farm Market, 184
Waiting Room, 76
Walden Galleria, 87, 122
Walden Golf Range, 118
Walden Pond Park, 119
Wallenwein's Hotel, 131
Walter's & Neptune's Restaurant & Tavern, 267, *267*
Walton Woods Bike Path, 100
Wardynski's, 22
Warner Museum, 150
War of 1812, 34, 43, 157
Wasabi, 104
Waterbike & Boat Adventure, 90
Waterbikes of Buffalo at Canalside, 50, *50*
Waterfalls, 25
  in Amherst, 100
  in Orchard Park and West Seneca, 136

Waterfront Trail, 264
Watermark Restaurant, 238
Water Street Landing, 181, *181*
Water Valley Inn, 147
*Waverly Beach, 221
*Wavery Beach, 22
Weather, 17
Webster's Bistro and Bar, 190
Wedding Company of Niagara, 233
Weddings, 17–18
  in Niagara Falls, New York, 162, *163*
  in Niagara Falls, Ontario, 233
Welland, 258
  eating in, 267
  green space in, 265
  shopping in, 268
  sightseeing in, 262, 263, *263*
  special events in, 269
Welland Canal, 232, 258
Welland Canal Corridor, 13, 258–269
  activities in, 264
  eating in, 266–267
  entertainment in, 267
  getting there, 259
  green space in, 264–265
  history of, 258
  lodging in, 265–266
  medical care in, 259
  museums in, 263
  shopping in, 267–269
  special events in, 269
Welland Canals Centre at Lock 3, 262, *262*
Welland International Flatwater Centre, 260
Welland Museum, 262, *263*
Welland Rose Festival, 269
Wellands Canals Trail, 264
The Wellington Pub, 73
Wendt Beach, 22, 143
West Canal Marina, 189, 190
The Western Door, 166
Western Lake Ontario Fishing Guide, 199
Western New York Southtowns Scenic Byway, 150
Western New York Wares, 30
West Falls. *See* Ski country
Westin Buffalo, 61
West Seneca, 135, 136, 141. *See also* Orchard Park and West Seneca
West Shore Trail, 113
West Side Bazaar, 74
West Side Rowing Club, 46
What a Woman Wants, 148
Wheatfield. *See* North Tonawanda and Wheatfield
Whirlpool Aero Car, 232–233, *233*
Whirlpool Jet Adventures, 177
Whirlpool Jet Boat Tours, 177, 244
Whirlpool Public Golf Course, 231
Whirlpool Rapids Trail, 180
Whirlpool Restaurant, 239
Whirlpool Rim Trail, 180
Whirlpool State Park, 163, 177
White, Stanford, 188

White Oaks Royal Niagara Spa Resort and Conference Center, 250, *250*
White Water Boardwalk, 235
White water rafting, 28
Wicks, William, 61
Wilcox, Ansley, 24, 43
Wilcox Mansion, 24, 43
Wildlife and Renaissance Festival, 134
Wildplay Mistrider to the Falls, 229
Wildplay Whirlpool Adventure Course, 229
Wild Things, 82
Wilkeson Point, 36, 57
William K's, 63
Williams, Jonas, 96, 97, 99
Williamsville, 34, 96, 99, 100
  eating in, 102–106
Williamsville Water Mill, 97
Willoughby Museum, 227
Willowbank Heritage Estates, 243
Willowbrook Golf Course & Restaurant, 209
Willow Ridge Bike Path, 100
Wilson, 196. *See also* Lake Ontario Shore
Wilson, Billy, Park, 98
Wilson, Luther, 195
Wilson, Reuben, 195
Wilson Boat House Restaurant, 201
Wilson Harborfront, 199, 203
Wilson Historical Society, 197
Wilson Pier, *198*
*Wilson Tuscarora, 22
*Wilson-Tuscarora State Park, 199, 200
Windows by Jamie Kennedy, 238
Windsor Village Artisan and Antique Market, 213, *214*
Wine, 19–20. *See also* Breweries and wineries
Wine on Third, 166
Wineries. *See* Breweries and wineries
Winfield, Mason, Haunted History Ghost Walks, 128
Winterfest, 139
Winter Festival of Lights, 240, *240*
WNY Book Art Center, 41
Wok & Roll, 106
Wolcottsburg, 110
Woodcock Brothers Brewing Company, 198
Woodlawn Beach, 22
  state park at, 143–144, *144*
Work of Art Frame Shop, 225
World Pumpkin Weigh Off, 112, 116
World's Largest Disco, 84
Woyshner's Christmas Shoppe, 82
Wright, Frank Lloyd, 13, 23, 28, 33, 42, 44, 45–46, *46*, 125, 141, 142–143
Wyndham Gardens Buffalo Williamsville, 101
Wyoming County, *275*, 275–276

Y
Yates Park, 136
The Yelling Goat, 121
Yolo, 102
Yoshi, 130
You and Me, 185

Young, Ed, Hardware, 108
Youngston. *See* North of the Falls
Youngstown Village Diner, 183, *183*
Youngstown Volunteer Field Days, 185–186
Youngstown Yacht Club, 177
Yummy Thai, 192

Z
Zee's Grill, 252
Zittel's Country Market, 147
Zoar Valley, 28, 278
Zoe, 102
Zoom Leisure Bicycle Tours and Rentals, 244